Dear Alicia,

Thank you for all you do for the students at Juilliard. You are keeping Juilliard at the highest standard for any dance program in the world.

Danny 8/11/20

Daniel Lewis

Donna Krasnow

DANIEL LEWIS

A Life in Choreography and the Art of Dance

DONNA H. KRASNOW *and*
DANIEL E. LEWIS

McFarland & Company, Inc., Publishers
Jefferson, North Carolina

LIBRARY OF CONGRESS CATALOGUING-IN-PUBLICATION DATA

Names: Krasnow, Donna, author. | Lewis, Daniel E., 1944– author.
Title: Daniel Lewis : a life in choreography and the art of dance /
Donna H. Krasnow and Daniel E. Lewis.
Description: Jefferson, North Carolina :
McFarland & Company, Inc., 2020 | Includes index.
Identifiers: LCCN 2020017973 | ISBN 9781476681917 (paperback) ∞
ISBN 9781476640174 (ebook)
Subjects: LCSH: Lewis, Daniel, 1944- | Dancers—United States—
Biography. | Choreographers—United States—Biography.
Classification: LCC GV1785.L465 K73 2020 | DDC 792.802/8092 [B]—dc23
LC record available at https://lccn.loc.gov/2020017973

BRITISH LIBRARY CATALOGUING DATA ARE AVAILABLE

ISBN (print) 978-1-4766-8191-7
ISBN (ebook) 978-1-4766-4017-4

Front cover image: Daniel Lewis in *La Malinche*,
choreography by José Limón, photograph by Eddie Effron,
courtesy Daniel Lewis archives

Printed in the United States of America

*McFarland & Company, Inc., Publishers
Box 611, Jefferson, North Carolina 28640
www.mcfarlandpub.com*

Acknowledgments

We would like to thank our families, friends, teachers, and mentors for their support and guidance over the years. We also want to thank Anastasia McCammon for her work in organizing and cataloguing the many boxes of archives that Danny has collected throughout his career. We wish to express our appreciation to all of Danny's friends, past students, and colleagues who contributed their thoughts, recollections, and experiences over many decades to this biography. We want to give special thanks to Maureen O'Rourke-Lewis, Nancy Scattergood Jordan, and Eddie Effron for their invaluable feedback about the manuscript as it was being written. We wish to acknowledge Karla Walsh for her extensive edits of the manuscript in its first draft. And finally, we wish to thank Layla Milholen and the staff at McFarland for bringing this project to fruition.

Table of Contents

Acknowledgments   v

Preface by Donna Krasnow   1

Daniel Lewis Timeline   4

1. The Beginning (1944–1963)   7

2. The Juilliard School (1962–1967)   20

3. The Limón Company (1962–1974)   44

4. Reminiscing About the Limón Company   60

5. Staging Limón Works Around the World   80

6. Contemporary Dance System and Daniel Lewis Dance:
     A Repertory Company   100

7. Other Facets of Danny's Life During His Company's Years   137

8. New World School of the Arts: The Beginning   150

9. Outreach and Special Events   165

10. Other Facets of Danny's Life During the NWSA Years   191

Appendix: Professional Accomplishments, 1960–2017   215

Index   221

Preface
by Donna Krasnow

It was a beautiful summer morning in 1980 in Portland, Oregon, when I arrived at Reed College. From 1973 to 1983, Reed hosted the Reed College Summer Dance Workshop, also called the Northwest Summer Dance Workshop, one of the largest summer dance festivals in the Pacific Northwest. I was invited that year by Keith Martin, who was organizing the workshop, to teach a course in anatomy as part of the program. Even more exciting than the opportunity to teach was the prospect of taking Graham technique classes with Armgard von Bardeleben, jazz classes with Nat Horne, ballet classes with Genia Melikova, and Limón technique classes with Daniel Lewis. I was in awe of this dazzling and renowned faculty. I was already an accomplished dancer in Graham, jazz, and ballet and the artistic director of my own professional dance company—Möbius in San Francisco—but I was a novice in the Limón technique.

My first impression upon seeing Danny was how unusual it was to see a dance teacher wearing jeans and boots. A cluster of keys dangled from a carabiner attached to a belt loop in his jeans. So much for dance attire. My second impression was his striking, handsome looks and his totally unaffected demeanor—relaxed and casual, without a single affectation of the dancer. Not even a hint of turnout in his gait. He introduced himself and his demonstrator, Jane Carrington, and the class began.

I was at once struck by his teaching style. He was soft-spoken but energetic. He was demanding about the work but entirely forgiving of our laughable attempts. In fact, I think I laughed more in that first class with Danny than I can ever recall laughing in a dance class. He told jokes and he told stories, but what moved me most of all was that he talked philosophy. He situated the technique in a larger vision of Limón as the choreographer, the musician, the artist. We were learning exquisitely gorgeous movement phrases with intricate rhythms, precarious balances, and complex multilimbed coordinations, but all the while, Danny was expressing in analysis and imagery the principles of the work: fall and rebound, fall and recovery, suspension, opposition, isolation, and always weight and breath, weight and breath. His approach to teaching provided a magnificent net of support and encouragement, even as we fumbled through the movement sequences. And as the class progressed, I experienced how he built the class structure so that simple phrases at the start introduced one idea at a time, which then layered to form rich combinations to explore and dance by the end of class.

I delighted in the way he would correct me: blunt but kind, respectful but without mercy, and always with laughter in his eyes. By the end of class, I had two thoughts: first, that I was hopelessly awkward at this new technique, and second, that I had found a way of dancing that felt just like home. I had to learn it. I knew I would follow Danny around the globe to learn Limón technique from him. And thus began years of doing just that. In the process, I embraced him as a mentor, a friend, an artistic director, a choreographer, and a role model for my own teaching career. It is a rare day in our lives when we know that an experience has been life changing, but the day of meeting Danny Lewis was just such a day for me.

In the summer of 2016, Danny Lewis called and asked me if I would be interested in writing his biography. Although all of my previous writing had been in dance science, I immediately decided to take on this project because of my respect for Danny and for his work, and because of its importance to the community of dancers. I knew from firsthand experience that his life covered every aspect of the field—dancer, teacher, choreographer, collaborator, artistic director, administrator, mentor, and benefactor. He has fulfilled so many roles for literally thousands of dancers and artists. I also knew from the wealth of his storytelling that he has had personal contact with many of the important dance artists of the past half century or more, throughout the world. Finally, I sensed that his personal and professional relationship with José Limón would provide deep insight into that great artist's work and vision. And soon after, this new chapter in our journey together began.

How does one begin writing the biography of someone who has experienced so much, over such a long period of time? Danny's life is not a clear linear through-line, moving from one aspect of his career to the next. At one point in his timeline, he was involved in teaching, dancing, choreographing, running his company, and staging Limón's work, moving from one role to the next with ease and what seemed like infinite energy. We decided early on not to tell his story chronologically, but rather to look at the various aspects of his work in a series of chapters: his early life, the years at the Juilliard School, dancing and touring with the José Limón Company, staging Limón's work around the world, directing his own company, Daniel Lewis Dance Repertory Company, additional work such as writing and choreographing operas and musicals, and finally his work as dean of dance at New World School of the Arts and in Miami.

The next question was how to gather all of the relevant information, and so began my trips to Miami to explore 60 archival boxes of photos, programs, letters, newspaper articles, reviews, posters, and even old airline tickets. Each piece of paper held in Danny's hand would stimulate stories, and he would freely talk as I recorded. The months between trips were spent transcribing tapes and organizing the material. But Danny and all of the written materials in his archives were not my only resources, as he gave me lists of names of people to contact and interview, past students, colleagues, and dance artists in cities across the world. One word kept re-appearing in all of these interviews—generosity. It became clear to me how much Danny has given to others and to dance, and I hope I was able to capture this spirit of his in the text.

Certainly, there are many biographies of modern dancers—Alvin Ailey, Pina Bausch, Merce Cunningham, Katherine Dunham, Martha Graham, Lester Horton, Doris Humphrey, Pauline Koner, José Limón, May O'Donnell, Anna Sokolow, Paul Taylor—but none have been written about Danny Lewis and none give insight into José Limón in the way that Danny does. None tell us about some of the great ballet dancers of our time learning modern dance works, and how that affected their dancing. And while some texts describe the teaching methods of a given renowned educator, Danny's unique approach to passing on the legacy of the Limón technique and its relationship to Limón's dances are important aspects of his story and of the history of modern dance. I hope that this exploration into the heart and mind of Danny Lewis and this testimony to his contributions to dance inspire the reader of this biography as much as he has inspired me.

Daniel Lewis Timeline

1944	1948	1958–1962	1962–1967	1962–1974	1972–1974	1977–1987	1987–2011	2002–
Born in New York City	Took first tap classes, doctor's orders	High School of Performing Arts	The Juilliard School: student	Limón Dance Company: dancer	Limón Company Artistic Director	Taught at London School of Contemporary Dance	Dean of Dance at New World School of the Arts	Dance4Life Lifetime Achievement Award
		1961–1967 Yiddish Theater	*1963–* Asia Tour with Limón	*1968–1972* José Limón's assistant	*1973–* Soviet Union tour	*1977–1985* New York University: faculty	*1988–* Founded Miami Dance Futures	*2003–present* Productions using Internet 2 technology
		1961–1972 Connecticut College	*1963–1987* Lincoln Center Student Programs: dancer and then director of three touring programs	*1968–1987* The Juilliard School: faculty	*1972–1987* Contemporary Dance System / Daniel Lewis Repertory Dance Company	*1978–1981* DLRDC in residence at Amherst College, Massachusetts	*1989–2011* Hosted numerous dance festivals and conferences	*2010–* Lifetime Achievement Award from the National Dance Education Organization
			1966–1974 Dance Uptown and Minor Latham Playhouse	*1968–present* Staged Limón works around the world	*1973 and 1984–1986* National Ballet of Canada School	*1984–* Founding Director of Limón Institute	*1994–2011* Hosted seven National High School Dance Festivals	*2011–* Martha Hill Lifetime Achievement Award
				1970–1972 Taught and choreographed at UCLA		*1984–* Published "The Illustrated Dance Technique of José Limón"	*1995–present* Miami Dance Samplers	*2011–* Retirement from New World School of the Arts

1

The Beginning
(1944–1963)

I was lucky to have been born at the right time, in the right place, and with the right talents. Because I never knew what the future would hold, at each turn in my life I have made sure never to let go of the people I have met or the situations that I encountered. This made it possible to always see dance in many different ways. In the early years, being born with a clubfoot was seen as a handicap, but now I realize it was a strange bit of luck that led me to dance. Life gives you many twists and turns and you never know where they're going to take you. The events in this first chapter shaped how I operate, making me who I am today. I hope you do enjoy my journey.—Daniel (Danny) Lewis

Childhood and Adolescence

Daniel Lewis was born on July 12, 1944, in Brooklyn, New York. His mother was originally Louise Lauria, and her mother, Anna Cezikova Lauria, was from Czechoslovakia, now the Czech Republic. Her father, Eduardo (known as Rocko) Lauria, was from Sicily, and was an iceman who delivered ice in Brooklyn. Danny's grandmother Anna and her brother Josef Cezik originally came to America to make money to build a house back home. Josef did go back, but Anna stayed and married Eduardo. Daniel's Jewish grandfather, Sam Bukinski, was from Poland; he went to Russia and married a Russian woman named Esther Cohen, and they came to America through Cuba. Upon coming to the United States, Sam decided to change his last name, and he chose the name Lewis, the first name of his father, Lewis Bukinski. Sam started a leather business with a man named Rosenthal, and the business supplied all the patent leather for Capezio (which was going to be an important connection for Danny later).

Danny's mother, Louise, did not get along with her mother Anna, and Louise left home right after high school, never speaking to her mother, even though she only lived ten minutes away. Danny didn't meet Anna, Eduardo, or Louise's younger brother, Edward, until Danny was eleven or twelve years old.[1] Danny's grandmother on his father's side died when Danny was an infant, so he never met her. Danny's father, Jerome (Jerry)

---

1. It was a family crisis that eventually brought Danny to meet his grandmother: Danny's cousin Ralphie was shot in the belly in a hunting accident. Danny's father went to upstate New York to be with the family, and Danny's mother went to tell Danny's grandmother.

Lewis, was a tool and dye maker and purchased tools for a company in New York City that made machines used to stuff dolls.

Danny was the middle son, Robert (Bob) was the eldest, Steven (Steve) was the youngest, and there were three years between each son. Danny's brother Bob was born with a bad clubfoot, and his foot was put in a cast as an infant. Danny was also born with a clubfoot, but his was not that bad, and his doctor prescribed dance classes to straighten his foot. This doctor, it turned out, was the father of a dancer. Later in life, Danny would say that his clubfoot was a piece of good luck!

From an early age, Danny knew that dance was his language of choice. Danny's first dance classes were in a house rather than a dance studio. There were several rooms in the family home with Masonite flooring. Danny had already been going to the house for weeks before, because his father was laying the floor. Danny had even assisted by putting down some of the screws for the flooring. His father made a deal so Danny could get tap classes for free. Danny was a bit nervous

Daniel Lewis and his mother Louise Lewis, leaving the hospital just after his birth, wrapped in a yellow blanket knit by his grandmother, Jamaica, Queens, New York, July 1944 (photograph by Jerome Lewis, courtesy Daniel Lewis archives).

that first day in class. Danny and his two brothers Bob and Steve were the only boys in a class of twenty to twenty-five girls. He learned flap ball change, shuffle, and other steps. Though his brothers were struggling, Danny had no problems; it came naturally to him. He took to it and enjoyed it! The age range in the class started at five years old. Danny's second class was more interesting; his brothers did not go again, so it was just Danny and all the girls, which made him unique. He felt special. It continued to come easily to him. By the third or fourth class, he was hooked. He began to look forward to going, although he did not know whether it was because of the movement, the feeling of being unique, or the experience of being the only guy. All he knew was that he felt good in the classes, and while he was there, he exploded with joy and movement. He thought of it as tap steps and sequences, not dancing. Finally, he began learning routines.

The man who ran the studio, Bob Bernissant, was French and originally from New Orleans. He would do annual recitals, which were real productions with sets, costumes, and live accompaniment. For classes, they used records—33s and 45s—but pianist Sandy Ross played every work for the recitals. In the programs, Danny was listed as Bob's student assistant. It was not talent that got a dancer a special part. The parents paid for their children to get good roles. Solos were $50, duets were $25, trios were $10, and so on. This included the cost of the costume, and Bob did well financially with the school. Danny got solos not because his family paid but because he was the only guy. The recitals always had a specific theme, such as Mardi Gras (New Orleans) or a Gershwin recital. Danny performed the very first year! The studio kept moving and getting bigger and bigger, and Bob ended up with three studios in Brooklyn. By the end of Danny's training with Bob, they were performing at the Recital Hall (now called the Harvey Theater) at the Brooklyn Academy of Music (BAM). These recitals were sold-out shows. Bob had a male partner named Arthur, a daughter from a previous marriage, and a small white poodle. Bob's mother ran the front desk for the school, and his father built the sets with Danny's father. After Bob left New York, he opened restaurants in New Orleans. Danny continued working with Bob about nine years, until he got into the High School of Performing Arts. Danny also took over teaching beginning tap classes to young girls, sometimes thirty in a class. Buddy Hackett picked up his niece at one of the schools a few times. The excitement of the BAM performances was overwhelming, even with only one pianist. In one work that Danny performed, he left out a final phrase and exited too soon, so Sandy just kept playing and playing. The sets were big paintings of New Orleans, on cardboard, that the dancers would hold up. Danny credits these early experiences through this school in his interest in the production end of dance.[2]

Daniel Lewis preparing for a tap dance recital in New York, circa 1950 (courtesy Daniel Lewis archives).

During this time, the Lewis family lived in the attic apartment of a private home that his grandfather Sam owned. Sam and Esther lived on the second floor. An Italian family, the Prevenzanos, lived on the first floor, and Danny's family had the top (attic) floor, with a side staircase leading up to the attic apartment. Danny's room had a slanted roof, and he shared a bunk bed with his brother Bob, who had the top bed. Steve had a small cot in the same room. After his grandfather Sam sold the house, they had to move to a different street in the same neighborhood. It was an Italian Catholic neighborhood, and Danny was often called "Jew boy"; neighborhood children convinced him that he personally killed Jesus. He was chased and beaten while in grade school, until he joined a gang called the 59th Street Boys for protection.

Danny openly told people

---

2. Years later, in 1991, Danny and his wife Maureen were driving out to Loveland, Colorado, where Maureen was taking a workshop in Anatomy in Clay. They stopped in New Orleans and looked in a phone book, and they found one listing for Bob Bernissant. They spoke on the phone, and Bob remembered Danny and his family well.

about his dancing when he was very young (five to eight years old); as he got older, though, he never told anyone at school or in the neighborhood. He had a secret life, especially when he started junior high school. Then when he was around twelve years old, he started doing television shows, such as *The Merry Mailman Show* (ABC), which was broadcast live. (In later years, he would do shows such as *Lamp Unto My Feet* and *Camera Three*, both on CBS.) On *The Merry Mailman Show*, the merry mailman was Ray Heatherton, father of singer and actress Joey Heatherton. One of Danny's appearances was when Rin Tin Tin was also on the show. He got paid with a case of marshmallow fluff, which he thought was fabulous. When Danny was about thirteen years old (in eighth grade), another student at the school saw Danny on TV in one of these shows. He was at John J. Pershing Junior High School, and some of the girls told the drama teacher, Mrs. Schroeder, that he was a dancer. She invited him to be in the ninth-grade show, even though he was only in eighth grade. He told the drama teacher no, because he did not want to be ridiculed and bullied. This became a big deal to her. The school decided to expel Danny for "poor citizenship." He was expelled for a day or two, and his mother had to fight the school to get him back into school.

In the junior high school yearbook, Danny drew beards on Mrs. Schroeder and on the boy on the top left, a wild kid at the school who burned Danny with a cigar behind his ear. One day the kid was smoking a cigar on the street as Danny walked by, and the boy burned him. When he got to school, Danny didn't say anything about it, even though it hurt terribly and developed a welt. One of his friends said something to the teacher, and Danny was sent to the principal's office, then ended up at the police station, because the kid had hurt other students. Overall, junior high school was a horror for Danny. He was very glad to get out of this school. Even though the school went through ninth grade, he left at the end of his eighth grade year to go to the High School of Performing Arts (the *Fame* school), a vocational high school in Manhattan that taught dance, theater, and music.

What Danny remembers most from his early years was that they were very poor. They never bought clothes but rather wore hand-me-downs. He came home one day and was shocked to find that someone in the neighborhood had left them a box of clothing on the staircase. The family just had no money. His dad was a machinist by trade and a buyer for the Almont Machine Company, which made machines that stuffed dolls. His dad would make a bit of extra money by going around and doing repairs on these machines. As a young boy, Danny spent a lot of time in doll factories, and he would bring home lots of dolls. His favorite was a dog with a collar and a small brass lock. Danny loved the little locks, and he took home dozens of them. His mother didn't work in the early years, but later on when Danny was in school, she became a school crossing guard at another school nearby. At lunchtime, Danny would leave Pershing JHS and go meet his mother where she worked. There was a candy store with a soda counter. She would bring him a sandwich, and he would sit at the counter and order an egg cream. Next door was a bakery where he would get a jelly doughnut. Both the beverage and doughnut were free because she worked at the corner and watched the kids.

Danny had reading issues that caused one of his high school teachers to suggest that he take reading courses at New York University (NYU) to help with this deficit. The reading problem dated back to his first school years. He spent two years in kindergarten, because he was too young when he was enrolled. Kindergarten through grade 5 was the worst education Danny ever received, thanks to an experiment the public school was trying at the time. He did not learn *a, e, i, o,* and *u.* Instead, the school taught him to read by drawing lines around the words and learning the shape of the word. Any time a new word came along, he had to learn a new shape. Danny did very poorly in school through those years, and he was generally third from the bottom of the class list in terms of academic rating. Teachers would say to his parents that it didn't matter because he was going to be a dancer! This is a very strong memory for Danny. When his family moved to a new neighborhood, Danny started a new school for sixth grade. He was so far behind the other students that it was humiliating. To this day, his spelling skills are very problematic because he never learned phonetics. This educational experiment in reading was clearly a failure of the educational system of the time, affecting hundreds of young children.

Even with this poor education, the school provided Danny with some important benefits and experiences. Each week, the administration brought in a series of guest speakers for a school-wide assembly. Two guests that were especially noteworthy and had an effect on Danny's life were Jackie Robinson, the first African American major league baseball player, and Helen Keller, an American author, political activist, and lecturer who was the first deaf and blind person to earn a bachelor of arts degree. Danny was very involved in the audio-visual group that supported these assemblies. Because Danny was setting up the microphones for these talks, he was to meet and interact with these guests. Due to these early events, throughout Danny's life, he always valued bringing in guest artists and exposing his students and dancers to new people and experiences.

When he got to high school, physics teacher Orving Orfuss let him take the physics class even though his GPA was not high enough, because he figured out that Danny knew all the answers to questions being asked and only lacked the writing skills. Danny would do well on multiple-choice questions because he could select the answers, but he could not write descriptive answers. Upon the teacher's recommendation that he take reading courses at NYU, his parents enrolled him in the classes, borrowing money from his aunt to pay for them.

Although Danny's family was poor, they never lacked what they wanted. At one point, he collected HO model trains. However, the switch tracks were very expensive. Since his dad was very talented in making things, he made a gauge; Danny would buy the track part, put it in the gauge, and file it until it fit and made the V. In this way, Danny made his own switch tracks. Once, Danny closed his finger in a door, and the finger became swollen as the area under the fingernail filled with blood. They had no medical insurance, so his dad took a small drill bit, sterilized it with heat, then turned it by hand to drill the fingernail and get the blood out. At one point, Danny's dad had three heart attacks in a row and could not work. The family's 8-millimeter film projector, with its three films that Danny would watch over and over, disappeared shortly thereafter; only years later did he realize that his parents had sold it to pay for living expenses. It was not until Danny started making money in high school that he could buy things. Yet he never felt deprived or inferior.

Danny had one good friend in those early years, Ronald Perlman, who went to a private school but lived in Danny's neighborhood. Ronald was the only one who understood about Danny's dancing, and later he became an audiologist. When they were in high school, Ronald's father had a Steelcraft boat with beds and bathroom facilities. The two boys were allowed to take it out on the weekdays, and they always had a fantastic time. They would take girlfriends out and pretend to run out of gas!

He did not have a close relationship with his two brothers when they were growing up. They had very separate lives and did not hang out much together. Steve was a musician and also ended up at the High School of Performing Arts. Bob went into business and was very successful. Danny and Bob have become close in these later years, and their families have Thanksgiving dinner together each year.

High School of Performing Arts (1958–1962)

While Danny was attending John J. Pershing Junior High School, he was miserable. He was called La Twinkle Toes and persecuted by the kids in the school. One day in 1958, Danny's mother saw an article about the High School of Performing Arts in the *New York Times*, and she and Danny applied for an audition. When his mother took him to the audition in New York, he was very nervous since he had no serious training. His mother, who was by this time an x-ray technician, gave him a pill (perhaps Valium or something similar) to relax him. (In fact, she often self-medicated and once ended up in the hospital as a result.) He did well and passed the preliminary audition, in which he did a tap dance, but he had to go back for a second audition. He passed that audition too and was accepted, and he received a letter stating that he needed two pairs of tights, two dance belts, white T-shirts, two pairs of ballet shoes, and white socks. Danny had none of this necessary attire, and they had no money. Because the business of Danny's grandfather Sam supplied all the patent leather for Capezio, a letter was sent on Lewis and Rosenthal stationery to Mr. Nick Tilize at Capezio saying that his daughter-in-law's son (Danny) was accepted to a special school for dance, and they should give Danny clothes at good wholesale prices. They outfitted Danny with tights and his first dance belt, a shock to Danny, who had previously worn underwear under his dance pants and never tights! He showed up at the school, totally unprepared for what he was about to experience. His first class was modern dance. Everyone applauded at the end of class, and Danny had no idea why; he thought he was supposed to bow. He had to learn a whole new etiquette and philosophy of dance training. David Wood, one of his teachers, had them doing Graham floor work. Bella Malinka, who had been with the Joffrey Ballet, taught him ballet, of which Danny had done very little. Surprisingly, there were five males in the class, and this was the first time he had seen other boys in dance. He realized that he was finally in a place where other boys did what he did, which was a major revelation.

One of his first teachers at the school was the preeminent world authority on dance notation, Ann Hutchinson Guest, who would later be present in the audience in 2010 as Danny accepted his Lifetime Achievement Award from the National Dance Education Organization (NDEO). David Wood, well-known dancer with the Martha Graham Dance Company, was Danny's favorite teacher at the High School of Performing Arts.

Danny loved the High School of Performing Arts (HSPA). He had a freedom he had never had before, and he could actually talk about what he was doing. In the past, he would do the performances and be so excited that he wanted to talk about it to someone, but he would close down. He would do a show on Saturday, go back to junior high school on Monday, and not tell anyone. Finally, at the high school, he could talk about what he was doing. In fact, he would get compliments after the shows, which felt rewarding. It was a fabulous time of transformation for him, from being a repressed dancer to becoming a dancer who could express and share what he was doing. One memorable work for Danny at the HSPA was *Cowboy in Black* by Norman Walker; the first year (1961) Danny was in the corps de ballet; then in the next year he was the cowboy.

This was an ideal place for Danny because he could be totally free to be himself. He worked as a dancer for the dance program but also did the lighting and sound for the theater program. Lawrence Olvin, the drama teacher, had a room in the back of the school that was the prop room.[3] Danny would clean up the prop room, which was always a mess. He had a key to the front door of the school and would go in on weekends to clean.

The head of the dance program at the High School of Performing Arts was Rachel Yocom, who hired a terrific faculty that trained well-known dancers such as Jacqulyn Buglisi, Cora Cahan, Laura Dean, Louis Falco, Eliot Feld, George Dela Peña, Bruce Marks, Arthur Mitchell, Eleo Pomare, Ben Vereen, Edward Villella, and Dudley Williams. Rachel was also known as a dance writer and photographer.

At the high school, Danny had friends, whereas in middle school his only friend had been Ron Perlman. He hung out with Eivind (Tim) Harrum, who went on to a full career as a dancer and an actor. He also met Nicholas (Nick) Cernovich, who was introduced to lighting by Tom Skelton. Tom Skelton was the first designer to start using side lighting for dance, giving depth to the body. Later, Nick Cernovich was to become a lighting designer for both dance and theater, working for dance companies such as Alvin Ailey American Dance Theater, José Limón Dance Company, and Les Grands Ballets Canadiens.

In 1960, there was an off-Broadway revival of *Oh, Kay*, with music by Gershwin, at the East 74th Street Theater. Mr. Olvin got Danny a job working on this show, and Danny worked with Nick Cernovich and another designer, Rick Nelson, doing the lighting. Danny was a high school student, and the show needed someone to run a follow spot. After that, he and Rick did a few other shows together, including lights for a jazz festival with Charles Mingus, Dave Brubeck, Max Roach, and other jazz musicians.

Tom Skelton, Nick Cernovich, Rick Nelson, and Chenault Spence (another lighting person) were some of the top people in the business, all of whom Danny worked with during these high school years, assisting on a show almost every night. One of the shows he worked on was called *Portrait of a Woman as an Artist*, which was performed off-Broadway at the Poor Man's Theater, in the sanctuary of a church in the Village. Rick Nelson lit it and then Danny ran it during the performances. On the first day, they taught him the lighting cues in one day, and then that evening there was a show. He had to run the show, having never seen it. The stage manager would tap him on the thigh whenever it was time to change the cue. It was a homemade dimmer board, and patching could be done with toggle switches. In addition to being paid well for these shows, Danny got an incredible background in lighting that he would later use for his company.

At the school, the academic faculty was quite lax about what the students were doing, and Danny got away with a lot. Danny was doing Yiddish Theater at night, and

---

3. Sadly, Mr. Lawrence Olvin later committed suicide. When Danny returned from touring Asia with the José Limón Dance Company in 1963, he called Mr. Olvin's home and was told that he had died.

he would finish quite late. Therefore, he moved into the city in 1961 (he was only about sixteen years old) and was living on his own, which was rare for someone so young. He rented an efficiency apartment at the Beacon Hotel. The whole world of dance and theater opened up to Danny, and he said yes to any work he was offered.

Yiddish Theater

In addition to his high school work, Yiddish Theater became a constant for Danny. Yiddish Theater had two parts: (1) actual Yiddish Theater that took place at the old Filmore on the lower east side, and (2) the more classical concert performances with Felix Fibich, where they did weddings, bar mitzvahs, and so on under the name Fibich Dance Company. When Felix choreographed for Yiddish Theater, he brought his company in to do the work. The important part of Yiddish Theater for Danny was the people—not just the big stars, like Burgess Meredith, Shelley Winters, Jan Peterson, and Edward G. Robinson, but the people there who also worked with Felix Fibich. Felix always went to the HSPA or Juilliard to find and recruit dancers. One of the first shows Danny ever did with Felix was a production that included Judith Willis, later a well-known choreographer but at that time a student at Juilliard, and Marsha Lerner, another Juilliard student. Backstage, they would walk up four flights of a spiral staircase; the dancers had to wait for their cues and then come down this long staircase. Danny fell in love with the older dancers from Juilliard, who seemed so sophisticated to a high schooler.

In addition to what he learned from his peers and from Felix, he learned important

The Wedding Dance, **choreography by Felix Fibich, in a Yiddish Theater performance at the Filmore Theater in the lower east side of Manhattan, circa 1963. Dancers, from left: Alice Condodina, Jim May, Laura Glenn, and Daniel Lewis (courtesy Daniel Lewis archives).**

lessons from the other types of performances at Yiddish Theater, which was the predecessor to Vaudeville. For example, Danny used to watch Max and Reizl Bozyk. They did a silly skit in which a wife tried to teach her husband to drink tea like an aristocrat. The way working-class men drank tea was to pour some into the saucer, put a sugar cube in the mouth, and drink from the saucer, which made the tea cooler. In the skit, they were at a formal reception, and she was showing him how to drink tea properly, but he could not hold his fingers correctly to achieve the form. At just the right moment, when she wasn't looking, he would put a sugar cube between each finger to create the right spacing and form, and he would lift the cup. The lights would go out, and the audience would roar with laughter. This taught Danny so much about theatrical timing, and how long you could draw an audience to a particular scene or theme without losing them. The audience in those days for Yiddish Theater was about 3,000 people per show and three shows a day. It was very popular. This experience was a very important part of Danny's life and taught him how to perform for very large audiences.

In the early days of the Yiddish Theater work, Danny would stay with Yiddish Theater friends who had an apartment, but that became too awkward when some of the homosexual men were coming onto him, so he got his own place at the Beacon Hotel. This was a weekly residence place where he had one room, kitchen facilities, a closet, a bed, and a toilet. It could be rented for about $50 a month. On one occasion, when visiting his family in Brooklyn, Danny said, "I think I'll go home now." His mother was quite shocked, because she did not know he had his own place by then. His dad simply wished him all the best! He did visit his parents a lot in those days, but he loved having a life with freedom, and he was making more money than his dad made. He was getting $60 a week from Yiddish Theater and getting extra pay for all the other shows, while his father's $63 a week had to support an entire family. Like any young guy, Danny saved none of the money.

One important dance partner from the that time in Danny's life was Aviva Passow. Unfortunately, Danny caused a hairline fracture to Aviva's arm when they were filming a TV show and he dropped her. The hospital put her in a cast, so they redid the costume to hide it and then finished the filming![4] The work they were filming was one of two television shows Danny did with Felix Fibich's company in a Sunday morning series called *Lamp Unto My Feet*, produced by the Public Affairs Department of CBS News. The show in which Danny partnered with Aviva was called "The 14th Day of Adar," about the Jewish holiday of Purim. Danny played King Achashverosh, and Aviva played his wife, Esther. Other dancers in the show were Kathryn Posin, Oshra Ronen, Donald Mark, and Anthony Masullo.

The other important person Danny met doing *Lamp Unto My Feet* was Vol Quitzow, who danced with the Limón Company before Danny did, and later founded Temple of the Wings in California with his family. While Danny was at the American Dance Festival (ADF) in his first summer there with José Limón, he met Vol's mother, Sylgwynn Barton, and father, Charles Quitzow, who came to Connecticut College each summer. Vol was not there the first summer, but Danny worked with Vol in Felix Fibich's company doing the Sunday morning series *Lamp Unto My Feet*. The show he did with Vol Quitzow was "A Hassidic Tale." Vol was the Soul, and James Howell was the Clerk, with music by Er-

4. Recently, Danny reconnected with Aviva Passow, now Aviva Stein, after finding her on the High School for Performing Arts website. He certainly enjoyed revisiting their friendship.

nest Bloch. The lighting designer was
Ralph Holmes, who did the lighting
for many black-and-white TV shows.
The producer was Pamela Ilott. In addition to Danny and Vol, the dancers
were Marsha Lerner, Carla DeSola
(dancer and later the founder of the
Omega Liturgical Dance Company),
Stanley Berke (later a choreographer
who ran New Dance Group), Marcia
Kurtz (later a well-known actress),
Jane Otley, and others. Eventually Vol
Quitzow ran the well-known school
called Temple of the Wings in Berkeley, California, based on the work of
Isadora Duncan. Many well-known
dancers started dancing with Vol
when they were young children.

Even in his first year at Juilliard,
Danny continued working with Yiddish Theater. However, he could no
longer do the weekly shows with Felix
and Judith Fibich; he did what they
called the "special shows." It should
be noted that Felix had a huge effect
on many young dancers and actors
who went on to have big careers. He
also gave these young people employment and salaries at a very early point
in their lives.

Poster for a Yiddish Theater performance in
Brooklyn, New York, directed by Ben Bonus and
Mina Bern, choreography by Felix Fibich. The
dancer on the left in the group picture is Daniel
Lewis (courtesy Daniel Lewis archives).

American Dance Festival

As stated earlier, David Wood was Danny's favorite teacher at the High School of
Performing Arts. What he loved about David was that he was the only man in dance
Danny knew who had a family—a wife and three young daughters. In Danny's first year
at the American Dance Festival (ADF) at Connecticut College in 1961, he went with
David Wood, who had a small company; his wife, Marnie; and some other dancers.
Claudia Pollack was another High School of Performing Arts student who was in the
company. Another of the High School of Performing Arts dancers who danced with
David was Don Bondi, who eventually ran the Los Angeles County School of the Arts.
Later, in 1963, 1964, and 1965, the Limón Company would rent a house at Connecticut College; one year the Woods had the house next door, so they would all do things
together.

Danny was at ADF as a demonstrator for David Wood, and he danced in one of David's company works as well. Many of the ADF faculty that summer were from Juilliard:

Martha Hill, Margaret Craske, and others. Also at ADF that summer were John Cage, Remy Charlip, Judith Dunn, Shareen Blair (who later danced with José), Steve Paxton, Valda Setterfield, and many other great dancers and artists. Robert Rauschenberg did the lighting for Merce Cunningham, and Tom Skelton did the lighting for José Limón. It was an amazing experience for Danny to meet all of these artists and interact with them.

In 1961, the fourteenth American Dance Festival was still held in New London, Connecticut, before the festival moved to North Carolina. The companies that performed that summer included Merce Cunningham, José Limón, Anna Sokolow, Paul Taylor, David Wood, Jack Moore, Doris Humphrey Repertory Group, and La Meri, and Tom Skelton was the lighting designer. He met so many dancers that year. He had seen the Limón Company before, and they were there, but Danny was not in the company yet, though he knew many of the Limón dancers in those performances. By the time of the Asia tour in 1963, the company members were Lucas Hoving, Betty Jones, Ruth Currier, Chester Wolenski, Halan McCallum, Louis Falco, Lola Huth, Sarah Stackhouse, Lucy Venable, Patricia Christopher, David Wynne, Ann Vachon, Lenore Latimer, Chase Robinson, Donato Capozzoli, Jennifer Scanlon, Jennifer Muller, Libby Nye, Daniel Lewis, Juan Carlos Bellini, and Fritz Ludin.

On a program from ADF from August 1961, Danny is listed with the Paul Taylor Company. Taylor had needed another dancer for the work *Insects and Heroes*, and David Wood recommended Danny. He ended up dancing with Paul Taylor, along with Linda Hodes, Maggie Newman, Dan Wagoner, Elizabeth Walton, and Elizabeth Keen. Danny did not do a lot of dancing in the work, and he learned it all in one rehearsal. The dancers were in rectangular cages, set up in a row with the fronts cut out. They would step in and out of the cages, doing different movements. This one performance made Danny an official alumnus of the Paul Taylor Dance Company, and he gets invited every year to all the events and galas.

That whole summer was incredible. First, Danny was out on his own, although only a junior in high school. Also, he was demonstrating for David Wood's classes every day. (One morning, after having been drunk the night before, Danny fell asleep while doing the bounces in David Wood's class. David threw him out!) Additionally, Danny met La Meri, who did Spanish dance and Indian dance, and these ethnic forms really excited Danny. He also got to see Merce Cunningham that year, who did a solo called *Collage 3*. The way Merce danced blew Danny's mind! The whole experience of ADF and Connecticut Col-

Daniel Lewis (left) and Paul Taylor. Paul spoke to the high school and college students and read from his biography about his dance *Insects and Heroes* and his love of insects at the New World School of Arts in 1989 (photograph by Karime Arabia).

lege exposed Danny to so many things that affected his life. Several years later he saw *Path*, Daniel Nagrin's 1965 work in which he walked across the stage with a two-by-four plank the whole time. It initially made Danny really angry, wondering why he was watching a dance like that. However, by the time Nagrin got halfway across the stage, it hit Danny—Nagrin's presence was astonishing. In Danny's words, "Nagrin can turn his back to you and dance."

Danny went to the American Dance Festival at Connecticut College each summer from 1961 through 1972. In 1964, he danced in *A Choreographic Offering*, in 1965 in *My Son, My Enemy*, in 1966 in *The Winged*, in 1967 in *Psalm*, and in 1968 in *Comedy* and *Legend*, all works by José Limón. In 1972, just after Limón's death, Danny went back to Connecticut College, but not with the Limón Company; he was invited by Charles Reinhart, the director of ADF, to stage Limón's dance *Emperor Jones* with the ADF repertory company. This was an important performance for Clay Taliaferro, who brilliantly replaced José in the lead role.

Those early years at Connecticut College really formed who Danny was and what he believed in as a dance artist. This is where he finally made the connection with what modern dance is. Before that, he was doing Yiddish Theater and was determined to be a Broadway dancer and tap dancer. Although he was training as a modern dancer at the High School of Performing Arts, he had no intention of going to college and no idea what he was going to do.

Spartacus

Spartacus was a ballet that the Bolshoi Ballet brought to New York in 1962, just after Danny's senior year at the High School of Performing Arts. It was performed at the Old Metropolitan Opera on 40th Street and Broadway, and they needed a large number of supers (short for *supernumerary*, amateur character actors in opera and ballet performances). They went to all the schools in New York City to get hundreds of supers. Danny auditioned, meaning that he went in and fit the costume! Unfortunately, the ballet did not do well. Reviews bombed, and they ended up canceling the run.

Two things were important to Danny about this experience: First, when the production occurred, there were several Russian dancers whose families Felix Fibich had known in Russia many years previously. Those dancers were told by their family members to look him up, and they all ended up in his apartment drinking vodka and telling stories all night. Danny was there, hearing all these fascinating dance stories. Second, it was amazing just being on stage at the Metropolitan Opera House in New York. He would stand backstage to watch the famous ballerina Maya Plisetskaya dance every night. She was such a beautiful dancer that he was spellbound watching her. The music by Aram Khachaturian is romantic and very Russian. Danny was just thrilled to be there. Danny even saved his backstage pass from Hurok Concerts, valid at the stage door only.[5]

---

5. Wendy Perron was also in *Spartacus*, which Danny did not know until he saw a Facebook posting in 2016. At the time, she was from the Irine Fokine School of Ballet in Ridgewood, NJ, but Danny had no idea that she was in the production. After her Facebook posting, other now-famous dancers began posting that they were also in it.

Arrival at Juilliard

At the time of working on *Spartacus*, Danny had no plans to attend college. He had auditioned and been accepted into *Anything Goes* off-Broadway, and his goal was to be a Broadway dancer. However, he received a letter from the U.S. government just after turning eighteen to register for the draft, and he was given notice that he was to go in for a physical. They sent him two train tokens to go get a physical examination in Brooklyn. He was taking a dance class at the Martha Graham Studio when one of the two class accompanists told him to think about going to Juilliard, because the government gave four-year deferments to any man in college. Danny called Juilliard and found out that there was going to be an audition in a few days, just a couple of weeks before the start of school. He auditioned and was accepted, which got him the deferment. At the start of the year, he showed up at Juilliard and saw Antony Tudor going into the elevator. Tudor looked at him and asked, "What are *you* doing here?" This initial experience at the school made Danny feel totally insecure!

Three months later, Danny was once again standing at the elevator when José Limón turned to him and said, "How would you like to go to Singapore, Hong Kong, Taiwan, Australia, and Cambodia?" Danny answered that he would love to; José said "OK" and walked away. He didn't say another word to Danny about it for months, so Danny assumed it wasn't really happening.

2

The Juilliard School
(1962–1967)

*All of the numerous, unanticipated people and events in the road I've taken
during my lifetime led to employment, enjoyment, and artistic fulfillment.
Connecting to José Limón and going on that first trip with the company to
Asia was a remarkable beginning to my dance career. And it was an extraordinary piece of luck that I met Martha Hill at Juilliard. She took me under
her wing, partly because of my rapport with José and his wife Pauline. My
friendship with all three of them would become a lifelong force in my life.*
—Danny Lewis

Martha Hill

Danny first met Martha Hill in 1962, when he went to Juilliard for his audition.
He not only got in but also received a full scholarship. Martha and Danny hit it off
right from the start. She would often bring Danny into the office to talk with him. Muriel Topaz said much later, when interviewed for a book about Martha Hill, that Martha relied on Danny to be able to communicate to the students. She would ask Danny
about what was going on, and she would use Danny as a sounding board for ideas and
to learn about what the students were going through at the time. Martha loved being
up to date about the current times and young people. Once, Martha asked Danny
and Teri Weksler (with whom he was living at the time) to go with her to see a show
called *Lemmings* at the Village Gate in Greenwich Village. From 1971 to 1973, a musical comedy revue called National Lampoon's ran at the Village Gate. The second half
of the show was "Woodshuck: Three Days of Peace, Love and Death," a parody of the
Woodstock music festival. "Woodshuck" featured spoofs of Woodstock performers,
including Joan Baez, Joe Cocker, John Denver, Bob Dylan, Mick Jagger, Pete Seeger,
James Taylor, and others. Martha Hill bought tickets for the three of them. Danny was
wondering what Martha was thinking and why she wanted to see this show. They left
the basement theater and went for coffee at a restaurant, and Danny asked her what
she thought of the show. She replied that Joe Cocker was not captured at all, though
with Mick Jagger they did all right. She went through all of them and knew them all by
name, what they sounded like, and whether the imitations were good or bad. He then
asked how she knew all this, and she said she watched Don Kirshner every Saturday

morning on the television show *Don Kirshner's Rock Concert* and learned all about the singers. She said that she really learned to understand her students through their music. Later in his life, Danny would sometimes ask his son Quinn to play his music for Danny for the same reason.

Through His Friends' Eyes—Elizabeth McPherson

Elizabeth McPherson is professor and director of the dance division at Montclair State University. She is the executive editor for the journal Dance Education in Practice *produced by the National Dance Education Organization. She has written extensively about dance, including co-authoring the book* Broadway, Balanchine, and Beyond: A Memoir *with Bettijane Sills.*

In her 2008 book The Contributions of Martha Hill to American Dance and Dance Education, 1900–1995, *she said, "I first met Danny when I auditioned for Juilliard in Atlanta, Georgia, in 1986. Michael Maule gave a ballet class; Danny gave some modern combinations; and then I performed a ballet solo. As I was putting on my pointe shoes, Danny leaned around the table and said, 'We don't really care about the pointe shoes. You don't need to put them on.' I was a little thrown off because I had rehearsed on pointe, but I kept my ballet slippers on. I knew he was trying to help me. Later on, as a student at Juilliard, I had Danny as a teacher twice a week for modern dance my first year. His teaching was clear and organized, but he didn't always teach a technique class. Sometimes he told us stories about the modern dance world. I found the stories fascinating."*

Beth interviewed Danny for her doctoral thesis in 2003 and again in 2005 about Martha Hill. In the interview, Danny said, "One thing I remember about Martha from the day I met her is that her bun was crooked. It never was straight. It stayed on that side. It had character like she had character. She really was an interesting person, and she certainly felt free to share her views. For Martha, teaching was about much more than the one course she taught. She was teaching in the hallway, on the street, in the studio, and in the theatre. She was at it 24 hours a day, every day of the week.

She critiqued everything you did: the way you walked, the way you talked, the way you went about life, and whether you should continue dancing or not. Or if she saw you in a performance, she critiqued the way you performed. Now she wasn't teaching us to choreograph. She wasn't teaching us to dance. She wasn't teaching us to do any of those things. She was teaching us to be human beings in an art form that she loved and respected. Therefore, we would do better art, better teaching, better everything. In that sense, she was always a teacher and mentor."

Throughout his years, Danny was to have three mentors. Martha Hill was Danny's mentor as an educator, and she prepared him for his future career in Florida. José Limón was his mentor as an artist, and he gave him opportunities to dance in some of the finest choreography of the twentieth century. And Anna Sokolow was his mentor as to how to stand firm for your principles.

Because Danny was earning a diploma and not a BFA degree, he did not take any academics at Juilliard, so there were periods of time in the day when he had no classes. Often, he would just show up in Martha's office. Sometimes Louis Horst was in the office too, and Danny had no inhibitions about just going in. Over time they developed a relationship that was very open and healthy. They had a kind of collegial relationship long before Danny officially joined the faculty.

The only person at Juilliard whom Danny did not get along with was Antony Tudor. Tudor would not talk to Danny, nor would he correct him in his class, which Danny took regularly. Sometimes Danny would go into Tudor's class in black tights, a white dress shirt, and a tie, just to see if he could get Tudor to say something to him. He never got a comment. Once Danny went to a party that Tudor was also attending. Libby Nye turned to Tudor and mentioned Danny's great dancing in a Limón work ("A Time to Be Born," a solo in *There Is a Time*). Tudor shrugged his shoulders and said, "Not really." Of course, this could be related to how much Danny disliked ballet, but Danny did not have any problems with Alfredo Corvino, another famous ballet teacher at Juilliard. Corvino would single Danny out to praise his magnificent elevation work. Danny's third ballet teacher during his Juilliard studies was Margaret Craske, who called Danny "boy" for all his years at the school. John Gifford was the other boy in the class, and they were "boy 1" and "boy 2."

In Danny's first year at Juilliard, Myron Nadel, now dean at the University of Texas in El Paso, choreographed *Once Upon a Mattress*. Alfredo Corvino was in it, as well as Jennifer Muller, Laura Glenn, and Danny. This was the only time Danny performed a ballet; he was the prince in the opening. Alfredo was the court jester.

For a long time during his Juilliard student years, Danny was teaching as a substitute for José when he couldn't be there, and demonstrating regularly for his classes, so Danny had a strange kind of in-between role as student and faculty. He was still friends with the students as well as having close ties with Martha Hill and José Limón. Finally, in 1967, Danny was hired by Martha as a regular faculty member, when he was only twenty-three years old. On the day of the official announcement, he walked into the faculty dressing room, and Tudor was there. Tudor said to him, "Well, what do you think of this year's class?" Danny told him what he thought, and they were fine after that; Tudor treated him as a colleague. In his first year as a regular faculty member, Danny remained in a kind of in-between world. He was still friends with the students, and dating students, who were approximately the same age. Once he became involved with Laura Glenn, it was a serious long-term relationship, and he stopped dating other dancers.

The other wonderful aspect to Juilliard was that at a very young age, he was colleagues with remarkable people in dance who had been his teachers. It was amazing that at the age of 23, all of Danny's teachers and other Juilliard faculty could now be considered his peers. In modern dance, this included June Dunbar (who was Martha Hill's assistant before Danny but left Juilliard to work with Mark Schubert at the Lincoln Center Institute), Mary Hinkson, Kazuko Hiraba-yashi, Hanya Holm, Betty Jones, José Limón, Bertram Ross (who brought his dog to class), and Ethel Winter. For ballet, he had teachers in three different styles: Alfredo Corvino and Margaret Craske (Cecchetti), Genia Melikova (Russian), and Antony Tudor (synthesis). Martha also brought in guests, such as James Clouser (a wild guy), Peter Gennaro (choreographer for the Perry Como show), and Kathleen Crofton, a tiny woman who wore a bun on the side of her head and demonstrated everything with her hands while she whistled. In those days, all the teachers smoked in the classroom while they taught. Danny also developed a long-term and creative relationship with accompanist Reed Hansen, and they

(From left) Anna Sokolow, Daniel Lewis and Kazuko Hirabayashi in front of Juilliard, New York, 1973 (photograph by Dwight Godwin, courtesy Juilliard School Archives).

mutually influenced each other's work. They found ways of teaching movement and musical phrasing that became unique to Danny's teaching approach and method.

In March 1972, Alma Hawkins, chair of dance at the University of California at Los Angeles (UCLA), brought Danny to UCLA for the start of the graduate program. While there, Danny choreographed a work for UCLA's dance department performances, called *Irving the Terrific*, with music by the Rolling Stones and costumes by Charles Berliner. It focused on the battle between the establishment and the hippies, set in a boxing ring. Reviewers said that the work lacked focus but that the dancers had good spirit! The work opened with flyers falling down from the ceiling all over the audience, advertising the fight of the century, the theme of the dance. When Danny returned to New York, he showed a video of it to Martha Hill, who loved it and wanted it remounted at Juilliard. The school flew Charles Berliner out from Los Angeles to supervise the building of the costumes and set. As they started working on it, Peter Mennin, the president of Juilliard, heard that they were using music by the Rolling

Irving the Terrific, choreography by Daniel Lewis, Juilliard, New York, 1973 (courtesy Daniel Lewis archives).

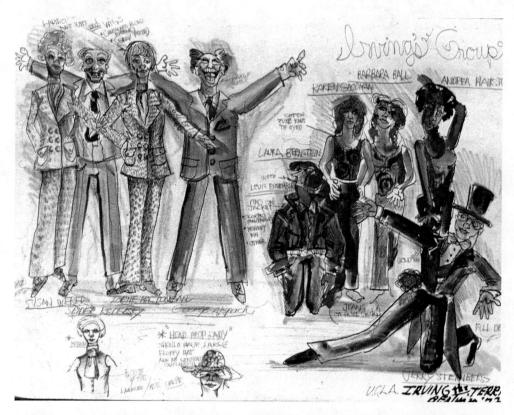

Costume design by Charles Berliner for *Irving the Terrific*, **choreography by Daniel Lewis, Juilliard, New York, 1973 (courtesy Daniel Lewis archives).**

Stones and decided this was out of the question. It was agreed that a composer would be commissioned to write a new score, with a similar feel to "You Can't Always Get What You Want," but more classical. The music was a good composition, but it did not accomplish what Danny wanted for the dance. In the end, Martha Hill went against Mennin and let the work go on with the Rolling Stones tune, but she was reprimanded for it.

José Limón: The Beginning

Months after Limón asked Danny whether he would be interested in going to Asia, he got a call from Harkey McCallum, telling Danny that rehearsals for the tour were starting and Danny was to learn *The Emperor Jones* and *Missa Brevis*. He and Harkey went to the old Dance Notation Bureau, and Harkey taught him all the parts. There was still no pay at this point, but Danny didn't care; he was just thrilled to be working with the Limón Company.

Then Danny began getting paperwork from Sue Pimsleur, who ran Musical Artists, the company that managed and booked the José Limón Company. This paperwork included contracts to go to Connecticut College. This was followed by calls from Chuck Tomlinson, the wardrobe manager, to get fitted for costumes. It finally struck Danny, at barely eighteen years old, that he was in a company! This was his first year at Juilliard, and Danny was just one year out of high school. Here he was about to tour with one of the great modern dance companies. At the time, Danny thought this must happen to lots of dancers and that it was perfectly normal.

Toward the end of Danny's first school year at Juilliard in 1963, Limón started rehearsals for the tour to Asia, which would run for four months, September through December. They went up to Connecticut College and rehearsed all that summer for performances that would take place before they left for the tour. The company performed *Missa Brevis, Concerto Grosso in D Minor, The Traitor, There Is a Time,* and *Passacaglia and Fugue in C Minor*. In addition to rehearsing and performing with the Limón Company, some of the company members performed in a show with students at the summer program. The student show included Fritz Ludin and Larry Richardson, who later formed his own company. Other dancers in this show were Marion Scott, Alice Condodina, Fred Strickler, Claudia Pollack (who had been in Danny's class at HSPA), Senta Driver, and Linda Rabin, who danced in Humphrey's *Shakers*. This show had many dancers who would later become well-known figures in the dance world.

In preparation for the Asia tour, the dancers had to get a full series of immunizations, including cholera, yellow fever, hepatitis, small pox, and malaria. They ended up performing with their arms swollen and sore. Just before they left, the company came to New York to perform *Missa Brevis* by invitation for the opening of the Philharmonic Hall (renamed Avery Fisher Hall in 1973 and David Geffen Hall in 2015). This was the first hall built at Lincoln Center. Chase Robinson, who was to perform a trio in *Missa Brevis*, became ill, so Danny performed this trio at Lincoln Center at only eighteen years old. This was a very special experience for Danny.

Also appearing at the Philharmonic that evening were the Donald McKayle Company (*Rainbow Round My Shoulder*), the Paul Taylor Company (*Aureole*), and the Merce Cunningham Company (*Septet* and *Antic Meet*). Tuesday evening, August 20, 1963, the Limón Company did *Passacaglia and Fugue in C Minor, There Is a Time, The Traitor,* and *Missa Brevis*. Dancers for this performance were José Limón, Betty Jones, Ruth Currier, and Lucas Hoving, with Juan Carlos Bellini, Donato Capozzoli, Patricia Christopher, Louis Falco, Lola Huth, Lenore Latimer, Daniel Lewis, Fritz Ludin, Harlan McCallum, Jennifer Muller, Libby Nye, Chase Robinson, Jennifer Scanlon, Sarah Stackhouse, Ann Vachon, Lucy Venable, Chester Wolinski, and David Wynne. Lighting was by Thomas Skelton, assisted by Jennifer Tipton; costumes were by Pauline Lawrence; and the musical director was Simon Sadoff. Shortly after this performance, they left for Asia.

The Asia Tour
of 1963

The Limón Compa-
ny's visit to Asia was the
first State Department tour
of any dance company in
Asia. Note that the four
State Department tours of
the Limón Company were
in 1954 (South America),
1957 (Europe), 1960 (Latin
America), and 1963 (the
Far East). José was awarded
the Capezio Award for
Dance Touring Abroad for
the State Department tours.
The 1973 Soviet Union
State Department tour is
discussed later.

(From left) Daniel Lewis, Chase Robinson (behind Daniel),
Lucas Hoving, Donato Capozzoli (behind Lucas), Betty
Jones, and a local dance teacher during the Asia tour, 1963
(courtesy Daniel Lewis archives).

The company started
on Northwest Orient Airlines, and it was the first time that Danny had flown in a large
jet. The first stop out of New York was on the west coast, and then they stopped in Honolulu for a whole day and an overnight rest stop. Danny and Jennifer Scanlon went up
into the mountains for a windy walk. After that they stopped in the Fiji Islands and from
there went to Australia. On August 30, 1963, the company performed in Sydney, Australia, the first stop on the tour, to an enthusiastic audience at the Elizabethan Theater.
They performed *The Traitor* and *There Is a Time* by Limón, and *Passacaglia and Fugue
in C Minor* by Doris Humphrey.

After Australia, they arrived in Singapore. The local hosts served them a dinner out
of steamboat pots on a long dining hall table, with no silverware, just ivory or plastic
chopsticks. In those days, few Americans had learned how to use them, and the chopsticks were slippery, making it even more difficult to eat. In the center of the long table
were several small dishes of sauces and dips for the food. As the American dancers ate
the meal, they were constantly dropping food, and the tablecloth became darker and
darker as time passed. By the end of the meal, the white tablecloth was black. On the
whole tour, they were treated like dignitaries because they were traveling for the U.S.
State Department. José always had to be "on" when meeting the many people, and he
was exhausted throughout this tour.

In Ipoh, Malaysia, the company performed at Saint John's Ambulance Hall. A
program was signed by everyone in the company. The musical director on the Asia
tour was Simon Sadoff; also on the tour were the pianist Howard Barr and the Lyrica
String Quartet. The performance was presented by the United States Information
Service (USIS) for the Perak Arts Council. The company performed *Passacaglia and
Fugue in C Minor*, *The Traitor*, *There Is a Time*, *Brandenburg Concerto*, and *The Moor's
Pavane*.

It was in Ipoh, Malaysia, that Danny had the one bad experience on the tour, a recommendation to a place in Restaurant Alley. It was a road filled with what were called "restaurants," but were only shacks with huge 60-gallon drums containing fires, plus a table and some chairs. They were told to get Indian pancakes, which were very special. After eating this dish, Danny became extremely ill for the next three days. To emphasize how sick he was, Danny spent so much time in the bathroom at the hotel that he was able to report that the bathroom had 9,887 black tiles and 8,277 white tiles. In Danny's words, "it was one of those illnesses where you think you are going to die, and then you're afraid you're *not* going to die!" This was the only time Danny was sick on the tour, while others were often sick. Jennifer Tipton got hepatitis on the tour, and she ended up in the hospital. The company went ahead without her, and then she caught up with them later.

The city of Penang was on a beautiful island in the northwest corner of Malaysia, and it was the most beautiful place Danny had ever seen. It had a phosphorescent bay, and they could swim with algae all around them. They performed *Passacaglia and Fugue in C Minor, The Traitor, There Is a Time, Brandenburg Concerto, The Moor's Pavane, Missa Brevis, Night Spell, Has the Last Train Left?* (by Lucas Hoving), *Strange, to Wish Wishes No Longer* (by Lucas Hoving), and *The Emperor Jones*. At this point, Danny was still dancing in the corps de ballet. The main dancers were Ruth Currier, Louis Falco, Betty Jones, Harkey McCallum, Sarah Stackhouse, Lucy Venable, and Chester Wolinski.

The best story about Malaysia is from their outdoor performance on Malaysia Day. This is the day that Malaya, North Borneo, Sarawak, and Singapore became the Malaysian Federation (with Singapore seceding in 1965). The company was performing *Passacaglia and Fugue in C Minor* in front of City Hall, for an audience of 18,000 people sitting on a hillside (they were expecting only 8,000), and it was televised all over Asia. They have huge hairy flying beetles in Asia. Patricia Christopher, a woman who danced with Lucas Hoving, had a switch (an additional hairpiece for performance) in her hair. It came out during the dance and fell onto the floor. While they were dancing the section called "The Bells," Patricia stepped on the hairpiece. She thought she had stepped on one of the beetles, and she froze and screamed.

The most important event for Danny on the Asia tour was the performance in which Danny replaced Chester Wolenski in *The Emperor Jones*. At the time, Danny was Chester's understudy. They were backstage, and Danny kept bugging and teasing Chester to let him dance the role. Eventually, Chester picked up his costume, threw it at Danny, and walked out of the room. Danny put on the costume and his makeup, and, when Chester still had not returned, Danny went onstage and danced the work. At the end, the dancers lifted José and dropped him back down, and it was at that moment that José and Danny made eye contact, and he realized Danny was in the work! Danny went back to the dressing room, nervous because he was sure he was going to be fired and sent home. (He had heard stories that in 1957, José had sent Pauline Koner home after a major disagreement during the South American tour.) After the show, Chuck Tomlinson (the costume person) came backstage to the dressing room and said, "Mr. Limón would like to see you in his dressing room." Danny reluctantly walked slowly to José's dressing room. Just as Danny reached the door, Pauline Lawrence Limón (José's wife) walked up, and pushed her way into the dressing room ahead of Danny. She said, "José, that was brilliant to put Danny in *The Emperor Jones*. He was wonderful! You should be so proud of him." As Danny walked in, José said "Oh yes, my boy, come here; you were very good." Danny was saved by Pauline![1]

The company's Asia tour went to the Philippines in October 1963. The company was performing at the Royal Theater with the cooperation of the Bayanihan Folk Arts Center in Manila. Amidst the confusion of assembling eighty crates of luggage, Limón stopped long enough to be interviewed, talking about learning so much from the dancers in the east and hoping to offer them something of the American techniques.

While the company was in Phnom Penh, the capital of Cambodia, they did a performance for Prince Sihanouk. The plan was that the Limón Company would perform for him, and then his royal dancers, the Royal Cambodian Ballet, would perform for the Limón dancers. The theater was scooped: the seats went way up, and the prince had to be seated at the highest point and in the front row, sitting in a tower built especially for this performance. When the performance was over, he came down to the stage and made the Limón dancers royal knights of Cambodia. The Gold Medal of Cambodia's Order of Artistic Merit was given to Limón, along with a handsome antique silver urn.

The next leg of the trip was to the ancient ruins of Angkor Wat, Cambodia, for a two-day holiday. The company boarded a Douglas DC-4 airplane, and just after takeoff, two of the engines caught fire. They immediately returned to the airport, and no one was too worried until they saw the fire trucks following the plane as it moved away from the terminal in case it exploded. The airlines only had a Douglas DC-3 available, a much smaller plane, so they needed volunteers to agree to remain in Phnom Penh for the two days. Danny and Libby Nye both went on the DC-3 with several other company members including José. During this holiday, Libby and Danny had the opportunity to travel by elephant through the ruins.

About a week later, when the company was in Thailand, Danny read in the newspaper that there had been a takeover of the Cambodian government. The new regime denounced everything American. About a month or two later, when the company was back in the United States, they learned that the new government military had gone into the palace and shot everyone connected to the royalty, including most of the royal dancers. Years later, in 1996, Danny and his wife Maureen went to Jakarta, Indonesia, for an international dance festival. The event was both meaningful and chaotic for a number of reasons. At one point, Danny and the dancers from Tsoying Senior High School were in the theater rehearsing "A Choreographic Offering" for the performance the next day. However, there was a political riot in the streets, and anyone who was in the theater was locked in for most of the day, due to the dangers. The next day, a dancer from Cambodia was presenting a paper at the festival, but his translator had not arrived. He was asking around whether anyone knew French to help him out, and Maureen volunteered to translate his paper. She took it to the hotel that night to read it over and recognized it as the same story Danny had told about the royal dancers. This man was one of those dancers, and he and a few others had managed to escape! The next day, Danny went up to the man and told him that he had been there with the Limón Company. There were

---

1. Many years later, when Pauline was ill, she instructed Danny, "Don't leave the company until José dies." Danny honored her wishes and stayed on until José's death, and he stayed an extra year as artistic director, until Ruth Currier stepped into the position and they had done the tour in the Soviet Union. After that, Danny sent the company to Paris, and he came home to New York. In the final couple of years with the company, Danny had tired of performing, but he had not left due to his promise to Pauline and the loyalty he felt towards José, Pauline, and the company.

Daniel Lewis and Libby Nye in Angkor Wat, Cambodia, with their guide during the Asia tour, 1963 (courtesy Daniel Lewis archives).

many tears and hugs, and this was a very moving moment for Danny. Because of the chaos of these few days, Danny never managed to get the name and contact information of this man.

The company performed *Missa Brevis* in Tokyo, Japan, and Simon Sadoff went to Tokyo several days ahead of the company to get the orchestra ready for the full Stokowski orchestration (rather than the organ version). The score is "Missa Brevis in Tempore Belli" ("A Short Mass in Time of War"), written by the Hungarian composer Zoltan Kodály in 1945. The company arrived in Tokyo, and they were scheduled to hear the music for the first time. They arrived at the theater and sat in the house to listen, and it was beautiful. The Japanese voices were stunning, and their Latin pronunciation was perfect. The orchestra was divine. They finished the work, the dancers all applauded, and José hurried over to the orchestra pit. He asked Simon how he had perfected it in such a short time. Simon replied jokingly, "I had to pay, and it wasn't through the nose." When the company toured on the bus with Simon, he carried a big flask, and every morning he would prepare martinis, olives and all, and walk down the aisle offering people martinis. It was like a ritual; José would always say, "Simon, it's eight o'clock in the morning!" Simon would reply, "Somewhere in the world it is four o'clock in the afternoon."

Maureen O'Rourke (right) at the World Dance Conference in Jakarta, Indonesia, July 1996 (photograph by Daniel Lewis, courtesy Daniel Lewis archives).

Five musicians traveled with the company as well: Howard Barr (piano) and the Lyrica String Quartet, which included Louis Simon (first violin), Barbara Long (violin), Michael Bloom (viola), and John Goberman (cello). The musical director was Simon Sadoff, lighting designer was Thomas Skelton, and costumes were by Pauline Lawrence Limón. A full crew also traveled with the company, including company manager Peter Inkey, production stage manager Jennifer Tipton, technical director Doug Maddox, stage manager Giovanni Esposito, master electrician Rell Thompson, wardrobe master Charles Tomlinson, and wardrobe assistant Lavina Nielsen, Lucas Hoving's wife.

The Asia tour was so special for Danny because everything he had done thus far had been local performances. This was the first time he had left the country to tour, other than some work in Canada, so Danny was very excited about going on this tour. He was also very ambitious and would learn other parts besides those that he was assigned. He found that the more he learned, the more he applied himself. By the time that they had left for the tour, he knew many different parts in the Limón and Humphrey repertory. It was during the Asia tour that Danny and Pauline Lawrence made a meaningful connection, and as with Martha Hill, Pauline decided to take Danny under her wing for reasons unknown to him. José took Danny on as his assistant the next year, very early in Danny's career in the company, and Danny attributes this position to Pauline. Aside from the fact that Danny learned material quickly and was always there, ready, willing, and able, he also knew many of the parts, so he was well suited to be Limón's assistant. Pauline arranged with Sue Pimsleur's business, Musical Artists, for Danny to receive a weekly salary of $25, starting right after the Asia tour. The exception was when everyone was on salary due to grants, and then the dancers, including Danny, received $50 a week. As soon as that stopped, Danny would go back to getting his $25 a week. Over the years, this amount increased. The only other people on a similar arrangement were Louis Falco and Sarah Stackhouse, for a short period of time, because José needed these two lead dancers. *The Exiles* was first danced by Limón and Letitia Ide (a very early dancer in the Humphrey/Weidman and Limón companies in the 1930s and 1940s, as well as on Broadway), followed by Limón and Ruth Currier (principal dancer with the Limón Company, as well as its artistic director immediately after Danny). After those couples, Louis Falco and Sarah Stackhouse were the next dancers to take on this work. In all the programs from the Asia tour, Falco and Stackhouse are always listed separately and highlighted.

On November 22, 1963, the company was in Korea. They were staying in a hotel where the walls were all made of rice paper, so it was fairly cold, and were sleeping on tatami mats, a type of mat used as a flooring material in traditional Japanese-style rooms. Danny was rooming with Libby Nye. One of the male cleaning staff knocked on the door and entered. He kept saying how sorry he was, but they had no idea what was wrong. Then word came around through the hallways that the Limón Company had to report to the dining area. They got dressed and went downstairs, where they found everyone huddled around a small television set. This is when they found out that President John F. Kennedy had been shot, and that he had died. The U.S. Embassy summoned all of the Americans to come to a military base, where they filed into Quonset huts, which are lightweight structures of corrugated galvanized steel that are used by the military. The U.S. government was afraid at that time that it might be a worldwide conspiracy and that Americans were in danger. On the base, they had a service for Kennedy. The company also paid tribute to Kennedy with their performance. As later reported in the article "José Limón Reports on Asia Tour" (*Dance Magazine*, February 1964), Limón went on stage to announce a program change, first asking the audience to stand in silent tribute: "For one minute an overhead spotlight shone on the center of an empty stage. Then the curtains closed and reopened on a performance of 'There Is a Time,' which the dancers dedicated to the memory of the President. The ceremony was repeated during the remainder of the tour."

The company had some strange performances on the Asia tour, in very small theaters. In Taiwan, the tallest building at that time was their hotel, and it was only two stories. The only taller buildings were in Chiang Kai-shek's palace. In one theater in Taiwan, the toilet facilities were outside, and they were disgusting. (That was *after* the theater people scrubbed them in preparation for the visiting company.) Back in the 1960s, most of Asia was very rural and not modernized at all. The company mainly rode around in rickshaws, although there were some taxis.

In Taipei, the company performed at City Hall, the government center. There was no room for an orchestra, so when they did *There Is a Time*, they put the string quartet in the wings of the theater, amplified with microphones. In the *Opening Circle*, there is a long viola note. Right at that moment in the performance, Michael Bloom's string broke, and he said aloud to Simon Sadoff, the conductor, "Simon, my string broke," which went out over the speaker system to the entire house! He changed his string, and they kept going. In Taipei, Danny met Lin Hwai-min, who would later start the dance company Cloud Gate. Lin was a poet who saw the Limón Company on this tour, and he came to New York to study dance.

One time, Danny and Libby went with Tom, a man they met in Taiwan, to a Buddhist monastery, and they spent the night there as well the following day. They went back to the hotel where the Limón Company was staying, and they got a room. They would periodically wake up, see that it was still dark, and go back to sleep. They finally opened the curtain and realized that there was no window, and it was much later than they thought. The company had already left on the bus for the airport. They hurriedly got ready and just barely made it to the airport in time for the flight.

Halan (Harkey) McCallum, the person who had taught Danny his first Limón dances, was Danny's primary roommate on the Asia tour, and Danny occasionally roomed with Libby Nye. Harkey was the son of a missionary in China, where he had grown up. When they went to Hong Kong, everyone stayed at the Hilton Hotel, but Harkey refused and booked the two of them into little dives for fifty cents a night, which saved them a lot of money. The per diem was about $115 a week, so Danny was saving about $80 a week during the stay in Hong Kong.

They met dignitaries all the time during this tour, and José would invite different company members to go with him for these meetings. Danny went to a couple of these events, and he found it very interesting to be with these higher-echelon people whom he would normally never meet. In every city in Asia, that area's ambassador from the United States would host an event to welcome the dancers. Danny actually saved all of the invitations, and he saved some drums from the tour as well. Danny also saved many of the Limón Company programs all through the 1960s and on.

Ruth Currier was to dance "A Time to Laugh" from *There Is a Time* on the tour, but she hurt her knee as soon as they were out on the road. José redid the choreography to include two men, Danny and David Wynne. Ruth did the whole dance, but they held her in the air the entire time! She did all the foot gestures and everything else, and they did the dance quite a bit on the road. At one point, there was discussion of sending her back to New York because she was doing so little, but they never did. Her knee got a bit better, and she finished the tour.

Toward the end of the tour, they were all getting very tired, and hungry for non–Asian food. At one of their later stops on the tour, the hotel had a full menu of Western food—the first one they had seen on the tour. The menu included filet mignon and baked Alaska. For four nights in a row, Danny had these two dishes for dinner! Even today when he goes out, he will joke about having filet mignon and baked Alaska. The hotel room also had a menu in English, and one of the items on it was an ice cream soda. Danny was thrilled, because he had not had an ice cream soda or any other milk products since coming to Asia. He called the kitchen and said he wanted a coffee ice cream soda. What arrived at the door fifteen minutes later was a cup of coffee, a scoop of vanilla ice cream, and a bottle of soda water! Apparently, it was a do-it-yourself delight.

For José, it was an exhausting tour. In a letter to Jane Dudley,[2] addressed as "Jane Darling," Limón talked about how busy they were—in his words "beyond description." José mentioned the visit to the Royal Palace (Pnom Penh, Cambodia) and the demon-stration they did. Flying home on the final day, Danny fell asleep. He woke up to find José lying in the aisle of the plane, and all the stewards were working on him, with oxy-gen. When Danny told Libby what was happening, she replied, "Oh my God, does that mean we're not going to have rehearsals?" In the end, it was nothing but exhaustion that José was experiencing.

After the company returned from the tour, an article from 1963 in *United Press International* described the political and financial aspect of the Asia tour and gave

---

2. Jane Dudley was part of the trio Jane Dudley, Sophie Maslow, and Bill Bales. She later taught at The London Contemporary Dance School, known as The Place.

insight into the U.S. political view of the arts. It cost the U.S. government $541,464 to send the Limón Company on the tour, called a cultural goodwill tour. This was actually discussed at the Congressional House Appropriations Subcommittee and made public. Subcommittee chairman John J. Rooney (Democrat from New York and a State Department nemesis) noted that the company appeared before 85,118 people during the tour, and he commented that this would be $6.30 per seat to see the company. He questioned how the American taxpayer could afford such things. However, Glen G. Wolfe, head of the State Department's cultural programs, said the tour was a big success and was well received. Rooney was also critical that Limón's wife Pauline went along as a company member and was paid $250 a week. Limón received $1,500 a week.[3] Wolfe remarked about the highly successful Singapore performance for 18,000 people. Rooney then asked how much the audience paid to see this show. Wolfe replied that for that particular show, the audience paid nothing, because it was in the open square. Rooney's nasty retort was "I imagine even a fellow doing an Irish jig would attract an audience if he was doing it without cost to the people looking at it." Rooney asked Wolfe which tour had been the most unsuccessful tour abroad and was told, "I would say that from a success standpoint, or lack of success in properly representing the United States, the Joey Adams troupe was by far the worst."

In the article "José Limón Reports on Asia Tour" (*Dance Magazine*, February 1964), Donald Duncan interviewed José Limón just after the Asia tour. José said that the tour had a disappointing start, because the Australians did not go all out for the company; evidently their heart belonged to the Australian Ballet. However, after they entered the "sensitive" (i.e., communist-threatened) areas, they scored hit after hit, despite the considerable anti–American feeling in some of these countries. A case in point was Singapore. The dancers were told to expect little applauding; the only way they would know that they were going over well would be to look out and see whether anyone was still in the audience! If they did not like the show, they would just leave. However, the Singapore audience of 18,000 remained standing in rapt attention for four dances!

Limón commented that a defect in the State Department tours was turning the performances over to local impresarios who would make them into money-making engagements. Because the ticket prices were only suitable for the upper classes and international guests, Limón saw a need to reform this practice in order to make the work more accessible to average people. He also commented on the U.S. Information Agency workers he met along the way—young, dedicated, able, and fluent in the local languages. He said how proud he was of America's overseas officials.

Duncan concluded his review by stating that Limón repeatedly stressed the urgency of increased contact between cultural exchange performers and the students. In José's words, "They are the ones who are going to matter tomorrow. And we learn so much from them."

---

3. It is probable that this amount of money was unremarkable to José himself, who had no sense of money. On one occasion, Danny witnessed a discussion in the hotel between José and his wife after Pauline had given José some money to go get some fruit. When José returned with a basket of different fruits, Pauline asked José where the change was. José said, "What change? I gave him the money; he gave me the fruit." Pauline was incredulous that José had given the man an outrageous amount of money for a bit of fruit, and the man had just taken it!

Performing After Asia

In 1963 after Danny returned from Asia, a performance at Juilliard included Danny, Susan Hess, and Martha Clarke performing together in Doris Humphrey's *Ruins and Visions*. Limón had been in the original cast, and it had not been performed for years. This was the first revival of this work. Danny also performed in *Two Essays for Large Ensemble* by José Limón.

In 1964, Danny danced with Oshra Elkayam Ronen and Kazuko Hirabayashi as part of the Kaufman Concert Series at the 92nd Street Y, where Danny did quite a few performances. Danny did several dances for Oshra, an Israeli dancer and wonderful choreographer who went to Juilliard. She later became a well-known actress in Israel. In 1964, Danny danced in her work with Hassidic music and dance.

Danny continued dancing with Felix Fibich in Yiddish Theater even after joining José's company. Other dancers were Jim May, Laura Glenn, and Alice Condodina. Danny actually got Alice the job with Felix, and they were paid $47 a week, whether on tour or in production. This group of dancers worked together for a long time. In 1964, the Yiddish Theater did a performance event called Festival Time at the Brooklyn Museum.

While on one tour in Québec, Canada, Danny and Alice went off to explore the French quarter of Montréal, and they found a charming place to have lunch. It was late afternoon and they had a glass of wine with the meal. They lost track of time, and when they came out onto the street, they could not find a cab. They went rushing back to the theater on foot. As they entered the backstage door, they could hear the orchestra playing the overture! There was no way they could get to the dressing room and onto the stage on time. However, the other dancers had brought their costumes down to the stage area, waiting for them to arrive. They barely got the costumes on and stepped out onto the stage. Felix was in the wings, in hysterics that they were missing. He never let the two of them forget this incident. In another theater where they performed, the dressing rooms were in the basement, and there was a huge mirror. On one occasion, Felix was standing in front of the mirror doing a variety of positions. Felix was marveling that the movements and positions that the arms could do were endless. Danny commented about how many more possibilities there were if he dropped to his knees. Felix said, "No, no! Then you would have to clean the costumes."

With the Felix Fibich Dance Company, Danny went out to Milwaukee, Wisconsin. To save money, they got people from the local synagogue to house the dancers. Laura Glenn and Danny ended up with Doran (Danni) and Sheldon (Shel) Gendelman. The Gendelmans were very friendly and took to Laura and Danny. She was an interior designer in the back of her husband's hardware store, Century Hardware. The store was doing well, but her business really took off. Her firm, InterPlan, was listed as the thirteenth largest woman-owned enterprise in Wisconsin, ranked in the top 500 of women's businesses in the country. The practice of billeting dancers was not uncommon in those days, and Danny lucked out with the Gendelmans because they were wonderful people. Many years later, their son Jeff sent Danny a package of Limón programs from 1951.

In 1966, Danny was still doing Yiddish Theater; was dancing with Felix Fibich, with Sophie Maslow, and with José Limón; and was a student at Juilliard! There were many performances in this Yiddish Theater collection, such as the Chanukah Festival in Madison Square Garden, with Sophie Maslow as choreographer. Also in the show were Theodore Bikel, Eli Wallach, Carmen de Lavallade, and the Sophie Maslow Dance Company. One year, Edward G. Robinson narrated as they danced. Other Yiddish Theater shows included Shelley Winters, Burgess Meredith, and Jan Peerce. Danny did quite a bit of Yiddish Theater with Ben Bonus and Mina Bern, a husband-and-wife team who did many Broadway shows.

All through his time at Juilliard, Danny was dancing with the Limón Company. He started dancing the Sleeper in *Night Spell* and other major roles by 1964; the transition was very rapid for Danny, as older dancers were leaving the company and Danny was taking on some of those roles. In 1965 in Flemington, Connecticut, at Miss Porter's School, Danny had to fill in for Louis Falco, who could not dance that night. This was a very informal showing but a good opportunity for Danny.

The company went to the American Dance Festival for many summers during Danny's time at Juilliard. Each year, the program would list all the works premiered at the festival over the years. Some of the oldest examples include Martha Graham's *Diversion of Angels* (1948), José Limón's *The Moor's Pavane* (1949) and *The Exiles* (1950), Doris Humphrey's *Night Spell* (1951), Merce Cunningham's *Antic Meet* (1958), and Paul Taylor's *Insects and Heroes* (1961).

A flyer for the seventeenth American Dance Festival in 1964 recalled several important aspects of that summer's program:

It listed a performance by Paul Draper, a tap dancer who incorporated ballet vocabulary and technique into his tap work. Paul and Danny shared their interest and love of photography, and they would go out and do photo shoots together. Paul's wife, Heidi, would tease them because they would spend hours and hours in the darkroom at Paul's house. Paul was a exceptional dance photographer, and he did a work called *Sonata for Tap Dancer*, which he performed without music but used the musical form of the sonata to structure the work. Paul was blacklisted during the McCarthy era, so his career never really took off as it should have.

Matteo was there and taught Danny how to play the castanets. Danny actually studied both Indian and Spanish dance with Matteo at the High School of Performing Arts. Danny still has the castanets and can play them!

They had a memorial program for Louis Horst, another one of Danny's teachers. When he was in Japan on the Asia tour, Danny had bought a little Panasonic tape machine that ran on batteries—a technology that did not yet exist in the United States. When Danny showed this machine to Louis Horst, he was incredibly impressed. He said that it would change the way people choreographed, because now they would be able to easily carry their music into the studio.

Danny danced with José that summer, doing *A Choreographic Offering*, which was the first work José worked on after the Asia tour. Note that when they got back from Asia, José wasn't planning on using any of the long-term company dancers, but he kept Danny, Fritz Ludin, Louis Falco, Sarah Stackhouse, Libby Nye, and Jennifer Muller. He kept these six dancers and added Michael Uthoff, John Parks, and Alice Condodina. He created this tribute to his mentor Doris Humphrey. At one point, José was going to dance in the work, but he hurt his knee. He called Betty Jones to come back, and she danced the one section he was going to do, which was the slower solo into the dance with the four men. *A Choreographic Offering* was a full-evening work, fifty-five minutes long. He started making the large sections of the work with twenty-eight dancers, using the Juilliard students, calling these sections "Two Essays for Large Ensemble." The original work had three large group sections. Danny edited the work in 1972 for the Soviet Union tour just after José died, to twenty minutes, figuring it was fine to play with it, because it was to Bach's music "A Musical Offering," which also is played in a variety of ways. Danny also made changes to two large sections. He used the end section of the middle large group section for the new finale.

An extensive list of works was done at Juilliard from the 1951–1952 season through the 1978–1979 season: Margaret (Maggie) Black, Valerie Bettis, Carolyn Brown, and so on. Danny shows up on the list for *Irving the Terrific*, May 1973; *The Waldstein Sonata*, April 1975; *Proliferation*, May 1976; *Mostly Beethoven*, February 1979; *Moments*, November 1982; and *Women*, March 1985. There were also many Limón works listed, and from 1972 on these were staged by Danny, including *The Winged* in 1972; *A Choreographic Offering* in 1974; *The Waldstein Sonata* in 1975; *There Is a Time* in 1970 and again in 1978; and *Missa Brevis* in 1977, with Ohad Naharin doing the lead role, and again in 1984, with Peter London doing the lead role.

American Dance Theater

American Dance Theater was a fabulous idea, co-founded by artistic director José Limón and producer Roger Englander, perhaps best known as the producer of CBS TV's *The New York Philharmonic Young People's Concerts with Leonard Bernstein*. American Dance Theater took place at the New York State Theater at Lincoln Center and was a combination of several companies—that is, a performance put together with dancers of all the different companies. It was sponsored by New York State Council on the Arts. José was listed as the artistic director. The musical director was Simon Sadoff, and the lighting designer was Thomas Skelton. The debut performance of the American Dance Theater in 1964 included dancers from the companies of José Limón, Donald McKayle, and Anna Sokolow.

They auditioned the dancers from each of those four companies and selected dancers, even including a couple of dancers from American Ballet Theatre. The program included Donald McKayle's *Workout* (music by Robert McBride), Doris Humphrey's *Lament for Ignacio Sanchez Mejias* (music by Norman Lloyd, with Louis Falco as the Bullfighter, Letitia Ide as Figure of Destiny, and Patricia Hammack as Figure of a Woman), Anna Sokolow's *The (Unanswered) Question* (music by Anton Webern), and José Limón's *A Choreographic Offering* (music by J.S. Bach).

Danny conducted the rehearsals of *A Choreographic Offering*, and the dancers were (in order of appearance) Libby Nye, Michael Uthoff, Jennifer Muller, Fritz Ludin, Alice Condodina, Daniel Lewis, Sarah Stackhouse, John Parks, Kelly Hogan, José Limón, Betty Jones, Laura Glenn, Louis Falco, Julie Arenal (Anna Sokolow's assistant and choreographer of the musical *Hair*), Lenore Latimer, Nancy Lewis, Joan Miller, Alma Robinson, Jennifer Scanlon, Nancy Stevens, Joseph Amaral, Richard Kuch (later a faculty member at North Carolina School of the Arts), Elbert Morris, Marcos Paredes (from American Ballet Theatre), Peter Randazzo (later one of the founders of Toronto Dance Theatre), and Larry Richardson. Other Limón dancers in the performance (but not in *A Choreographic Offering*) were Patricia Christopher, Chase Robinson, Miguel Godreau (later with DLDRC and Alvin Ailey), and many more. This project was very successful in its first year, with full houses. American Dance Theater received a lot of press, and it was a big deal at the time.

They repeated this format in the second year (1965) with choreographers Valerie Bettis (*As I Lay Dying*), Merce Cunningham (*Summerspace* and *Winterbranch*), Lucas Hoving (*Icarus*), Doris Humphrey (*Passacaglia and Fugue in C Minor*), Pearl Lang

(*Shirah* and *Apasionada*), José Limón (*Missa Brevis*),[4] Sophie Maslow (*Poem* and *The Village I Knew*), Alwin Nikolais (*Imago* excerpts), and Anna Sokolow (*Ballade*). The musical director was Jorge Mester, lighting designer was Thomas Skelton, and once again José was the artistic director. In this show, the dancers were not so mixed; the dancers did the work from the choreographer with whom they normally danced. Thus, it became more like a usual festival, and this was the final performance of this incredible idea of American Dance Theater. Although the dancers thought it was going to become an ongoing event, it lasted only these two years.

Lincoln Center Student Programs

In early 1963, Danny was in his first year at Juilliard, and Lincoln Center was just opening. The Philharmonic Hall was the first hall finished, and the Limón Company was among the companies that performed at the venue's opening. In that first dance event at Philharmonic Hall, Limón presented two of his most famous works, *The Moor's Pavane* and *Missa Brevis*. In this performance, as mentioned previously, Danny did the trio in *Missa Brevis* because Chase Robinson was ill.

At the same time, June Dunbar (the assistant director of the Juilliard dance division from 1957 to 1967) and Mark Schubert started what was known as the Lincoln Center Institute. They would send out programs all over the northeast United States to perform. An article by Thomas Putnam in the *Buffalo New York Courier Express* from January 20, 1963, described one of these tours:

> Through the Lincoln Center Student Program, two ensembles from the Juilliard School are presenting about 125 dance concerts in schools throughout New York state. The eight dancers who presented the program Friday morning at Cardinal O'Hara High School, town of Tonawanda, are graduates of the dance department of the Juilliard School. They are spreading the word about dance. The program offered modern works by José Limón and Anna Sokolow, and a pas de deux from "Coppelia" which was choreographed by James Clouser, after the original of Arthur Saint-Leon, and prepared under the supervision of Antony Tudor. The jazzy, thoroughly contemporary "Session of Six" of Anna Sokolow made an immediate impression. It is a lively romp, a young and swinging bit of fun which keeps the dancers running across the stage in early conflicting paths. Teo Macero's jazz score is an impetus to the fun. The dancers were Diana Byer, Carla Maxwell, Diane Mohrmann, Eric Hampton, Daniel Lewis, and Dennis Nahat. Improvised impressions of the popular dance scene by the dancers were combined with Sokolow's choreography, but one never had the impression of anything but a totally organized experience. José Limón's "La Malinche" is a dramatic exploration of Cortes's conquest of Mexico. One had to be impressed with Limón's strangely rugged movements, his angular forms; but lyricism is not excluded. The characters of El Conquistador, La Malinche, and El Indio were danced by Dennis Nahat, Carla Maxwell, and Daniel Lewis. Miss Maxwell and Lewis danced a warm duet, one which expressed the victory of two sympathetic natures.... These young dancers are getting wonderful experience from this program. And they surely must enjoy hearing such an enthusiastic response as they received from the students at Cardinal O'Hara High School.

---

4. Dancers in *Missa Brevis* were José Limón, Louis Falco, Betty Jones, Sarah Stackhouse, Libby Nye, Jennifer Muller, Alice Condodina, Kelly Hogan, Lenore Latimer, Ann Vachon, Shareen Blair, Jennifer Scanlon, Laura Glenn, Marjorie Mussman, Fritz Ludin, Michael Uthoff, Daniel Lewis, John Parks, Peter Randazzo, Moss Cohen, David Krohn, and Clyde Morgan. The piece was conducted by Abraham Kaplan, with the Camerata Singers and Clara Tilton Neu as organist.

Through His Friends' Eyes—Jennifer Scanlon

Jennifer Scanlon attended Juilliard and danced with the Limón Company, starting with the Asia tour, for twenty-one years. She taught Limón and Alexander Technique at Boston Conservatory for twenty years. Jennifer said, "I was with Danny on many of the Lincoln Center Student Programs tours when Danny and I were Juilliard alumni. At one of these shows, we were performing Doris Humphrey's Night Spell *and the bench tipped over, causing Danny and me to tumble to the floor. I blamed Danny for the mishap, but he was not the cause of the falling bench—we had simply leaned too far in one direction, and the bench slowly went over. For the students, this moment was the highlight of the performance, and many of them wrote about it in their follow-up letters and drawings. Danny liked to cause laughter in the audience, especially in the school shows. He was quite the comic on tour for the schools.*

One of Danny's best qualities is that he thought everything was possible with a great attitude, and he lived life with that optimism. Also, he was a natural born mover, which was a gift, and he had great talent. He had the ability to get along with people—a real people-person—and he was passionate, but not too disciplined, as he did not like to rehearse much. He was very intuitive as a dancer, and he depended on his intuition. He was a big part of the whole Limón experience for me."

Tony Salatino and Serpa Jorasmaa (from Finland) were two of the dancers on the Lincoln Center Student Programs tours, and they were a couple. Tony and Serpa performed three pas de deux together on the tour, one from *Sleeping Beauty*, one from *Don Quixote*, and one from a work by Anna Sokolow. Once when they were out, Danny and some other dancers put some speakers under their bed. At 2:00 a.m., they put on the music for *Coppelia* as loud as possible! They would also cook in the hotel rooms until the management would throw them out. Once during a tour of southern New Jersey they went out and bought crabs. They steamed the crabs in the motel room with hot plates, and the entire motel smelled of crabs as the scent traveled through the vent system.

While Danny performed in the Juilliard Lincoln Center Student Programs in the early years, he was later the artistic director (AD) for the student programs, and he ran it for about ten years. They did such prestigious works as *Day on Earth*. The director of the Lincoln Center Student Programs was Richard Killough, who hired Danny to be the AD. Over the ten years, they performed a wide range of choreography and did many performances. They would often do two shows a day, for many days in a row, and they would do these tours for a month at a time. In one program in 1967 (Danny's last year as a student at Juilliard), they presented *Badinage*[5] by Fredbjørn Bjørnsson, Ruins and Visions[6]

---

5. Choreographed by Fredbjørn Bjørnsson (Royal Danish Ballet); lights by Sidney Bennett; music by Johan Halvorsen; dancers Sue Knapp (now stages Tudor works), Eric Hampton (danced with Netherlands Dance Theater, artistic director of the ballet company Eric Hampton Dance in Washington), Diane Mohrmann (danced with the José Limón Company), Robert Lupone (Patty Lupone's brother, went into Broadway work and worked on *A Chorus Line*), Lee Wagner (later on faculty at Florida International University and on the committee that interviewed Danny for his New World School of the Arts position), Lance Westergard (danced with the Metropolitan Opera Ballet), Lulu Puertollano, Janet Sumner (ran the dance program at Southern Mississippi and was Robert Lupone's girlfriend), and Stephen Reinhardt (Broadway music director, eventually moved to Los Angeles to work in television).

6. Choreographed by Doris Humphrey; music by Benjamin Britton; costumes by Pauline Lawrence Limón; dancers Robyn Cutler (danced with Don Redlich and José Limón), Danny, Linda Rabin (from Canada, and an original member of CDS), and Martha Clarke.

and *Ritmo Jondo*[7] by Doris Humphrey, *Under Green Leaves*[8] by Charles Bennett, and *Session for Six*[9] by Anna Sokolow.

The Juilliard Lincoln Center Student Programs was one of the first series of its kind, and it also supported a multicultural program. They performed these concerts on tour in several locations and presented works by a wide range of choreographers, but the towns they were going to in upstate New York had schools with a largely African American population. Danny felt that they needed to expand the type of work. Therefore, Danny suggested that they add a multicultural program to serve this population. In 1977, Richard Killough hired Danny, who was by then on the faculty at Juilliard, to run the multicultural program. They expanded outside New York, doing all of southern New Jersey one year. Danny put the programs together, selecting repertory, created the programs, and sent them out. By then, Danny was no longer dancing in these programs. Note that the Lincoln Center Student Programs ran out of Juilliard, because they had all the dancers, and the dancers got paid about $40 per performance, which was quite a lot in those days.

Eventually, the Lincoln Center Student Programs hired Danny's company, Daniel Lewis Dance: A Repertory Company (DLDRC), to do these tours. In addition to the performances, they did events such as classes. The dancers in the company at that time included Randall Faxon Parker, Jim May, and Risa Steinberg.

Several groups participated in the Lincoln Center Student Programs in 1975 to 1976: Lincoln Center for the Performing Arts, the New York Philharmonic, the Juilliard School, the Metropolitan Opera, the Metropolitan Opera Guild, New York Shakespeare Festival, Lincoln Center/City Center of Music and Drama, New York City Ballet, New York City Opera, the New York Public Library, the Chamber Music Society of Lincoln Center, and the Film Society of Lincoln Center. The Lincoln Center Student Programs were presented by these organizations. Danny's company represented the Juilliard Dance program because they were all Juilliard graduates; in the program, the company was listed as "the Juilliard dancers." In fact, Daniel Lewis Dance: A Repertory Company had so many Juilliard alumni that they filled some of these events with DLDRC works.

The Lincoln Center Student Programs continued for many years. In a program from 1984, the Juilliard School presented *Day on Earth* and other works at the Mary Louis Academy in Jamaica, New York, for 600 eleventh- and twelfth-grade students. This school and others were visited multiple times in the 1980s.

The Lincoln Center Student Programs were incredibly important for Danny as a dancer, because he was getting extensive performance experience. Danny became a very seasoned performer during this time.

---

7. Choreographed by Doris Humphrey; with several previously named dancers plus John Giffin (another founding member of CDS, also danced with Les Grands Ballets Canadians and Pina Bausch, and taught at Ohio State). Lee Wagner and Eric Hampton later did *Little Improvisations* by Antony Tudor, a marvelous work for children in the public schools.

8. Choreographed by Charles Bennett, who had the First Chamber Dance Quartet; music by Telemann; dancers Linda Kent (danced with Alvin Ailey and Paul Taylor), Diane Mohrmann, Robert Lupone, and Robert Iscove (became a filmmaker). Danny staged two ballets, *La Malinche* and *The Moor's Pavane* for Bennett's chamber dance quartet. Danny would go out to Port Townsend in the summers and teach and stage works for Bennett.

9. Choreographed by Anna Sokolow; jazz score by Cantzaro; lighting by Sydney Bennett and Larry Berger (Juilliard graduate, and creator of the dance program at the University of South Florida); and the same group of dancers.

Juilliard Work Continues

After Danny's years as a student at Juilliard, he continued his affiliation with the school as a faculty member and assistant to Martha Hill until 1987. This was a rich time for Danny in terms of developing his pedagogy and forming his company often with Juilliard alumni, and in his relationships.

Through His Friends' Eyes—Nancy Scattergood Jordan

Nancy Scattergood Jordan met Danny during her years at Juilliard, and later became his assistant and rehearsal director. She said, "I met Danny at Juilliard in 1971, and I came from the ballet world, so the look of him—in his jeans and Frye boots—was weird, but he could do everything in those boots. I gravitated to Limón technique because it was close to what I could relate to from my ballet background. Its concepts and dance-related information opened a whole new world. In fact, generally Danny's classes opened people up quickly to positive input, and he built a class that made sense, one exercise building to the next. He spoke of Limón as physics, especially in terms of the use of weight and isolation. After I graduated from Juilliard, I eventually joined the dance faculty as the rehearsal director at the invitation of Muriel Topaz. During my fourteen years in this position (under Muriel and then Ben Harkarvy), I worked on original choreographies or restaging works of over thirty choreographers, retiring in 2000. I also staged the works of Michael Uthoff, Lila York, Daniel Lewis, and José Limón on companies nationally and internationally."

In the November issue of *Dance Magazine* in 1982, there was an article about the Juilliard Dance Ensemble. The evening closed with the premiere of Danny Lewis' work *Moments*, subtitled *The Tribute to José Limón*. The article stated that "his new dance

Daniel Lewis teaching class at Juilliard in New York, 1983 (photograph © Peter Schaaf, courtesy Juilliard School Archives).

distills moments of kinetic power from eleven of Limón's dances. This approach risks being a plastered together catalogue of Limón's hits, but Lewis navigated the hazards gracefully, producing a seamless work of new composition by Edgar David Grana, costumes by John Lee." The review went on to give some biographical information about Danny, his work at Juilliard, and his company.

About *Moments*, Danny Lewis created the following program note:

> There are moments in every dance that a dancer remembers in his body as very special. This dance is composed of such moments from the following works of José Limón: "Missa Brevis," "The Unsung," "The Traitor," "The Emperor Jones," "The Moor's Pavane," "There Is a Time," "Concerto Grosso," "A Choreographic Offering," "Legend," "The Winged," and "Psalm."

In March 1984, the Juilliard students performed *Missa Brevis* with Peter London in the lead role originally danced by José Limón. Danny felt that Peter came close to doing the role as José danced it—so close that it was like watching José return. Jennifer Dunning reviewed the work on March 18, 1984, for the *New York Times*, saying, "a modern dance antiwar classic, directed by faculty member and former Limón artist Daniel Lewis, ended the evening on a majestic note. Outstanding were Natalie Rogers in the Crucifix, and Megan Williams in the Hosanna."

Through His Friends' Eyes—Peter London

In 1985, Peter London, then in the Juilliard Dance Ensemble, danced in a reconstruction of Emperor Jones *with music by Villa Lobos and staged by Danny. Later, Peter London danced with several companies, including the Martha Graham Dance Company and the José Limón Company, and became director of Peter London Global Dance Company. He was a Juilliard graduate and long-time faculty at New World School of the Arts. He said, "As a student at Juilliard, I loved Danny's classes. He organized the class in a very simple, direct manner, starting with the torso and the breath, and then adding the arms and gestures. There was no chance that the hand could move unless it was coming from the back and deep inside the torso. Then he added the legs, then the head. I loved the exercises sitting crossed-legged on the floor (a special series that José did) with the hands. I feel that Danny's classes truly prepared me for doing José's roles, such as in* Missa Brevis, The Traitor, *and* Emperor Jones. *What I loved about working with Danny was the trust he placed in the dancer. I had come to Juilliard with no knowledge of Limón work. Despite that, Danny gave me major roles, often José's parts, in Limón repertory right from the start of my years at the school. I appreciated that Danny would give me such a huge responsibility, which made me feel that I was being treated as an adult."*

Through His Friends' Eyes—Solveig Olsen Santillano

Another student of Danny's at Juilliard was Solveig Olsen, later Solveig Santillano. After being Danny's student at Juilliard, she danced with Anna Sokolow's Player's Project, Ruby Shang and Dancers, Neta Pulvermacher's Off the Wall Dance Company, and toured internationally with Momix. She eventually co-founded her own company SoMar Dance Works, and she joined the dance faculty at Mercyhurst University in Erie, Pennsylvania. Solveig said, "My first memories of Danny at Juilliard were of his nonchalant stride and his easygoing nature: shirt buttoned low, long hair, keys dangling from his blue jeans. Stories and projects wove their way into our warm-up and dance phrases, drawn from his personal experience with the masters and the famous works of his time. And it was Danny who taught our production seminars, his own company acting as a model for our senior class as we choreographed; created a budget; designed costumes, plots, and programs; hung the lights; and swept the floor. Although I didn't realize the importance of it then, I was given, through his presence, the model of a teaching artist. The model we were given was of a generative, working professional, someone who had rubbed elbows with, worked alongside, and eventually became the right hand to more than one of the most important figures of modern dance. What it must have been like to dance with legends like José Limón, all the while facilitating a thriving company in New York. He had everything we could imagine: his own company, board of directors, and his own dance space. He traveled in circles we dreamed about, coached us, and helped facilitate the staging of important works we were given to explore. He always treated us as though we were his equal, as though our work in the world mattered, and granted opportunities to those who were ready for them."

In 1985, Danny made a work at Juilliard called *Women*. He used music by Martin Swerdlow, a Canadian composer from Toronto, who came to Juilliard to see the work.[10] The theme of the work was women, and it featured one little girl. He had a wonderful lead named Sally Sullivan who looked about twelve years old but was actually a college student. There were also two men in the work, who acted as conductors of the work. Danny brought in actress Marian Seldes to critique the work, which she did often for him. Danny found her to be a joy to work with. One year, Ethel Winter, member of the Juilliard School dance faculty and early dancer with Martha Graham, received the Martha Hill Award. Seldes was the Mistress of Ceremonies. Danny was to introduce Ethel, and Marian was to introduce Danny. When Marian got up, she first talked about Martha Hill and the award. Then she began introducing Danny, and at one point said that Danny didn't know something: She announced in a very dramatic fashion that she was *madly* in love with him!

In 1986 a letter was received from Mr. Bao You-yu, president of the National Institute of the Arts, inviting the Juilliard Dance Ensemble to the Hong Kong Academy of the Performing Arts in July. Muriel Topaz, in her first year as dance director at Juilliard, arranged this trip, and it was Danny's first visit to the academy. They took Juilliard students to perform in a festival, doing *The Traitor* by José Limón, directed by Daniel Lewis, with dancers Torbjörn Stenberg as the Christ figure and Peter London as the Traitor. Two of the followers were Kraig Patterson, who danced later with Mark Morris, and Bruce Harris, later a Broadway producer. They also did *New England Triptych* by Michael Uthoff, assisted by Nancy Scattergood Jordan. This was just before Danny's final year at Juilliard. The conference and festival were organized by Carl Wolz, who went to Hong Kong in 1982 as part of a team that established the Hong Kong Academy of the Performing Arts, and he became its first dean of dance. The festival programs were in both English and Chinese, and dancers from schools and companies from around the world participated. Wolz did a fabulous job organizing that year's festival and more festivals after that year.

Later in July as part of this same tour, the Juilliard dancers did the same works at the Taipei Festival of International Dance Academies. This was another amazing festival, with dancers and companies from all over the world. At this festival, Danny reconnected with Lin Hwai-min, who was the artistic director of Cloud Gate, a major dance

---

10. When Danny called him in 2016 to ask about the music, Swerdlow no longer had any of the electronically produced scores.

company by then. During one of the performances, there was an earthquake, so the crew had to continuously refocus the lights throughout the show, because the lights all moved when the earth shook. Lin Hwai-min came on stage to tell everyone in the audience that everything was fine and that the show would go on.

On the other side of Hong Kong Island, there was a famous flea market in the city of Stanley. Martha Hill insisted that they must go to the flea market because it had a wonderful atmosphere and fascinating merchandise. Danny, Alfredo Corvino, and Peter London were invited to go with Martha. As they were getting ready to go, Danny suggested a nearby taxi stand. Martha said no, they would take a bus, because it was a real experience. By now she was eighty-six years old! In spite of this, they took the bus, and it was packed, so they were all standing. When they got to the market, it was unbearably hot. After they all walked around for a while, Martha said, "Alfredo doesn't look very good, I think we should get him back to the hotel." Danny turned to Alfredo, who was seventy years old at the time, and quietly told him that they needed to get Martha out of there. Martha was ready to get back on a bus, but Alfredo (out of a gentlemanly concern for Martha) asked that they not take a bus, saying that he needed an air-conditioned taxi.

Daniel Lewis and Martha Hill in Taiwan, 1986 (courtesy Daniel Lewis archives).

3

The Limón Company
(1962–1974)

Dancing with José Limón's company for over a decade was one of the luckiest opportunities of my life. The experience of touring, performing, and having dances created on me by a master artist shaped me not only as a dancer, but as a choreographer and person. While Limón's death was a tragedy for all of us in the company, the experience of serving as the artistic director for the tour of the Soviet Union pushed me to grow into the role of leader, and find new skills which I would need for future endeavors.—Danny Lewis

Dancing with Limón

After Danny graduated from Juilliard in 1967, he continued dancing with the Limón Company and acting as José's assistant. He performed several works by José and would later travel the world to stage many of them.

One of the more difficult works that Danny performed was *Legend*, choreographed in 1968. *Legend* was the story of Nat Turner, an enslaved African American who led a rebellion of slaves and free blacks in Virginia on August 21, 1831, resulting in the death of 55 to 65 white people. The dancers were Danny, José Limón, and Clyde Morgan. Danny was the Master, Clyde was Nat Turner, and José was the Dark Angel. This was an emotionally difficult dance for Danny and Clyde to do because Danny had to be so brutal to Clyde in the performance, and they would hug each other both before and after the work. *Legend* was not a work that the company did a lot, but it was an important work for José. Due to his early life, moving from Mexico to Texas and transitioning from an aristocratic life to that of a Chicano farm worker, he understood the master-slave relationship. An article written on August 19, 1968, by Don McDonagh from New London, Connecticut, included an excellent review of Danny's portrayal of the Master in *Legend*. The early reviews of *Legend* were bad, but the work obviously was important to José, because he continued to work on it. The dance progressively improved, and the reviews got better and better. Shortly after the premiere performance, Louis Falco took over José's role as the Dark Angel.

The company toured the work *Comedy*, choreographed in 1968 and based on the play *Lysistrata*, with Sarah Stackhouse as the protagonist. The work was about mistresses and wives withholding their sexual favors to end a war. The company performed

Comedy at the Billy Rose Theater, although it was first done at Connecticut College in 1968; Joseph Wittman (married to choreographer Martha Wittman) wrote the music, lighting was by Thomas Skelton, and costumes were by Pauline Lawrence Limón. They wore combat boots and other odd costumes. José sent dancers Daniel Lewis, Carla Maxwell, Louis Falco, and Jennifer Muller to do a photo shoot for the *New York Times* photographer Jack Mitchell, but the way the photo was posed was distasteful to José, and he left notes on the callboard for the dancers expressing his sentiment. They actually performed *Comedy* quite a bit. What José liked about the work is that he loved controversy. If a dance got bad reviews, he was actually encouraged.

In the 1969 American Dance Festival (ADF) performance at Connecticut College in New London, Connecticut, the Limón Company performed along with other companies, including Paul Taylor, Lotte Goslar, and the First Chamber Dance Quartet, as well as four Humphrey fellows commissioned by ADF to choreograph new works. Limón did two new works (*Comedy* and *Legend*), and three revivals (*La Malinche* from 1947, *There Is a Time* from 1957, and *Traitor* from 1954). In Marcia B. Siegel's review "Old at Twenty-One" in *New York* magazine (September 16, 1968), Siegel said that both the revivals and the new works were narrative and specific, rather than abstract, and she was not particularly positive about the works. She did comment that the works "offered the gratifying experience of seeing the young members of the company in roles of real stature. Sarah Stackhouse, Jennifer Muller, Daniel Lewis, Clyde Morgan, and Carla Maxwell were outstandingly good. They have all been with Limón for the bulk of their professional careers ... and I'm delighted to see them given challenges worthy of their talents."

There Is a Time, **choreography by José Limón, 1963. Dancers from left: John Parks, Daniel Lewis, and Edward DeSoto (photograph by Eddie Effron, courtesy Daniel Lewis archives).**

Through His Friends' Eyes—Carla Maxwell

Carla Maxwell and Danny danced together for several years, starting at Juilliard. She eventually joined the Limón Company in 1965, and she was a principal dancer for many years. She became artistic director in 1978; during her tenure, the company emerged as one of the finest repertory dance ensembles in the world. After her retirement as artistic director, she became the legacy director of the Limón Company. Carla said, "Danny always had a sense of humor and a playfulness, which lightened the working atmosphere. We did many early morning performances, and he was fun to work with. Danny had so much curiosity, and he loved life. He had to work for everything, coming from a poor family, so he took nothing for granted. His work ethic was a gift, one that he received from his family and early experiences. He did not like rehearsing much, but he never failed onstage. He had many interests, including an intense interest in photography, which opened his mind. José was like a second father to Danny, which had a huge impact on Danny. He knew that after José passed, he wanted to do something else and wanted to give back to the dance community, so New World School of the Arts (NWSA) was a huge fulfillment for him. Danny always had a generous and good-natured soul, and he had a big heart. He always cared about other people and had compassion."

A year later, in the June issue 1969 of *Dance Magazine*, Marcia Marks wrote a review of *Legend*. According to Marks, after the Connecticut premiere of *Legend*, José said that the piece still needed work. Marks felt that the revised version was much improved, with Louis Falco as the Dark Angel and with the emphasis in the work being shifted to Clyde Morgan as the Slave. Daniel Lewis danced the role of the Master. She stated, "Briefly, 'Legend' depicts Southern expression of the slave, the slave's uprising and his final hanging. The Dark Angel goads the Slave on to kill his Master, then sees the Slave hanged." The African American friend who Marks brought to the performance felt that the work embraced hopelessness, whereas hope was the very essence of the history of black martyrdom. She did, however, have high praise for the authentic rendering of the spirituals. The review also discussed *The Traitor*, *La Malinche* (well danced by Carla Maxwell, Daniel Lewis, and Edward DeSoto), and *The Exiles* (Sarah Stackhouse and Louis Falco), calling it "an odd evening of violent works performed by very few dancers."

It is important to note the historical context of this work José was creating in this time period. In the 1960s, when Limón was doing work of dramatic intention and filled with lush movement, modern dance was moving in the direction of postmodernism, the Judson Church, and abstract minimalism. Limón was doing magnificent work, but critics were often very negative about his work, saying that it had too much movement, too much color, too much music, and so on. Works that are now considered masterpieces were being panned due to the context of what was happening in dance. It actually wounded José when reviews came out and 90 percent of the coverage was for the small Judson Church performances while José's large, grandiose evenings were mentioned as a minor afterthought.

José was very aware that this shift in perspective on modern dance was occurring in the mid to late 1960s. On October 5, 1966, Limón gave the convocation speech for the sixty-second academic year at Juilliard in the Concert Hall, with president Dr. Mennin presiding. After opening remarks by Mennin, Limón stated that his subject was "music and dance, musicians and dancers, composers and choreographers."

I have always maintained that musicians are dancers, and that dancers can be good dancers only when they are also good musicians.... Early in our adventure as humans on this planet, very early, even before language was invented, as pre-humans, or sub-humans, or humanoids, we had that supremely instinctual urge and capacity to dance. From this was born percussion and song and music and ritual and painting and sculpture, and from these, architecture and poetry. But all this is another story. Let me, today, only point to that supremely choreographic composer, that incomparable dancer of the spirit, J.S. Bach.... Dance, as you know, is of all kinds and categories. There is a dance for every single human experience. What, may I ask, can we call the impassioned procreative act; what else but dance is the convulsion of birth; what is the perpetual delight of infancy and childhood but a dance; and what of the frenetic rituals of adolescence; and the sober solemnities of maturity, the weddings, academic processions, inaugurations, coronations, funerals; what are these but the dances with which we are conceived, are born, grow, live, and die? All this is dance, both profane and sacred. Bach contains it all in his music, whether secular or religious. He was irrepressively a dancer.... Doris Humphrey and Martha Graham, in the early days of American dance, when they were pregnant with an indigenous art, conceived it as gloriously free of the dead hand of an effete and decayed past. Doris Humphrey created dances, almost symphonic in dimension, entirely without musical accompaniment.... She accomplished some revolutionary works, the repercussions of which are with us to this day. I was privileged, as a young member of her company, to perform in some of these.... I was astonished when, one day, she returned to J.S. Bach. To the Passacaglia and Fugue in C Minor. Bach, her first love. And to the contemporary composers.

Limón went on to speak of Isadora Duncan, and her use of classical composers, such as Tchaikovsky and Schubert. Returning to Humphrey, he said,

I asked Doris Humphrey, who would always speak of Pavlova and Nijinsky with reverence and adoration, if it was really true that these two lived up to the legend that has grown about them. She said that it was true and much more. In these two, she saw perfection. Flawless artistry. Then came the supreme accolade, "They did not dance to music. They were music," she said.

Limón told an anecdote about his wife Pauline Lawrence, and her experience with a famous dancer:

My wife as a young girl just out of high school, as a talented pianist, found herself playing the piano for dancers' rehearsals. She speaks of these days as completely fascinating. A new and exciting world, the world of art and glamour was opened to her. One rehearsal she finds memorable. She was playing for a famous dancer. The concluding bars of a solo passage were causing trouble. The dance and the music just simply would not end simultaneously. This happened over and over again. In utter exasperation, the dancer stalked to the piano, pointed a trembling finger at the music, and demanded to know why the final chord was not being played. My wife explained that there was no such chord, that she was playing the music as it was on the paper. The dancer, by now very irritated, pointed to a mark on the music and demanded, "What's that?" "That's a rest," said my wife. "Well, play it anyway!" My wife did. She played the rest.

Limón went on to talk about his work with various composers, Heitor Villa-Lobos, Arnold Schoenberg, Norman Dello Joio, Gunther Schuller, Hugh Aitken, and Paul Hindemith. He told the story of setting his work *The Demon* to Hindemith music, and how Hindemith reacted when he first saw the piece. Limón had been warned that Hindemith was difficult, with a vile temper, so when he heard the commotion out front after the piece, he was sure that Hindemith was having "an apoplectic seizure." It turned out that Hindemith was applauding and shouting his approval. After that, he conducted the work and was a joy to work with, insisting that the dancers could ask for whatever they needed.

At the end of his talk he told the graduating students how privileged they were to be artists:

I adjure you to the courage and probity of the artist, to a terrible daring, to fortitude in the face of the challenge of nihilism, and lunatic horror. Some of you here will work with tradition. Others will find new roads. I hope the first will revere and conserve, but not embalm, the treasure of the past. There is a great difference between a pantheon and a mausoleum. The others, I hope, will not spit in the face of tradition. Remember the old girl is your mother, and there is a commandment, the fifth, if you will recall. Be truly revolutionary, not a mere mutineer or rebel. Revolutions, after the ax and the guillotine and the firing squad have finished their untidy work, can be glorious. Make yours one such. Remember you are peerless. Remember that art is redemptive, that your life will be half debacle, half apotheosis. You will be wounded. Wear your scars as the most exalted of decorations.

The Festival of Dance series took place for several years at the Brooklyn Academy of Music in Brooklyn, New York, and was an astonishing collection of dancers, companies, and choreography from New York. In August 1966, dancers included Patricia McBride (New York City Ballet), Edward Villella (New York City Ballet), and Glen Tetley Dance Company. In 1968–1969, companies in this festival included Martha Graham, José Limón, Yvonne Rainer, Twyla Tharp, Anna Sokolow, Don Redlich, Paul Taylor, Meredith Monk, Erick Hawkins, Alwin Nikolais, Merce Cunningham, Alvin Ailey, and American Ballet Theatre. The festival went on for over three weeks. The Limón Company did *Comedy*, *Missa Brevis*, *Psalm*, *There Is a Time*, *The Winged*, and *Tragedy*. Danny said that *Comedy* and *Tragedy* were probably two of José's weakest works. The music for *Comedy* was by Joe Wittman. *Tragedy* (also called *My Son, My Enemy*) was choreographed in 1965. The music for *My Son, My Enemy* was by Vivian Fine, and it was scored for objects like chains, broken glass, falling bricks, and glasses of water (to be rubbed). The work also had acrobats and swimmers in it. Vivian sent a piano reduction of the work, which the dancers couldn't count. José invited Vivian to rehearsal to help the dancers with the music. She brought the score and a tape recorder, with a recording of the score. Vivian counted as they danced, but she simply called out what sounded to the dancers like random numbers: "1 [long pause], 1, 2 [long pause], 1 [long pause], 1, 2, 3, 1," and so on for 15 minutes. When the work ended, José told Vivian how very helpful the session was and thanked her. He walked her to the door, she left, and José turned to the dancers and said "Just keep dancing." They only did the work once or twice after that session!

The Limón Company did lengthy bus tours in the early years of Danny's time in the company, often for the public schools and colleges. The most famous bus driver of all was Tiny, who was actually pretty big! The company would do a performance, immediately get on the bus, ride for two to four hours to a hotel, and go to sleep. They would then wake up the next morning, drive another two to three hours, get to the theater, unpack and set up, warm up, rehearse and space the works, do the performance, and get back on the bus to repeat the whole cycle again. This would go on for thirty days and thirty nights with twenty-seven performances. They would get at least one day off per week, partly because they were members of American Guild of Musical Artists (AGMA), so it was required to have one day off each week. There were dozens (if not hundreds) of these performances on the bus tours.

Through His Friends' Eyes—Laura Glenn

Laura Glenn was one of the dancers on these bus tours, and she reminisced about Danny's nature throughout his life, and how it manifested on the bus tours. She said, "In public school, there are always children who were the teacher helpers, like running the projector. Danny was one of those kids, always volunteering to help. He was a great caregiver all his life. He was always doing extra deeds for José and other dancers. For example, he got a tape machine and a pillow for José to put on his lap on the bus tours, so José could listen to music, which he loved. He was also a good dance partner, making sure no harm came to people."

Sometimes the rides were really long—they might be in Ohio one day and in South Carolina the next. The day they went through the Appalachian Mountains, everyone on the bus became sick to their stomachs from all the winding roads. In one place in North Carolina, there was a blizzard, and Tiny got lost, so they were very late getting to the performance. The show was supposed to start at 8:00 p.m., and they were still on the bus. They stopped to phone ahead to let them know that they would be there; the venue was already filled with the audience. As soon as they arrived, José went onto the stage to talk to the audience while the dancers warmed up in front of the audience; hence it was a very abbreviated warm-up. José was very nice and explained the situation to everyone. He told the dancers that *A Choreographic Offering* was on the program, but they would only do the first four sections and the finale, or they would be there late into the night.

The company also did lectures/demonstrations on these tours. For these demonstrations, the dancers were divided into the Sunrise Group (the early morning dancers) and the Sunset Group (the evening dancers). Danny and Alice paired up for the early morning shows, and they would do sections of the dances with lots of lifts. Once at a performance for children, José described Danny and Alice by saying, "Miss Condodina could not get in the air without Mr. Lewis." After one appearance at a junior high school, one of the students sent a letter to Danny afterward speculating that Danny and Alice must be a couple who were in love with each other, which is why they were dancing that way together!

Through His Friends' Eyes—Alice Condodina

Alice Condodina danced with Danny during his early years with the José Limón Company, and with Felix Fibich. In the 1960s and 1970s she was a Limón master dance artist and principal dancer. She had her own company in New York and later in California where she taught in the dance department at University of California at Santa Barbara from 1975 to 1994, returning annually as a research faculty member. Alice said, "Danny had incredible dedication to the art of dance, and extraordinary respect and love for the art of José Limón. His belief in the ability to make a dream happen was obvious, starting with his pulling himself up to become the hardworking artist he was in José's company. He clearly demonstrated this ability with his own company, with what he achieved, the support that the dancers gave to him, and the integrity of how he worked. He had amazing strength as a dancer. I first saw Danny dance The Unsung *when it had its premiere performance at the Juilliard Theater in 1970. I can still see him dancing his remarkable solo, and no one has equaled it. Even though I had been a dancer my whole life, he made me feel the essence of what it would be to have an urgency to dance. I wanted to get up and fly and roll and jump! It had to be love and commitment that put his body in space and time so vehemently that it could cause such a reaction in someone who was a dancer. He became a real dance poet."*

Once, coming back from a long tour, they stopped to do a performance at Colgate College in Pennsylvania. The auditorium had a church-like front, with a platform stage and a drop-off at the end. They moved chairs and used the floor space down below the stage area to dance. For the crossover, they had to go over the pedals of the organ and then through a door to get back to the dance space. It was very difficult to do the work, because the stage was so small and the works they had prepared (*A Choreographic Offering* and *Missa Brevis*) had large casts and used huge amounts of space. On stage right, when the women would exit leaping, the men had to form a human wall to catch them. On stage left, there was a grand piano that the dancers had to crawl under to get to the stage. Of course, the audience saw none of this!

Another funny on-tour story occurred at Stockton State College in New Jersey, where they were performing *There Is a Time.* They got to the point in the dance for "A Time to Embrace," and Danny and Sarah Stackhouse entered the stage and went into the

opening position, holding each other. The sound technician always worked with two tape machines so they could go from one recording to the other easily and cue up one work while another was playing. Apparently, the person running the machine didn't thread the tape correctly for "A Time to Embrace"; as the tape started, the sound was garbled, as it were speeding up and slowing down constantly. Danny and Sarah just kept dancing; they were doing fine until Danny heard the company in the wings laughing and laughing. In the meantime, José was screaming into a headset, asking the technicians what was going on and telling them to fix it. Through all of it, Danny and Sarah just kept going, but by then were literally biting their lips to keep themselves from laughing. Then they heard the audience starting to giggle. José screamed out, "There's going to be an investigation!" José pulled the curtain and stepped out to speak to the audience. He apologized and said that they would start from the beginning of that section, because the audience needed to see the entire section with the music. Sarah was back-

José Limón and Pauline Koner at North Carolina School of the Arts, 1968, one of the few known photographs of the two of them together after their split in 1957 (photograph by Daniel Lewis, courtesy Daniel Lewis archives).

stage saying, "Don't make me go out there again!" José did indeed make the two of them go back onstage and do the whole section again.

Another performance was in 1968 at North Carolina School of the Arts, with Nick Cernovich touring with them for lighting. José had not spoken to Pauline Koner since he had split with her in South America in 1957. It was agreed that the two of them would meet and go out on stage to reminisce about the early days of the company. For the dancers who were backstage, seeing them onstage together again was a warm and beautiful moment.

The company did many performances in Chicago, a few of them at the Harper Theater, which sponsored a fabulous dance series. In November 1968, while performing at the Harper Theater, one of the works in the show was *The Moor's Pavane*.[1] At one point in the work, a handkerchief comes out, and Othello gives it to Desdemona. Something went wrong, and the handkerchief got caught on Emilia's dress, long before she was supposed to have it in the choreography. Emilia kept trying to get rid of it, and finally she threw it, and it ended up with Iago. The handkerchief kept getting passed around until it eventually made its way back to Desdemona.

Brooklyn Academy of Music (1968)

On February 3, 1968, the company performed at the Brooklyn Academy of Music (BAM). They did *The Winged* and *Missa Brevis*. Dancers in this show were the full company,[2] with Betty Jones as guest artist. Danny danced in both works. Costumes were by Pauline Lawrence and Charles Tomlinson, company stage manager was Judy Daykin, and assistants to Limón were Sarah Stackhouse and Daniel Lewis. The lighting for this concert was by Thomas Skelton, incidental music for *The Winged* was by Hank Johnson, and a tape score put together by Simon Sadoff and Daniel Lewis of background sounds. *The Winged* was danced by Louis Falco, Sarah Stackhouse, guest artist Betty Jones, and the full company. In Clive Barnes' review entitled "Dance: Limon Company in Brooklyn" in the *New York Times* on February 5, 1968, Barnes noted that the company was in excellent performing condition. He called *The Winged* the major attraction of the evening. He stated that since its 1966 premiere, Limón had trimmed and shaped it, courageously omitting his own role, and the work could hold its own with the finest of Limón's work. "Indeed, in the matter of sheer dance invention, it is probably his most effortless achievement.... Light, airy and impressively buoyant, the ballet sweeps along with admirable momentum. The young company performs with a well-judged mixture of vigor and tension.... Betty Jones, Sarah Stackhouse, and particularly the exciting Louis Falco were outstanding, but now the ensemble is more evenly matched, and other dancers, such as Clyde Morgan and Daniel Lewis, show considerable potentiality." Barnes also discussed *Missa Brevis*, noting that the work had strength, beauty, and a passionate poignancy. "As in 'The Winged,' the ensemble supported the ballet with

1. *The Moor's Pavane* is based on Shakespeare's *Othello* and condenses the story of the four main characters (Othello, his wife Desdemona, his friend Iago, and his friend's wife Emilia), danced in the form of the pavane.
2. Company dancers were Louis Falco, Sarah Stackhouse, Jennifer Muller, Laura Glenn, Diane Mohrmann, Daniel Lewis, Avner Vered, Lenore Latimer, Carla Maxwell, Fritz Ludin, Edward DeSoto, Jennifer Scanlon, Tamara Woshakiwsky, Alice Condodina, Clyde Morgan, and Louis Solino.

excellently controlled dancing." He ended the review by remarking on Limón's "remarkable choreographic imagination."

Billy Rose Theatre (1969)

The Billy Rose Theatre was a Broadway theater on 41st Street in New York. In January 1969, Richard Barr and Edward Albee presented a series of shows at the theater, produced by Charles Reinhart (executive producer) and Michael Kasdan (associate producer), including an extended series by the Limón Company.

Dancers were the full company.[3] The musical director was Simon Sadoff, and lighting was by Nicholas Cernovich. Danny performed "A Time to Be Born and a Time to Die" and "A Time to Embrace and a Time to Refrain from Embracing" with Sarah Stackhouse in *There Is a Time*, *Swifts* with Diane Mohrmann, the solo "Hopper" and the group section "Flight of Furies" in *The Winged*, and Iago in *The Moor's Pavane*; was among the group Psalmists in *Psalm*; and was in *Comedy* and *Missa Brevis*.

At one point, there was a series of performances at the Billy Rose Theatre by modern dance masters, with combined programs—that is, more than one company in a given show. Lotte Goslar, a famous dancer and mime known for her eccentric and whimsical comedy, was a short, roly-poly woman with a round, expressive face. As a performer, she brought bugs, flowers, and mushrooms vividly to life. In one of her most famous solos, "Grandma Always Danced," she was seen first as a baby and then as a bride, a mother, and finally an old woman. Because of her quirky subject matter, no one wanted to share a program with her. José was a magnanimous gentleman, and he agreed to share an evening with her. In his view, she was an artist, and he didn't care what her subject matter was.

The Billy Rose Theatre was a fabulous season, and Danny loved the fact that it was mainstream Broadway, where all the major musicals took place. Here they were presenting modern dance in the same space and making a statement by moving onto the next level of performance.

In Frances Herridge's review in the *New York Post* on January 21, 1969, titled "José Limón Begins Broadway Run," Herridge began by talking about how rare it was to see modern dance companies on Broadway. This week-long run included the premiere of *The Winged*, plus *There Is a Time* and *The Moor's Pavane*, which the reviewer called "the most dramatically perfect work that Limón has ever done." Limón danced as Othello, with Sarah Stackhouse as Desdemona, Louis Falco as Iago, and Jennifer Muller as Emilia. The review had mixed comments about *The Winged*, calling some of the sections superb but finding other variations not as successful, feeling that overall the work was too long, but praising Limón's movement inventiveness. The final discussion was about *There Is a Time*, especially noting the lovely duet "A Time to Embrace and a Time to Refrain from Embracing."

In 1969, other reviews would mention the brilliant, younger dancers Clyde Morgan,

3. Company dancers were Louis Falco, Sarah Stackhouse, Jennifer Muller, Daniel Lewis, Jennifer Scanlon, Lenore Latimer, Laura Glenn, Carla Maxwell, Diane Mohrmann, Tamara Woshakiwsky, Alice Condodina, Clyde Morgan, Edward, DeSoto, Louis Solino, Avner Vered, and Charles Hayward.

Daniel Lewis, and Edward DeSoto in the company. There are multiple reviews of *The Moor's Pavane*, which may have been reviewed more than any other modern dance in history.

University of California at Los Angeles (1969)

In 1969, the company toured California, performing at the University of California at Los Angeles (UCLA). The dancers were the full company.[4] When the Limón Company went to Royce Hall at UCLA, it was an incredible time for José because his entire family lived in California, so many came to the performance. One brother had already passed away, but the brother's two children came, and they were enthralled by Uncle José, having never seen him or his work. The company met all the family members backstage.

Thirteen years later, Danny received a letter dated April 15, 1982, from Lavinia Limón, a niece of José Limón, in which she expressed her appreciation for Danny's piece *Moments: The Tribute to José Limón*, which premiered that year. In her words, "I know very well what pieces inspire, affect, and move me, and 'Moments' did all of that. I really felt that you caught the spirit and soul of my uncle in the piece.... Also, I saw 'And David Wept' on television and thought you were marvelous. I would greatly enjoy seeing your company at some time in the future."

Brooklyn Academy of Music (1969)

The company performed for the second time at BAM in the 1968–1969 festival. This was the more important BAM concert, because these were the last performances that José did with the company. Dancers were the full company,[5] with Letitia Ide and Marian Seldes as guest artists, performing in *Lament for Ignacio Sanchez Mejias*. The conductor was Simon Sadoff, lighting was by Chenault Spence, and costumes were by Pauline Lawrence.

On April 29 and May 3, they performed *A Choreographic Offering, Lament for Ignacio Sanchez Mejias*, and *The Moor's Pavane* (with José Limón dancing the part of Othello). On April 30 and May 2, they performed *La Malinche* (dancers Carla Maxwell, Danny Lewis, and Edward DeSoto; music by Norman Lloyd), *The Exiles* (dancers Louis Falco and Sarah Stackhouse, music by Arnold Schoenbert), *Legend* (dancers Clyde Morgan, Danny Lewis, and José Limón), and *The Traitor* (with José Limón as the Leader; Louis Falco as the Traitor; and Followers Danny Lewis, Clyde Morgan, Edward DeSoto, Louis Solino, Avner Vered, and Charles Hayward). It was at the end of these performances that Pauline Limón urged José to retire and let people remember him as a great dancer. He was sixty-one years old at the time.

---

4. Company dancers were Louis Falco, Sarah Stackhouse, Jennifer Muller, Daniel Lewis, Jennifer Scanlon, Lenore Latimer, Laura Glenn, Carla Maxwell, Diane Mohrmann, Tamara Woshakiwsky, Alice Condodina, Clyde Morgan, Edward DeSoto, Louis Solino, Avner Vered, and Charles Hayward.

5. Company dancers were Louis Falco, Sarah Stackhouse, Jennifer Muller, Daniel Lewis, Jennifer Scanlon, Clyde Morgan, Laura Glenn, Alice Condodina, Carla Maxwell, Diane Mohrmann, Tamara Woshakiwsky, Edward DeSoto, Louis Solino, Avner Vered, and Charles Hayward.

While they were in Brooklyn for this performance, Danny took his blue Volkswagen (the car that he bought just after the Asia tour) to the repair shop at the dealership because the generator was not working. The technician at the shop, Julio Berlingeri, had just come from Argentina a few weeks earlier. They ended up talking for a while, and Julio asked Danny what he did. Normally, Danny did not tell men he met that he was a dancer, but he felt it would be OK to tell Julio, who then asked him what company he danced with. When Danny answered José Limón, Julio started talking to him in Spanish! Danny told him that he did not speak any Spanish, so Julio switched back to English to explain that he was the pilot who had flown the Limón Company all around Argentina and South America when they toured there. Danny got Julio tickets for their upcoming performance at BAM. When the show was over, he brought Julio backstage and took him to José's dressing room. The moment the door opened, José called to Julio by name and began talking to him in Spanish. They hugged like old friends. Later when Danny needed to replace the blue Volkswagen, Julio helped Danny find an orange Volkswagen (which he called "Pumpkin"). Julio had a beautiful wife named Carmen, and the couple became good friends with Danny's parents, who lived nearby in Brooklyn.[6]

Adirondack Champlain Festival (1971)

The Limón Company toured upstate New York, and the Adirondack Champlain Festival (now called Adirondack Harvest Festival) was one of the events they did. They performed *La Malinche* (danced by Laura Glenn, Aaron Osborne, and Edward DeSoto), *The Exiles* (danced by Carla Maxwell and Clyde Morgan), *Night Spell* (with José's solo danced by Danny Lewis), and *The Moor's Pavane* (with Danny doing Iago). On this tour, they performed in one venue that looked like a summer resort place, with a space that was a dining room in the daytime and a ballroom at night. When they were rehearsing, the floor was really slippery. So to give the floor a bit of stickiness, they put down cola syrup diluted in water, which they brought on tour for this purpose. The four dancers stepped out on stage for *The Moor's Pavane* and started the first leg gesture, which was a plié with a rond de jambe. All four dancers left their ballet slippers stuck to the floor. They had obviously used too much cola! In some places the floor was tacky, and in other places the floor was still wet. The dancers were slipping and sliding and sticking all over the place. In Danny's words, the performance was "ludicrous."

Limón's Death

Limón died on December 2, 1972. Afterward, there was a controversy over who owned his ballets. The Dance Notation Bureau (DNB) took it upon themselves to start selling the work to various companies.[7] The issue of ownership of Limón's work was

---

6. Danny lost track of Julio and Carmen, but years later he received an email from Carmen asking if she had reached the right Danny Lewis. She had since divorced Julio and had moved to India, working for UNESCO as an administrative officer.

7. Eventually, Danny had to get the DNB to pay the Limón Foundation back. Muriel Topaz (then with the DNB) made a deal with Danny that she would notate certain works for free in exchange for the money they had collected.

Night Spell, **choreography by Doris Humphrey. Dancers from left: Laura Glenn, Jennifer Scanlon and Daniel Lewis in the air (photograph by Martha Swope, courtesy José Limón Dance Foundation).**

unclear, because the choreographic works were not specifically mentioned in the will, so the court decision was that the family owned the works. The Limón Institute was then in the difficult position of trying to divide the royalties among nine brothers and sisters, including one brother who died and whose share would go to his two children. It wasn't that much money to divide nine ways. One of the brothers said it was ridiculous, because it would not be that much money, and the family should accept an offer from the institute for the rights to the work. Each family member was given $2,500 for his or her share of the work. The two children of the deceased brother refused to sell the rights back (especially the son who was an actor), so Danny went out to Los Angeles and talked to them at length. Carla Maxwell and her sister Paula Maxwell Guerrero also made a trip to meet with the family, because Paula spoke Spanish. Carla thought that some of the family feared they would lose José's spirit if they gave up the rights to the work. Carla emphasized to them that this would be how José would live on—by keeping his work alive by the institute's continued staging of his work. The Limón Foundation now owns all of the works except *The Waldstein Sonata*, which is owned by Danny, because this piece was completed by Danny and did not premiere until after Limón's death.[8]

The Soviet Union Tour (1973)

With Danny as acting artistic director, the Soviet Union tour took place shortly after Limón died. This was Danny's last tour with the Limón Company. Programs from the tour were all in Russian and included several pictures of Risa Steinberg, Edward DeSoto, Carla Maxwell, and Peter Sparling. Also in these photos were Laura Glenn, Jennifer Scanlon, and Danny. HI Enterprises was the company that took over the Limón Company management during this period. Judy Hankins of HI Enterprises accompanied the company to the Soviet Union in 1973.

An article in the *Leningrad Press* dated February 26, 1973, described the opening night at the Opera Studio in Leningrad. It mentioned that the end of the show was met with seven minutes of rhythmic handclapping, the traditional sign of approval in eastern Europe and the U.S.S.R. The audience had 1,850 Leningraders—a packed house—and they watched *There Is a Time*, *The Unsung*, and *The Moor's Pavane*.

While all the pieces were met with interest and attention—through *The Unsung*, twenty-six and a half minutes of dance only to the sound of eight solo male dancers' feet, the theater was completely silent—it was the final two numbers that elicited the dance-wise crowd's most enthusiastic response. As the curtain fell on *The Unsung*'s final scene, an American Indian receding into the silent distance, a cloud of applause broke that called the dancers back singly and together, again and again. It was the last piece, however, the late José Limón's classic treatment of Othello—*The Moor's Pavane*—that brought the house down. The audience sat forward tensely as Iago (Daniel Lewis) whispered his deadly insinuations into the ear of the Moor (Edward DeSoto) while his wife stole Desdemona's handkerchief. As in its Shakespearean source, tension mounted as the inevitability of the tragedy became increasingly evident. In the words of one viewer, "The Moor's tragedy was magnificently translated, and enhanced by the dance medium in Limón's hands." "A dramatic dance spectacular," said another, referring to the richly costumed figures—Moor in blood-red velvet and Desdemona in traditional white against a background of Iago's ochre—moving to the stately Renaissance rhythms of Purcell's Abdelazar Suite. Tuesday night the group performs *Concerto Grosso*, choreographed by Limón in 1945 to the music of Vivaldi; *Orfeo*, another Limón piece to Beethoven's Opus 95, No. 11 in F minor, done in 1972; *Dances of Isadora*, a Limón piece choreographed in 1971 to music of Chopin and dedicated to the great American interpretive dancer, once married to Russian poet Sergei Yesenin; and finishing with Limón's famous *Emperor Jones*, a 1956 work done to the music of Heitor Villa-Lobos, especially commissioned for the piece.

---

8. After the dispute over Limón's works was resolved, a similar issue occurred with the works of Martha Graham, and the rights to her works were battled over in court. Both the Martha Graham Foundation and Ron Protas (caretaker of Graham in her last years) claimed the rights, but the courts uncovered documents in which the foundation had commissioned and paid Graham to choreograph the works, so it was the foundation that owned them, not Martha. Similarly, José might have been paid by Juilliard or by the Limón Company or by a commissioning organization to create the works and may have never actually owned them. Unfortunately, Sue Pimsleur, the Musical Artists company manager, had disposed of all of the contracts and other paperwork, and there was no proof of ownership of the work.

Before they had left for the Soviet Union, Konstantin Sergeyev, the artistic director of the Kirov Ballet, came to the United States to see and approve all of the works they would be dancing in Moscow. He looked at every repertory work for the tour except for *The Exiles*, because they had not yet rehearsed it. The plan was to stage it and then show it to him when they got to Moscow. The company arrived in Moscow, and Carla Maxwell and Danny performed it for him in rehearsal, alone in the huge Rossiya Concert Hall in Red Square. Afterwards, Sergeyev came up on stage, kissed them both, said he loved the work and that it was beautiful and there would be no problem performing it. However, on the opening night performance in Leningrad, Laura Glenn and Aaron Osborne performed it. Danny and Carla had danced it like innocent thirteen-year-olds leaving the Garden of Eden, but Laura and Aaron performed it more like nineteen-year-old adults. Toward the end of the performance of the work, Danny started hearing noise backstage. The audience was giving the work a standing ovation, but meanwhile the Soviet officials backstage were reacting to the work with outrage. Danny was called over to where the commotion was going on and was told the company could not perform this ballet again. Danny suggested that he and Carla do it, but he was told that if they performed that ballet again the company would be sent home. Danny and management had a meeting that evening to change the programming for the whole tour. The next morning, Sergeyev came to Danny's hotel by himself to have breakfast with Danny. He apologized and

Daniel Lewis and Carla Maxwell in *The Moor's Pavane*, choreography by José Limón, in Moscow during the Soviet tour, 1973 (photograph by V. Bliokh, courtesy José Limón Dance Foundation).

said that his government wasn't ready for that work. Maybe on another tour at a future date they could do it.

When the company was in Riga, Latvia, Danny was having meetings at the embassies regularly, and everything about the tour had to be negotiated. The dancers all felt that the Aeroflot Airlines was terrible, with extremely harsh takeoffs and landings (which were cheaper for the airline than takeoffs and landings with slower ascents and descents). On the first flight, everyone got sick. After that, they decided that they wanted to take the train, rather than fly, and this had to be negotiated with the government. The problem was the dance floor they traveled with. If it was put on the train for the many hours of travel, it would become frozen and take two days to thaw out. Therefore, they had to fly the floor and put the dancers on the train! The train ride was a grand experience, with wooden cars and potbelly stoves.

At every performance, there was a KGB agent backstage, and their bags were continually searched. Danny had brought some art books (works of Kadinski) to give as presents from dancers of the New York City Ballet to their friends in companies in the Soviet Union. Danny packed them in the costume boxes to hide them. He would take the books, get picked up by a car, go several blocks, get out, and walk through an alley way to get to the Russian dancers. It was a smuggling operation— for something as harmless as art books! Back at the hotel, the Soviet agents were very upset that Danny disappeared for hours. When he got back, he was interrogated about where he had gone.

The lack of freedom on this tour was strange to the dancers. They were not allowed to take pictures at the airport. At one point, Danny left a copy of *Time* magazine in his hotel room, and they brought it to him at the airport so that it would not be not left in the room for anyone to find and read. At one point, Edward DeSoto came to Danny to say that he had forgotten that he had a joint in his hat, and he wondered what he should do. Danny said that they should go out-

Daniel Lewis in Moscow during the Soviet tour, 1973 (courtesy Daniel Lewis archives).

side in Red Square and smoke it rather than waste it! They did this with many people walking around the Square, but because the Russians all smoked various cigarettes with strong odors they felt safe doing it. When people started looking at them, though, they became worried. Then they realized that it was not the joint that was drawing attention—it was their white leather coats. Everyone else was dressed in the standard green coat and hat with the Soviet star on it.

While they were in Riga, Danny received a phone call that Risa Steinberg's father had passed away. He went to her room to tell her, and he suggested that they go for a walk. They went for a long walk to talk and ended up lost and wandering the city at 2:00 a.m.; they couldn't find the hotel. They saw a militia man with his green coat and machine gun. They made some noise approaching him so that he would see them coming and not react. Danny said they were looking for the Hotel Riga, but the man only heard "Riga." He just kept saying "Riga" and walked away. They finally bumped into a group of teenagers, who understood and led them back to the hotel.

This tour was the last time that Danny performed with the Limón Company. It was in Moscow, which was to be the last performance, that Danny let it be known that he would be retiring from the company. Previous to this evening, Danny had taught master classes at the Moiseyev School and at the Bolshoi School. Students from the two schools and company members were all there at the Moscow performance, joining with the audience in rhythmic handclapping. Danny recalls the bows for *The Moor's Pavane*; he remembers going out one at a time, then all four dancers, then again one at a time, then all four—the ovation went on and on and on. Danny remembered thinking during these curtain calls, "What a way to end my time with the company!"

4

Reminiscing About
the Limón Company

At the time I was dancing in Jose's works, I knew how lucky I was to be dancing masterpieces and observing how they developed. The work was physically satisfying, as I loved his movement, but also it was a gift to dance in works that had a deeper emotional and philosophical context. There were so many aspects to dancing his work that influenced me. It was such a fantastic time in the company, and I was so lucky to work with such amazing and dedicated dancers.—Danny Lewis

Interview with Danny about José Limón[1]

There are several reasons I was attracted to working with José rather than with other choreographers. José was very open to the idea of the dancer being part of his creative process. I felt I had the freedom of interpretation, and then José would tell me what he did or didn't like. Of any choreographer I had met, he was the one with whom I could have the most natural relationship and open conversation, sharing humor and common values. He respected me as a dancer as well as a person. When I first met José, he drove a red jeep rather than a car, which I enjoyed, and after a time, I learned that he drove a riding lawnmower at his farm near Stockton, New Jersey. Once I was in the company, I spent quite a bit of time at the farm with José and Pauline.

The most exciting and rewarding experience was being choreographed on by José. His imagery and his stories leading up to the movement gave me so much information to allow interpretation of the choreography. Movement phrases were not precious to José; a movement on Tuesday did not necessarily work for him Wednesday. He was more idea driven, and as a work developed, he would go back and change or fix phrases to suit the concept of the work. Every day at Juilliard, he would arrive with another story that the garage attendant in New Jersey told him while he waited to board the train to New York. These stories were, at times, crass and not to be told to a refined audience, but I really loved them and laughed with José. He was always a gentleman in rehearsals

---

1. In this interview with Donna Krasnow in Miami, Florida, in October 2016, Danny expressed his personal thoughts and experiences dancing in José's work, and the works that were profoundly meaningful to him.

and treated dancers with kindness and respect. In all my years of working with José, I only saw him lose his temper in a rehearsal a few times. In one instance, I was assisting José while he was choreographing *Mac Aber's Dance* in the Juilliard Theater. A young stagehand walked onto the stage and said it was time to stop rehearsal. When José asked why, he was told that the rehearsal was over. José stood up from his chair and threw the chair into the orchestra pit, knocking over the music stands and chairs, and ended the rehearsal abruptly. I could see in his face that his creative process was being slit with a knife.

There is a story about *Mac Aber's Dance*. It was a good work for the Juilliard students as it displayed their talents well, and the music was excellent, but as a choreographic work it was not very strong, and José did not consider it one of his masterpieces. In the dance, there is an orchestra pit, and the dancers kept sliding into the pit. The music was by Jacob Druckman, Muriel Topaz's husband. One day, they were rehearsing *A Choreographic Offering*, and José announced that Rebecca Harkness wanted a Limón work for the Harkness Ballet. The company dancers were very excited, as it was a great opportunity and hopefully would bring in good money. José went to dinner with Rebecca Harkness, and the next day, José came back to rehearsal and when asked about the dinner, he said, "The woman has the taste of a chambermaid. You know what she asked for? *Mac Aber's Dance!*" The company then asked him what he said to her, and he remarked, "I said no."

The first work of José's that I ever danced in was *Missa Brevis*. The first work I actually learned was *The Emperor Jones*, but *Missa Brevis* was my first experience performing a Limón work. When José asked me to go to Asia, I was a first-year student at Juilliard. I said yes, but I did not hear from him all year. Then I got a call from Halan (Harkey) McCallum to come and learn *The Emperor Jones*, just the two of us. I went to the rehearsals and learned the parts in the work. When the company was called together, I was the understudy, and the men who had been in the company for a while did the work. At the same time, I learned *Missa Brevis*, and that was the first work I performed at Connecticut College that summer. I also danced in *There Is a Time* at Connecticut. After that the company came to New York for the opening of the Philharmonic, where I did a trio and a quartet in *Missa Brevis*, because Chase Robinson was sick. Then we headed to Asia. This was the same summer that Ruth Currier was injured, and her solo "A Time to Laugh" was changed to a trio, with David Wynne and me carrying her around the stage for the whole work.

The first work that José choreographed on me specifically was *A Choreographic Offering*, which was still during my Juilliard years. I was in the large group sections, called "Two Essays for Large Ensemble." When I came back from Asia in 1963, José did not invite many of the old company members to return, and he formed the company with the newer dancers: me, Jennifer Muller, Libby Nye, Sarah Stackhouse, and Louis Falco. José started working on the fast quintet with me, Jennifer Muller, Libby Nye, Michael Uthoff, and John Parks. We rehearsed at Socrates Birsky's studio, a strange place with wooden floors. After the Asia tour, José did the work *The Demon* (1963), and he did *Two Essays for Large Ensemble* at Connecticut College with the summer dance program students. The following year he developed *A Choreographic Offering* (1964) at Juilliard with the dance students, and he was working with his company outside Juilliard for the smaller sections. He also did *Variations on a Theme of Paganini* (1965) with the Juilliard students (but I was not in this work), and *My Son, My Enemy* (1965) at Connecticut

College. For me, after the early performances and the Asia tour, which was a major experience, working on these works felt like part of the job. Because I had already learned so much work, and performed so much, learning *A Choreographic Offering* did not feel like a huge deal.

As for my favorite Limón works to dance, a highlight was dancing *The Moor's Pavane* with José as Othello. And doing the men's trio in *Missa Brevis* with José in the lead role was also very special. I truly loved dancing onstage with José; he was a big guy who pulled you around the stage. José also danced one section of *A Choreographic Offering*, but he got injured and brought Betty Jones back to do his part.

Carla Maxwell and Daniel Lewis in *The Moor's Pavane*, choreography by José Limón (photograph by Martha Swope, courtesy the José Limón Dance Foundation).

Daniel Lewis in *The Unsung* premiere, choreography by José Limón, Juilliard Theater, 1971 (courtesy José Limón Dance Foundation).

Originally it was a trio at the beginning of the work, and it became a solo with four men entering later, who carried Betty off the stage. Falco and Stackhouse danced the fast duets, and she did the very slow solo later in the work. Probably the most interesting work to do that José choreographed was *The Winged*, because it was working with abstract ideas, and each dancer had solos and duets. Other works like *My Son, My Enemy* were large group works, but *The Winged* felt very individual. My favorite section wasn't even my own solo, which was "Hopper," about a bird that hopped but never took flight; it was "Borrowed Wings," about two birds that couldn't fly but borrowed someone else's wings. It was a wonderful duet and the only section that had actual music by Hank Johnson, a Juilliard student who had given José jazz scores that he had composed. Originally José did not want music for *The Winged*, but Pauline Limón convinced him that he had to have some background music. Simon Sadoff and I found bird sounds and made a collage for "Harpies." José decided to use Johnson's music for "Borrowed Wings." *The Winged* was certainly the most fun to work on in the choreographic process.

The next work of importance to me was *The Unsung* (1970), as this was again working on individual solos and duets. *The Unsung* was José's homage to the Native American chiefs, and I danced the role of Sitting Bull. When José began the work, I was traveling, staging José's work at various places, so I did not know a lot of it. When I first came home, I learned "Pantheon," which is the opening section. José choreographed my solo in one rehearsal. I came back the next day, and José cut it and made it shorter. It was a simple solo, but José knew me so well by then that he could create all the movement very quickly. José would show me what he wanted, and I would, off on the side, start doing it, and José would say, "Oh, I like that better, do it that way." That is why I made the decision many years ago to dance for José rather than Martha Graham; with her, you did material exactly as she wanted, but with José, you were given a lot of liberty. (Paul Taylor also gave his dancers liberty, and he used to say that the choreographer is only

50 percent of the dance. Merce Cunningham was much more like Martha Graham in this respect.)

At the end, working on *The Unsung*, when José was very ill, he could only work for short periods and then have to lie down for a while. For the dancers, this was a period of the unknown, but José was still working, so the dancers weren't worried about him yet. However, there was a point at which they didn't think he would make it to a rehearsal. I would go to get him, and he would be in a piano practice room, playing the piano and writing notes. I would tell him it was time to come to the rehearsal studio, and José would crumple up the music he had just written and throw it in the garbage. I am sorry that I did not go back and retrieve it later.

The company went to Honolulu in December 1972, and by then José was ill, and he was not touring with the company. I was more or less running the company, as acting artistic director. When the company was in New York, José was choreographing a bit of *The Waldstein Sonata*. He had also begun a trio with me, Ann Vachon, and, as memory recalls, Louis Solino, but it was only some movement ideas. He had just completed the last finished work he did, which was *Carlota*, and just before that *Orfeo* and *The Unsung*. People in Asia had not seen the Limón Company since 1963, almost ten years prior, so people flew in from all over Asia to see the company in Hawaii. We were performing only two works, *The Moor's Pavane* and *The Emperor Jones*, because there was a musical piece on the program before the company. The orchestra then played live for the two Limón works.[2]

The day of the performance, December 3, we were rehearsing like mad with the orchestra, and the dancers were being so picky about the tempos, saying they wanted one section faster, another slower, and it was so crazy that I did not know why the conductor didn't just walk out. My approach is just to let the musicians do what they are comfortable playing unless the tempo is really way off. At this time, HI Enterprises was the booking agent for the company and was run by Judy Hankins and Mary Jane Ingram, who were traveling with the company. When the rehearsal ended, they called the dancers into the office to go over some business, and at one point, I asked how José was doing. One of them said in a very matter-of-fact manner, "At 6:07 p.m., Eastern standard time, at Hunterdon Medical Center, Flemington, New Jersey, José Limón passed away."

The company fell apart, and we had a performance that night. We also found out that the conductor had already been told and knew during the rehearsal. It was a very difficult performance. We announced at the start of it that José had passed away, and we were doing the performance because that is what José would want. It was probably one of the most emotional performances I ever did. Afterward, the critics who were there came backstage and interviewed the dancers for a long time, because it became a story, not just a review. Edward DeSoto and I were the last two dancers to leave. The next day

---

2. John Anderson of the Honolulu newspaper Sunday Star Bulletin interviewed Danny just prior to the performances of the company for an article titled "Limón Director Hooked on Dance," published December 3, 1972. Danny said about dance, "It's almost like a drug. Once you start doing it, you're hooked on it. Your body becomes dependent upon the movement." It was the first time the company had been to Honolulu and one of the few times that the company would perform with an American orchestra. Danny was quoted as saying that "the success of the concerts will depend primarily upon how well the troupe and the orchestra can coordinate their talents. The central figure will be Maestro Robert LaMarchina, Honolulu Symphony Orchestra conductor ... the company always favors a conductor who is sensitive to the tempos and the dancers' special needs. It's a matter of coordinating rhythms.... It's a give and take sort of thing—we dance to the music and he plays to our dancing. If a dancer is feeling really up one night, it's up to the conductor to see it and conduct accordingly."

we had the day off. Most of the dancers went off to other islands. I went with Bonnie Oder to her house, had a few Mai Tai cocktails, and passed out.[3]

After the second performance, it was time to fly home to New York and figure out what we were going to do with the company. It was a difficult time to figure everything out about the company, where it would go, etcetera. I had previously announced that I would stay on as acting artistic director until José died, as I had promised Pauline Lawrence I would, and then I said that I would stay until they found a new artistic director, which took a year. (Eventually management convinced Ruth Currier to leave her tenure-track position at Ohio State, move back to New York, and take on the position. In the meantime, during that year, we toured all over. It was decided that Currier would start in 1974, right after the tour to the Soviet Union. After that tour, I arranged for the company to go on to Paris, and I went back to New York.)

I was already acting artistic director even before José died, so I was making all the decisions for the company. Hence, it seemed like a natural evolution for me to be the acting artistic director after José's death. This is not always the case with companies when their founder passes away. It was a difficult time in general for me, as the acting artistic director, dealing with all of the women, their concerns on the road, and their desire to give ongoing advice. The men tended to be easier to work with, and shortly after José passed away, a few of the men quit the company. So many of the men were there for José. I also felt that after José passed away, I no longer wanted to perform.

When I edited *A Choreographic Offering* from its original fifty-five minutes down to under twenty-five minutes for the Soviet tour, I posted the sections and who would be dancing what parts on the board. No one said a word about the fact that I had cut so much of the work. Their only interest was in what sections they would get to dance. I justified these cuts because José had taken the music by J.S. Bach, "A Musical Offering," and cut it to fit the needs of the dance. Thus, I had no qualms whatsoever about the cuts of various sections. I reworked the fast dance and gave it an ending that would complete the entire work. Much later, Carla Maxwell did her own version of *A Choreographic Offering* for the company.

Interview with Danny About His Fellow Limón Company Dancers

Louis Falco and Sarah Stackhouse were truly the great dancers of José's company in my generation, dancing both *The Exiles* and *A Choreographic Offering* duets. They were truly brilliant together. They knew how to take a dance performed years before by José and Letitia Ide, who were very different dancers, and bring it to the current times with the newer techniques, and not lose the essence of the ballet. It was an improvement rather than a new version of the work. They were truly gorgeous dancers. Falco

---

3. After his death, Catherine S. Cunningham wrote an article about José in which she described how the company had initially wanted to cancel the performance for that night, but Danny (as acting artistic director) decided that José would have wanted them to perform. "There was a moment of silence before the concert, and afterwards there was a standing ovation. It was a fitting tribute to Limón." An article titled "Remembering José Limón: Reminiscence" was written by Jean Battey Lewis, the well-known critic who oversaw The Washington Post's dance coverage for nearly fifteen years. She wrote this as a tribute to José after he passed away.

was actually a star in Europe. He would go to Amsterdam with his company all the time, and he was really well-known. Sadly, he died too soon from AIDS-related illnesses.

Jennifer Scanlon and I were very good dance partners together. She is a beautiful dancer and a very sensitive creature, and she could joke and have a fine time in the process. For me, Sarah Stackhouse was a difficult partner, though I did dance quite a bit with her. She was a perfectionist, and there was never enough rehearsal for her. We had to do material over and over and over, and she was never satisfied. I was just not that way; once I knew how to do the material, I was satisfied. Carla was fine as a partner; I liked dancing with her and we communicated well. The dancer with whom I had the most fun was Alice Condodina. We did *A Choreographic Offering*, and other small parts together, and I really enjoyed her. She went on to work at UC Santa Barbara. She would come during the summer terms to NWSA and teach performance techniques.

The two men with whom I danced the most were Edward DeSoto and Clyde Morgan. With Ed, I did *The Moor's Pavane*, and with Clyde I did *Legend*. These works were performed quite a bit. I also did *The Moor's Pavane* with Clyde, but not as much as with

Daniel Lewis and Clyde Morgan in *Legend*, choreography by José Limón (photograph by Martha Swope, courtesy Daniel Lewis archives).

Ed, as Clyde had left the company. Clay Taliaferro came into the company just as I was leaving, and I taught *The Emperor Jones* to him. There is a connection to the other man when you do *The Moor's Pavane* together, as you are fighting all the way through the work. This is in contrast to a work like *The Unsung* where I had little to do with the other men, and I was not even around when their solos were choreographed. Most of the group sections were transitions between solos. The only long group section in that work was "Pantheon," the opening. It was a very hard dance to do, as we had to find a group rhythm that worked for everyone and maintain it. With the solos, the men could each find their own rhythm and do it the way they wanted. My method of having dancers in technique class do material in silence was developed from doing *The Unsung*.

Through His Friends' Eyes—Clay Taliaferro

Clay Taliaferro was a principal dancer and guest artist with the José Limón Dance Company for many years, and he was assistant artistic director to Ruth Currier. Additionally, he was acting artistic director and principal dancer with the Donald McKayle Dance Company and danced with Anna Sokolow, Stuart Hodes, Sophie Maslow, and Lotte Goslar. Clay Taliaferro wrote to Danny, expressing his feelings about those early days in the company. He said, "I often think how different my later dance life would have been had you not left the company when I was just getting in—not so much about dancing, but how you thought. On the very first day dancing in front of José, with you standing at his shoulder with a reassuring big smile as I received my first notes, I was scared to death, more of the other dancers than of José. At one point, Jim May told me to watch a video of The Waldstein Sonata, *which I had never seen. I was transfixed, moved, envious, excited, respectful and appreciative all at the same instant. The alternative thought was that if only I could have danced in that work with dancers of that caliber, doing what I feel is the most gorgeous Limón I've seen—the kind of gorgeous dancing I always felt to be an example of the natural growth of the master Limón. I had a terrific time in the company, but I also know that as the 'new boy on the block' as José called me, I was at a juncture in my dance life where I felt desperately in need of a master. Seeing your relationship and work with José was like a beacon for me—José, as my master, would make the kind of demands on me that I so needed at that time to get on with any growth—then along came death, a death I cursed for depriving me of the life I envisioned I could have. Know that your interest, Danny, in keeping the company alive, inspired me to stay and test the journey, one that I am happy I took."*

Libby Nye and I danced together on the Asian tour. We roomed together during part of the tour, and we went on several excursions together. One was the trip to Angkor Wat, Cambodia, where we rode an elephant through the ruins for two days. This was not a serious relationship but more one of companionship. Libby taught in Toronto and in Germany quite a bit. Libby and I had very different backgrounds and approaches to teaching. I didn't see her for many years, until Nina Watt brought all of the early Limón dancers to Bennington to make a video about Limón's technique, including me, James Payton, Carla Maxwell, Libby Nye, and Robyn Cutler, a Juilliard graduate who joined the company after the Asia tour. Nina was associate professor of dance at the University of Hartford in Connecticut, and as part of her tenure research she chose to do a video documentary with the early Limón dancers. It was called *Limón Teachers Workshop*, and it was done at Jacob's Pillow. Disc 1 was center and floor work. Disc 2 was barre.

Discs 3 and 4 were about across-the-floor material. It was an entire day of shooting. Payton and I were the only men there. I was late, as I was coming from another job, and when I arrived, Payton exclaimed, "Another man! Thank you!"

Limón's Approach to Music

In the early days of José's choreographic life, dance and music were inseparable. These dances mimicked the music.[4] He knew music well, because his father was a musician, conductor, and music teacher. Then, as José developed further, he began to move away from relying on music in this way. He liked Bach and Beethoven and did wonderful dances to them, and he did collaborations with Heitor Villa-Lobos and Norman Dello Joio. Yet he really wanted to get rid of music in his choreography. By the end, *The Unsung* and *Carlota* were done without music. It is astonishing that sometimes people who see *The Unsung* ask who wrote the music, not realizing that the only sounds are clapping, stomping, and breathing that the dancers create to the rhythm of the dance. The section "A Time to Keep Silence and a Time to Speak" in the work *There Is a Time* gives the same feeling. In March 1978, Danny invited Norman Dello Joio to come see *There Is a Time* when he staged it with the Juilliard dancers. Danny asked Norman to come backstage before the performance to say something to the dancers, to inspire them before their first performance of the work. When they got backstage, Danny asked Norman to tell the dancers how he and José had collaborated. Norman said it was simple: They met once in the Juilliard cafeteria; José listed the sections he wanted to do, and he made it clear that the "A Time to Keep Silence and a Time to Speak" section was to be done without music but with a "clapping" score. Then they went their separate ways, and Norman would send music to José. It all just came together perfectly.

Atypically, two of the last dances José was working on, *The Waldstein Sonata* and *Orfeo*, were both set to Beethoven music. He seemed to be getting back into his earlier life as a choreographer. José was dying as he was working on *The Waldstein Sonata* and only got about halfway through it. Fortunately, Danny filmed it before José died, so he had all of the movements and ideas on film from which to work. It was in 1975 (three years after José's death) that Martha Hill went to Peter Mennin, president at Juilliard, to talk to him about the work. Danny met with Mennin and showed him the film, and Mennin told Danny that he wanted him to finish it. José had actually done an ending for the work, but it continued after the music ended. Mennin told Danny to make sure to end the dance with the music. Danny was actually surprised to receive the OK for this project, because Mennin was not a huge fan of dance, unless it was dance in the opera, which he loved.

At one point when José was ill, Danny was in Amsterdam, Holland, and he bought José a tape machine. Up until this time, José was always hauling around heavy and bulky Wollensak tape machines. There was a new German company that made

4. When Danny was in Moscow, serving as acting artistic director of the Limón Company, he had dinner with Madam Prokofiev, wife of composer Sergei Prokofiev. Madam Prokofiev asked whether José had ever set anything to her husband's music. Being diplomatic, Danny said that there was only so much a man can do in his lifetime. Actually, he knew that José hated the romantics and did not particularly like the music of Prokofiev. However, later, when Danny returned home and starting working on his book (The Illustrated Dance Technique of José Limón), he discovered that José had done a lot of work to Prokofiev in the early days of his choreographic life, mainly solos.

a machine called an Uher with five-inch reels. They were really good machines, with professional-quality sound; were smaller, lighter, and easier to carry; and ran on batteries or electricity. At one point, José commented that he was spending more time at the farm and would love to have the complete Beethoven sonatas. Danny bought the album *Complete Piano Sonatas by Ludwig von Beethoven* with Wilhelm Kempff playing the sonatas, and he recorded all of them on about twenty tapes, in five-inch reels. He gave José the tape machine from Holland and all of the tapes, and José headed out to the farm. The next day, José called to say that the machine didn't work, so Danny agreed to come out to the farm to see what the problem was. When he arrived around dinnertime, Danny found that there was a button that directed the sound to external speakers when pulled to the out position, and directed the sound to the internal speakers when pushed in. Danny pushed it in, and then the music was audible from the machine. José was very annoyed and cursed at the button! José did get to hear all the Beethoven sonatas, and that is when he began *The Waldstein Sonata*. Around the same time, José started working on movement themes for another Beethoven trio. After José died, Danny took these movement themes and made the *Beethoven Duet* for Naomi Sorkin (from ABT) and Bill Carter (from ABT and the Graham Company). They danced it at a gala for the Dance Notation Bureau. Later Danny turned it into a trio for his company, and then a sextet for other companies and school performances. The names of the works were straightforward: *Beethoven Duet*, *Beethoven Trio*, and *Beethoven Sextet*. The movement was so rich that it could be arranged for any number of dancers.

Limón's Works

Note that all of José's works are listed in Danny's book *The Illustrated Dance Technique of José Limón*. The *Waldstein Sonata* is listed under Other Works, which also included *1935*, a drama produced at Steamboat Springs, Colorado; *Yerma*, with Santa Fe Opera Company; a piece called "And David Wept" done for *Lamp Unto My Feet*, a CBS television series with Danny, Jennifer Muller, and Aaron Osborne; and several soldier revues done while José was in the U.S. Army, from 1942 to 1945.[5] The last piece José choreographed and danced in was *Luther* (1972), also for CBS, but not broadcast until 1986.

La Malinche

A documentary film, released on DVD, about choreographer José Limón and his work *La Malinche* was published in 2004. This documentary—conceived, written, and directed by Patty Harrington Delaney—included interviews with performers and dance scholars as well as a performance of *La Malinche* by the José Limón Dance Company.

Danny performed and staged *La Malinche* many times. After the Asian tour, Danny was still a student at Juilliard. (In fact, it took him five years to complete his studies because he was touring so often.) José was planning to perform *La Malinche* for a Lincoln Center Student Programs tour. Danny was chosen to do El Indio (the Indian),

---

5. It was Pauline who wrote to someone in charge in the military and got José placed in special services, entertaining the troupes, rather than in a combat role.

Dennis Nahat was chosen to do El Conquistador (the Conqueror), and Carla Maxwell was La Malinche (the Traitor). He learned it directly from José and was the first to do it after José no longer danced it. It was quite an experience, as it was the only time José sat down and taught him a role from beginning to end, describing every movement along the way, what it meant, and why they were doing it. (Normally, once a dancer was a known quantity in the company, he just threw material at the dancer and assumed he or she knew how to do it.)

El Indio begins by banging his hand on the ground (showing his anger about every-thing that has happened). José would jokingly say, "And make those tortillas really thin!" In the direction that José gave Danny, he would refer to "flying over the mountains, looking at the landscape, enjoying your land, feeling the desert." He would talk about the anger at La Malinche and pounding at El Conquistador. The dynamics for El Indio are very strong. There is the juxtaposition of the hard movement and then the softness, representing the beauty of Mexico against the anger going out against La Malinche and El Conquistador. The nicest part for El Indio is at the end when he resolves his conflict and accepts La Malinche back, and then the whole work relaxes; the dancer bows, even before the end of the work.

Danny brought a film of the work to Mexico when he went to teach in Mexico City. Someone there told him that he had staged La Malinche a long time before, and it had not been received well. This was because José made a hero out of a traitor, and in the early days of the work (the 1950s), it was still too close to their feelings about that time. There were interesting restagings of the work. Because it is like a play, the people dancing it had a hard time stripping themselves of the drama and letting the movement project the drama. The dancers did not need to act or express the story; the movement did it so clearly. If it was danced with the right dynamics, the story worked.

When Pauline Koner, who was teaching at the North Carolina School of the Arts, asked José if someone could come to stage La Malinche for her students, Danny actually asked José not to send him. Pauline was a powerful woman and a strong creator in her own right, and she felt as though she owned her roles in José's works. (This was largely because José gave the dancers a lot of freedom when he was choreographing. He was open to letting the dancer have input into the development of the work.) Danny asked José what he should do if Pauline said something should be done differently than what Danny was teaching. José told Danny to do whatever she wanted to do, not to argue with her, and if she did not stop talking, just push the button on the tape machine and she would start dancing. In the end, it was a good experience, and they had a good time doing it.

The work is powerful today because it is a story piece that a three-year-old can understand. It is clear and straightforward, and it is a wonderful story with a resolution in the end. Like The Moor's Pavane (Danny's favorite Limón work), La Malinche was a work in which he felt a sense of completeness from beginning to end: the dancer devel-oped a character, and he resolved who the character was and what the ballet was.

The Limón Company would do school performances at 8:00 a.m. The danc-ers would all get into two cars or station wagons, drive around the state, go to a the-ater or school very early, warm up, and do an assembly program. At each school, the dancers would talk about the work and then perform it, and then there would be a question-and-answer period. They would do La Malinche, Sokolow's Session for Six, and then maybe a ballet pas de deux. Danny literally did hundreds of these school shows

Daniel Lewis and Laura Glenn in *La Malinche*, choreography by José Limón, 92nd Street Y, New York, 1969 (photograph by Eddie Effron, courtesy Daniel Lewis archives).

over the years. Dennis Nahat, who later was to become artistic director of the Cleveland Ballet, was on these tours.[6] At the start of the work, the three characters come in, they bow, and they start the dance. A different instrument represents each character. The drum is El Indio, the voice is La Malinche, the trumpet is El Conquistador, and the piano holds it all together. Each dancer has a solo, and at one point, El Conquistador stands with his sword downstage right, and El Indio does his solo against him, with everything going at him. One morning, Danny was focused on Dennis (as El Conquistador), and Dennis slowly worked his way offstage, got on his hands and knees in the wings, and

6. Dennis Nahat was asked by Lucia Chase to join American Ballet Theatre that year. He told her that he had already committed to José Limón to do La Malinche on the tour, so he could not come to ABT. Danny thought this was incredible, showing real integrity. Lucia Chase told him they would wait for him for the year! So he did the tour.

started vomiting. Danny was onstage pounding and stomping away, and it came time
for the three of them to meet up again. Dennis made it back onstage to finish the work.

The Winged

The Winged first premiered on August 20, 1966, at Connecticut College. When
José first talked about doing *The Winged* in 1966, Danny thought he was out of his mind!
José talked about birds, harpies, and flying monkeys, and he did not want music. He had
finally reached that point where he wanted no music at all for his work. Pauline Lawrence (his wife) insisted that he could not do that. Simon Sadoff and Danny put together
a score of background music with bird sounds and sounds from the woods, all from
sound effect records. There was also a jazz score by Hank Johnson, a Juilliard student,
that José like, so he asked Sadoff and Danny to use that music as well. Danny went to the
Juilliard music library and got some records by Henry Cowell, an American composer,
music theorist, pianist, teacher, publisher, and impresario. Sadoff and Danny had some
Wollensak tape machines, so they would record the music and then turn the tape upside
down and play it. The final score for the dance was a whole array of these sounds and
altered musical compositions. What was interesting about this work is that because
they did not dance to the music, sections could be longer or shorter in performance,
depending on the energy of the dancers. Hence, they always performed with two tape
machines and white leader tape between them, so that as the person running sound saw
one group exiting, he would fade out that music section and fade in the next one on the
other machine. It was very complicated to make this process work.

The Limón Company did a season at the Washington National Cathedral, the
second-largest cathedral in the United States, a gorgeous church that they had been
building for decades. It is the official church of Washington, D.C., where all the dignitaries go. They built a stage in the nave of the church for this week-long series of performances, and behind the stage was the organ.[7] On opening night on February 21, 1968,
they performed *The Winged*, *Exiles*, and *Missa Brevis*. On February 22, the company
performed *Psalm*, *There Is a Time*, and *Missa Brevis*. The soloists included José Limón,
Louis Falco, and Sarah Stackhouse. *The Winged* was the big hit of this series. When they
were at the Washington National Cathedral, a film company wanted to film *The Winged*
for a television show. When the dancers showed up at 8 a.m., they learned that this
filming was going to be a full 30-minute show, and only José was being paid. In the end,
José gave all the money to the dancers for their work.

The company performed at the Harper Theater in Chicago every year for many
years. In a *Chicago Tribune* review titled "Winged Creatures Soar at the Harper" on
November 14, 1968, Thomas Willis told the reader that Limón was "part bird" and that
the work *The Winged*, leading off the company's first bill of the week, made that clear. He
stated that Limón's stamp was on every move of the choreography, and "the creatures
which glide in sweeping curves, flutter, fight, mate, and play cannibal during its course
are all in some mysterious way extensions of his own powerful presence." This was the

---

7. José did a lot of religious-themed works (There Is a Time, The Traitor, The Exiles, Psalm), because
he had been raised as a Catholic in Mexico, so it was not strange to him to perform in churches. He was
able to make these stories universal. He condensed these mammoth stories into their central themes.
For example, in The Traitor (the story of Christ's betrayal by Judas), the characters were the Leader, his
followers, and the Traitor.

first performance of the work in Chicago. He remarked that "although the sound effects exist only for atmosphere, rhythm is alive and well, displayed in every movement." He then went on to describe various sections of the dance and the characters, "a group of harpies, masochists all, glare and bite at their own legs. A sphinx, Jennifer Muller, riddles the audience with a siren's body and a beseeching glance. Louis Falco who is everything a dancer should be, preens and struts as a winged sentinel, then returns as a fire-breathing Pegasus."[8]

Psalm

Eugene Lester was commissioned to write the music for *Psalm*, created in 1967, and based on *Last of the Just*, a novel by André Schwarz-Bart. It describes the destructive consequences of bigotry and hatred. Note that when *Psalm* was originally performed, the program mentioned that it was about the persecution of the Jews, but current programs do not specify this intention. Louis Falco was the soloist in the dance, and the music was voice (sung in Hebrew by Tom Love) and percussion. Limón was going through a time when he wanted the dance to be the music. Lester came to the rehearsals while the work was being created, counted out the measures, wrote some music, and gave it to José, who would then discuss removing certain measures. This went on day after day until Lester got fed up with this process, so he stopped giving the music to Limón. Instead he would give it to Danny and Jennifer Muller, who acted as intermediaries and peacekeepers and who would then bring the music to Limón. They would then take the changes to Lester, who would make them. It was a difficult working situation. Amazingly, however, it worked! It turned out to be a good composer-choreographer collaboration.[9]

A review by Ernestine Stodelle titled "Limón's Psalm Unveiled as 20th Season Ends" dated August 21, 1967, in the *New London Day* talked about the premiere of Limón's work *Psalm*. Stodelle was a dear friend to both José Limón and Doris Humphrey. In the review, she discussed this performance at the Palmer Auditorium at Connecticut College as part of the American Dance Festival's twentieth anniversary. It described the performance by the sixteen members of the Limón Company as eloquent: "a work of great compassion, beauty, and meaning." She remarked that the sold-out house gave a richly deserved ovation. In her words, "The theme of 'Psalm' is religious persecution, specifically that of the Jewish people. Without any historical references, it takes the spectator into the heart of a Christ-like figure, called The Burden Bearer, who personally absorbs the sufferings of an oppressed race as it moves through the ages." She noted that it is not a dance of despair, but it is about the passion of faith. "Even when we hear the Burden Bearer's eternal lament 'My bones are broken. My life is in ashes. My God, why

8. The review also described Comedy: "an updated Lysistrata which knows how things really would have turned out." Once again, Willis was thoroughly taken with dancers' performances, especially Sarah Stackhouse and Louis Falco, the general who "languishes midway between destructive frustration and impotence." Willis finished the review with Missa Brevis, which Willis had also seen two years before. He described the work as "a moving interpretation of Zoltán Kodály's war-tinged score. Mr. Limón, as the perturbed visitor to the bomb-wrecked church, dances the 'Qui Tollis' sections. His movements are rich in symbolism—of Christ, of a suppliant at ordination, and of guilt represented in the vocabulary of the earlier days of Graham and Doris Humphrey."

9. Note that the work was remounted under Carla Maxwell in 2002 with newly commissioned music by Jon Magnussen.

hast thou forsaken me?' there is redemption and exultation." She described the score as marvelous, creating a mood of intense emotion, with increasing power. She had highly positive comments about Louis Falco, Jennifer Muller, and Sarah Stackhouse and went on to say that the entire extraordinary company was to be praised: Lenore Latimer, Jennifer Scanlon, Laura Glenn, Carla Maxwell, Tamara Woshakiwsky, Diane Mohrmann, Alice Condodina, Daniel Lewis, Fritz Ludin, Clyde Morgan, Avner Vered, Jim May, and Edward DeSoto.[10]

Reviews of Other Limón Works

On February 19, 1967, Jean Battey of *The Washington Post* wrote, "No more important dance event has taken place at the White House than the performance February 9 of José Limón's 'The Moor's Pavane' on the occasion of President and Mrs. Johnson's dinner for the King Hassan II of Morocco. Because it honored Limón, an artist who has been enthusiastically received on four overseas tours; because it is a dance of such superb quality; and because, in practical terms, its cast of four and its beautiful formal design fit so well on the small White House stage, this was an occasion to treasure both for its inner and outer significance."

"All-Limón: His Dances of 25 Years Given in New London" was a review of the Connecticut College performance written by Don McDonagh in the *New York Times* on July 11, 1972. McDonagh started by saying that in the twenty-five-year history of the American Dance Festival, no single name was associated longer with the festival than that of José Limón. In this performance, Limón offered a retrospective of his works, focusing attention on the "special and varied performing skills of his finely schooled dancers. The present Limón Company ... is one of the strongest in terms of energy and sheer exuberance. It was a pleasure to see a beautiful work such as *There Is a Time* handled with a freshness that one normally associates with new work.... Daniel Lewis, a mainstay of the company in its styling and attack, danced with fury and tenderness in his first solo 'A Time to be Born and a Time to Die,' and Edward DeSoto later followed with the brilliantly driving intensity that he brings to bear on his roles. Jennifer Scanlon in 'A Time to Laugh.... A Time to Dance' created a mood of movement that touched all with the abandon and joyousness that the headlong velocity of an accomplished dancer can create." McDonagh gave high praise to the performers, saying, "One should name each and every performer but that is impossible, so to all, a collective congratulations."

Other Performance Opportunities

During his years dancing in the Limón Company, Danny also had opportunities to dance with other choreographers. Danny danced in several works by an excellent choreographer named Judith Willis. The best work of hers was called *Songs for Young Lovers*,

---

10. Stodelle also discussed other works on the program. She described The Moor's Pavane as an unforgettable performance by José Limón (the Moor), Betty Jones (Desdemona), Lucas Hoving (Iago), and Pauline Koner (Emilia), all the original cast. Stodelle noted that the work was acclaimed in Europe and Asia since its 1949 origins. Regarding The Winged, Stodelle commented on the virtuoso dancing and the imaginative daring of the choreographer's concept.

done in the mid–1960s, with Carla Maxwell, Anna Mittel- holzer, Judyth Ofsowitz, Sara Rudner, Edward DeSoto, David Earle, Eddie (Edward) Effron, and Daniel Lewis. This work was created at Juilliard and would eventually be performed by the Alvin Ailey American Dance Theater. Danny per- formed the work at the dance festival at the Delacorte Theater in Central Park on September 2, 1966, with Carmen de Laval- lade and Judith Willis. Other dancers at this festival included Edward DeSoto, Eddie Effron, Carla Maxwell, Laura Glenn, and Glen Tetley. Danny per- formed *Songs for Young Lovers* on several occasions, includ- ing the Kaufman Concert Hall series, where Danny also per- formed in a full evening with Ruth Currier. In March 1971, Danny and Charles Weidman were guest stars with Miriam Pandor's company, Repertory Dancers. Other dancers in that

Songs for Young Lovers, **choreography by Judith Willis, 1965. Dancers, back row, from left: David Earle and Daniel Lewis; dancers, front row, from left: Edward DeSoto and Eddie Effron (courtesy Daniel Lewis archives).**

company were Ann Vachon, Ruth Draper, Blondell Cummings, Judy Lasko, Dian Dong, and Susan Epstein. Danny performed in *Day on Earth* with Ann Vachon, Dian Dong, and Susan Epstein as the child. In this show, they also danced Weidman's works *Bargain Counter* and *Lynchtown*, which Danny had danced when he first met Charles in the High School of Performing Arts.

Dance Uptown and the Minor Latham Playhouse

Danny was beginning to develop his own work and company during these years working with Limón. Janet Soares, the head of Barnard College Dance, founded and ran Dance Uptown, and she commissioned two works from Danny, *Man Made* and *The Minding of the Flesh Is Death*. These works were performed at the Minor Latham Playhouse at Barnard College (116th Street and Broadway, across the street from Co- lumbia College), which was just down the street from Juilliard at that time (122nd Street and Claremont Avenue). He choreographed *Man Made* in 1966, which used ancient Tibetan chants and rhythmic rituals, and had as dancers Danny, John Giffin (who even- tually danced with Pina Bausch), Linda Rabin, and Laura Glenn, all Juilliard dancers

David Earle (left) and Daniel Lewis in *Songs for Young Lovers*, **choreography by Judith Willis, 1965 (courtesy Daniel Lewis archives).**

who were in the start of Danny's company. The next year, 1967, he choreographed *The Minding of the Flesh Is Death*, originally performed at the Palmer Auditorium with Jim May, Laura Glenn, and Eddie Effron; Danny did his own lighting for the work. The story of how *The Minding of the Flesh Is Death* came about is fascinating. One day on 42nd Street, Danny was handed a pamphlet by some stranger, a preacher. The flyer was titled "The Modern Dance," and it had on the front a drawing of a woman dancing with a skeleton, captioned "The Minding of the Flesh is DEATH." Around the drawing was the text "The Dance with Death," "On the Brink of a Volcano," and "The Lust of the Flesh." The pamphlet began, "Dr. E.S. Sonners, eminent specialist in nervous disorders, of Chicago and Los Angeles, makes this terrific indictment of the modern dance: I attack the modern dance as a reversion toward savagery. As a medical man, I flatly charge that modern social dancing is fundamentally sinful and evil. I charge that dancing's charm is based entirely upon sex appeal. I charge that dancing is the most advanced and most insidious of the maneuvers preliminary to sex betrayal. It is nothing more or less than a damnable, diabolical, animal, physical dissipation." Danny thought it was funny, so he gave his work this same name. Danny redid *The Minding of the Flesh Is Death* for the Dance Uptown series at the Minor Latham Playhouse.

At one show at the Minor Latham Playhouse, October 27, 1967, Gay Delanghe (a dancer with Lucas Hoving and later chair of dance at the University of Michigan) danced in a work that the review said was only a little longer than its title! In that show, Danny presented *Man Made* and *The Minding of the Flesh Is Death*. The review described the dances in philosophical terms, speaking to themes of cynicism, man's sincerity, and dance as a preliminary to sexual betrayal. Danny just laughed at this review.

On January 18, 1970, Anna Kisseldorf wrote a review of the Dance Uptown Series at the Minor Latham Playhouse at Barnard College. The review was titled "Mother/Son Strife Is Theme of Dance at Barnard Series," and it discussed the new works of the Saturday evening show. It named the most substantial work as Danny's work *Lallan Schoenstein Presents the Bokinski Brothers*. The review went on to say that the work "took a fresh, facile, and comic look at the overbearing mother and son theme." It then described the two groups of dancers: the pot-smoking friends of the son, and the family around the dinner table. (The joints were actually just Bull Durham tobacco.)

Deborah Jowitt reviewed the same work, calling it a "familiar affair." She noted that it featured an all-American family, and that most of the cast were actually relatives of the choreographer. Performers included Laura Glenn, Peter Sparling, Lallan Schoenstein, Margie Fargnoli, Mark Stevens (a dancer in the Limón Company), Aaron Osborne (hero of the work), and Danny's brother Steven Lewis, who did magic tricks in the work. Laura's brother was wheeled in on a windowed staircase. Candy Lewis and Martha Glenn, playing the part of two of the children, sat at the table eating a meal for the entire dance. The work had a great deal of yelling between the mother and brother. Jowitt went on to describe in detail the group of friends bouncing around to The Who, smoking grass, and screwing a little. She noted the theme of freedom versus conformity, and she remarked how cool it was to see smoking onstage! Jowitt observed that all the dialogue was in clichés and that the dancers all dragged on their joints on the same count. She called the work "odd" but seemed to enjoy it.

Janet Soares and Kenneth James got faculty grants to take dancers to Glastonbury to perform at the Glastonbury Festival. Kenneth James ran and sponsored the dance festival. He was originally from Glastonbury but moved to the United States and became a professor at Barnard College and director of Minor Latham Playhouse.[11] The Glastonbury Festival had both the music festival (small at that time) and the dance festival, and the dance part of the festival took place in a church. In the summer of 1971, they traveled to Glastonbury and performed *Man Made* in an abbey; only the walls of the church existed, so it was outdoors. Myth has it that part of King Arthur's body is buried there, but there are many places in England where he was said to be buried. It was about two miles from Tintagel, the place where Merlin the Magician's Cave is located. Dancers who performed included Danny, Suzanne Vega, Peter Sparling, Chris Palladian, Hannah Kahn, Rae (Carol-rae) Kraus, Henry Van Kuiken, Carol Hess, Jessica Fogel, Holly Williams, Gay DeLanghe (later a faculty member at the University of Michigan), and other illustrious dancers. They also performed *La Malinche* at the festival, with Janet Soares as La Malinche, Danny as El Indio, and Peter Sparling as El Conquistador. Six of those listed became heads of dance departments, and one became a famous recording artist. Nancy Topf, who also danced in these Dance Uptown shows, became very well known in both the dance community and the somatic practice world, developing a tech-

11. James Bakery on High Street was owned by Kenneth James' brother. The dancers practically lived on double cream and scones from the bakery.

nique of neuromuscular retraining. She died in the Swiss Air flight 111 plane crash off of Nova Scotia when she was on her way to teach in Geneva.

At the Glastonbury Festival, all the neighboring restaurants and pubs had posted "No hippies allowed" signs, because the locals did not like the festival people invading the town. When Danny and the dancers would walk into these places, they were refused service and told to leave.

Peter Sparling and Danny did not stay in the bed and breakfast where the other dancers were but in a field behind the B&B. Carol-rae and Peter stayed in a tent together (although they were only platonic friends). They paid the B&B for breakfast and the use of the shower and water closet (restroom). The dancers returned from the performance one evening to find a cow lying on Peter's tent. Since Danny and Peter were city boys, they were afraid to go near the cow. They went to the house and got the farmer. He kicked the cow, and it moved on. After that, they set up the tent again. Danny waited a while and then went behind Peter's tent and started to push it. Peter came out naked, screaming, "They're back!" The next day they moved to the fenced-in area in front of the house.

Glastonbury is near a town called Street. Street is the town where the main factory is for Clark Shoes. Nathan Clark, whose family ran Clark Shoes, was a man who loved dance and went to ADF at Connecticut College every summer.[12] Danny once went to Street to visit Nathan, and he was not there; however, the people there said that they knew Danny was coming. They took Danny, Peter Sparling, Rae Kraus, and Sharon Bouck out to dinner and treated them really well.

Sharon and Danny had a wonderful affair that summer. She was not performing at the festival but was traveling to Europe to go to France. Sharon was booked on a charter flight to London, and Danny bought a ticket on the same flight so they could fly together. The plane, a charter, was diverted to Belgium, where they were given coupons to take the ferry to Dover and then a train to London. They ran to catch the ferry, but missed it by minutes; in fact, they arrived in time to stand on the dock watching the ferry leave. They could not find a spare room anywhere, so they ended up sleeping in a park that night, and their summer affair started. When they arrived in London, she changed her plans and went to Glastonbury with Danny. Sharon did manage to get to France for a few days, and then she returned to Glastonbury.

Through His Friends' Eyes—Sharon Bouck

Sharon Bouck recalled her time that summer: "When we left on the flight from New York, our plane was diverted from London to Belgium due to problems at the London airport. That day we took a bus to Ostend, Belgium, in order to catch the last ferry of the day to Dover, England. We missed the ferry, and could not find a hotel room, as they were all booked. We ended up sleeping in what we thought was a secluded area in a park, but when we woke the next day, people were all around us playing tennis. That day we took the train to London and spent the night with Jane Dudley. The next morning, I went to Paris and you went to Glastonbury to join the dancers.

---

12. Nathan Clark generally spent his time in New York rather than England. He had an apartment in a brownstone in New York, and one room had nothing in it but a huge hot tub—the kind you would put outdoors. He loved inviting the female dancers up to his place to get naked in the hot tub. Once Danny was there with Martha Hill; Theodore (Teddy) Wiesner, head of Brooklyn College and later of the American Dance Festival; and other dancers. Nathan was telling everyone to get undressed, and Martha and Teddy could not believe they were even there! Of course, Martha and Teddy did not get into the tub.

Later, I joined you and Peter Sparling as you were finishing your stint in Glaston-bury. Janet Soares was very suspicious when I showed up, but I had time to explore Glastonbury, which I adored; I was on a huge King Arthur kick at that time.

After the end of the Festival I rented a car, and you, Carol-rae, Peter, and I went to Cornwall together. We even explored the Dartmoor. Peter made a drawing of us taking a nap somewhere along those cliffs and gave it to me. I will never forget, as long as I live, watching the sun set at 11:00 at night at Land's End, already a month after the solstice at that. After the Cornwall trip, Peter and Carol-rae departed, and you and I went to Wales together, including Snowdonia National Park. We camped out, and I bought a single-burner Swedish stove. After Wales, we drove up to Scotland, got rather bogged down with the never-ending, Maine-like western coastline, so we crossed over to Edinburgh. I learned that August in the British Isles is rainy—we began to stay in huge castle-like B&Bs because the camping got too soggy—and I swore that if I ever went back to England or Scotland it would be during July! I remember the fondness with which you talked about José during those days we spent together, how you cared for him during his last months."[13]

In 1974, the company performed at Dance Uptown, where they did Danny's work *No Strings*, which Danny had created at Barnard College, and the work of three other choreographers: Janet Soares, Deborah Jowitt, and Dianne McIntyre. Dancers in *No Strings* were Teri Weksler and Leigh Warren, with Daryl Bratches, Dianne Hulburt, Nancy Scattergood, and Andrew Miller. In the dance, Teri Weksler and Leigh Warren rise out of a moving chair composed of two people under drop cloths to perform a romantic duet that is interrupted with occasional slapstick. Weksler is dropped on the floor twice. The work included some exaggerated 1940s movie musical dancing, a few moments of Russian folk dance, and other odds and ends.

During these years, Danny had just started his company. These performances were the early days of his developing his choreographic voice, and he was beginning to find the dancers with whom he wanted to work.

---

13. José was preceded in death by his wife. During the Glastonbury Festival, Danny received the letter from José saying that Pauline had passed away. José had written in the letter that Diablo (Spanish for "the devil") came and took her.

5

Staging Limón Works
Around the World

It was a great stroke of luck that José trusted me to stage his works in many cities and countries. I was able to travel throughout the United States and to Israel, Sweden, Denmark, England, Canada, the Netherlands, and Hong Kong, working with some of the finest schools and companies in the world. It was during this time that I met some of the best dancers of the era and forged connections with people whom I would know over my lifetime. These connections also led to future artistic opportunities for me.—Danny Lewis

Danny staged the works of José Limón, Daniel Lewis, and Doris Humphrey all over the world for fifty years. He worked with the schools and companies that are listed in the Appendix; only the most significant or lengthy residencies are discussed in detail. Danny did several summer programs over many years, often staging works during these residencies. He did much of his guest teaching in the summers because he was committed to Juilliard during the year.

Through His Friends' Eyes—Colin Connor

Colin Connor is the fifth artistic director of the Limón Company in the Limón Foundation's seventy-year history. He danced for eight years as a soloist with the Limón Dance Company and has created over fifty commissioned works of choreography. Colin said, "Danny was gone by the time I got into the Limón Company, but I wanted to know a male who had worked closely with José in the early years. The main attribute I admire in Danny is his big love for life—he has an attitude that says, 'let's not look back, let's keep looking forward.' I appreciate Danny's willingness to look at something—even if he thinks it won't work—and be open-minded, look at it with fresh eyes, and not get stuck in preconceptions. I made a choice to do The Exiles *with the Limón Company using different music and costumes. Danny's positivity about this idea was fabulous. Danny believes that because the Limón work is so strong, it can be treated in the way Shakespeare is done, with a wide range of different production values. If you don't take risks and try different approaches to a dance, it becomes stale, like a museum piece. I am sure that this approach fueled Danny's vision of dance training at New World School of the Arts (NWSA), and that the immense success of so many students there is due to this approach that embraced both the value of the past and new possibilities of the present and future."*

Batsheva Dance Company (1969)

Danny staged José's works all over the world, and he learned from José what to do. The best lesson he learned was while working on *The Exiles* for Batsheva Dance Company in Israel in 1969. José flew over to view the work. Danny had staged it with Laura Glenn, and they had done a wonderful job transposing the work onto these two very young dancers, Rahamim Ron and Nurit Cohen. The two mature soloists in the company had expected to get the parts. When they did not, the two were very angry, and the male went into faculty member Jane Dudley's office and vehemently expressed their anger at her. They also called Batsheva De Rothschild (cofounder, with Martha Graham, of Batsheva Dance Company) to complain. When they asked Danny why he did not use the company's soloists, he said he was directed by José to select the best two dancers for the work. The work was about Adam and Eve coming out of the Garden of Eden, and they were supposed to be thirteen-year-old adolescents, so the dancers selected were the right dancers for the roles. They were beautiful dancers, and the staging was excellent. When José flew in to view the work, they danced brilliantly for him. When they were finished, José said, "Children, come and sit down, and I will tell you the story of Adam and Eve." He talked about their innocence, about putting on the clothing and leaving the Garden of Eden. Then he asked to see a section in the second part, and he redid the choreography for a few minutes of a twenty-minute dance. Danny was bewildered, because it looked like a lot of changes, and he did not understand why José was changing the choreography. That evening over dinner, Danny asked José why he changed it when the dancers looked so good. José agreed that they looked stunning but said they had no ownership of the ballet. By changing the choreography, now they felt that the dance was part of them. He told Danny to watch the work over the next few days. Sure enough, the work grew beautifully. After that experience, whenever Danny staged a Limón work, he would say, "That part doesn't look right on you," and he changed it so that people felt that they had ownership. It was one of the joys of being a dancer in Limón's company; he never asked you to do a part the way someone else did it. He always asked you to do it the way you would do it best.

After Batsheva, Laura and Danny went to Istanbul, Turkey, for a few days and visited Sebnem Selisik Aksan. Because of a strike at the airport in Istanbul, there were no buses to take them into the city. A man with a taxi offered to drive them. After an hour in the car, he dropped them on a street with huge apartment buildings and said it was

(From left) José Limón, Daniel Lewis and Laura Glenn at the Dead Sea, Israel, 1969 (photograph by Linda Rabin, courtesy Daniel Lewis archives).

(From left) Daniel Lewis, Laura Glenn, José Limón, and Linda Rabin at the Mount of Olives, Jerusalem, Israel, 1969 (courtesy Daniel Lewis archives).

the right place. They got out of the cab, and he drove away. It was 2:00 a.m., with no one on the street, and they had no idea where they were! They walked to the first building and saw a little note taped to the door, saying, "Ring buzzer #3." They rang it, and out came a man in a sleeping gown and cap, who was expecting them. He took them upstairs to the top apartment, where Sebnem had left a note saying she would be by in the morning to get them, which was an incredible relief.[1]

American Ballet Theatre (1970)

American Ballet Theatre (ABT) did both *The Moor's Pavane* and *The Traitor* in June 1970. It was very unusual at this time for ABT to do work of this nature. They were

---

1. After Turkey, Danny and Laura went on to Greece, where they intended to visit the childhood home of Laura's grandfather. They could not find the home or any records for her grandfather. At the police station, where they kept the records, the policeman who was helping them pulled Danny aside to ask whether Laura's grandfather was Jewish, because during the war, they had separated the records of the Jews. This helped him find the records of the grandfather and finally the area where he had lived.

a very classical company who did not do modern-based work in those days. This was the first staging of *The Moor's Pavane* outside the Limón Company.

On June 27, 1970, ABT performed at the State Theater. *The Moor's Pavane* opened the show, and *Giselle* closed the show, and these were the only works on the program. The ABT directors at that time were Lucia Chase and Oliver Smith, and it was very unusual to see a modern masterpiece and a ballet classic on the same program together.

Danny thought that *The Moor's Pavane* was a good choice because Bruce Marks was dancing with ABT and was a well-known ballet and modern dancer. ABT also had Toni Lander, Sallie Wilson, and Royes Fernandez, all excellent dancers. Sallie Wilson was known for her dancing in Tudor works such as *Dark Elegies*, and when she retired from ABT, she became a modern dancer and danced with Patrice Regnier, a Juilliard graduate, and other modern companies. The four of them made a terrific cast, and they did a wonderful job with *The Moor's Pavane*.

Through His Friends' Eyes—Bruce Marks

Bruce Marks had the following comments about learning his role in The Moor's Pavane *from Danny: "Transmitting the body of information called a dance is a delicate matter. Dances—the great ones—have a soul. That soul exists in the muscle, mind, and memory of the performer. The complexities of the work are musical and stylistic and often dramatic. Daniel Lewis came to me with a deep and abiding love and respect for José Limón, the person who had entrusted him with the caring for and transmitting of his greatest work. While Danny knew the work inside and out, he was extremely aware of the latitude I would need to make Jose's Othello into Bruce's Othello. Danny never asked me to imitate José; he knew that a carbon copy would not suffice, and he was going to allow me to be myself, as he trusted my modern dance background and my knowledge of Limon's work. The* Moor's Pavane *turned out to be a signature work for me, one of the joys of my life. This gift that he gave me came through his ability to turn movement into meaning. He was exacting in his demands as well as giving and gracious, allowing me to take ownership, for a time, of these treasures."*

Clive Barnes wrote a review titled "Dance: Moor's Pavane" in *The New York Times*, dated June 29, 1970, about the ABT performance of the work. It acknowledged all of the people who worked on or contributed to this version: music by Henry Purcell (arranged by Simon Sadoff); costumes by Pauline Lawrence; execution supervised by Charles Tomlinson; conductor Akira Endo; with dancers Bruce Marks, Royes Fernandez, Sallie Wilson, and Toni Lander. The review described the work as "a totally engrossing work and likely to remain among Mr. Limón's most enduring works."

> It is unique in all Shakespearean ballets in that it dives deep for the art rather than the matter.... What Mr. Limón has set out to do is to picture the corrosive force of jealousy and the destruction of good by evil, and to encapsulate this into the patterns of a ballroom dance.... He has been fortunate here in an ideal cast. I will never forget Mr. Limón himself and Lucas Hoving as the original Othello and Iago.... Yet now Bruce Marks and Royes Fernandez are no less impressive, Mr. Marks, bearded, noble, anguished and with all the passion and agony of the world on his broad shoulders, is brought low by a sinuously insinuating Mr. Fernandez, a very proper villain with the graceful movements of a snake. This admirable cast is completed by Sallie Wilson as the wicked Emilia (Mr. Limón is less charitable with her than is Shakespeare) and Toni Lander as the yielding and wronged Desdemona. It is a shrewd and subtle work, that will be a credit to Ballet Theater.

Danny was concerned, however, about staging *The Traitor*, because it would take many men, and they would need to have men who could do the Leader and the Traitor roles. *The Traitor* premiered at the American Dance Festival at Connecticut College in 1954, with music by Gunther Schuller (*Symphony for Brasses*), original costumes by Pauline Lawrence, and with Royes Fernandez as the Leader (originally Lucas Hoving), Bruce Marks the Traitor (originally José Limón), and six ABT male dancers as the Followers.[2] The work was performed in June 1970, and the men all did excellent work adjusting to the Limón style; they were beautiful and very strong dancers.

Bruce Marks (left) and José Limón rehearsing *The Moor's Pavane*, choreography by José Limón, at the State Theater, New York, 1970 (photograph by Daniel Lewis, courtesy Daniel Lewis archives).

On the night of the premiere of *The Traitor*, José and Danny went out shopping to get gifts for the dancers (Royes as Christ and Bruce as the Traitor). Bruce was easy: some pieces of silver and a little leather case to represent the twenty pieces of silver that Judas was paid. But what do you get for Christ? They were on 72nd Street and Broadway, and there was a new building being constructed. There were fences and barbed wire to keep people off the site. José asked Danny to climb over the fence and get a rusty piece of barbed wire. Then they went to a florist, who wove the barbed wire into a crown of thorns using roses. It was truly a beautiful object when it was completed. They put it in a box with green tissue paper. When they gave it to Royes, he was in tears. Danny was moved by the fact that José was so sensitive in finding something to give to Christ.

Royal Swedish Ballet (1970, 1971)

1970 with Laura Glenn

The performance of the Royal Swedish Ballet in Stockholm, Sweden, was on April 25, 1970, although the residency began in March. Danny and Laura flew to Stockholm

---

2. The Followers were Robert Brassel, William Carter, Robert Gladstein, Keith Lee, Dennis Nahat, Marcos Parades, Frank Smith, and Vane Vest.

right after staging *Missa Brevis* at UCLA, and they were in Sweden for the Spring Equinox on March 20. Danny and Laura Glenn staged *There Is a Time*, *The Exiles*, and *Missa Brevis*, a full evening of Limón work. This was a very special time for Danny, and he got to know the dancers well. The dancers in *The Exiles* were Gerd Andersson[3] and Jonas Kåge, and the main dancer in *Missa Brevis* was Verner Klavsen.

Danny and Laura stayed in an apartment in the old city or old town called Gamla Stan, which was an easy walk from the theater. The apartment was in an old brownstone, a very narrow place with a spiral staircase, and it was owned by the author Susan Sontag. Each room had its own fireplace, and this was the only heating system for the apartment. When they first arrived, wood had been ordered for the apartment but was not going to arrive for a couple of days. The Swedish phone book was in several volumes because it was for the whole country, and they ended up burning the phone books for heat those first few days. Since they were starting in March, it was very cold and was dark most of the day, with only about three hours of full sunshine each day. The food was fabulous, and they had so much fun in the wonderful country of Sweden.

This was the first time that Danny had been in a situation with dancers who were fully dedicated to what they were doing and gave their all. But if rehearsal was scheduled to end at 4:00 p.m., no matter what they were doing, they stopped and left. The union representative would call out "Quit" at 4 p.m., and that was it.

In addition to the rehearsals that Danny was doing with the dancers, Danny had given Limón classes. When Danny came to the theater in the evening to see the opening performance of *There Is a Time*, he went backstage to talk to the dancers. He came upon a row of women in their tutus, ready for the first ballet work of the evening, doing Limón body swings. He was viewing them from the back, so he could see the tutus circling in the air with each drop as their heads dropped to the floor and their bottoms flew upward. The dancers said that they had never found any exercise that warmed up the body so well and gave them such freedom of movement.

Laura remarked that one of the most difficult aspects of staging the work was dealing with the raked stages and dance studios, especially doing sections like "A Time to Laugh" in *There Is a Time*. Also, everything was a fight with the theater staff, because it was an opera house and dance was considered a secondary event, so there were always negotiations to get more rehearsal time in the space. Limón did come over to Sweden to see the works. The performances were fabulous, and José was very pleased.

Danny and Laura had some interesting outings while in Sweden. A former neighbor of Laura's from Queens was living and working in Sweden at the time. He had a small airplane, and he flew them up to northern Sweden to see the ice caps, which terrified Laura. Another time, Danny and Laura rented a car on a free weekend, and they decided to drive up to see the Viking burial mounds. The map they had led them down a road that went right up to a lake. They stopped at the edge of the water, assuming that they had made a wrong turn. Cars started piling up behind them on the road. Eventually the drivers got out of their cars and came over to Danny and Laura. They told them to just drive, explaining as best as they could to people who spoke very little

---

3. Gerd Andersson's husband was Veit Bethky, general manager for the opera (who later invited DLDRC back to perform in Stockholm). Their son was Lars Bethky. At Gerd's suggestion, Lars came to New World School of the Arts years later to hold an audition for a project he was doing. On one occasion, Danny had Gerd and Viveka Ljung, another dancer in the Royal Swedish Ballet, in his New York apartment for dinner. He prepared a Stouffer's frozen spinach soufflé; they both loved it and kept asking for the recipe!

Swedish that the water level was quite low, and it was six feet of solid ice under the water. Thus, in the winter, you could drive out onto the lake, where there were signs pointing which way to go to different cities. Once you were 100 feet out, there was no more water, just the ice.

1971 with Jennifer Scanlon

Danny returned to Stockholm a second time in 1971 with Jennifer Scanlon and staged *The Moor's Pavane*; Teri Weksler came with Danny as his partner. Jennifer was coming to Stockholm from the west coast, where she had been teaching for First Chamber Dancers. She flew across the country, met Danny in New York, and then they flew over to Sweden. As it turned out, going through customs was quite the adventure. In her words, "I looked like Miss Norm, and he looked like Mr. Hippie." They did not have their work visas yet, because they had been told by the opera to come as tourists and they would be given their visas when they arrived. Customs officials asked how much cash they had on them, and they only had a small amount. This triggered a full baggage search. The customs officials went through Jennifer's carry-on luggage, where she had bottles and bottle of vitamins. Then they went through all of Danny's bags but found nothing. Finally, a supervisor came over and asked how they would support themselves while in Sweden, and Danny showed his American Express card. This was sufficient for the officials.

The Royal Swedish Ballet was the first time Jennifer staged *The Moor's Pavane*. There were two casts for the work. Cast 1 was Verner Klavsen as Othello, Gerd Andersson as Desdemona, Jens Graff as Iago, and Mariane Orlando as Emilia. Cast 2 was Markku Heinonen as Othello, Margit Lithander as Desdemona, Imre Dózsa as Iago, and Viveka Ljung as Emilia.

Through His Friends' Eyes—Beth Corning

In 1983, Danny returned to Stockholm when Beth Corning, later director of Corning Works in Pittsburgh, wanted to do The Exiles *in Sweden with Jens Graff. At that point, Danny was the founding director of the Limón Institute, so he wrote the contract, went over to Sweden with his wife Jane Carrington, and taught the work to Beth and Jens. They did a fabulous job dancing the work.*

Beth Corning wrote the following about her experiences with Limón work and with Danny: "In the mid 1970s while a student at the University of Michigan's dance department, I met Danny, who had come to the department to set Jose's and Danny's work The Waldstein Sonata, *and Danny and I became friends. Then, in the early 1980s, I was living, dancing, and running my own company, Corning Dances and Company, in Stockholm, Sweden. I called Danny and asked him to set* The Exiles *on Jens Graff and me, and he came with Jane. I remember much laughter. I remember Danny sitting and directing, and then jumping up to demonstrate so elegantly with Jane. I remember Danny being generous and warmly complimentary to the two of us. It's such a challenging and fulfilling work to dance! To work with that level of artistry, that brilliant choreography, that wonderful partner, that wonderful coaching—it's a memory that, still after forty-some years of dancing some pretty amazing work, stays close to my heart. I clearly remember Danny's warmth and love of sharing the work, and José's voice gently, gentlemanly, elegantly speaking through Danny's love and understanding."*

University of California at Los Angeles (1970–1972)

Danny was teaching in London when he was offered a guest faculty position at UCLA in the next winter quarter. He had to sign a contract, which required him to sign a statement and swear an oath of allegiance to the constitution of the state of California. According to the regulations, the only person who has the authority to notarize such a statement when you are outside the United States is the ambassador or an attaché general at an embassy. Danny went to the U.S. Embassy in London and asked to see the ambassador. He did not see the ambassador, but he did meet with someone in a high position at the embassy, who told Danny it was no problem to do this service for him. They went through the paperwork, and the document was stamped. When the process was finished, the person told Danny that he had to charge him for it. Danny responded that it said on the form that it was illegal to charge for it. The person replied that the rule only applied in the United States! The fee was only about five pounds, so after much discussion, Danny decided it was easier just to pay it. They went to the cashier, and Danny paid the fee and left. He was about two blocks from the embassy when he discovered that a Marine in full uniform was chasing him, trying to tell Danny he was needed back at the embassy. When he got there, he realized that he had not actually raised his right hand to swear the oath of allegiance!

From 1970 to 1972, Danny taught at UCLA for the winter quarter each year. He would commute twice a week from Juilliard in New York. Danny was initially staying with Laura Glenn in UCLA faculty housing. The accommodations were bleak, and Danny mentioned to the dancers at UCLA that he was looking for a place to stay. A dancer at UCLA named Les Ditson introduced Danny and Laura to Dennis Weinreich, whose brother Michael had just left for Europe, so Dennis was staying in a large, empty house on Bundy Drive.[4] Danny and Laura ended up staying with Dennis for the 1970 UCLA residency, and Danny bought a junk car to get to the school. In 1971, Danny stayed at the apartment of David Hall, an actor, and his first wife Susan Petroni. (David would later be well known in film and in shows such as *CSI: Crime Scene Investigation*.) Danny shared a bed with a young woman who worked nights at the Veterans Administration Hospital, so Danny slept in the bed at night, and she slept in the bed during the day. They shared the rent. When the big San Fernando earthquake in Los Angeles happened on February 9, the hospital where she worked collapsed. She was now out of a job and did not want to sleep days anymore. Michael Weinreich lived upstairs, and he cleared out his junk room and added a mattress so that Danny could move in with him with his first wife Karen. When he moved in with Michael and Karen, Danny asked what he would be charged for rent. They said no, they would not take rent, but Danny could help by cleaning up and doing dishes. The next morning, Danny went to Sears and bought them a dishwasher.

In 1970 at UCLA, while he was staging *Missa Brevis*, he worked with Nina Watt, a student in the program. He told her that when she came to New York, she should come and see him. She did just that; she literally just showed up on his doorstep in New York one day with her backpack on! Danny introduced her to José, and this was the start of

---

4. Dennis Weinreich later moved to London and met Li, who would become his wife. They formed their own company, VideoSonics, which did work for BBC and on many major movies. Whenever Danny was at the London Contemporary Dance School, Dennis and Li would give him a place to stay in their house. To this day, Danny and the Weinreich family are the closest of friends.

her career with the Limón Company. She was eventually a soloist and danced with the company from 1972 to 2001.

Through His Friends' Eyes—Robert Small

Robert Small was another one of the dancers in Missa Brevis, *and he wrote the following comments: "We performed* Missa Brevis *at UCLA, and what an experience it was with you and Laura. You know, working and learning from you both inspired so many of us to come to NYC, and most of us did join companies during the golden days of the NEA Touring Program in the late 1960s through the '70s. Nina Watt and I were juniors, and she left UCLA immediately after her* Missa Brevis *experience with you and joined the Limón Company. Susie MacDermaid finished her master's degree that year and went to NYC to dance with you, but she got into the Nikolais Dance Theatre. I came to NYC in 1971 with Lisbeth Bagnold (my girlfriend), who finished her master's degree. I got my BFA that same year and joined Murray Louis' company in August 1971. Lisbeth joined Nik's company [Nikolais Dance Theatre] soon thereafter. Also from that* Missa Brevis *group were Anne and Les Ditson, who joined Murray's company in 1970, a year before I arrived on the scene. So, thanks to that period when UCLA had the funding to invite guest artists to set work on us, we all flocked to NYC. How times have changed! But the memories and life-changing influences that you had on us are profound to this day. I am now a landscape designer, designing rooftop and terrace gardens here in NYC since 1993, but the motional sensations of my twenty-year career in dance still inform my design choices and aesthetic. And, as Phyllis Lamhut and I keep reiterating, 'Motion is the engine for creative thinking, acting, and being.'"*

Royal Danish Ballet (1971)

The Royal Danish Ballet performed regularly at Kongelige Teater (KGL Theatre) in Copenhagen, Denmark. Danny and Carla Maxwell staged *The Moor's Pavane* with dancers Vivi Flindt (Emilia), Toni Lander (Desdemona), Bruce Marks (Othello), and Henning Kronstam (Iago). Toni and Bruce, who were married, had done the work previously with American Ballet Theatre, dancing with Sallie Wilson and Royes Fernandez. The Danish cast was a divine one. Carla only had to teach Vivi her part, and Danny only had to teach Henning his part, because the other two already knew their parts. It so happened that when Bruce and Toni came to do these performances, it was the heyday of dance in Denmark during that period of time. There was lots of funding for dance, and they were able to bring in many guest choreographers.

It was an interesting performance because King Frederick IX and Queen Ingrid of Denmark came to the opening night and sat up in the corner box. At the very start of the concert, the national anthem was played and everyone had to stand and face the king and queen. At the end of the work, the audience could not applaud until the king and queen applauded. Danny had acquired a Lee Hawkins High School marching band jacket, which was red with a blue collar and blue cuffs, with little stars on it, and Danny wore it to opening night. He did not look at all out of place with all the royalty there! (José flew in just before the opening to look at the work, and he thought this attire was very funny.) Carla and Danny had wonderful times staging the work in Denmark.

One night, Danny and Carla were having dinner with José, and he mentioned that he had never been to Florence, Italy. He remarked on how close they were and remarked that he wanted to go there with the two of them. José bought the tickets, and the three of them flew into Rome, but José was not happy in Rome, because the city was too big for him. Then they went to Florence, and José took them through the Galleria degli Uffizi (Uffizi Gallery), describing every painting. He knew the history of each painting, including who the artist was sleeping with at the time! They had wonderful meals in Italy, and they went into small stores to buy items to take home, including a beautiful red velvet tie that Danny bought. Carla loved big brimmed hats, and she saw a gorgeous one in dark chocolate brown with light beige feathers in the window of one of the shops. When they walked into the shop, with Danny and Carla dressed like two hippies and José was in his usual elegant suit and hat, the woman running the shop exclaimed "What a spectacle!" in Italian. (Danny admits they were "a strange group"—this 6'4" bald man with these two young kids.) José helped with the purchase of the hat, because he spoke Spanish, which is similar to Italian (another Romance language). Carla still has this hat, but Danny got rid of the tie which was stained with soup and gravy.

Through His Friends' Eyes—Vivi Flindt

At the NDEO conference in 2016, Danny and Donna Krasnow had dinner with Knud Arne Jürgensen, who is a Danish music, opera, ballet, and theater historian, dramaturg, and curator of exhibitions; he was the curator of the archives at the Royal Danish Library. He remarked about those grand days in Denmark with all the funding for dance. He then texted Vivi Flindt, who sent the following statement about working with Danny: "It is always so great to talk about The Moor's Pavane *and to go back in time and remember the wonderful time, first in the studio and then on the stage. For me, it is really one of the highlights in my career. I shall never forget the feeling when we danced at the Bolshoi, that huge stage and four dancers; it was just fantastic and it was a huge success with the very traditional (let´s say old-fashioned) audience. What a fond memory!"*

National Ballet of Canada (1973)

After the Limón Company tour in the Soviet Union, Danny sent the company to Paris, and he returned to New York. He then had a month in which he had no commitments to the Limón Company, so he took a real vacation and went camping in Colorado. He got a call from Sue Pimsleur that he needed to go to the National Ballet of Canada in Toronto, Canada, because Sol Hurok had purchased *The Moor's Pavane* for $25,000 as a birthday gift for Rudolf Nureyev, who would be guest dancing with the company. Danny left his car in Colorado, jumped on a plane, and met Edward DeSoto in Toronto. The two of them worked on *The Moor's Pavane*, and the dancers were Rudolf Nureyev as Othello, Winthrop Corey as Iago, Maria Barrios as Emilia, and Mary Jago as Desdemona. They got to the end of the work, where Emilia and Iago's bodies and costumes cover Othello as he is killing Desdemona. All the audience would see were Othello's fists rising over the costumes one at a time and then coming down several times. Nureyev turned to Danny and said, "This needs to be seen." Danny asked him what he meant, to which Nureyev replied that the murder was very important and needed to be seen. Danny politely explained that from the beginning everyone knows the story and knows she is going to be killed, and José did not want the actual murder to be seen. They had a disagreement about it, but finally Nureyev agreed.

Several months after Danny left, he received a call from Nureyev that the National Ballet Company was coming to the State Theater in New York, and he wanted Danny to come and see the production. Danny went to the box office to get his tickets, and he sat down in the theater. When the time came for the killing of Desdemona, Iago and Emilia did chaine turns out to the sides of the stage, and the audience saw Nureyev killing her. Danny was livid, and he went backstage, where he and Nureyev had words. Danny was angry, so his words were harsh. The next day, Danny received a call from Hurok's office, asking Danny to come to the office with Sue Pimsleur to clear up the whole situation. Hurok pulled out the contract, turned to a particular page, and told Danny to read it. It stated, "Mr. Nureyev can perform 'The Moor's Pavane' whenever, wherever, and however he pleases." Danny asked Sue why she had signed it. She replied that the discussion had been that Nureyev had AIDS and might need to change a jump or a leap or something to accommodate his health issues. Danny said he felt it was reasonable for changes to be made to his role, but not to change the choreography of other dancers (referring to the chaine turns of Iago and Emilia). Hurok said that did not matter—the contract was very clear, so Nureyev could do what he wanted. They were stuck with that contract for years, until Nureyev became the artistic director of the Paris Opera Ballet in 1983. At that point, he was no longer dancing; he wanted to stage the work with other dancers and therefore had to draw up a new and better contract. Sarah Stackhouse went to Paris to stage it.

Alvin Ailey American Dance Theater (1973)

In December 1973, Danny and Laura Glenn staged *Missa Brevis* with the Alvin Ailey American Dance Theater. Dudley Williams, Clive Thompson, Ulysses Dove danced as the men's trio, and Judith Jamison danced Hosanna, Betty Jones' part. When Danny first cast Judith, she said she was not suited for that role and could not do it, but Danny told her she could indeed do it. He said she was wonderful and cooperative to work with, and she worked diligently on the style. John Parks, a Juilliard graduate and Limón Company dancer, danced José's part. The music was live organ and chorus.

On December 4, 1973, the Alvin Ailey American Dance Theater performed at the City Center 55th Street Theater. The program included *Hidden Rites* (1973) by Ailey, *According to Eve* (1972) by John Butler, and *Missa Brevis* (1958) by José Limón. The dancers for *Missa Brevis* were the full company, but special roles were danced by John Parks in the section "Qui Tollis"; Dudley Williams, Clive Thompson, and Ulysses Dove in the sections "Cum Sancto Spiritu" and "Credo"; with Sylvia Waters, Estelle Spurlock, and Dana Sapiro also in "Credo"; Sara Yarborough in the section "Crucifix"; and Judith Jameson in the section "Hosanna."[5] New York City has a large dance audience, but it

---

5. Other dancers in the company were Mari Kajiwara, Linda Kent, Tina Yuan, Masazumi Chaya, Hector Mercado, Michihiko Oka, Kenneth Pearl, Kevin Rotardier, Nerissa Barnes, Melvin Jones, Christa Mueller, Edward Love, Elbert Watson, Donna Wood, and Peter Woodin.

tends to be divided around companies and genre. This performance was so well received that it brought a whole new audience to Limón's work.

New York University (1977–1985)

Danny taught at NYU as an adjunct professor from 1977 to 1985 in the School of Education–Health, Nursing, and Arts Professionals, along with Chair of the School of Education Patricia Rowe and faculty members Laura Brittain, Marcia Leventhal, Judith Schwartz, Ernestine Stodelle, Martha Eddy, and Jane Carrington. This was an important and long-standing position for Danny. Present at the first faculty meeting he attended were Ruth Abrahams, Elmer Baker, Christine Dunbar, Karen Gillespie, Gail Oakland, Patricia Rowe, Louise Scripps, Andrea Wilson, and Charles Woodford. Patricia Rowe and Danny were good friends, and he did a lot of work for her over many years.[6]

Jacqui Von Honts, a graduate student at NYU, did a painting around 1980 based on one of the posters from Danny's first company, Contemporary Dance System (CDS). This flier shows (from left to right) Martial Roumain, Miguel Godreau, Rae Kraus, Teri Weksler, and Peter Sparling. Patricia Rowe had this painting in her office for many years. Patricia had said one of her paintings was to be given to Danny after she passed away, and in 2017, Ruth Abrahams gifted this company painting to Danny from the estate of Dr. Patricia A. Rowe, in her memory. It is currently hanging in the Dance Division at the University of Florida, as part of the Daniel Lewis Dance Research Collection in the George A. Smathers Libraries.

Ruth Abrahams donated this Jacqui Von Honts painting (left) from Patricia Rowe's office to Daniel Lewis, taken from this CDS company poster (right) (poster design and photograph by Paul Perlow, courtesy Daniel Lewis archives).

6. Danny spoke at her memorial, which was held at the Joyce Theater on Monday, September 27, 2010. Other speakers and performers at the memorial included Judith G. Schwartz, Genevieve Oswald, Ralph Samuelson, Magda Saleh, Beth Griffith, Nancy Meehan, Jim May, Ruth Abrahams, and Jeanne Bresciani.

Through His Friends' Eyes—Rae Kraus

Rae (Carol-rae) Kraus was studying acting at Carnegie Mellon University in Pittsburgh when Graham company dancer Ethel Winter saw Rae and wanted her to go to Juilliard. Although for various reasons Rae did not attend Juilliard, it put the idea in her head to dance. She transferred to Barnard College, where Janet Soares choreographed a solo The Brentwood Pieces *on her. Shortly after, Rae became an Affiliate Artist. Janet took Rae's solo to the Glastonbury Festival in 1971, along with Danny and Peter Sparling, and this is when Rae and Danny became good friends.*

About this early time with Danny, Rae said, "He was passionate about dancing and just as passionate about living life! This was an important lesson that I learned from Danny. After the festival was over, we all went camping on the moors. Danny taught me that you work and dance intensely, and then you rebuild yourself by giving your body a rest but opening up your emotional mind. Danny had excellent insight and instincts about people. He took me into his company with only a few months of training. One day in rehearsal, he asked me to do a double back attitude turn, and I said I would do it if he could show me what an attitude was! Despite my lack of training, he put me on the path to become a professional dancer, as he saw my potential and my gift as a performer. My time with CDS was crucial to my becoming a dancer. I learned amazing repertory, and I danced with great dancers such as Peter Sparling, Teri Weksler, and Miguel Godreau. Danny created a wonderful, supportive atmosphere in the company and trusted each dancer to find the qualities he needed in his work. Danny became a powerful influence in the dance world, as an artist and as an educator, because of his instincts about people. Danny had a truly magnificent career and was an extraordinary dancer, but then he decided to give back. His generosity, and his love of seeing people accomplish, led him to start many people down the path to becoming dancers. He elevated the field of dance beyond anyone who was my contemporary. Danny has given dance to the world."

Danny also emceed many events at NYU, including the "50 Years of Dance Education" presentation in April 1982. This event marked NYU's history in the start of BFA programs for dance across the United States. NYU had been the first school to move dance studies from physical education into arts and education. This occurred in 1932 under Martha Hill, who felt that dance should not be part of physical education.

London Contemporary Dance School (1977–1987)

London Contemporary Dance School (LCDS), also known as The Place, was located at 17 Dukes Road in London. Robin Howard was the founder of the London Contemporary Dance School. He had lost both his legs in World War II but saw the Martha Graham Company in 1954 and was mesmerized. Therefore, when he started the school, it was based on Graham technique. Initially, Danny was brought to the school as a contrast to and balance for the Graham work.

Jane Dudley, originally a prominent dancer in the Martha Graham Company in New York, had moved to London to teach at LCDS in 1970. Jane Dudley was the rehearsal director of the Batsheva Company and its artistic director from 1968 to 1970, just before she came to London. It was in Israel that Danny and Jane first became friends, as he was there staging two works. She and Nina Fonaroff, also previously with the Graham Company, were the two who convinced those in charge at LCDS (such as Richard Ralph, the school principal) to bring Danny there to stage Limón works and give workshops in the technique. The fact that this continued for nine summers was due to the quality of the work and also that Danny and Richard got along really well.

There were letters from Jack Norton, general manager at LCDS, co-signed by Jane Dudley, at the start in 1977, setting up the terms of the residency and the terms of the contract. In the first year, he staged *A Choreographic Offering*. An earlier letter in 1976 had suggested that they wanted Danny to stage his work *The Waldstein Sonata*, but that never actually happened. Jane Dudley had seen Danny rehearsing the work at Juilliard and thought it was beautiful. Danny wanted Nancy Jordan to go over and stage it, and then Danny would go over and direct it, but the school felt it could not afford the cost of bringing in two people at that time. Also, Jane wanted Limón works, but Ruth Currier did not want students dancing his work. (This policy changed when Carla Maxwell became the artistic director of the Limón Company.) Overall, the negotiations with LCDS were complex and difficult; nevertheless, Danny ended up going many times. One of the precedents his visit set was how his fee was defined. In essence, the school bought the Limón work and then paid Danny to show them how to use the work. In this way, he was not an employee of the school.

In 1977, in addition to teaching at LCDS, he brought his company, and they performed in Stockholm, Sweden, and Kuopio, Finland. The school tried again in this year to get *The Waldstein Sonata*, but Danny was still unwilling and refused, because he felt Nancy Jordan must be the person to stage it, and then Danny would follow to coach it. In 1978, he returned to LCDS; he staged *There Is a Time*, and his fee doubled from what he was paid in 1977.

In 1981, Danny had a schedule conflict that would make him unable to go to Reed College in Portland, Oregon, for the summer program because the dates overlapped with his teaching at LCDS. So he asked LCDS for an increase in his fee to match what Reed would have paid him. In the end, Danny did both Reed and London Contemporary Dance School that year, because LCDS shifted the dates to accommodate him.

In 1982, Danny staged *Missa Brevis* for the school. Julian Moss, who ended up in the London Contemporary Dance Theatre, danced in this production. The work was performed in Southwark Cathedral in London, with the King's College singers. After the performance, the Anglican priest came to Danny and said that they needed to have dance performances more often; he had never seen so many people in the church! They performed *Missa Brevis* all over London. Danny also taught at the summer school that year, along with Kazuko Hirabayashi and others.

In 1983, the main show presented works by students at the school, plus *A Choreographic Offering*, staged by Danny and Jane Carrington. Jane was an outstanding regisseur, and she had assisted Danny many times all over the world. She could learn material and immediately be able to show it, and she had a photographic memory. By this time, Danny and Jane had been married since October 1980. The version they staged was the one Danny had edited and arranged for the State Department tour of the Soviet Union in 1973.

London Contemporary Dance School dancers came and performed at Brooklyn Academy of Music. Dancers included Julian Moss, Darshan Singh Bhuller (later the director of Phoenix Dance Theater and choreographer of several works at NWSA), Robert North (who performed by permission of Ballet Rambert), and Siobhan Davies (who later formed her own company). All of these dancers were Danny's students at LCDS. Also in 1983, London Contemporary Dance Theater asked Danny to consider becoming the artistic director, to replace Robert Cohan, who was going to leave; in the end, Robert decided to stay on.[7]

In 1987, his final year at LCDS, Danny and Jane staged *There Is a Time*. Later, Danny rented the *There Is a Time* costumes from London Contemporary Dance School to use at the New World School of the Arts performance. It became a hassle, because after they were shipped, the customs officials would not let them into the country. They were shipped back to London, and the staff at LCDS shipped them back to Florida again.

Through His Friends' Eyes—Adriana Urdaneta

Three dancers from the London Contemporary Dance School—Adriana Urdaneta, Jacques Broquet (now Adriana's husband), and her sister Luz Urdaneta—moved back to Caracas, Venezuela, and formed a company called Danzahoy (Dance Today). Danza-hoy performed at the Riverside Dance Festival in 1983.[8] At this time, Danzahoy invited Danny and Jane to come to Venezuela to teach and stage Humphrey's Night Spell. *They were already to be in Mexico working, so Danzahoy flew them from Mexico to Venezuela, and then back to New York.*

Adriana wrote the following about the residency at Danzahoy's studio in Caracas: "We staged the piece in fifteen days, working all day long like crazy. It was a 'first-click' love story, and that was why it just happened in such a manner. It was a fascinating and intense process. We honored the American modern dance pioneers, as we ourselves were pioneers in Venezuela. The fact that a small company in Venezuela could access the work was already a gift. What a pleasure and lesson of life it was to be able to dance such a magnificent work of dance! Another aspect of the process that I could point out was the contrast between Danny and Jane in terms of how you both transmitted the steps. Danny was always talking about the dramatic aspect of the motions, so the story could 'appear' in our bodies. He did it in a very simple, easy to understand, sometimes even humorous way, like a children's story: 'Now he is sleeping and dreams of these monsters coming and terrorizing him. Then he discovers that one of them is actually beautiful and falls in love! Oh, my God! What will he do now?' We definitely grasped the essential elements and dove into the choreography with a childlike innocence and pas-sion. Doris Humphrey's work was full of emotional colors, and that was key to achieving such results in such a short time. Then Jane came with the mathematics of the technical difficulties and precise details of the steps of the piece. Great combination! It was an unforgettable experience to us all, especially for Jacques, Luz, and myself. Thank you for making it possible! What a magnificent opportunity! And finally, I admire the way you admire your masters. You have dedicated your life to do so, and that is a beautiful and generous way of living."

Over the ten summers at the London Contemporary Dance School, Danny did a tremendous amount of work, teaching for both the school and the company and stag-ing Limón works. He was highly regarded and trusted by the faculty and adored by the

---

7. In 2006, when Peter London staged Martha Graham's Diversion of Angels for the students at NWSA, Robert Cohan attended and talked to the high school students about Martha's choreographing of the work and how important the tilts are in the work, representing the off-balance nature of love.

8. There was a work in the program by Carlos Orta, who danced with the Limón Company and did many of José's roles. He was from Caracas, Venezuela, and died suddenly at age 60 in 2004.

dancers, and he created a beautiful balance in the technical training at a Graham-based school.

Reed College (1980–1981)

In 1980, Danny went to teach Limón classes with Jane Carrington at the Reed College Summer Institute. Danny and Jane drove to Portland, Oregon, with Esther Friedman, one of his Juilliard students, as his demonstrator. Jane had her own classes to teach and therefore was not demonstrating for him. Danny and Jane returned in the summer of 1981. The director of the program was Keith Martin, who ran Northwest Repertory Dance Company in Portland at the time, and Danny set Humphrey's *Night Spell* on Joe Morales, Amy Bennett-Gaehler (Morales' favorite partner), Kelly Schleigh, and Alice van Fleet. Of dancing in the work, Morales said, "*Night Spell* was a high point for me. As a Hispanic, it really meant something to me to perform José Limón's role in that." It was in 1980 at Reed College that Donna Krasnow and Danny met, and she studied Limón for the first time. In 1981, Danny taught composition at Reed. Danny told the students that they all had to go find music for their dances. One young man brought in *Nefertiti*, the Broadway musical Danny had choreographed years before. He told the man to bring the album in, and Danny pointed to his own name on the cover! On the last day of Limón classes, Danny brought a large box of fresh chocolate-covered strawberries to class. Every time a dancer did something well, Danny would reward him or her with a strawberry. He made sure that by the end of class everyone had received a strawberry.

National Ballet of Canada (1984–1986)

The 1980s were incredibly busy years for Danny, and he made several trips to Canada, including Toronto and Calgary. Danny had an ongoing relationship with the National Ballet School of Canada (NBS) in Toronto, and he was there for full residencies in 1984, 1985, and 1986. Erik Bruhn was the artistic director at Royal Swedish Ballet before coming to the National Ballet of Canada, and he had recommended Limón work for the company. He recommended that Danny teach at NBS, because the dancers needed some Limón training. (This was before Betty Oliphant was getting ready to retire in 1989, and Mavis Staines was preparing to take over.) In that first year, Danny only taught classes. In 1985, the program at the National Ballet School included Limón's *There Is a Time*. Danny received a letter from Mary Anne Beamish, director of public relations at the NBS, mentioning how large the audiences were, how well the dancers performed *There Is a Time*, and how many people commented on how impressed they were with the performance and with the students' ability to dance with maturity and presence.

A May 1985 review by William Littler, dance critic for the *Toronto Star*, also talked about the NBS students doing *There Is a Time*. He said, "What on earth are ballet dancers to-be doing dancing Limón? In the first place, the school graduates do not invariably enter ballet companies. David Hatch Walker, for example, wound up in the Martha Graham Company, while Robert Desrosiers formed his own major company. In the second place, Daniel Lewis argues that today's dancer can ill afford to be a narrow specialist unable to adapt to a variety of choreographic styles." This is a great testament to Danny's vision of the well-rounded dancer and his contribution to this development in dance training, as well as a foretelling of his future program at New World School of the Arts.

It was during these years that Danny met and worked with Lisa Drake, an exquisite dancer who went on to dance with Netherlands Dance Theater and later became the rehearsal director for Cullberg Ballet. Betty Oliphant, the school director, allowed Lisa to perform as a soloist in *There Is a Time* in 1985 but took her out of *A Choreographic Offering* in 1986 because the costume was a bright yellow unitard. This outfit showed her weight to be above the restrictive standards of the NBS during that time period. Danny adored Lisa, and he thought that she could dance Limón like no other ballet dancer he had seen, even though she was only about fourteen years old at the time.[9] Lisa's brilliant dancing didn't matter to Betty, who refused to let her dance in the work.

Through His Friends' Eyes—Lisa Drake

Lisa Drake made the following comments about her time with Danny: "Danny was my first real meeting with contemporary dance, when I was a student at the National Ballet School of Canada. He showed us a video portrayed by puppets: first the ethereal approach of classical ballet, then the deep humanism of modern dance. In that moment I felt connected. The clarity of my desired path was revealed. This is best explained as a fundamental paradigm shift; my perception of beauty and dance transformed in an instant. I felt excited! This profound acknowledgment came hand in hand with Danny's perception of me. He recognized me not just as a teenage dancing body but as a focused young woman, full of passion and the wish to express. His interaction and collaborative means were my first encounter with both professionalism and adulthood. It was empowering. Working with Danny was the most positively formative and inspiring experience of my career. I have often returned to that time in my memory to access encouragement and trust."

The National Ballet of Canada, on its twenty-fifth anniversary in 1984, produced a commemorative book that had many old pictures of the school and important people and faculty. They had all the dancers sign the copy that they sent to Danny. What is memorable to Danny in this book is a photograph from a creative movement class in 1967 at the National Ballet School. The photo included Gerard Ebitz (later ballet faculty at NWSA) and James Kudelka (later artistic director of the National Ballet Company), as young children. Danny had this picture on his wall in his NWSA office, not realizing that Gerard was in it, and Gerard walked in one day and exclaimed that he was in the picture!

In 1988, Danny was flown to Toronto to participate as one of five guest speakers on a panel for the opening of the new Betty Oliphant Theater. This theater was built specifically as part of the performance training for NBS. The year after this opening, Betty Oliphant retired as cofounder and artistic director of NBS, and Mavis Staines took over as director. Graduates of NBS included Mavis Staines, James Kudelka, Lindsay Fischer, John Alleyne, Rex Harrington, Jennifer Fournier, Martine Lamy, Frank Augustyn, Gizella Witkowsky, Robert Desrosiers, Peter Ottmann, Raymond Smith, Michael Greyeyes, Neve Campbell, Johan Persson, and Dominique Dumais. These are some of the

9. For all of these years, Danny has stayed in touch with Lisa. For Danny, it is always amazing when he can watch a dancer from a very young age, all the way through to his or her professional career. This is the true artist-educator in Danny. Danny and Lisa continue to email and use social media to communicate on a regular basis.

most well-known dancers and actors in Canada and internationally, and many probably had classes with Danny at some point.

Through His Friends' Eyes—Mavis Staines

The following is from a letter written much later by Mavis Staines: "Hello, dear Danny. As you can see from the date, I have definitely missed the official Christmas card deadline. Rather than admitting defeat, I will now focus on wishing you and Maureen all the very best in 1995. It would be wonderful if 1995 meant that we occasionally had the opportunity to see one another again. Menaka Thakkar was telling me about the joint project with you in the fall of 1995. She is a very talented woman, so the two of your talents combined should provide impressive results. Life at NBS is hard to describe, not because there is a shortage of energy or determination within, but because funding difficulties push us closer to the edge of the cliff than we have been for the past few years. I am used to skating on the edge of the precipice, but it is getting a little thinner than any of the past 25 years with the Canada Council, in its funding within the next year. The arts community is acknowledging the shortage of money but begging to be an equal partner. Please keep your fingers crossed for us. I refuse to believe we cannot solve this problem. I am grateful for the extraordinary talent of staff and students. Looking forward to our next meeting. Much love, Mavis."

University of Calgary (1984, 1986)

In 1984, Danny and Jane were invited by faculty member Donna Krasnow and Keith Burgess, head of the dance program, to head a six-week residency in Alberta, Canada, at the University of Calgary. Donna had asked Danny to bring several Limón films to show to the university students, and he exited the plane loaded down with suitcases. When asked why he was carrying it all, he said, "I'm not checking these films; they're one of a kind!" In addition to teaching Limón classes every morning, Danny staged Limón's *A Choreographic Offering* on eighteen dancers, including Donna and Jane. He also choreographed *Atomic Ambience*, with music by Jean Piché, for the students. Jane choreographed a work for the students, plus the duet *Living on the Ceiling* for herself and Donna. Jane danced two other solos in this show: *Miracle* (a premiere) and *History Full of Song* (1979). They rented an apartment in the outskirts of town near Donna's apartment. On the day that they arrived in May, there was a snow blizzard!

In the summer of 1986, they returned for a second six-week residency. This time, Danny staged *There Is a Time* and choreographed "Bibleland" on the students for the show *Summerdance*. Jane choreographed a work for students called *Bittersweet Sister* and another duet for herself and Donna called *Buddy Monday*. This time they stayed at the house of music professor Charles Foreman, who was performing live piano music for another guest faculty work by Andrea Olsen. Elaine Bowman and Peter Hoff, directors of Dancers Studio West, produced a full evening of solos danced by Jane, including "A Time to Laugh" and "A Time to Hate" from *There Is a Time* by José Limón; *History Full of Song* by Jane; "Allegro Mysterioso," a solo from *Lyric Suite* by Anna Sokolow; a solo from *Ballade* by Sokolow, and *Plain Song* by Jane. The beauty of these two residencies is that they were long enough (six weeks) and intensive enough (three or four classes each day) for the students to see real progress and improvement in their work.

Danskern Amsterdam (1985)

Adriaan Kans and Ellen Crawford worked together to form the dance company Danskern. Adriaan had come to the United States to study dance, and he fell in love with the works of Doris Humphrey and José Limón. He invited Danny to come to his studio in the Netherlands in May and June of 1985. Danny and Jane stayed in a nice third-floor apartment right in the red-light district, which is a totally safe area of Amsterdam. Danny would stand at the window, watching the kids in the street pooling their money to see who could get in for a visit with one of the women in the windows!

Danny and Jane staged *Day on Earth*, *The Exiles*, and *There Is a Time* for Danskern. A rehearsal and class schedule for the Danskern program showed *Suspension*, choreographed in 1943 by May O'Donell; *Day on Earth* by Doris Humphrey; plus morning Limón classes with Danny and floor barre once a week with Jane. Adriaan's request for film showings included *La Malinche*, *The Emperor Jones*, *There Is a Time*, *The Unsung*, and *The Moor's Pavane*, all by Limón. Adriaan also requested a showing for the company of Sokolow's *Dreams*, plus an introduction to the public of Danny's book *The Illustrated Dance Technique of José Limón*. This evolved into a long relationship, and they had many visits.

Through His Friends' Eyes—Adriaan Kans

Adriaan Kans took his first classes with Danny at The Place in London. While mining the archives of the Jerome Robbins Dance Division of the New York Public Library, he came upon Daniel's work with his company, Daniel Lewis Dance: A Repertory Company. Then, at Danny's invitation, he went to see some of his Limón repertory classes at Juilliard. Adriaan said, "What I saw were inspired revivals, superbly danced by young dancers who obviously knew what they were dancing about: motivation, style, kinetics. When Danny staged Humphrey and Limón dances with my company Danskern, his wonderful coaching brought this tradition into crystal clear immediacy. It brought to my mind the following quote by José Limón: 'It is important to preserve the traditional. It is part of our heritage, and as such is to be cherished. But the modern idioms should be left to the individual to be kept resilient, venturesome, experimental, unhampered.' The night I danced the Danskern premiere of Humphrey's Day on Earth, *staged by Danny and Jane, the eyes of May O'Donnell, composer-husband Ray Green, and lifelong assistant Gertrude Shurr (Danny's first Graham teacher at the High School of Performing Arts) were watching over the company. They were all seated at dead center on the first balcony of a packed Amsterdam Municipal Theatre. Some forty years before, the three of them had seen their good friend José Limón dance the original 1947 premiere. May O'Donnell commented, 'I don't remember the dance being this alive, this vital, Adriaan.' That was when I knew that I was right in what I had experienced, time and again, staging these magical works with Danny."*

Hong Kong Academy for the Performing Arts (1988, 1993)

Soon after moving to Miami, Danny received a call from Carl Wolz at the Hong Kong Academy of the Performing Arts (HKAPA). He wanted to do two works, *A Choreographic Offering* and *Missa Brevis*, but Carla Maxwell was concerned that the works would not get enough rehearsal time with Danny. The plan was to have Tom Brown, faculty member and notator at HKAPA, do some of the rehearsing and staging before Danny would arrive in Hong Kong, due to time constraints. Danny spoke to Carla, assuring her that he could get the work done in the time allotted. It turned out to be a wonderful production in Hong Kong. He staged *A Choreographic Offering* in 1988 and *Missa Brevis* in 1993. The dancers were devoted to the whole work process and were completely focused. A. Christina Giannini, the woman who was going to design new costumes for *Missa Brevis*, was flying through Miami on her way to Hong Kong. Danny met her at a restaurant before her next flight, and he gave her input on how to design the costumes.

6

Contemporary Dance System and Daniel Lewis Dance

A Repertory Company

I was lucky at this point in my life to have the opportunity to form my company, first called Contemporary Dance System and later Daniel Lewis Dance: A Repertory Company. The timing was perfect, with chances for an impressive amount of performing, touring, and residencies. I also had the vision to make it a repertory company. I was lucky to know wonderful choreographers, such as Anna Sokolow, José Limón, and Doris Humphrey, and be able to stage their work on my dancers. The financial support from both the residencies and private donors gave me the ability to give my dancers work all year round.
—Danny Lewis

Early Years

During all of these years traveling and staging Limón works, and teaching at Juilliard, Danny was choreographing and directing his own company, first called Contemporary Dance Sextet, then named Contemporary Dance System (CDS), and finally called Daniel Lewis Dance: A Repertory Company (DLDRC). Paul Perlow, art director and graphics designer and later an adjunct professor at New York City College of Technology, did the CDS and DLDRC logos and all the artwork for the company.

Through His Friends' Eyes—Nancy Scattergood Jordan

Nancy Scattergood Jordan told of her experiences working on his choreography: "In fall 1975 and winter 1976, I worked with Danny when he set The Waldstein Sonata *on Juilliard dancers, at the suggestion of Martha Hill. Danny then wanted to set it on his company. My first experience working with CDS was staging* The Waldstein Sonata, *and then Danny invited me to stay on as rehearsal director. I only danced with the company on rare occasion when I was needed, such as when someone was injured, because I knew the whole repertory. For example, at Riverside in October 1976, I ended up dancing Hannah Kahn's part in* The Waldstein Sonata *because Hannah's back went into spasm. Danny preferred the coaching end of rehearsing, while I did the nuts and bolts. He would come into rehearsal and talk about the ballets, the characters, and the meaning of it all.*
My favorite works were The Waldstein Sonata *and* There's Nothing Here of Me *but*

Me. Open Book *was a tough one for me to stage, because it is very esoteric and hard to nail down, relying so much on what the individual dancer brings to it. It was better to be a coach for that work than the person setting the material. Throughout the years of the company, I was one of the constants, always working in the background, and was able to watch the entire arc of the company.*

Danny was one of the luckiest men on the planet. He was a natural dancer, and he was the right gender at the right time. Because of that particular combination, he was given great opportunities that he might not have otherwise had. Additionally, he had the most incredible mentors in the world, so he really received knowledge from the horse's mouth and took from everyone all that he could. He was incredibly gifted, and he was smart enough to understand the importance of these gifts and his responsibility to other dancers and to the art form. He continued the incredible tradition that he learned from his mentors, but he also opened and expanded it, including multicultural dance, technology, and more. His mind has always been open, but he never forgot the lessons that his mentors taught him, the building blocks of everything he's done. He had much love for José Limón and thought of José and Martha Hill as his two dance parents."

Allen M. Turek was one of the two men who handled the closing of Danny's apartment in New York. Turek came to see the dance company and was very impressed with its caliber, so in December 1983, he decided to join the board of directors for the company. By March 1984, Danny had put together a diverse and influential group of people for the board, including Daniel Lewis (president), Nancy Scattergood Jordan (vice president), Allen Turek (secretary), Marcia Van Buren (treasurer), Martha Hill (artistic advisor), Phil Scottie (the owner of Century Café), Gloria Londino (who was with the *New York Times*),[1] Steve Hirsch (Operation Prime Time and involved in the television show *Wheel of Fortune* at the beginning), and Wayne Rooks (a lawyer from CBS Records). Danny pulled together quite the impressive group for his board. The board authorized Martha Hill to organize an artistic advisory board for the company consisting of dance people in the community. Its purpose was to give artistic direction, comments, advice, and evaluation of the company.

Contemporary Dance Sextet was the name of Danny's company prior to being called Contemporary Dance System. The original six dancers in the work *Dance Sextet* were Eddie Effron, Irene Feigenheimer (Eddie Effron's girlfriend), Laura Glenn (Danny's girlfriend), Kathryn Posin, Danny Lewis, and Chester Wolenski, and this group evolved into Danny's company. Some of these dancers were from Anna Sokolow's company and some were from the Limón Company. This group of six would take repertory excerpts from work by Sokolow and Limón and get performance bookings with them. The photo for the first flyer for Contemporary Dance System looks, in Danny's words, "like a bunch of hippies"!

Danny had a long and important connection with Anna Sokolow, and he had weekly dinners with her. She would call Danny to ask him out to dinner, but Danny always paid, because when the time came to pay, she would grab the check, open her purse, and say that she had no money with her. This became an ongoing ritual. They had wonderful conversations about her work, and often Danny would ask about the works she had done in the 1920s through the 1940s, when she was an artist working

1. Gloria Londino was a friend of the mother of Jane Carrington. Phil Scottie was Jane's boss; she worked in two of his restaurants.

Flier of the first dance company CDS, 1972. From left: Margie Fargnoli, Laura Glenn, Carol-rae Kraus (behind), Daniel Lewis, Peter Sparling (behind), Eddie Effron, Kathy Posin, Mark Stevens (John Giffin, Linda Rabin, and Chester Wolinski not pictured) (photograph by Paul Perlow, courtesy Daniel Lewis archives).

with the needle trade unions and much of her work was political. She did some really exciting works at that time: *Lament for the Death of a Bullfighter* (1945, danced by Jane Carrington in later years), *Ballade in a Popular Style* (1936), and *Kaddish* (1945, danced by Risa Steinberg in later years). When Danny would ask about these older works, Anna would say that she could not remember them. One day, Danny told her to just do what she remembered! That is how the three-part work called *As I Remember* came about, and it consisted of these three solos.[2] His relationship with Anna was important but at times contentious. A story by Nancy Scattergood Jordan related one of the rare times that Danny ever became angry. Anna was rehearsing one of her works on the company in costume. Anna, dissatisfied with one of the dancers, went over to her and yanked on the costume, shredding it. Danny became furious and stormed out, slamming the door. After a time, he calmed down and returned, but it was a rare moment of fury.

In 1971, Contemporary Dance Sextet did a tour at Cuyahoga Community College in Cleveland, Ohio, supported by the Ohio Arts Council. Larry Berger, a Juilliard graduate and stage manager for the Lincoln Center Student Programs, taught at Cuyahoga Community College in Cleveland, and he invited Danny's company there. Larry applied for and got a large grant to fund this visit, which was a two-week residency.

The performances received support from the Arts Council, and they did a

---

2. Danny told this story at her memorial at the Joyce Theater in 2000.

two-week run. Dancers for Sokolow's opening solos in *Lyric Suite* were Chester Wolenski, Irene Feigenheimer, Kathy Posin, and Eddie Effron. Laura Glenn and Chester did a duet, also from *Lyric Suite*. Kathy Posin did the solo *The Cold*. Also on the program was *The Minding of the Flesh Is Death*. The review by Miriam Cramer Andorn stated that it was rare for the students there to see a concert of such high caliber. According to Andorn, the audience cheered and loved the show. The review went on to talk about the students in Cleveland and the surrounding towns welcoming the opportunity to study, as they did classes as well. The review called Danny an exceptional performer and choreographer.

Danny did dozens and dozens of performances and classes in the educational system—younger years in the public schools as well as colleges and universities—and Danny has many boxes of letters of appreciation. A letter from the Cleveland Mayor's Committee on Cultural Policy in 1974 makes it clear that there was an awareness at all levels—city, state, and national—that Danny and his company were doing important work in the school system.

In 1972, a program of five premieres by CDS was dedicated to the memory of José Limón, who had passed away that year. The program was *The Bather and the Lady* by Peter Sparling; *Full Songs* by Laura Glenn; *My Echo, My Shadow, and Me* by Daniel Lewis, with music by the Ink Spots and dancers Laura Glenn, Rae Kraus (soloist), Aaron Osborne, and Mark Stevens; *Let Us Now Praise Famous Men* by Margie Fargnoli; and *December Prose* by Peter Sparling (in which Danny danced). At this point, Castalia Enterprises was managing CDS.

In March 1974, Danny's company was doing *Lyric Suite* at the 92nd Street Y, a popular dance performance space in New York City. It was choreographed by Anna Sokolow to a six-movement work for string quartet written by Alban Berg in the 1920s, using methods derived from Arnold Schoenberg's twelve-tone technique. The company had not worked out any licensing arrangement to use the music. Danny assumed that Anna had the licensing agreement because Alban Berg had told Anna they she could use the music. Eugene Moon from Theodore Presser Company, the distributers of the music, contacted Danny's manager about the fact that the company had not made any arrangements to use the music. The letter said that under no circumstances could they grant gratuitous performance rights for any works in their catalogue; it did not matter that Berg had given permission, because Theodore Presser Company owned the rights. Initially they wanted $175 per performance, but the entire box office receipts were only about $200 each evening. Danny went to the office of Theodore Presser Company and met with a woman at the company who knew Danny from the dance world. She finally gave them the rights at the very low cost of $25 per performance. They ended up doing *Lyric Suite* a lot, so they could not have afforded what was originally being charged.

The Waldstein Sonata

The Waldstein Sonata is a very important work to Danny because it was a transition. His life with José had ended and by 1975, Danny had nothing to do with the Limón company. Then Martha Hill saw the film of what José had done on the work prior to his death; she thought it was worthwhile to reconstruct and finish it. However, she had to get Juilliard President Peter Mennin's permission for this to happen.³ Danny ended up in a one-on-one meeting with Mennin, which felt strange because he did not have a close relationship with him. They sat together and looked at the film, and Mennin said yes to the project and paid for it.⁴

The Waldstein Sonata premiered on April 26, 1975, at the Juilliard Theater. The music is Piano Sonata Number 21, in C Major, Opus 53, by Ludwig von Beethoven. Later in 1975, Danny's company performed the work, and this was one of the first performances with the new name Daniel Lewis Dance: A Repertory Company. The dancers were Laura Glenn, Hannah Kahn, Teri Weksler, Tony Balcena, Randall Faxon Parker, Jim May, Pierre Barreau, and Peter Healey.

On April 29, 1975, a review by Clive Barnes in the *New York Times* titled "Dance:

The Waldstein Sonata, **choreography by Daniel Lewis and José Limón. Dancers from left: Teri Weksler, Jim May, Peter Healey, Randall Faxon Parker (photograph by Martha Swope, courtesy Daniel Lewis archives).**

Juilliard Ensemble Presents 3 New Works" summarized the performance at the Juilliard Theater. Barnes regularly reviewed this annual event for the graduating seniors, but he said this performance was special, because they were presenting three new premieres: *The Waldstein Sonata*, started by José Limón in 1971 and completed by Daniel Lewis in 1975, *Mask of Night* by Kazuko Hirabayashi, and *Ride the Culture Loop* by Anna Sokolow. There were two casts for *The Waldstein Sonata* in this series. Cast 1 was Roxolana Babiuk, Dian Dong, Virginia Edmands, Dianne Hulburt, Pierre Barreau, William Belle, Robert Swinston, and Leigh Warren. Cast 2 was Shirley Brown, Linda Spriggs, Catherine Sullivan, Collette Yglesias, Anthony Balcena, William Belle, Hsueh-Tung Chen, and Barry Weiss. The pianist was Emanuel Krasovsky. Barnes found *The Waldstein Sonata* of particular interest, partly because of its history, with Danny echoing

---

3. The founding president of Juilliard was William Schuman, who brought Martha Hill to Juilliard to start the dance program. Mennin became president in 1962, the year Danny became a student at Juilliard. Danny knew and worked with Mennin for over twenty years. After Mennin's death in 1984, Joseph Polisi became president.

4. After the Limón Foundation bought the rights to Limón's work from his family, Danny maintained the rights to The Waldstein Sonata (mentioned earlier). Danny has agreed that after he passes away, the rights will go to the Limón Foundation.

the 1971 motifs by Limón as much as possible, and also because the work was "most gratifying" and "an interesting work." He loved the Beethoven music and its structure, and he complimented Limón and Lewis for recognizing this "taut and brilliant sense of structure." He also commented on the "eccentric but oddly appropriate arm gestures" and the work's use of stillness: "One dancer might provide a static focus for the dance, and at times the choreography would hurtle impetuously along matching headlong arpeggios, at other times it would halve or quarter the music's time, providing a different kind of visual commentary and symmetry." Barnes highly praised the dancers, calling them equally talented, and was also positive about the other two works on the program, making note that Sokolow had forty-one dancers in her work! Overall it was a strong review, especially for *The Waldstein Sonata*.

Several companies performed *The Waldstein Sonata* over the years. In 1976, Elizabeth (Liz) Bergmann invited Danny to Ann Arbor, Michigan, where she headed the university dance program, and asked him to bring CDS men to the university to perform *The Waldstein Sonata*, along with other Limón and Lewis works. He also staged *The Waldstein Sonata* on the university dancers. Because the university program had no men, CDS male dancers joined the university dancers to do the work, using two casts of university women to give the opportunity to as many students as possible.

Danny allowed Ann Vachon's company, Dance Conduit, to perform *The Waldstein Sonata* for many years, starting in 1984. Nancy Scattergood Jordan staged it. Janet Pilla, who ended up with Dance Fusion in Philadelphia, was one of the dancers. After the initial staging of *The Waldstein Sonata* by Nancy, Janet would do the staging for Conduit in subsequent years, and she was very good at remounting it for new dancers in the company in terms of the form and musicality. Nancy Scattergood Jordan, an expert at remounting, also brought weight and dynamics to the work.

In 2012, Janet Pilla staged and Risa Steinberg directed *The Waldstein Sonata* on the Juilliard Dance Ensemble, and Danny came in to look at it before the performance, to add his own voice about the work. Ann Vachon's company had changed the way it was listed on the program, and Janet used those program notes for this staging. Danny asked to put the listing the original way, with the choreography as "(1971, 1975), José Limón, Daniel Lewis." They did new costumes for the work at this time, and Danny was very pleased with these costumes and the way the performers danced.

Ray Cook created a Labanotation score of *The Waldstein Sonata*, which Danny and the Dance Notation Bureau still possess, although it has never actually been checked. Cook, originally a ballet dancer from Australia, became a professional notator for several choreographers, including Doris Humphrey, Martha Graham, Jeff Duncan, Anna Sokolow, Paul Taylor, George Balanchine, Michel Fokine, Dan Wagoner, José Limón, Gerald Arpino, Lester Horton, Norman Walker, and Lin Hwai-Min. He also danced with several modern companies and was a professor at Vassar College.

The Dance Company's Golden Era

In the late 1970s, Bob Reiter, Danny's manager and an attorney, ran out of bookings for Danny's company. So to keep the company from being stagnant (and not breaking new ground), Bob connected Contemporary Dance System with music producer and booking agent Max Gershunoff. Max took on the dance company. Whenever he was booking a music series, he would tag Danny's company onto it. Max felt that it was difficult to book the group because its name had "System" in it, so Danny followed his advice and changed the company name to Daniel Lewis Dance: A Repertory Company (DLDRC), which Max felt was much more appealing to a broad audience.

Max was excellent as a producer and got the company a lot of bookings. They toured everywhere, and the situation was financially lucrative for Max, so it was a win for everyone.[5]

Through His Friends' Eyes—Teri Weksler

Teri Weksler first met Danny at Juilliard, where she graduated in 1974. Besides dancing in DLDRC, she was a founding member of the Mark Morris Dance Group and danced with Five by Two (directed by Jane Kosminsky) and with Baryshnikov's White Oak Dance Project. Teri talked about her personal and professional life with Danny: "I lived with Danny for about seven years, and Danny was my first long-term relationship. I fell in love with him initially because he was the most gorgeous dancer. In addition to working with his company, Danny and I took many personal trips together, and I accom-

panied him on some of the trips to stage Limón's dances.

The one work of Danny's that stands out in my mind from the days of dancing in his company is And First They Slaughtered the Angels. *I loved the poetry and the music in the work, thought it was a truly lovely work, and enjoyed dancing with Shelly Washington and the rest of the dancers. He has an uncanny ability to take on events and undertakings that no one else can do. He has amazing organizational skills, including his memory of details, which is why he was able to put together very complicated and immense events, such as the high school dance festivals. He just always knew how to figure out what was needed to make something happen and how to make people feel comfortable in these large settings. He always took care of artists and managed everything with such delicacy. It took a rare combination of organizational ability and artistry. Additionally,*

And First They Slaughtered the Angels, **choreography by Daniel Lewis. Dancers from left: Laura Glenn, Peter Healey (on the floor), Victor Vargas, and Randall Faxon Parker (photograph by Martha Swope, courtesy Daniel Lewis archives).**

5. When Danny presented the first BFA concert at NWSA many years later, Max and his partner saw Danny's name in the newspaper and wrote to him. They were living in Boca, Florida, and they came to the first NWSA college graduation performance.

he had tremendous vision, and no sense of boundaries, something that is rare and unusual. No one does it like Danny. He doesn't say no, and is an incredibly generous soul, as well as very loyal to anyone who ever worked for him. And Danny was really born to dance, with the most beautiful, natural quality."

The company performed *My Echo, My Shadow, and Me* with Kat de Blois. Danny truly loved Kat and created many roles for her while she was in the company. She had an artistic energy that Danny really liked. Works for her included *Open Book*, and Danny cast her as a man in *My Echo, My Shadow, and Me*. Danny really appreciated her willingness to take on challenges and her ability to have total trust in what he doing.

Kat de Blois graduated from the Boston Conservatory. In 1978, Tony Balcena, a dancer in Danny's company, came to Kat to say that Danny was looking for a new dancer; Tony suggested that Kat take Danny's class so that she could be Tony's partner in the company. Danny immediately invited her into the company. After dancing in DLDRC, she did a tour of *West Side Story* in Europe and then went to Paris to dance, sing, and act in musical theater, also working at Euro Disney in Paris as a performer and creative director.[6]

Through His Friends' Eyes—Kat de Blois

In Open Book, *Kat's role was that of a young soul, with her movement vocabulary suggesting youthfulness and curiosity. Kat said, "Danny's choreography was fabulous, and the Limón technique was very challenging, but once you learned to let go, then it was possible to dance with freedom in the phrasing. It felt so good and organic and fell in line with my spirit. Danny would say, 'Dancing is not the steps, it is what happens when you go from step to step, and what is in between the steps.' I did experience this work as a dark work, a departure for Danny from his usual dances, which were typically humorous. It was not an easy work for him, and he spent many months developing this dance. It was hard for me, given my conservative background, to strip and be nearly nude, in a flesh-colored leotard, but it made me think about fully investing in being an artist and letting go of inhibitions. Danny guided me in that way; I trusted him and knew it would all be fine. In the end, I felt beautiful in the dance. This dance and* There's Nothing Here of Me but Me *were the two works that were important to me, because I was fortunate enough to be part of the creative process.*

What impressed me most were Danny's unselfishness and generosity, and his teaching method of having the students analyze and watch each other and help each other. He helped me develop a style that is very active and present. I modeled my teaching after what I learned from Danny. He is someone who wanted to share and genuinely help the students, wanting to ignite energy in young dancers. He was also super organized, and he made sure all of his dancers had enough work to survive and get unemployment benefits in their time off. Danny got my parents interested in modern dance after seeing his work. Working in Danny's company was a definite high point in my career. He is a very important man in my life!"

6. When Danny; his wife, Maureen; and his son, Quinn, were in Paris many years ago, Kat took Quinn on a tour of Disney. There was one show with cartoons that spoke in various languages (French, English, German, etc.) The cartoon character would point to a child in the audience and say, "You! Stand up!" The child would stand, and they would start having an interactive conversation. When Quinn was there, the cartoon character pointed into the audience and said, "Quinn! Stand up!" He stood up, and the cartoon character asked him what he was doing in Paris. They were taken backstage to see how it all worked, and the technology was very exciting.

The years 1975 and 1976 were very good years for Danny and the company, and both years were extremely busy with performances and workshops. A typical day in the life of CDS had this schedule: On Monday, October 18, 1976, Danny ran errands for the company from 8:00 a.m. until 12:00 p.m., including buying a tape recorder, picking up the bench for *Day on Earth*, picking up an additional chair for *Rooms*, buying two white shirts for costumes, picking up the audio tapes by Gary Harris, and calling musicians for one of the works. The company's day would always begin with a company warm-up. Then Danny and Nancy ran company rehearsals of *Dead Heat* from 12:00 to 1:00 p.m., *And First They Slaughtered the Angels* from 1:00 to 2:00 p.m., *Steps of Silence* with Anna Sokolow from 2:00 to 3:30 p.m., and *Night Spell* from 3:30 to 5:00 p.m. In the evening, Danny did managerial work for the company. On days when Danny taught at Juilliard, he would send Nancy, Eddie Effron, and David Rosenberg with the company for performances at various locations. During these years the company would rehearse at multiple locations, including Larry Richardson Studio (where Danny taught classes outside Juilliard), Francis Alenikoff Studio, Paul Sanasardo Studio, Bernhard-Link Studio, Kazuko Hirabayashi Studio, Tokunaga Dance Studio, the Juilliard School, Dance Theater Workshop, the Dance Notation Bureau, Jim and Lorry May's loft, and Laura Glenn's loft.

Anna Sokolow directing her dance *Scriabin* for DLDRC at the Dance Notation Bureau, 1975. Dancers from left: Victor Vargas, Randall Faxon Parker, Teri Weksler, Pierre Barreau, Laura Glenn, Peter Healey, Ko Yukihiro (photograph by M. B. Hunnewell, courtesy Daniel Lewis archives).

In 1975, at Town Hall at 43rd Street in New York, DLDRC was invited to perform *Steps of Silence* and *Lyric Suite*, both by Anna Sokolow, including a discussion afterwards with Anna. Other companies that performed in the Town Hall series were Murray Louis, Twyla Tharp, Pearl Lang, Lynn Kellogg, and Chris Conners. These were one-hour concerts that were essentially informal lecture/demonstrations. They were called "interludes" and cost $2.50 to see.

In 1975 CDS received an NEA grant for Anna Sokolow to stage a new full-evening work called *Scriabin* based on the composer's music. It was a nightmare to work with her on this work. She was in love with the music, and nothing could satisfy her. They did these rehearsals for six weeks in New York and then at Amherst for two weeks. The dancers were in pain the whole time! In the end, the work was magnificent. This is the work from which they would later do excerpts at the Spoleto Festival in 1977.

DLDRC performed for Repertory Dance Theater (RDT) in Salt Lake City in July 1975. The RDT dancers were fabulous and had strong repertory but always felt like they had no competition. They invited DLDRC to come perform with them, and they were blown away by Danny's group. They performed *Night Spell* (with Danny doing the Sleeper), *Dead Heat* (with Danny and Matthew Diamond), *And First They Slaughtered the Angels*, and *Day on Earth*. Other dancers in the show included José Coronado (who had danced in the Hunting Dance with the Joffrey Ballet), Pierre Barreau, Elizabeth (Betsy) Fisher, Hannah Kahn, Rae Kraus, and Teri Weksler. Danny had hired Carol out of Barnard, and then she met Matthew, whom she eventually married. The lighting was by Eddie Effron, who also stage managed; the musical director was Stanley Sussman; and Danny was the artistic director.

Betsy Fisher from the company (who later danced with Murray Louis and ended up at the University of Hawaii) had a boyfriend at the time named David Kauser, an actor from Juilliard. Betsy did not fly to Salt Lake City with the company; instead, she and David drove in his Volkswagen van to Salt Lake City to meet the company there. After the tour, Betsy (and her two dogs, Blue Streak and Sneakers), her boyfriend David, Teri Weksler, and Danny (and his dog, Quay) got into David's van and did a cross-country trip. From Salt Lake City, they went

Daniel Lewis in *Night Spell*, choreography by Doris Humphrey (photograph by Eddie Effron, courtesy Daniel Lewis archives).

to California, up the west coast, all the way across Canada, and back down to New York. This was not the only road trip for Danny and Teri—in fact, at the start of their relationship, Teri had gone out to University of California at Santa Cruz to take a summer dance workshop. Danny drove all the way across the country to get her, and then they drove back to New York together. It was a very romantic time, as were other road travels they did together, which included camping in many of America's most beautiful places! In 2010, Danny and Betsy met up by chance at the National Association of Schools of Dance (NASD) conference, and they were having dinner with Christopher Pilafian. Christopher had been Danny's student at the Juilliard School and later was a founding member of Jennifer Muller/The Works. At that point, Danny realized he had never told Betsy he loved her when she was dancing in his company. He took this moment to let her know.

Eddie Effron (dancer, dance photographer, lighting designer, and stage manager), was Danny's main lighting designer for most of the company's years. As a young man, Eddie had plans to become a doctor. When Eddie decided not to go to medical school and wanted to see if he liked dance, Jim Payton (a dancer with José Limón) told him he should go to the American Dance Festival and dance 12 hours a day to see if he really liked it. He was waiting in line to register, and Danny walked up to him, asking him if he were Eddie Effron. Eddie said yes, and Danny told him that Mr. Limón wanted to speak to him. From that point, Eddie viewed Danny as "an angel appointed by God," and they became good friends from then on.

Through His Friends' Eyes—Eddie Effron

Eddie danced at Juilliard and went on to dance with various professional companies, including Danny's first company, Contemporary Dance System. He started doing photography for dance, which made him very conscious of light, and he was also very aware of light as a performer onstage. He later donated all of his dance photography to the New York Public Library of Performing Arts. He became interested in lighting for dance, doing some work for José Limón while still dancing in José's works. After a knee injury in the mid 1970s, he decided to transition from dancer to lighting designer, working with Trisha Brown, Kathy Posin, Dance Theatre of Harlem, Merce Cunningham (as lighting coordinator), Anna Sokolow, and Nacho Duato, among others. Because he had done so much of the repertory for several of these choreographers, it was an easy transition to lighting the dances. Eddie said, "Working with choreographers as a dancer is more like being a 'tool' for the artist, but as a lighting designer, you are a collaborator in the creative process."

About Danny, Eddie commented, "The beauty of working with Danny as his lighting designer was that we knew each other so well. There was a trust established right from the start, which made the choreographer-designer relationship very easy. I understood, from twenty-five years of working with Anna Sokolow, the importance of transition. Because I knew Danny's work so well, I already knew when the transitions were happening and how to time them, so I could go in and light a work in a day; with other choreographers I would spend weeks in rehearsals trying to understand the dance. I also liked Danny's work, and the other repertory the company did, which made it fun for me to light the dances.

Danny always had a passion for dance and worked hard, but he also had a joyfulness and a sense of humor when he worked. I felt that Danny had a unique quality to make things his own, such as his solo in The Unsung. *Danny owns that part. Danny truly loved the life of the dancer, the work, and the touring and traveling. Although I was initially surprised that Danny took the job in Miami, I am proud of what Danny created at NWSA and I feel that they were lucky to have him. As an educator, Danny was 'José at his best' in terms of explaining why you were doing the movement a certain way and what ideas were underlying the form. One of Danny's unique qualities is that he does not alienate people at all. He doesn't burn bridges in his professional life, which has served him well all his dance life. He always shows respect to people in the dance world and keeps the lines of communication open. This is a rare quality in a person."*

Another program in January 1975 showed that they were touring with Stanley Sussman, the musical conductor. On this tour, three of the dancers were Miguel Godreau (in Broadway musicals and with Alvin Ailey American Dance Theater), Shelley Washington (dancer and assistant with Twyla Tharp, and married at one point to Peter Sparling), and Edward DeSoto, who were all on leave from their usual companies and so were able to do this tour with Danny's company.

The company did several seasons at American Place Theater in New York City. One season, December 1975, Danny's company did a tribute to Anna Sokolow. This was an important event for the company, and there were several reviews. The dancers included José Coronado (who danced with Joffrey Ballet), Pierre Barreau, Matthew Diamond (courtesy of Jennifer Muller and The Works), Jeff Duncan, Ko Yukihiro, and some of the regulars. The works they danced were several Sokolow works plus other works by Diamond and Lewis: *Moods, Ballade, Rooms, Lyric Suite, Dead Heat, Night Spell*, and *And First They Slaughtered the Angels*. Jeff Duncan was dancing in *Rooms* in the role he first danced for the filming of the work in 1968. He began his career with Alwin Nikolais at the Henry Street Playhouse. He was also a protégée and assistant to Doris Humphrey for two years and was a principal dancer in the Anna Sokolow Dance Company for twelve years. He started Dance Theater Workshop, co-founded with Jack Moore and Art Bauman, in New York in 1965. In 1975, when he became director of the Jeff Duncan Repertory Dance Company. He passed away in 1999 from AIDS-related complications. Ko Yukihiro received his dance degree at the University of Hawaii. He danced with Ethel Winter, Betty Jones, Fritz Ludin, Takako Asakawa, David Hatch Walker, Paul Sanasardo, and others. Danny commented on how difficult Anna was to work with, and how Randall Faxon Parker said on the first day of rehearsals with her, "I hope she remembers that she likes me!" Musical director for the tribute was Stanley Sussman (music teacher at Juilliard and principal conductor for the Martha Graham Company), and the stage manager was David Rosenberg. Anna Kisselgoff reviewed the performance in the *New York Times*. She spoke highly of the future of the company and its potential. She stated that by inviting Anna Sokolow to be their resident choreographer, they defined more clearly the kind of dances they wished to do. Although they would also be presenting choreography by Lewis and company members, working with Sokolow gave them a ready-made store of Sokolow classics.

Through His Friends' Eyes—Matthew Diamond

Matthew Diamond danced from the time he was sixteen years old until his early thirties, performing with companies such as Louis Falco, Jennifer Muller, Paul Sanasardo, Norman Walker, and briefly with José Limón, eventually forming his own company in New York. Matthew danced for several years in Danny's company and eventually moved to Los Angeles with Rae Kraus to work mainly in television.

Matthew related his experiences working with Danny's company. "The first work of mine that Danny commissioned for his company was Dead Heat *in 1975, originally danced by me and Leigh Warren from Australia. Danny had decided to produce a concert of work by his company dancers, and after this concert, Danny asked me if he could keep the work in the repertory and dance Leigh's part himself. This surprised me, because Danny had essentially stopped dancing by this time. Danny was beyond perfect for the part, and I was thrilled. The work stayed in the repertory for many years. For me, being in Danny's company was exceptional, because Danny was as concerned about the experience of the dancer as he was about his own experience as a choreographer. He had by far the most generous attitude and set the most generous culture of any company I was ever in. Danny was always finding ways to give his dancers work—whether performing in schools or teaching—so that they could survive as dancers in such a difficult financial time. In fact, the exposure that Danny gave* Dead Heat *in years of performances eventually led to my being asked to stage it on Utah Repertory Dance Theater (URDT), and URDT later commissioned me to do another work. This was a doorway for me in my career as a choreographer.*

Danny helped all the people with whom he came into contact, which was quite unique in the dance world. Although choreographers were often abrasive, difficult, and self-centered, Danny was well liked by everyone. Danny was generous, organized, and all-embracing, and he had a broad view of what the world could be and how his job was helping others. He was a wonderful artistic director, producer, and entrepreneur, and did a fantastic job in the creation of NWSA. He had the insight to see what

Matthew Diamond (left) and Daniel Lewis in *Dead Heat*, choreography by Matthew Diamond (courtesy Daniel Lewis archives).

wasn't there for the field and the people he cared about, and then he went and supplied it, making him a great facilitator, with a magnetic, all-embracing personality. He was truly rare."

Dancing with the company in these years (1974–1976) were Peter Sparling, Martial Roumain, Richard Caceres, Matthew Diamond, Rae Kraus, Laura Glenn, Leigh Warren, Teri Weksler, José Coronado, Hannah Kahn, Andrew Miller, and Dianne Hulburt.

After Dianne Hulburt danced with Danny, she changed her name to Dunya McPherson in the 1980s, because she wanted to do Middle Eastern dance. She eventually became the spiritual guide of the Dancemeditation Sufis. She wrote a book published in 2008 called *Skin of Glass: Finding the Spirit in the Flesh,* which chronicles her journey of dance and mysticism. In the book, which she sent a signed copy of to Danny, she describes him, starting on page 20:

> Daniel Lewis, a Limón Company soloist and faculty, looked like Jim Morrison walking down the hall in faded bell-bottom blue jeans and a work shirt, his long dark hair tossed back. Other teachers changed into special outfits to teach, but Danny taught in his jeans and desert boots. A sheaf of keys clipped to his belt jingled when he landed from demonstrating a jump or came smoothly out of a turn. Then he ran his fingers through his hair to pull it off his face. A little dangerous, he kept us all on the flirting edge. One sunny March afternoon, he took me to one of the Japanese restaurants along Columbus Avenue to eat sashimi, introducing me to raw fish for the first time. I hoped I wouldn't look naïve. Danny popped apart his wooden chopsticks. "You'll like it. It's protein, no fat! Dancers can eat this forever." He poured tamari into a little dish and mixed in a bit of green paste. "Wasabi. Don't put too much. It's hot!" I snuck a nibble of tuna while he wasn't looking. It was sweet, tender, deep red flesh. I smeared it around my tongue, my eyelids sinking down lost in the flavor. "Delicious, really delicious." My splintery chopsticks reached for the second piece of their own accord, and suddenly snapped back. He was watching me smiling. "Good, huh?" He'd seen it, my veneer down lost in sensuous pleasure. I pulled in like a snail foot retracting and agreed. Casually triumphant, his eyes returned to the piece he was dipping. I watched his rough, unshaven chin as he chewed. He stopped, raised his eyes deliberately, and looked at me for a long moment. "How do you like it?" I froze, skewered. What if he asked me to sleep with him? What would I say? How did I smell? Was my make-up smeared? Casting couch, casting couch! Was I that girl? Utter confusion made the food taste fabulous. "It's really good!" I stuttered. "You aren't eating the wasabi. You gotta try it." He stirred the green paste and sauce as if stirring my befuddled desire. "You can add more if you want it spicier." As he chattered about the dances for Spring Concert, my guts tumbled around and unruly like a mass of hot electrical cables strewed over the table. As soon as I closed some in, others slid out. He picked up the check and we walked back to Juilliard. Immersed in my confusion, I barely noticed that for the first time, a dancer had talked to me about how to eat for a sustainable dance life.

This was actually the point in time when Danny asked Dianne to join his company.

From the beginning, the company paid royalties for *Day on Earth* to Charles Woodford, Doris Humphrey's son, every time they performed it, and this was true regarding other choreographers as well. This was a motivation for Danny to work with Carla Maxwell and the Limón Foundation to buy back the rights to the Limón works from the family members who had inherited them. Danny dealt similarly with rights for music he was using, such as the music for Anna Sokolow's *Lyric Suite* by Alban Berg. In April 1982, Carl Fisher, music publisher of the music for *Ballade*, wrote a letter complimenting Danny in his efficiency in planning the staging of Sokolow's ballet. Danny paid regular small royalties every time they did Elizabeth Keen's work *Taking the Air*. Similarly, Danny paid royalties for use of the music for Keen's work *Etudes;* the composer, Virgil Thomson, thanked Danny for being one of the few dance companies that paid royalties for using his work. Virgil Thomson came to the premiere performance of the work and spoke to the audience.

In the 1975–1976 season, Danny's company was invited to the State University of New York (SUNY). *And First They Slaughtered the Angels* was in the performance that they did at SUNY Potsdam in September 1975. Over time, they performed at several of the SUNY campuses. Also in 1976, Danny went to West Michigan University to teach classes. Even while the company was doing extensive touring, Danny was taking on additional jobs teaching workshops. In 1977, the company went to the University of Minnesota in Minneapolis. Additionally, Danny taught Limón classes and did film showings and discussions.

In 1976, the company did a residency at Plymouth State College in New Hampshire and received NEA grant money for touring. They received a full-page review in the college newspaper. Danny gave a free master class called The Essence of Movement. The program was *And First They Slaughtered the Angels*; *Day on Earth*; *Debussy Dances*; *My Echo, My Shadow, and Me*; and *The Waldstein Sonata*. Danny generally ended shows with either *And First They Slaughtered the Angels* or with *The Waldstein Sonata*. At one point, the women's costumes for *And First They Slaughtered the Angels* were becoming worn out and ragged looking due to so many performances. José Coronado, who came from Mexico and worked in a sewing shop, bought fabric and made new costumes to replace them. This type of dedication represents the community atmosphere that existed in Danny's company.

In the fall of 1976, DLDRC went to Virginia Commonwealth University for a residency; the NEA grant subsidized one-third of the expenses of the residency. The dancers all had to drive down to Richmond, Virginia, and complained endlessly that they had to perform and teach workshops in a gymnasium. This residency was one of the first times the company worked without Danny present. Mary Joiner was the administrator who handled the paperwork for these jobs. The company continued in the NEA touring program for several years and received many NEA grants. The grants were significant amounts of money (some as much as $35,500), which allowed for the costs of new works as well as touring expenses.

Pictures in the DLDRC files from 1976 include Danny's company and Kathy Posin's company, who also performed in the 1976 performance series at Virginia Commonwealth. By this time, Eddie Effron was the lighting designer for Danny, not dancing anymore, and Nancy Scattergood-Jordan continued as rehearsal director. In future years, she continued staging Danny's works.

An October 12, 1976, program of DLDRC listed Daniel Lewis as artistic director, Anna Sokolow as resident choreographer, Bob Reiter as general manager, Eddie Effron as lighting designer, and David Rosenberg as production and stage manager. David was (and is) the husband of Robyn Cutler, who danced with the Limón Company. David left a teaching position at Hunter College to get involved in carpentry and then Eddie convinced him to become a stage manager for Danny's company. Eventually he was the stage manager for Eliot Feld and later took over I. Weiss and Son, a business that made curtains for theaters.

A program from 1976 at Castleton State College in Vermont shows an early picture of the company with Peter Healey, Hannah Kahn, Teri Weksler, Pierre Barreau, Jane Carrington, Laura Glenn, and Jim May. Danny was still dancing, but not as much.

He did the part of the rock star in *And First They Slaughtered the Angels*, but this was a walk-around part in which he played an imaginary guitar. They did a six-day residency at this college.

This photo is one of the most beautiful images of the company, and it was used on many brochures and posters.

In the 1976–1977 season, the Dance Umbrella at the Roundabout Theater in New York (23rd Street and 6th Avenue) presented showcase evenings for dance, sponsored

And First They Slaughtered the Angels, **choreography by Daniel Lewis. Dancers from left: Peter Healey, Pierre Barreau, and Daniel Lewis (photograph by Martha Swope, courtesy Daniel Lewis archives).**

by the Tag Foundation. They produced a huge number of dance companies, and DLDRC performed October 27–31, 1976. There were three separate programs: Program A was *Night Spell* (Doris Humphrey), *Steps of Silence* (Anna Sokolow), *And First They Slaughtered the Angels* (Daniel Lewis), and *The Waldstein Sonata* (Daniel Lewis). Program B was *Debussy Dances* (Hannah Kahn), *Steps of Silence* (Anna Sokolow), *Day on Earth* (Doris Humphrey), and *The Waldstein Sonata* (Daniel Lewis). Program C was *Rooms* (Anna Sokolow), *Dead Heat* (Matthew Diamond), and *The Waldstein Sonata* (Daniel Lewis). Danny was still dancing, so he did the second man's part in *Dead Heat*. The

DANIEL
LEWIS
DANCE
REPERTORY
COMPANY
Daniel Lewis,
Artistic Director
Anna Sokolow,
Resident Choreographer

Company Premiere of Jose
Limon's "EXILES"

Area Premiere of Daniel Lewis'
"LIFE AND OTHER THINGS"

Works by Doris Humphrey
and Hannah Kahn

KIRBY THEATER AMHERST COLLEGE
MARCH 30, 31, 8 p.m.
RESERVATIONS 542-2277 10 a.m.-5 p.m.
ADMISSION $2.50 or Amherst College I.D. (Senior Citizens $1.50)

Poster for DLDRC company. Dancers clockwise from top: Jim May, Peter Healey, Hannah Kahn, Pierre Barreau, Laura Glenn, and Teri Weksler (poster design and photograph by Paul Perlow, courtesy Daniel Lewis archives).

music director was Stanley Sussman, and the conductor was David Fein. They did *Steps of Silence* with a string quartet plus percussion; they always did this work with live music due to the fact that there was no recorded score, and the publisher would not allow them to make a recording. They had two pianos, two violins, a cello, a viola, and percussion. For *Debussy Dances*, it was a quartet of Juilliard musicians and for *The Waldstein Sonata*, Emanuel Krasovsky—Juilliard student and master class teacher—was the pianist. In *And First They Slaughtered the Angels*, there are two couples who cross over in the back, and Danny used management people to do these roles! When the company toured this work, it was manager Bob Reiter who would teach young students from the college or local studios the sequence of the two crossover couples, and he really enjoyed stepping out of his attorney and manager roles to do this work! Bob Reiter and Judith Lamb did the role of one of the crossover couples in some of the productions.[7] Maggie Ramsey worked with Bob, and she and her husband, Jim Ramsey, were the other crossover couple.

Don McDonaugh wrote a review about this performance titled "Dance: A New Umbrella Season" in the *New York Times* in October. He discussed the serious nature

of the work and the forceful, dynamic presentation of the repertory. He was particularly impressed with Sokolow's *Rooms*, saying, "in addition to its unsparing look at urban isolation, it has several juicy solos, including.... Hannah Kahn and Pierre Barreau.... Daniel Lewis, the company's artistic director, was nicely tortured by panic, and the company, Randall Faxon Parker, Laura Glenn, Teri Weksler, and Peter Healey, all contributed to the pervading atmosphere of malaise and anxiety. It's unsparing but excellent."

Other companies that the Roundabout presented were Kei Takei (Moving Earth), Jamie Cunningham (Acme), Annabel Gamson, Phyllis Lamhut Company, Jennifer Muller and the Works, Don Redlich Dance Company, and Rod Rodgers

Teri Weksler and Daniel Lewis in *Night Spell*, choreography by Doris Humphrey (photograph by Martha Swope, courtesy Daniel Lewis archives).

---

7. Bob and Judith now live in upstate New York. Every year Danny receives a gallon of real maple syrup from them.

Dance Company. The Roundabout series lasted a couple of years and then had to fold due to financial reasons.

In April 1977, the company was asked by CBS producer Roger Englander to participate in the filming of Anna Sokolow's *Dreams*. This work deals with the Holocaust, and in order to replicate the environment, they did the filming on location in a gutted, unoccupied building at Hudson and Clarkson in New York City. They used the roof, the eighth floor, and the basement. The filming took two days, April 16 and 17, and it was incredibly cold. This circumstance made it a terrible environment for the dancers. However, the discomfort did add to the impact of the film. Dancers were Daniel Lewis (artistic director) with Pierre Barreau, Laura Glenn, Peter Healey, Hannah Kahn, Jessica May, Jim May, Lorry May, Victor Vargas, and Teri Weksler. The film was showed on CBS, and it was one of the first times that a dance was filmed in a way that was specifically designed for the camera. Roger, Anna, and Danny worked diligently to make this effort a success. One conflict that occurred in the process was that Roger wanted the dancers in one scene to wear military hats to represent the storm troopers. Anna, who felt that the movement expressed the idea, refused. Danny solved the disagreement by deliberately not bringing the hats to the filming on the second day.

In 1977, Danny asked Lucas Hoving if the company could perform his work *Icarus*, and he agreed. Lucas had concerns about casting, especially who would dance his role. Randall Faxon Parker, who was tall and slim, played the Sun, originally danced by Patricia Christopher. Lucas' part, Daedalus, was danced by Pierre Barreau. Chase Robinson's part, Icarus, was danced by Peter Healey.

In 1977, the company performed in Minnesota. At the end of the residency, Danny was paid in one large check. He went to the bank and cashed the whole amount and then paid everyone in cash, because they were all going different directions. He still had $30,000 in cash to carry back with him to New York!

In June 1977, Veit Bethke, general manager of the Royal Swedish Ballet and the husband of Gerd Andersson, brought Danny's company to Stockholm, Sweden, to perform. Before going to Sweden, they performed at a festival in Kuopio, Finland, on June 11 and 12. No one spoke any English in Kuopio, which created major problems for the company; they could not even order food at a restaurant. They ended up going to a marketplace, where they could point at the food. Danny loved the central square with this wonderful marketplace. Because they had twenty-four-hour sunlight at that time of year, they had a dance festival in Kuopio that went on all through the day and night. Danny's company performed at 2:00 a.m. When they returned to the rooms, they needed to darken the windows. At first they were covering them with blankets and towels, until the Soviet dancers showed how to crank down the shades that were between two panes of thermal glass.

The Stockholm part of the tour was three performances, on June 14, 15, and 16. Danny has many good reviews from the tour, but they are all in Swedish. A letter from the cultural attaché provided a partial translation of one, which stated that *Day on Earth* was one of the absolute master works of modern dance. The review ended by thanking the company and its leader Daniel Lewis. It went on to say that the group had very high technical standards and succeeded in making full use of the Maxim Teatern (Theater) stage. The reviewer emphasized *The Waldstein Sonata*, saying the structure was incredibly rich. At Maxim Teatern in Stockholm, Sweden, the company performed *Day on Earth* by Humphrey, *Steps of Silence* by Sokolow, *Dead Heat* by Diamond, *And First*

They Slaughtered the Angels by Lewis, *The Waldstein Sonata* by Limón and Lewis, and *Rooms* by Sokolow. Matthew Diamond was not on the tour, so Jim May did his part in *Dead Heat.*

DLDRC went to Charleston, South Carolina, in 1977 to be part of the Spoleto Festival, an international dance festival produced by Joseph Wishy.[8] This was an important event for both the dance world at large and for DLDRC. That year the festival presented six world premieres by major choreographers, as part of the day-long celebration of the composer Alexander Scriabin. The choreographers for the June 4 Scriabin Dance Gala included Anna Sokolow (choreography performed by DLDRC) and five pas de deux: George Balanchine (for Patricia McBride and Jean-Pierre Bonnefous), Glen Tetley (for Carla Fracci and Charles Ward), Lar Lubovich (for Martine van Hamel and Rob Besser), Frederick Ashton (for Lynn Seymour and Robert North), and Alberto Mendez (for Alicia Alonso and Jorge Esquivel). Danny's dancers guided Alonso on and off the stage for the bows, because her eyesight was quite compromised by this point. In addition to the six premieres, there were revivals of early solo works by choreographers Ninette de Valois, Isadora Duncan, and Ted Shawn, performed by Maina Gielgud, Anabelle Gamson, and Dennis Wayne. Note that all the works were done to Scriabin compositions. This was the same time that Danny was working on *Nefertiti* at the Blackstone Theater in Chicago, and he was not able to be at the festival. The DLDRC dancers who performed at Spoleto were Teri Weksler, Victor Vargas, Jim May, Hannah Kahn, Peter Healey, Laura Glenn, Randall Faxon Parker, and Pierre Barreau. Also at the festival were the manager Bob Reiter, rehearsal director Nancy Scattergood Jordan, and Eddie Effron for lighting. Danny had commissioned a full evening of Scriabin works, but they did not perform all of that work at Spoleto, because Wishy cut it down to excerpts, favoring the ballet works. Other evenings in the Spoleto festival presented Eliot Feld, Ohio Ballet, Black Medea, and Mark Morris, as well as many musical groups, and there were dozens of newspaper and magazine reviewers present. Clive Barnes' review called this festival "a chance to see dancers at their own parties."

DLDRC performed in October 1977 at Hopkins Center at Dartmouth College in New Hampshire. The October 10 review, titled "Dancers: Technical Wizards," said, "Rarely at Dartmouth do we see a professional dance company with the quality and technique exhibited by DLDRC, which performed two different programs in the Center Theater last Friday and Saturday.... The works of straight dancing were truly compelling to watch. 'The Waldstein Sonata' and 'La Malinche' let DLDRC display its dazzling technical wizardry." The review mentioned that Danny had finished *The Waldstein Sonata* after José's death and called it an exhilarating work. The reviewer described *And First They Slaughtered the Angels* as "a humorous piece danced between whimsical angels and blue-jean clad Hells Angels with lyrical music. DLDRC played a charming joke on the audience in this dance, and the audience loved it." The reviewer's favorite work of the two evenings was Humphrey's *Day on Earth,* which was called a masterpiece; the reviewer said it was superbly danced by Hannah Kahn, Teri Weksler, Jim May, and Jessica May (Jim's young daughter). "This piece was emotionally moving and close to technically perfect. Jim in particular gave a stunning performance. He was easily the best dancer in the company, no small feat for a company as accomplished as DLDRC."

---

8. One night many years later, Danny was sitting next to Joseph Wishy at the State Theater in New York at a performance of a European ballet company that Wishy had produced. The show was awful, and Joe explained, "I took it unseen."

The Hungarian composer Zoltán Kodály, best known as the creator of the Kodály method of musical education for children, had previously taught at Dartmouth. They also had a mural by Mexican painter José Clemente Orozco at the college. These famous artists and their works influenced Danny and his choreography, so this performance at Dartmouth was very special to him. In his speeches, Limón spoke about meeting Kodály when he was brought by Jac Venza, public television producer, to New York to see a video of *Missa Brevis*. Kodály did not like the work, saying it was "crude," but Martha Hill asked him if he had ever seen modern dance, to which he replied no, he had only seen ballet. After she described modern dance to him, he asked to see it again; upon rewatching it, he hugged José and said it was a beautiful ballet.

In 1977–1978, DLDRC had the opportunity to have Arthur (Art) Bauman restage his solo dance work *Dialogue*, which Danny loved. It was first choreographed in 1973 and used a film. This work was part of the early years for Danny to learn about technology and dance.

In 1978, DLDRC went to the University of California campuses of Riverside and Irvine. At UC Riverside, they performed several works, including *Life and Other Things*, a weird work by Danny in which the dancers wore green hospital surgical scrubs, borrowed from the Hoag Hospital in California. The music was a collage ranging from Beethoven's "Moonlight Sonata" to 1930s jazz. While at Riverside, Danny also taught master classes. At the performance, they did *The Beethoven Duet*, Sokolow's *Dreams*, and Hoving's *Icarus*.

At UC Irvine, the company did a one-week residency. At the Fine Arts Village Theatre, they performed *Beethoven Duet* by Danny, *Dreams* by Sokolow, *Icarus* by Hoving, *Day on Earth* by Humphrey, *Glint* by Kahn (a trio that would later be danced by Hannah Kahn, Mark Morris, and Teri Weksler), *And First They Slaughtered the Angels*, and *Life and Other Things* by Danny. Both Teri Weksler and Jane Carrington were dancing in the company at this time. The application from the university for the NEA grant was sent in after the deadline, but they had a way to get funding from the university. Loring commented on how excellent Danny's dancers were, and Committee for the Arts Director Betty Tesman commented that it was a fabulous opportunity that the students would see the works of Sokolow, Humphrey, and Lewis on campus. *Beethoven Duet* was the work Danny created for Naomi Sorkin and William (Bill) Carter in New York, but Danny's company performed it for the first time at UC Irvine a few weeks after the New York premiere.

Jennifer Dunning wrote a review titled "Daniel Lewis Dancers Perform 'Beethoven Sextet'" for the *New York Times* of January 13, 1979, describing DLDRC's home season and gala at the Entermedia Theater in New York. She said that the company dancers were "among the best dancers on the smaller modern dance company circuit today." Dunning called the company "a labor of love for Mr. Lewis" and said that "the rewards are great." She also noted that the season contained "vital dance that spanned six decades and performing that was impressive both for its technical excellence and exhilarating spirit." Dunning commented that Lewis had gone preservation one better with *The Beethoven Sextet*, calling it "a buoyant little opening dance of simple diagonal runs and shifting geometric patterns. Both lyrical and percussive, the dance has such Limón signatures as rounded, soft arms and bodies, but the feet are flexed at unexpected moments and the pace decidedly brisk." Of Lewis' work *Life and Other Things*, Dunning commented that the piece "refuses to allow fairly straightforward Limónesque dance based to flow uninterrupted, but characteristically juxtaposes it with bizarre gesture and quirkily accented jazz stretches and spins."

The 1979–1980 Artists Series was in Huntington, Pennsylvania, at Juniata College. The company performed *The Beethoven Trio*; *My Echo, My Shadow, and Me*; *The Exiles*; *Night Spell*; and *And First They Slaughtered the Angels*. This was one of an extensive series of performances in the late 1970s and early 1980s. The stage manager was Alyce Dissette. Alyce was Gilbert Vaughn Hemsley's assistant. Gilbert was the production supervisor and lighting designer and director of the New York City Opera. Danny did three shows with him: *Nefertiti*, *Aida*, and *Dido and Aeneas*.

In the 1980s, Danny's company did many performances at the Riverside Dance Festival, held at the Riverside Church in New York, a popular theater for dance performance. The artistic director of the festival was David K. Manion, who became the executive director for the International Committee for the Dance Library of Israel, where Danny sent videotapes of Felix Fibich's choreography. Manion became a founding member of the Martha Hill Dance Fund and was on the board of directors of the Martha Hill Foundation. In 1982, Elizabeth Keen joined Anna Sokolow as resident choreographer for the company, and Ze'eva Cohen (who would later invite the company to Princeton University in 1984) was a guest choreographer. For the 1982–1983 season, Danny commissioned a work by Elizabeth Keen for the company. Dancers in the company included Kristen Borg, Jane Carrington, Kathleen Casey, Randall Faxon Parker, Jim May, and Steven Sabado. Works included a solo for Randall called *Randall's Island* by Ze'eva Cohen and the world premiere of *Taking the Air* by Elizabeth Keen, with music by Virgil Thomson and costumes by Charles Berliner. Berliner had previously done the costumes for *Irving the Terrific*, done at UCLA in 1972. Danny has all the original drawings of the costumes for *Taking the Air* for the five dancers in the work.

Also at the Riverside festival that year were Mercury Ballet, Gus Solomons, Billy Siegenfield, Greenhouse Dance Ensemble, Contemporary Chamber Ballet of Caracas, Tandy Beal, Dancemakers from Toronto, Maria Formolo and Keith Urban from Edmonton, and Margi Gillis from Montréal. The Riverside Church seasons were clearly international events, but the festival ended in 1987 due to financial constraints. This was devastating to many companies in New York City, because the festival provided an eclectic range of programming (ballet, modern, ethnic, tap, and social dance) as well as an affordable stage for small companies and a home for out-of-town companies.

The company held a gala event on March 5, 1981, at Marymount Manhattan Theater and presented the first full evening of works by Daniel Lewis: *Beethoven Trio*, *Open Book*, *And First They Slaughtered the Angels*, *No Strings*, and *There's Nothing Here of Me but Me*. Prior to this performance, Danny always presented repertory with different choreographers, so this was the first time he did a show entirely of his own work. The gala board who presented this concert included William Bales, William Como, Louis Falco, Pauline Koner, Carla Maxwell, Jennifer Muller, Jack O'Brien, and Paul Taylor. Dancers were Antony Balcena, Kat de Blois, Randall Faxon Parker, Jane Carrington Lewis, Jim May, Ernest Pagnano, Clifford Shulman, and Kristen Borg.

Jennifer Dunning reviewed the performance at Marymount Manhattan Theater in the *New York Times* on March 7, 1981:

> "I am an open book to my boss," a dancer proclaimed about halfway through Daniel Lewis's new "Open Book." "And a complete mystery to my closest friends," another dancer said. Count this perplexed observer on the side of the angels. Odd dance succeeded odd dance on a program of five

pieces choreographed by Mr. Lewis and performed by the Daniel Lewis Dance: A Repertory Company on Thursday at the Marymount Manhattan Theater. The one exception was "Beethoven Trio," a pretty, buoyant little opening dance. But the fact that the choreography was "after José Limón" may explain its sensible, deliberately crafted look.

"And First They Slaughtered the Angels" is probably Mr. Lewis's best-known bit of mystification. Thuggish bikers, fluttering angels and some types in sleek evening dress meet and part and meet again. But its undertone of violence gives "Angels" a lunatic cohesiveness. Silver screen adagio dance and two mobile armchairs made "No Strings" the most enjoyable oddity on the program. And "There's Nothing Here of Me but Me" provided a touching look behind the curtain at a performer haunted by the theater.

The company is a close-knit ensemble of skilled and very personable dancers, among them Antony Balcena, Randall Faxon Parker, Cliff Shulman and Jane Carrington-Lewis. The deft Mr. May is alone worth a trip to the theater, with his sensitive phrasing, lyrical arms and use of fluidly shifting lightness and weight. The group will perform at Marymount through tomorrow in works by Mr. Lewis, Mr. Limon, Doris Humphrey and the resident choreographer, Anna Sokolow.

Through His Friends' Eyes—Jim May

Jim May is the artistic director of the Sokolow Theatre Dance Ensemble, working with Anna Sokolow since 1967, and a former dancer with José Limón and Daniel Lewis Dance: A Repertory Company. Jim said, "I met Danny four and a half decades ago while performing in the Yiddish Theatre on 2nd Avenue in New York, with choreographer Felix Fibich. Danny came backstage and said that José Limón was looking for dancers and asked whether I was interested; I did not know who José Limón was, but I said yes. I performed on Broadway in musicals and was a member of the Eliot Feld Ballet, but it was Danny's guidance that led me to focus and dedicate myself to American contemporary dance for the past fifty years. Danny introduced me to Martha Hill, Antony Tudor, Anna Sokolow, and American modern dance. A few years later, I became a soloist in Danny's company. When Danny retired from performing, I felt that I had a special role, because I became Danny's 'body' in the work. I felt that I was that part of Danny, and I wanted to live up to that role. At the time, modern choreographers concentrated on their own work, but Danny's company performed the repertory of different artists, including José Limón, Doris Humphrey's Day on Earth, *and Anna Sokolow's* Dreams. *My five-year-old daughter danced in the last two works for seven years. At one point, the company went to Finland, and we flew all night. When we got off the plane, we immediately had to face a press conference. Little Jessica fell asleep in my arms, and the photo of her sleeping made the newspaper the next day, with the caption 'What dancers think about the press.'*

I believed Danny was a truly talented choreographer. Danny's movement really poured out of him when he choreographed, and he was like José in that way. One of my all-time favorite works of Danny's was There's Nothing Here of Me but Me. *I loved the start of the work, which begins with bows (like at the end of a dance), and I loved how it bewildered the audience. I thought that by starting with the bows, Danny was dealing with the issue of the audience and the idea of theater. In this light, I thought of three works as a trilogy: In* Mostly Beethoven, *the 'audience' was actually onstage, with the chairs along the front that the dancers inhabited, and Jane Carrington was an usher. In* Bibleland, *the audience saw backstage, with the cameraman and the preacher. This idea of the offstage material coming onstage was playing with the idea of theater. For me,* There's Nothing Here of Me but Me *was other worldly and very surreal. Dancing it felt like I was in a painting by Magritte or another of the surrealist painters, and yet it all made sense.*

The company was amazing at that time, and they were all very close friends, which I felt when performing this work. After the bows at the opening, we could just be ourselves. All of the dancers also loved how collaborative the process was in working with Danny. In the chariot section on the diagonal across the stage in There's Nothing Here of Me but Me, *Danny was not sure what music to use, so Nancy Scattergood Jordan brought in the music from* Planets *by Gustav Holst.*

Alvin Ailey was the only other company outside ballet doing repertory. Danny called his company Contemporary Dance System, the first to use the word contemporary. Danny was also the first to use the computer for his music, while others were

There's Nothing Here of Me but Me, **choreography by Daniel Lewis. Dancers clockwise from left: Kat deBlois, Jim May, Jane Carrington, and Randall Faxon Parker (photograph by BO PARKER, NYC).**

still using fifty-pound reel-to-reel tape recorders. They did not know that the iPod was coming!

Over the years, I would visit and teach at NWSA. I have taught all over the world, and everywhere I go, dancers, teachers, and students have been touched by Danny, and call him Danny, not Mr. Lewis. His footprint is amazing, and countless artists and educators are guided and touched by his generosity, selflessness, infectious curiosity, and tireless effort to allow dreams to thrive."

In 1982, Sophie Maslow agreed to stage her work *Poem* on Danny's company for their tenth-anniversary season. *Poem* is one of Danny's all-time favorite dances. The work is done to a percussion score (drumming) composed by the famous jazz musician Duke Ellington and based on Lawrence Ferlinghetti's poem "Autobiography," from the book *A Coney Island of the Mind*, published in 1958. Ferlinghetti was from Brooklyn, as was Danny.[9] The setting is a cafe called Mike's Coffeehouse in present time. *Poem* is interwoven with group dancing, one duet and three solos, and has five dancers altogether, plus an actor reciting the poem onstage. Danny was thrilled to have the work performed by his company, and when he came to Miami many years later, Book Fair International (the largest book fair in North America) asked Danny to provide some dance for one of their events. Danny chose *Poem* because it had written words by a well-known, respected author. It was a huge success at the Book Fair.

On December 3, 1983, the company participated in a benefit performance at the Emanu-el YM/YWHA, in honor of Charles Weidman, partner to Doris Humphrey, who had passed away in 1975. They performed *Day on Earth* by Doris Humphrey. The whole program included *Flying Colors* by Fred Matthews, *Dances for Isadora* by José Limón (with Carla Maxwell dancing), *Brahms Waltzes* by Charles Weidman (danced by Deborah Carr Theatre Dance Ensemble), *Danse Americaine* by Ted Shawn, *The Kitchen Table* by Bill Cratty (danced by Jane Carrington, Risa Steinberg, Bill Cratty, and Michael Kraus), *Fables for Our Time* by Charles Weidman (danced by the Mary Anthony Dance Theater), *Solitary Songs* by Pauline Koner (danced by Evelyn Shepard), *Day on Earth* by Doris Humphrey (danced by Jim May, Randall Faxon Parker, Jane Carrington, and Jessica Poletti as the child), and *Lynchtown* by Charles Weidman, a large group work with soloist Carol Mezzacappa.

In April 1983, Danny's company did a performance at the Juilliard Dance Theater. The dancers included Jim May, Jane Carrington, Randall Faxon Parker, Clifford Shulman, Cathy Casey, Stephen Nunley, Diane Butler, and several others. In 1983, Pentacle became the management company for CDS/DLDRC when Danny decided he needed a full-fledged managerial company. The management company was run by Mara Greenberg and Ivan Sygoda. Pentacle remained the manager until 1987, when Danny moved to Florida and the company disbanded.

In 1983–1984, the company did performances and workshops in 20 district schools in the New York area, including District 15 in Brooklyn, Hillside Elementary School, PS 175, PS 5, and Clara Barton High School. In 1985, they repeated the tours in another fourteen New York area schools. These workshops in the schools were an important part of the educational outreach aspect of the company, because bringing

9. The poem "Autobiography" by Ferlinghetti is what Danny wants read at his funeral. His favorite quote from the poem is "I once started out to walk around the world but ended up in Brooklyn. That Bridge was too much for me."

dance and the arts to children and adolescents was always a goal of Danny's and a focus of his work.

In 1984, Daniel Lewis Dance: A Repertory Company had a tenth-anniversary celebration, performing at the theater of Riverside Church. Daniel Lewis was the artistic director, Anna Sokolow was the resident choreographer, Nancy S. Jordan was the associate director, Eddie Effron was the lighting designer, and Stephen Cobb was the production stage manager. The program included five premieres and three commissioned scores by American composers (Louis Levin, Peter Wetzler, and Edgar D. Grana).[10] It should be noted that the early company had consisted mainly of Juilliard dancers, but by this time the dancers came from a much broader dance background.

Jennifer Dunning reviewed this concert series in the *New York Times* on January 22, 1984, in "Dance: Daniel Lewis and Anna Sokolow." Dunning was very good to Danny's company and fully understood what he was trying to do. Her review is as follows:

> Daniel Lewis is a noted graduate of the Juilliard School, where he now teaches, and he danced with José Limón, whose works he has staged. Given that background, it wasn't surprising that a program by Daniel Lewis Dance on Thursday at the Theater of the Riverside Church was an evening of solid choreography performed by capable dancers.
>
> Most noteworthy was a striking new work by Anna Sokolow, based on three solos choreographed in the 1930's. In "As I Remember," set to music by Silvestre Revueltas, Chick Corea and Maurice Ravel, Miss Sokolow expresses deep emotion almost entirely through posture.[11]
>
> The opening solo, called "Lament for the Death of a Bullfighter," has Jane Carrington standing erect and almost still, but for one crumpled fall and a pull or two at her long black dress, revealing scarlet lining. It is a forbidding view of formal grief. The tone becomes lighter as Evelyn Shepard skips with her usual warmth through the second solo, "Ballade in a Popular Style." Youthful gaiety becomes manifest in the slight tilt of her body and the way her feet and hands are poised, as if supporting her in air.
>
> The work closes with "Kaddish," in which a black-clothed mourner is pulled into herself, hunched in an anguish that also finds expression in the straining upward of her livid arms and face, bathed in light. That solo is danced, with extraordinary power, by Risa Steinberg. "As I Remember" is dedicated to the late Louis Horst, the teacher, composer and critic and a mentor to Miss Sokolow, in this centennial of Horst's birth.
>
> Mr. Lewis's new "Textured Lighting" is as dark and formal a work, but its formality is very much of the 1980's. Set to a score by Edgar David Grana, the work is all subdued athletics in its stage crosses and partnering for four men. Edward Effron's chill lighting provides the turbulent landscape through which they dance, as strong an element as any in a dance dedicated to the late Gilbert Hemsley Jr., the lighting designer. Jim May, one of the most sensitive modern dancers around,

---

10. Program A was Out of Sink by Nancy S. Jordan (world premiere) with dancer Jane Carrington, and music by Eddie Sauter; Textured Lightning by Daniel Lewis (world premiere) with dancers Brian Carbee, Michael Kraus, Jim May, and Stephen Nunley, and commissioned music by Edgar David Grana; As I Remember by Anna Sokolow (world premiere) with three sections: "Lament for the Death of a Bullfighter" (dancer Jane Carrington), "Ballade in a Popular Style" (dancer Evelyn Shepard), and "Kaddish" (dancer Risa Steinberg, and music by Revueltas, Chick Corea, and Ravel); The Exiles by José Limón (1950) with dancers Jane Carrington and Jim May, and music by Arnold Schoenberg; and There's Nothing Here of Me but Me by Daniel Lewis (1980) with dancers Jim May, Brian Carbee, Michael Kraus, Stephen Nunley, Randall Faxon Parker, and Risa Steinberg, and Daniel Lewis as the stage manager, with music by Holst, Massenet, Locatelli (tape collage). Program B was Day on Earth by Doris Humphrey (1947) with dancers Jim May, Randall Faxon Parker, Risa Steinberg, and Jessica Poletti as the child), and music by Aaron Copeland; As I Remember, Duet in Passage by Jane Carrington (world premiere) with dancers Michael Kraus and Risa Steinberg, and commissioned music by Louis Levin; Repetition by Jim May (world premiere) with dancers Brian Carbee, Jane Carrington, Nancy S. Jordan, Stephen Nunley, and Randall Faxon Parker, and commissioned music by Peter Wetzler; and There's Nothing Here of Me but Me.

11. Anna and Danny had searched for the original music, contacting her former friends in Mexico, but no one could find it. Instead Danny and Anna found the Corea music, which worked well for the piece.

is the quiet trailblazer in the quartet, which included Brian Carbee, Michael Kraus and Stephen Nunley.

The power of the dance was somewhat diluted, however, by the score's distracting chants and by the sense that the dance had some deeper meaning to the choreographer than was clear to the viewer. That sense of missed connections also diminished Nancy S. Jordan's new "Out of Sink," though the brightness of its jazz score by Eddie Sauter was evoked well in Miss Carrington's performance of the wandering solo.

The program was completed by Mr. Lewis's "There's Nothing Here of Me but Me" and "The Exiles," Mr. Limon's probing look at the loss of Eden, danced dramatically by Mr. May and Miss Carrington. The company will perform at Riverside through today.

In January 1984, Jane Rigney also reviewed this tenth-anniversary show in the *New York Tribune*. She wrote many reviews of the company, and in this one, she talked about Jim May and Jane Carrington dancing *The Exiles* at Riverside Dance Festival. She referred to Danny's company as doing true, unadulterated modern movement and offering a "normal" dance forum. In the performance series, the company did five premiere works. She noted that outstanding dancers included Jim May, Jane Carrington, Risa Steinberg, Michael Kraus, Brian Carbee, and Steven Nunley.

Danny wrote a lovely letter to the company at the end of the 1984 season. He thanked them and stated that it was the most beautiful and successful season that they ever had. He said that not only did the dancers prove themselves, but the seasoned members made the new members feel right at home, which showed onstage. He added his thanks to the choreographers. He went on to tell them about a fundraising event planned for April 1985 at the Century Café. He announced that his book *The Illustrated Dance Technique of José Limón* would come out later in 1984.

On Monday, April 15, 1985, a gala fundraising event occurred in New York at the Century Café at 132 West 43rd and Broadway, run by Phil Scottie, who closed the restaurant for the night and donated all the food and drinks. Scottie lost income that night by closing the restaurant for the evening, but he was a man who would start restaurants for people and invest in them, and he was also on Danny's board of directors. The Gala Committee was headed by Tony Randall (actor) and Morley Safer (news anchor). The Gala Committee was Ze'eva Cohen, William Como (*Dance Magazine* editor), Louis Falco, Laura Glenn, Lotte Goslar (German dancer), Edgar D. Grana (composer), Erick Hawkins, Martha Hill, Pauline Koner, Phyllis Lamhut, Carla Maxwell, Don Redlich, Marian Seldes (actress), John Shea (actor), Peter Sparling, Lee Theodore (lighting designer), Linda Wayne, Dyan Wiley (cousin of Jane Carrington), and Anita Zeidman (Jane's mother who worked at the *New York Times*). Company members for this gala were Jane Carrington, Randall Faxon Parker, Donna Krasnow, Megan Williams, Jim May, Kraig Patterson, Evelyn Shepard, Natalie Rogers, Peter Smith, Clifford Shulman, and Risa Steinberg. The funds being raised were for the Emerging Artists Series, and it was also a celebration of fifty years of dance. For the fundraising raffle, they had a color television, three original signed line drawings by Edward C. Scattergood from Danny's book *The Illustrated Dance Technique of José Limón*, and a case of wine donated by the Century Café.

Some of those attending the gala were William Bales (of the Dudley-Maslow-Bales Trio), Bonnie Bird, Betsy Carden (head of Brooklyn College dance department), Ernestine Stodelle, John Chamberlain (her husband and noted newsman), Alfredo Corvino, Edgar D. Grana (composer), Martha Hill, John Erwin (CBS television), Anna Kisselgoff, Ruth Lloyd (wife of Norman Lloyd, composer), Matteo (Spanish dancer), Thelma Dickson Murphy, Charles Reinhart, Stephanie Reinhart (co-director of ADF), Ben Sommers (head of the Capezio Foundation), Estelle Sommers, Michael Uthoff, and Hortense Zera (original Martha Graham Company dancer). Speakers were Daniel Lewis, Jerrold Ross (head of Arts and Arts Education at NYU), Martha Hill, Dr. Daniel E. Griffiths (School of Education, Health, Nursing, and Arts Profession at NYU), Leonard Fleischer (senior advisor to the Arts Program at Exxon Corporation), and Patricia Rowe (chair of the Department of Dance and Dance Education at NYU). Danny came away from this event feeling exhilarated about the future of the company.

Through His Friends' Eyes—Donna Krasnow

Donna Krasnow recalled a funny story from dancing with the company in 1985, when she ended up dancing in And First They Slaughtered the Angels *in New York. At intermission, one of the women in the work, Natalie Rogers, became very ill. There was one section of couples waltzing in the background, so Danny needed a woman for that role. Donna said, "Danny told me to put on the costume and get ready to go onstage. He said not to worry—just to follow my partner—and that is exactly what I did. The dress was too long, as Natalie was taller than I am, so I just had to make sure not to step on the hem as I moved around the stage. It was my only experience as a dancer performing a work onstage that I had never rehearsed!"*

In 1985, the company danced in a Limón Foundation performance at the Limón Studio, along with Clay Taliaferro Company dancers and Martha Partridge Company dancers. Other dancers with Danny included Juilliard graduates Kraig Patterson, Natalie Rogers (who became one of Garth Fagan's assistants and worked with him on *The Lion King, Ellington Elation* for NYC Ballet, and *Jukebox* for Alvin Ailey), Evelyn Shepard (well-known New York dancer), Peter Smith, Megan Williams (who later danced with Mark Morris), plus Donna Krasnow, and his usual company members Risa Steinberg, Jane Carrington, Randall Faxon Parker, Jim May, and Clifford Shulman. Everyone involved in this show sent Danny their text for the flyer, which Danny gave to director Frank Barth, expecting Frank to take it to the designer for layout. Instead, Frank had it printed exactly as Danny gave it to him, which was not very attractive! The other companies were very angry about this result, especially since Danny had submitted more information, and submitted his first, so he had a much larger section of the flyer.

DLDRC was doing an astonishing amount of performance work during these years, more than many professional companies were doing.[12] And through all of this, Danny

---

12. Additional performances from 1975 to 1984 included Nassau County Department of Recreation and Parks (1975), American Stage Festival, Milford, New Hampshire (1976), Flagstaff Dance Festival in Arizona (1976), Manhattanville College in Purchase, New York (1976), Middlebury College in Middlebury, Vermont (October 5, 1977), Washington Square Park (New York Auditorium) (1977), Castleton State College in Vermont (1977), Northrup Auditorium at the University of Minnesota in Minneapolis (1977), American Theater Laboratory in New York City (1977), St. Paul's School in Concord, New Hampshire (October 1976), Swarthmore College in Pennsylvania (1978, 1979), Westchester Community College (1978), Tompkins College Center, Cedar Crest College, Allentown, Pennsylvania (1979), Catawba College, North Carolina (1979), Marymount Manhattan College (1980), Nashville Institute of the Arts, Tennessee (1980), Mt. Holyoke College, Massachusetts (March 1981), Atrium (April 1981), Citicorp Center, New York (April 1981), Stockton State College (May 1981), Blair Academy, New Jersey (May 1981), Nashville Institute for the Arts (1981), Columbia Dance Theater, Maryland (1982), Maurice Levin Theater, New Jersey (1982), Washington and Jefferson College Arts Festival in Washington, Pennsylvania (1983), City of Yonkers Bureau of Parks and Recreation (1983), Princeton University (1984), Queens Community College (1984), and Rockland Center for the Arts, West Nyack, New York (1984).

was teaching at Juilliard, teaching and staging work at other schools and companies, and staging work internationally.

On January 15, 1981, Julinda Lewis Williams wrote an article that was referred to as "Daniel's Den" in the teaser on the cover of *Other Stages* magazine. The article, on page 3 in the magazine, was titled "The Book of Daniel." It looked at Danny's work *Life Is an Open Book*, based on a poem by Danny written in 1961 called "Life Is an Open Book, Only the Book Is Missing." In Danny's words, "Now I want to find the book and open it up." Inside the covers, he expects to find the special, magical moments that people treasure: the little experiences that happen maybe once a year that stand out, and the relationships (between people and between people and objects) that on rare occasion make you step back and reflect. Williams talks about Danny's process, starting with movement and finding music: *Open Book* began with the idea of magic, a magician and his tricks. Eventually the magician disappears, because in Danny's words, "You don't need a magician. The magician's not around in real life; I think it's just circumstances.... But I needed something in the beginning to let the audience know that there's some outside force." Danny went on in the article to talk about his influences: Limón formed the basis of his craft, from Sokolow he acquired a sense of the dramatic and the psychology of theater, and from Yiddish Theater he gained a sense of obligation to the audience, to entertain them and make them want more. The article also speaks of other works of Danny's and how they reflect a similar process and style. Williams says that *There's Nothing Here of Me but Me* from 1980 is a reflective work that explores the backstage life of the dancer. It is made up of small sections strung together by a common theme: aloneness or estrangement. She wrote, "Whether one saw in it a James Thurberish theme or Walter Mitty's fantasy, the work communicates as Lewis intended it should." In examining *And First They Slaughtered the Angels* from 1974, she describes the use of narrative at the beginning and the end, using fleeting images, illusions, fragments of drama and humor, that together tell the entire story. Lewis has great respect for his audience, and their intelligence, and wants them to understand his work. He found a happy balance between artistic concept and commercial product, using Broadway and Hollywood theatrics, for which he holds a respectful opinion. The article goes on to talk about the biography of Limón he was working on. Danny stated, "Everything about his process as an artist, I've learned. The way he carried himself as an artist, the way he worked, his thought patterns, right from his conception of an idea through to the finished product. The only place I didn't understand José was on an intellectual level ... he was brilliant. He could write piano sonatas, he painted, played the piano, he was a choreographer. Intellectually, you could sit down and have a conversation and there were times he was just way above my head to a point of embarrassment. I wouldn't even tell him; after I talked to him, I'd go home and look up these long words in dictionaries, and I'd know he was laughing in the back of his mind, seeing that I didn't know what the word meant, but that I wasn't going to ask him." Williams finishes the article with the following observation: "Lewis learned his lessons well. The company has been praised for successfully mounting works of Humphrey and Limón, for its well-trained dancers, for the powerful and original choreography, and for the preservation and revitalization of the repertory dances."

Interview with Danny About His Work[13]

I choreographed about twenty-five works over my career, which is not a huge amount of repertory for a professional choreographer. My two favorites are *There's Nothing Here of Me but Me* and *Open Book*.

My Echo, My Shadow, and Me was choreographed in 1972. I loved the musical group the Ink Spots as a boy, so I choreographed the work to their music. I chose two men and a woman to be three men in pin-striped gangster suits. The work also had a black angel, originally played by Rae Kraus. Different women danced the part of the man: Kat de Blois (the original in this role), Laura Glenn, etc. This work was done on an NEA choreographic fellowship.

Cabbage Patch was the Americana work, made in 1976 for the American Wind Symphony. In 1976 I received a call from Robert Boudreau, the conductor of the American Wind Symphony, telling me that he was planning a bicentennial tour and had arranged to have a river barge built to go down the Mississippi River, around the state of Florida, all the way up the Atlantic coast to the St. Lawrence seaway, and back down the Mississippi River again. This was to take a year, and he wanted a dance group to travel with the symphony to do Americana-type dance. The conductor had seen a review in the newspaper about my company doing Anna Sokolow's work, and he wanted to take that work. I put together a program and asked Anna to do a square dance, which she did, but it only had three sides, so the audience could see "into" the form. I did a work called *Cabbage Patch*, which dealt with early American pioneers. We also did two sections from *The Unsung* (about Native Americans), and we did a small lecture/demonstration for some of the shows as well. The dancers were called The Riverboat Dancers. The actual final program listed "Indians," a solo dance choreographed by José Limón (this was actually from *The Unsung*); *Square Dance* by Anna Sokolow; *Jelly Roll*, another solo by Sokolow; *Modern Quartet* by me; and *Charleston* by Sokolow.

I also hired Sandman (Howard) Sims to do sand dancing; he was the originator of this form. The show opened in Biloxi, Mississippi, and they had to call in the Army Corps of Engineers to finish building the river barge. It had a top that would lift up, and the symphony was underneath it, with a space for the dancers. I hired two dance captains, who stayed for the entire year, and many dancers for the tour. Since a year is a long time to tour, we had to replace some of the dancers along the way. The dancers traveled in vans, not on the boat, and a truck with fireworks traveled with them, for Handel's "Music for the Royal Fireworks," for which they would do the fireworks display during this work. I would meet the group in some of the bigger cities, just to check in and see how things were going. When I was there, Sandman Sims and I would dance together. I did buck and wing and Sandman Sims did sand dance. Interestingly, for his sand dance, he did not use sand, he used powdered glass, because it had a better sound. He danced on a platform he had made that was about four inches thick, with a steel plate on it and a hole on the side where he would stick a microphone to amplify the sound.

Along the way, the dancers stayed in people's homes. This arrangement worked fine, although there were occasional minor problems. The dancers got paid a decent sal-

---

13. In this interview with Donna Krasnow in Miami, Florida, in October 2016, Danny expressed his personal thoughts and experiences about his choreography, what works were the most meaningful to him, and how they evolved.

ary for a full year, as they were paid at musician's rates! The dancers were Joan Schwenk, Francine Figgott, Mercie Hinton, Kathleen Quinlan-Krichels (dance captain), Andrew Quinlan-Krichels (dance captain), Agnes Denis, Walther Tjon, Pang Gi, Keir Hangin, and Michael Ferguson.[14]

Tour A began in April 1976 in Biloxi and ended July 9, 1976, in Providence, Rhode Island. (When the tour began in Biloxi, the barge was not actually finished; they were still working on the acoustic paneling for the first performance.) Tour B began July 23, 1976, in Watertown, New York, and ended October 3, 1976, in Lake Charles, Louisiana. At one point, Robert Boudreau was charged with not meeting Coast Guard regulations when the barge was to sail across Lake Michigan, and he was arrested right before a concert![15]

And First They Slaughtered the Angels was choreographed in 1974, with eight dancers (four men, four women) with music by Johann Pachelbel, Hector Berlioz, and Otto Luening. This was my first really fun work. I loved working on this dance and loved the music. This is when I discovered my love of juxtaposing good against bad. *Irving the Terrific*, done two years earlier, was a boxing match of a hippie and the establishment, but it was so literal that it was almost sophomoric. *And First They Slaughtered the Angels*, on the other hand, isn't literal; it is image based. For example, with the angels, there can be Hell's Angels, white angels, dark angels, angels of death, angels of life, angels of mercy, and I had many different kinds of angels in the work. Mainly I used the Hell's Angels, the black angels (the bad ones), and the white angels (the good ones). I then chose music and added the French text in the beginning, because I didn't want to be literal, and I figured that not that many people in the audience would know French. It was also at such a low volume that even for those who spoke French, it would be too difficult to hear what was being said. It really served more as mumbling than any text meant to be heard, which gave the work a mysterious quality.

There is a moment that is quite ominous in this work. The three angels are lying on the floor downstage, and the men enter upstage and stand watching them in a creepy way. Then the angels run and jump on the men, and the men catch them. It received a laugh from the audience, but it is actually quite threatening and menacing. The funny part is when they are all rolling on the floor, and the men stick their heads out from under the women's dresses. It is typical of my work to have comic moments, and this was a comic relief moment. This work was a fun dance to choreograph. It had a superhero, and it had all the angels. Through the years, Randall has had various partners, mainly myself and Jim May. Even after I retired from performing, I would still perform that role, as it had very little dancing. There was one phrase with rolling and jumping, but it was quite easy for me. The text for parts of the work was from a poet named Lenore Kandel, as was the title of the work. I tried to contact her a while back (before the internet) but was unable to do so.

No Strings, choreographed in 1974, first premiered at Barnard College. The work

14. The two dancers Danny knew the best were Kathleen Quinlan-Krichels and Andrew Quinlan-Krichels, a married couple who were in charge on the road; they were paid extra for this work.
15. The tour included Biloxi and Gulfport in Mississippi; Pensacola, Panama City, Clearwater, Tampa, Stuart, Boca Raton, West Palm Beach, and Cocoa in Florida; Brunswick, Georgia; Charleston, South Carolina; Wilmington and New Bern in North Carolina; Norfolk, Virginia; Cambridge and Baltimore in Maryland; Wilmington, Delaware; Lancaster and Philadelphia in Pennsylvania; Newcastle, Delaware; Cape May, New Jersey; Dobbs Ferry, New York; Milford, Greenwich, and East Greenwich in Connecticut; Portsmouth, New Hampshire; Quincy, Boston, and Fall River in Massachusetts; and Providence, Rhode Island.

had three men and three women, and it was to music by David Rose and Gabriel Fauré. I considered *No Strings* a throwaway work, a love duet. There is one couple in the work, and other people are flitting around them, trying to pull him away from her. At one point, he seems to go off with two other women, but he essentially stays with his main relationship. The music by David Rose is called "Symphony for Strings." Eddie Effron jokingly renamed the dance *No Steps*, because there is very little choreography in the work. I loved the chairs in the work, created by people underneath huge pieces of fabric, which become dogs, and then the dogs become something else—constant evolution. The dance has been performed quite a bit. It was loved in the public school system in the Lincoln Center tours, and I set it at Hampshire College in Amherst, Massachusetts. This college also did *My Echo, My Shadow, and Me.*

Proliferation was made in 1976 at Juilliard to music by Saul Goodman and was a wonderful vehicle for men. Part of the set was a tree stump about three feet wide, and the crew loved this work because they finally saw some real "macho" dancing. This work really showed off the talents of the Juilliard dancers.

Mostly Beethoven was created at Juilliard in 1979. I used an entire Beethoven string quartet and ten dancers. The musicians were placed on the stage on a platform. There were also chairs on the stage, where dancers sat (as audience) facing the stage area. The opening scene was as if one were closing his eyes and having a fantasy to the music. It was a really good work, and Martha Hill came to see me after viewing it to let me know that she enjoyed it and thought it was a wonderful work. She told me that she had a meeting with Hanya Holm, and that Hanya had some great ideas for the work. I arranged to meet with Hanya, and we went to lunch. She told me that my biggest mistake was putting the string quartet on a platform at center stage; they should have been halfway in the wing on the side, and there would have been a lot more room for the dance. She also discussed movement development and other aspects of the work for quite a while. At the end, I thanked her for the useful advice and said that I was going to work on the work. She said "Ah, throw it out and now do something new!"

Beethoven Duet was made in 1980 using movement motifs from an unfinished work by José Limón, and it was eventually made into a trio and a sextet.

There's Nothing Here of Me but Me was choreographed in 1980, with its world premiere in March 1980 at Amherst College. The work had four men and three women, was about sixteen minutes long, and had music by Gustav Theodore Holst, Jules Émile Frédéric Massenet, and Pietro Antonio Locatelli. The DLDRC company dancers in the work were Jim May, Brian Carbee, Antony Balcena, Pierre Barreau, Jane Carrington, Randall Faxon Parker, and Kat de Blois. This is the one work that I did that is autobiographical, about myself and my fantasies. It is probably one of the most cohesive works I ever made. It has a beginning, middle, and end, and it has a story line. It still uses my juxtaposition of joy and avoidance during the work. There are symbolic gestures such as looking at the watch to see what time it is. The work is basically a fantasy. The curtain rises on a blank, brightly lit stage. Small groups of dancers and a solo dancer come out in sequence taking bows, so it is essentially at the end of a show. Hence the work tells the story from the end of the bows for a show to leaving the theater for the evening. After the bows, the lights go out, and the work lights come on. Dancers hug and kiss and do the usual goodbyes for the evening. Jim May remains onstage, weird music starts to play, and Jim begins turning around while removing his jacket.

As to the autobiographical nature of the work, it demonstrates confusion about being onstage and offstage. When you are a dancer and also the director, you almost have to have this split existence. We toured a lot, and my responsibility was to talk to the host who brought us to the location, and this was all acting, pretending. I did not like this role, so I had to put on an act. I began to find it very hard to separate the two roles of being offstage acting and onstage performing. Being onstage became so much harder. Even after many years of performing, I remember standing in the wings getting very nervous when the cue came to enter. (This was especially true for performing *The Unsung*, where the first action was to run onstage and leap and leap and leap over and over.) It was the nightmare of not knowing when you're a performer and when you're just a person. In the work, there is the moment when the fantasy that Jim May is having comes to an end, and people start coming onstage talking to him normally. He is disoriented and does not even realize he has been in a fantasy. In the work, Jim is always stepping out of himself and looking at himself as if to say "look at me." He does this action over and over, bending over and pulling himself out, and he does this with the other dancers too. He also has struggles with others. The two pas de deux have women lifting men. My company had women strong enough to accomplish this feat. One of the wonderful aspects of this work is that it has both gorgeous movement and tells a strong story. All of the movement is reversed throughout the work. There are a few humorous moments, one of my trademarks.

The original concept of *There's Nothing Here of Me but Me* was to do a dance backward, meaning that it would start with the end of the dance and then reflect back into the dance. I felt that I accomplished this idea in how the work turned out, by having the bows come first, followed by a retrospect of what it was like being onstage and not knowing why you are in a particular character or what the character is. At that time, I was very tired of having to be literal; I wanted to be more abstract. I don't think that the work says anything special, but it does say that this man, as he reflects back in his life onstage, meets all sorts of characters. Some of these are comical, some serious. The work has an ethereal quality, somewhat like the music of Holst, used early in the work. The wind blowing across Jim's face, as the dancers come blowing across the stage, helps to create this quality. Time seems to be the one thing that holds his character, as he is constantly looking at his watch and then pushing it away, because time is the essence of where you are and what you are doing. It wasn't really meant to be a deep ballet of any kind, but as it developed, it became one of the clearer ballets that I ever made, in terms of the audience seeing what is happening. It was strikingly simple, and people were really surprised at the end when everyone walked across the stage in their street clothes, leaving the theater. The audience finally got that this entire work was Jim's dream after the performance ended. At that point, I (as stage manager) would come out onstage with this attitude, because in the beginning I was onstage telling Jim to put his costumes away, since the "star" was always leaving his costumes around. I would toss the costumes at him and tell him to hang them up. As simple as this dance was, it worked, and it had everything I wanted to say in it, without giving away any deep secrets. This work was Jim May's favorite work to dance, because it feels so complete. Also, he got to do some truly gorgeous movement, and he did it so well. Jim was truly at the peak of his dancing during this period, and he was an incredible dancer—truly magnificent, both technically and dramatically. The whole company always got exquisite reviews for their dancing.

Open Book was choreographed in 1981, on my company, with its premiere at

Marymount Manhattan College in New York. The music is by Gustav Mahler, Richard Wagner, and Gioachino Antonio Rossini, and it had six dancers: Kat de Blois, Jim May, Randall Faxon Parker, Jane Carrington, Tony Balcena, and Clifford Shulman. The original title was *Life Is an Open Book*, but I shortened it to *Open Book*. The work was in memory of and dedicated to my cousin Joan Shapiro, my father's sister's daughter, who committed suicide. It is a downer work, as it is dealing with death and mourning, but the movement is beautiful. I consider this work the best work I ever did. It is indeed my favorite work, and I felt that I truly hit on something different. In all of my works, the music was always cut and spliced (collage format). The sound score for this work was made from several pieces of music, all classical. I always made the music fit what I wanted and always used classical pieces to build my scores.

Jim May and Randall Faxon Parker are the father and mother in *Open Book*, and Kat de Blois is the lead, the child. No character in the work is specifically my cousin, but it is a work about the pain of death. Tony Balcena, Jane Carrington, and Brian Carbee were also in the dance.[16] The work contains a lot of very sharp movements and a lot of broken lines. Nancy Scattergood Jordan was the rehearsal director, and the work was amazingly clean, especially given how quirky much of the movement is. Nancy was truly an exceptional rehearsal director, and the dancers were stunning. Although there was something very different about this work from my other dances, the movement was certainly "signature" Lewis. The men wore flesh-colored briefs in the work, and the women wore flesh-colored leotards, and all of the dancers had darkly colored see-through costuming over these briefs and leotards. When Kat removed the top layer, it was quite striking in creating a nude effect. The way she took it off was actually so elegant. The work received mixed reviews. One person who wrote about the work complained that they couldn't hear the words, but to me that didn't matter. You only needed to hear little bits and pieces of text.

Although in my view the work is my best dance, it is not my most popular work. It is the best because I really dealt with subject matter that isn't funny, that is serious and deep. I always had comedy in my work, no matter what I was choreographing—always a few cute moments. *Open Book* did have a few cute moments, but they didn't override the seriousness of the work. The moments when the dancers did little funny things were just to give the audience a moment of relief; otherwise it would have been a very heavy ballet. The loss of a child has to be the worst thing that can happen to a parent and to society in general. It doesn't take much to set off a revolution when you see children being hurt. What caused all the problems in Vietnam—besides it being a nasty, terrible war that should not have been fought—was seeing the pictures of children suffering, such as the famous image of the little burned girl running naked down the street. Children should not die. My cousin Joan wasn't a child; she was an adult, but she died (through suicide) before her parents died. This shouldn't happen. She was a disturbed child who had her issues, and I dedicated the ballet to her, although I didn't think that the work was really about her. It was about the opening line (which is also the closing line): "The graves of our children are the best places to hear pleas for mercy." That line is paraphrased from a line in the prologue of the book 'In Cold Blood' by Truman Capote. In fact, much of the text for the dance was paraphrased from that prologue. I added other lines, such as "I'm an open book to my boss, and a complete mystery to my closest

---

16. Tony passed away in 1995, and Jane passed in 2015.

friends." This line is a paraphrase from Lawrence Ferlinghetti's poem called "Autobiography." Joan's suicide was shocking to the whole family, but it was actually the second death. My other cousin, the son of my mother's sister, was shot by a shotgun during a hunting accident. He lived for about a week, during which time my father traveled to upstate New York to be with the family.

Moments was first choreographed for the Juilliard Dance Ensemble in 1982, and it is a work that I have done several times. After Juilliard, I staged *Moments* for one of the Limón summer programs. The work was a tribute to José Limón, and the music for this work was composed by Edgar David Grana, a Juilliard graduate in music. Martha Hill introduced us, and I actually created three dances to his music. After José died, I was commissioned by Martha Hill to do this work for the tenth-anniversary celebration of José's death. The work was a large group work, and I interspersed motifs from many of José's works exactly as José had choreographed them. The dance would be going along, and suddenly something from José's solo in *Missa Brevis* would appear. Michael Schumacher originally played José in the work.

The Morning after the Night Before was choreographed in 1988 at Towson State College in Maryland. I created this work when I first moved to Miami. When NWSA hired me, I told them that I already had this commitment in Maryland, so I went there several times to make the work. I made this work very differently than the way I normally made dances. I had the dancers at the college make up the movement, and I organized it. I was pleased with how the work turned out.

In 1988, when I became dean of dance at NWSA, I stopped choreographing.

Through His Friends' Eyes—Jack O'Brien

Danny received a letter dated February 6, 1974, from Jack O'Brien, known for his musical theater work on Broadway. O'Brien has won three Tony Awards and been nominated for seven more and won five Drama Desk Awards. He was the artistic director of the Old Globe Theatre in San Diego, California, from 1981 through the end of 2007. In the letter, O'Brien talked about seeing Irving the Terrific *the previous spring and having seen Danny's company the night before writing the letter.* "I saw things in your work that spoke to me directly on a totally theatrical level. I was genuinely moved, and I saw 'it' being born—the event, the company, the individual works, everything. It can confirm or deny a basic direction, a lifestyle, a sense of excitement in your commitment—the feeling of being 'right.' The evening was built masterfully, with the first half being promising, eager, a sense of event not completely delivered, but still one was grateful, provoked even, just being there. It was a smooth, positive beginning. And then you brought it all together, the way you obviously intended. 'Angels' [referring to* And First They Slaughtered the Angels*] seems to be you on a deeper level than 'Irving' was. Still there was the sense of the totally theatrical, the juxtaposition of polar opposites, the great bracing dash of humor, and the deep insistence of something beneath. Just wonderful. Astonishing even. The audience became utterly alive, during and after, and not just with the kind of enthusiasm that 'friends' have for 'our' work. They were engaged. They were involved. They were right! I sensed levels of the work—three transparent sets of images seen around and through each other—this consummate respect for form itself, its structure, so to speak, which we often overlook in our searching for the 'meaning' of things—this meticulous control over an animal which doesn't want to be tamed, all these things are uniquely your gifts, and make me proud and happy to be in the presence of an original thinker. I loved the use* *of the spoken word in the work, and the beauty of merging dance and spoken theater to-gether. This letter is a fan letter, but something more. I congratulate you, Danny, for your taste, your control, and your accuracy, and the precision and sensitivity with which you handled* Day on Earth *was the frosting on a considerable cake."*

Company Supporters

There were various donors and benefactors to the company over the years, mainly family, friends, and dance community members. Some of the early donors included Nathan Clark, Jerry Lewis (Danny's father), and Alfred and Mary Kahn (Hannah's parents). Alfred Kahn was the person who deregulated the airlines. In 1974, he became chairman of the New York Public Service Commission. He later served as chairman of the Civil Aeronautics Board, advisor to the president on inflation under Jimmy Carter, and chairman of the Council on Wage and Price Stability (Carter's "inflation czar") through 1980.

Throughout the late 1970s, the budget of the company continued to increase, both in grants and in sales and receipts for touring and performing. The New York State Council on the Arts (NYSCA) gave considerable funding to CDS/DLDRC for many years.

A 1983 letter about the company's residency at Amherst College came from Alfonse D'Amato, a U.S. senator from New York from 1981 to 1999. The letter was about the approval of Danny's NEA grant application requesting $36,000 for the 1984–1985 season. He said that in monitoring federal grants, it was his desire as a U.S. senator to see to it that those projects from the state of New York most in need of federal aid be offered assistance during these times of financial stress. He then congratulated Danny.

Danny applied to the NYSCA for a grant in the 1984–1985 season, and he received the grant. Beverly D'Anne was the director of the NYSCA dance program, and she was later on the committee that searched for the new director of the Limón Company in 2016. Other grant application panelists were Carolyn Adams, Senta Driver, Garth Fagan, Maria Grande, Elisa Monte, Renee Perez, Marcia Preiss, Peter Rosenwald, Philip Semark, Clive Thompson, Catherine Turocy, and David Vaughan. These are all people with established careers: dancers in companies, company directors, and so on. Danny also knows these people personally.

The company received a total of ten grants from the NYSCA, and then the money suddenly stopped coming. Because of budget issues with the council, the funding dried up.

Through His Friends' Eyes—Nancy Scattergood Jordan

Nancy Scattergood Jordan spoke about the end of Danny's company from her perspective. "By the mid 1980s, the company started to lose funding and became a different entity. In the final two years, I was unpaid, and it was truly a labor of love. However, the process became very difficult: Jane Carrington had problems with me, which made me unhappy in my role. I felt that my job was being taken away from me by a company member. In the fall of 1985, I took Danny to dinner one evening and said it was time for me to leave—Danny and Jane could run the company. Danny replied that he thought this was telling him that it was time to fold the company. By December 1985, Danny started the process of ending the company. The company continued officially until the summer of 1988. Danny had an NEA grant to finish, and the NEA allowed Danny to give the money to Jane Carrington and Leslie Neal to produce a concert in Miami, where he and Jane had just moved."

7

Other Facets
of Danny's Life During
His Company's Years

It was my wide-ranging artistic interests as well as luck that gave me a myriad of opportunities in related fields. I worked as an author, as a choreographer for opera, plays, and musicals, and as the founding director of the Limón Institute. With Juilliard as my training ground, I was also able to expand my teaching jobs and develop my pedagogical style. The dual talents of choreography and teaching opened many doors in various institutions for me. I have never backed away from going where chance and opportunity takes me, even if it is an unexpected ride.—Danny Lewis

Teaching and Staging His Work During the Company Years

Danny has staged and directed his choreography in many schools and companies all over the world. (The full list can be found in the Appendix.) One major school where Danny and his company were in residence for many years was Amherst College in Massachusetts.

Amherst College

In 1965, a four-college consortium was formed with Amherst College, Mount Holyoke College, Smith College, and the University of Massachusetts at Amherst[1]; then in 1966, Hampshire College was founded and added to the consortium. This five-college consortium in western Massachusetts was intended to promote the broad educational and cultural objectives of its member institutions. In 1978, a five-college dance department was formed. In addition, each college would maintain its own dance department as well. Each already had its own dance program, except for Amherst College. John William Ward, the president of Amherst College from 1971 to 1979, called Bob Reiter,

---

1. In 2014, Danny did a visit at the University of Massachusetts at Amherst at the invitation of Paul Dennis, who had danced with the Limón Company. It was a consultative visit to advise on what they needed to do to receive accreditation.

Danny's manager, because he wanted a one-semester residency for movement for actors and other classes with Anna Sokolow. Bob called Anna Sokolow, but he already knew she would not do a whole residency. Therefore, Bob suggested that Anna come a few times at the start and end of the semester to give master classes, with DLDRC being in residence for the full semester. After the first year, Amherst liked the arrangement so much that they asked for the company to do an ongoing residency.

Danny's company went there for several years, from 1974 to 1980. They would rent a house every year, and the company would go there for two weeks, then later for another two weeks, and some company members would stay on and teach throughout the semester. The residency was usually January through May. This was a wonderful experience for both Danny and the company, and it also ensured year-long work to his dancers, with all of their other performances. Students from any of the five colleges could come to Amherst and take classes. Theater professor Helene Keyssar coordinated the company's visit. Additionally, company members would teach master classes at the other campuses. Susan Hunt was hired full time by the school a year after the company started going to Amherst, but she left when she did not receive tenure. There was additional funding for the company visits and performances from the NEA. Danny and company members also accepted special projects during the residencies that included choreography for musicals and plays at Amherst College.

At one point, Martha Hill wrote an important letter of support to Helene Keyssar, speaking of the five-college dance department as a model for others to follow. She felt that dance and arts training should be a part of any well-rounded liberal arts education program. She also commented on the importance of the students having direct contact with practicing artists and with young practitioners in the field. She stated that she was impressed by the variety of students in the program and by the number of young men who were participating. (The soccer and football coaches sent their team players over to take modern dance classes with Nancy Scattergood Jordan and other company members because they appreciated that modern dance would give them balance, coordination, timing, and flexibility.) Martha Hill felt that Danny's dynamic young group contributed to this interest in dance, as well as the year-to-year continuity of the residency program. This letter was in part a response to the presence of people at the University of Massachusetts who did not want Danny's company there because they thought that Amherst should hire full-time dance faculty.

After the president of the college left, dean Catherine Bateson made the decision to end the company's residency at Amherst. In 1981, the school sent a letter expressing disappointment that Danny and the company would not be returning to Amherst the next year. The letter commented on how sad the people at the five colleges were, and it expressed appreciation for the extent of importance that the company had been to Amherst's dance program, and to the educational program of the five-college dance consortium. The letter stated that the students from all five colleges had benefited from the classes and contact with Danny and the company members. It even stated that students (especially the more advanced dancers) would arrange their schedules to accommodate Danny's classes. It went on to mention staging *Passacaglia and Fugue in C Minor*, and how the students had been able to study technique in a way not offered anywhere in the area, as well as receiving assistance with their choreography. It commented on the help Danny had given to Susan Hunt in developing the program.

Additional Teaching

In 1976, Danny went to Towson State College in Maryland and staged his work *No Strings* on the college students. This was a work that DLDRC performed, but Danny was already being asked to go to various schools to stage his work. In 1988, Danny returned to the school, now called Towson State University, to stage *The Morning after the Night Before*. Danny listed himself on the program as a motor movement engineer, not as choreographer, because he had each of the dancers make up thematic material, and Danny arranged it.

How the engagement at Towson State came about was a funny coincidence. Laura Glenn and Danny moved into an apartment at 122nd Street and Broadway. This sixth-floor walk-up apartment was in a building owned by Columbia Teachers College. They moved in and started paying the rent, which was $42.25 a month because it was a rent-controlled building. They were there for about a year when one Saturday morning, someone rang the bell at the front door. At the front door were Helene Breazeale and her son. She explained, "My son grew up in this apartment, and I want to bring him up to show it to him." They said fine, and Helene and her son came up to the apartment, where she showed him around and talked a bit of family history. At one point, she asked Danny what he did, and when he said he taught at Juilliard, she said that she was a Juilliard graduate, from before Danny's time. She said she was now at Towson, and they exchanged phone numbers. This is how he ended up going to Towson to stage works.

Another teaching stint was at the University of Alabama. Affiliated Artists was a group in New York that raised money and sent professional performers out to do eight-week arts workshops in different places. In August 1976, Matthew Diamond received one of their grants to go to the University of Alabama in Tuscaloosa, Alabama, to teach for legendary coach Paul (Bear) Bryant. Matthew went to teach dance to the Crimson Tide football team, with Danny assisting. Well-known football players included Johnny Davis, a fullback, and Ozzie Newsome, a split end. Danny said that it might have been just as well that Bryant did not see his football players doing two weeks of ballet taught by a 135-pound dancer from Manhattan. At the end of the eight weeks, the grant said that Matthew had to do a full evening concert, so he chose to do *Dead Heat* with Danny. It received a lot of publicity in all the newspapers in the surrounding states, because the 1976 Olympics had just ended, so there was nothing much for the sports people to write about. The whole residency was a lot of fun for both of them.

In 1978, Danny taught a Limón course for teachers, advanced professionals, and graduate students at City Center in New York. The application process was quite extensive, and no walk-ins were allowed for any of the classes. Danny was contacted by Bonnie Wickoff, one of the dancers at the Joffrey Ballet and a former principal dancer with the Royal Winnipeg Ballet. She felt that the repertory she was performing at Joffrey required stylistic versatility, and thus her interest in the course. Naturally, Danny accepted her, even though attendance was limited to twenty-five students. Other applicants for the course included Stephen Petronio, Steve Paxton, Moss Cohen from the Graham Company, Fay Levow (married to Pierre Barreau, from Danny's company), Sandra Stratton (now Stratton-Gonzalez, who was a good friend of Jane Carrington and to this day is connected to Danny through NDEO), Adriana Urdaneta from Venezuela, Bruyere France from Montréal (who studied with Les Grands Ballets Canadiens and Toronto Dance Theatre), and Jennifer Diggs from Amherst College. There were students in attendance from all over the world. Kat de Blois was a student in the course, and she was then being considered for the company. In the course, Nancy Scattergood would warm the dancers up with a ballet warm-up, and then Danny would come in and teach the Limón class. At the end of the course, the students wrote evaluations, talking about how the classes affected the dancers, what they learned about alignment and use of weight, and how they appreciated Danny's teaching. Danny did several more of these workshops and courses for teachers and professionals. So many dancers were showing up each year that they continued to do preregistration.

In May 1981, the company went to Stockton State College in New Jersey, and Danny went to Portland State University to teach workshops. Throughout the late 1970s and 1980s, the company did massive amounts of touring and performing, while Danny continued guest teaching and choreographing in addition to his Juilliard job.

In 1982, Danny taught at the Choreographic Institute (Centro Superior de Coreografia Grupo Piloto de Danza Contemporanea) in Mexico at the invitation of Lynn Duran. This was a very large music and dance school where she was working. Danny spent a lot of time teaching there with Lynn Duran over a two-year period, and she was a good representative of the Limón technique. She also did the first translation of Danny's book into Spanish, and Ofelia Chávez de la Lama did the second translation with all the diagrams. The dancer, teacher, and researcher Ofelia Chávez de la Lama was appointed by the National Institute of Fine Arts (INBA) as director of the National Center for Research, Documentation and Information of the José Limón Dance (Cenidi Danza José Limón). In March 2017, Danny traveled to Chetumal, Mexico, with Dance NOW! Miami, who were performing *Ritmo Jondo*, choreographed by Doris Humphrey and staged by Danny. On the way to Chetumal, they went to Mexico City, where Danny visited with Ofelia. A group of the dance students from the 1980s at the Choreographic Institute came to observe him teaching and lecturing about José Limón, and he was very moved to see these familiar faces. This group of people were by this time very involved as authorities and faculty at the Escuela Nacional de Danza Clásica y Contemporánea (ENDCC) del Instituto Nacional de Bella Artes. The authorities included Ofelia Chávez, the Director of Cenidi Danza José Limón, Rodolfo Hechavarría, the Director of ENDCC, Sonia Oliva, the Secretario Académico de la Licenciatura en Danza Contemporánea, and Rocío Flores, the Coordinatora of the Licenciatura en Danza Contemporánea. Two of the faculty professors included legendary figures of ballet: Socorro Bastida, the first dancer of Mexico National Dance Company and of Cuba, and Luis Fandiño, recognized first dancer of Ballet Nacional and faculty member for decades at ENDCC. Also present were other faculty members Mireya Perea, Laura Rocha, and Barro Rojo Arte Escénico, and co-founders of Dance NOW! Miami Hannah Baumgarten and Diego Salterini.

In June 1983, Elsa Piperno brought Danny to Italy to teach a two-week workshop at Danza Comtemporanea da Roma. Jane was supposed to accompany him, and in addition to teaching, she was going to dance in a lecture/demonstration staged by Danny. He requested that the company come in the third week of June and perform at the festival, following performances they did in Turkey. In the end, the company did not come, because the performances in Turkey and Rome did not happen. Jane ended up not coming either. Danny recalls going to the downstairs pizzeria every evening by himself. A problem with this job was that Piperno promised to pay Danny in U.S. dollars, but she paid him in Italian lira, which were not supposed to be taken out of the country. Danny had to sneak wads of Italian cash into London! He ended up giving

Daniel Lewis in Mexico City in 2017 at the National Institute of Fine Arts, meeting with the group who had been his dance students in the early 1980s. Standing, from left: Ofelia Chávez de la Lama, Sonia Oliva, Rodolfo Hechavarría, Diego Salterini, Rocío Flores (in front of Diego), Daniel Lewis, Hannah Baumgarten, Luis Fandiño. Seated, from left: Mireya Perea, Laura Rocha, Socorro Bastida (courtesy Daniel Lewis Archives).

quantities of it to various students at The Place, and they would go to the bank and exchange it for him.

In 1985, Danny was invited back to Reed College in Portland, Oregon. This was not for the summer dance program but for a lecture on José Limón for the Division of the Arts. The division felt it was time for a dance guest speaker, and they were impressed with Danny's work and his background. They had heard that he might be in Calgary in January and could perhaps include Reed on this trip. (Actually, Danny's visits to Calgary were always in the summer.)

Danny also taught many workshops at Larry Richardson's Dance Gallery in New York in the 1980s. Some of these workshops were done in partnership with Nancy Scattergood Jordan, who would teach a ballet class prior to Danny's Limón class. Later he taught classes at the 92nd Street Y. Other places he taught workshops were New York City Center and the Limón Center.

Publications

Over the years, Danny has written articles for journals and magazines as well as his book *The Illustrated Dance Technique of José Limón,* now published in Japanese, Spanish, German, and English. A full list of his publications can be found in the Appendix.

A package Danny received from Yugoslavia contained two magazines with articles on Limón (with a picture of Danny) and a letter with a translation of one of the articles,

The book covers of *The Illustrated Dance Technique of José Limón* by Daniel Lewis in (1) English (upper left), (2) Spanish (upper right), (3) Japanese (bottom left), and (4) German (bottom right) (photographs of 1–3 by Daniel Lewis, illustration on 4 by Edward C. Scattergood, all courtesy Daniel Lewis archives).

called "Keeping Dance Traditions Alive." The article was an interview with Danny that had been done during the period when Danny was writing *The Illustrated Dance Technique of José Limón.* The author mentions seeing *The Exiles* in March 1982, so this article was written after that date, probably in late 1983 or early 1984. This interview speaks eloquently about Danny's approach to teaching and how he developed a system, outlined in his book, to best convey the technique to dancers, dance teachers, and students.

In the interview, Danny talked about Limón and Doris Humphrey. He commented that Doris and José had never created a school but rather wanted to teach the dancers how to achieve what was needed for the choreography. A series of exercises was created that included dance phrases, and Doris' concepts were applied to every movement. To José's isolation movements, Danny added the concept of "a center" where the oppositional energies of the body meet. In this way, they could train people from different companies and different ways of moving. José would select dancers who were able to do his style of movement, but he did not necessarily teach them. It was Danny who combined the work of Humphrey and Limón in the process of creating the way he taught the technique. Everyone who worked with Limón teaches in their own way. Most claim that they teach the "Limón style" because there isn't really a technique. (In fact, John Martin once said that modern technique is not a technique but a point of view—a system that creates a certain quality of movement, and every teacher has to develop an adequate system of exercises.) Danny disagrees and believes that Limón *is* a technique due to the foundation and principles upon which the movement is developed; it is not simply a style or quality, even though it is taught in many different ways.

Danny said in the interview that when he was learning isolation with Limón, it usually referred to movements of the head, shoulders, and chest. Danny's dancers, he said, had a more organic sense of movement. Consequently, if the head moves, the movement registers down along the spine all the way to the lumbar area. He added one more thing: Using a system of oppositions in the body, he had created the concept of a "high point." This may be the single most important contribution on Danny's part to the technique. José would ask the dancers when working on choreography to bend as far as possible to the right, for example, and then turn. The dancers always had to figure out how to find the balance. If the concept of a high point is correctly understood, the dancer can execute this kind of movement more gracefully and organically. One should not use too much muscular force, because that tends to interrupt the flow of the movement. The dancer wants the audience to gasp in wonder and say, "My God, how can they move like that!" The upper body moves, although there is no movement in the lower part except for the imaginary opposition, which creates the grounded feeling that the audience perceives. As the body goes off balance, it looks like it is going to fall, but it does not. Instead, it glides to the next movement. To achieve this effect, the technique must be organic. As long as the dancer has a center, it will look organic. Danny stated that when he teaches, he usually would use demonstrators because one must see the movement in order to believe it is possible to do it! It is not enough to use verbal direction ("Body this way, legs that way"). It is very difficult to explain all this in words; movement has to be seen.

When asked whether studying this technique alone is enough, Danny responded that he would never advise a student to study just this technique. It was his conviction that a dancer's technique should be a combination of different ways of moving. Limón's technique, as he himself used to say, came after half an hour of ballet barre and floor exercises. Ballet over centuries has proven itself and is a precise, well-rounded technique. It has its own vocabulary and is, in a sense, independent. Danny advised students to take not only ballet and his classes but Graham and Cunningham as well, and any other technique that has proven successful. For example, Cunningham technique is the result of over fifteen years of experimentation and fits very well with the needs of Mr. Cunningham. A dancer should be able to take different classes and to dance in different companies. One should not limit herself or himself. Even the ballet companies are more and more being introduced to modern dance. In Sweden, Danny taught their first modern classes; ever since, they have continued doing some modern exercises regularly. Danny said, "For example, I went backstage before their performance of 'Romeo and Juliet,' and noticed that some of the dancers had incorporated modern dance exercises in their usual warm-up. 'Bravo!' I congratulated them, and their response was 'We do it before each performance because it warms up the back and gives us freedom of movement.' I think the ballet companies are beginning to realize that in modern dance, there is something they can use to their advantage, and which will expand their range of movement. It doesn't mean they will start to look like modern dancers. They will remain classical but with better knowledge about training their bodies for contemporary choreography."

The article then went on to discuss Danny as one of those personalities in American modern dance who is trying to bring the past into the future. It quotes Anna Kisselgoff (dance critic for the *New York Times*) as having once said, "Lewis contributes his talent to the further development of style within the main currents of modern dance at a time when many young choreographers choose to limit their vocabulary and create inarticulate combinations, which is the trend of the so-called post-modern dance scene." (Note that this is the article's rewording of Kisselgoff's comments.) The article pointed out that Danny and his company performed with different choreographers, while the majority of companies perform only works by the founding choreographer: "His company's emphasis lies in keeping alive modern dance histories in spite of ever-growing diversity of styles."

In January 1985, Jane Rigney wrote a review of Danny's book *The Illustrated Dance Technique of José Limón*. She called it an unusually easy-to-follow manual for both students and teachers of dance. The review described the excellent verbal descriptions of movements, the photos in the book, and the excellent line drawings by Edward C. Scattergood, modeled after Jane Carrington.

In 2006, *Dance Teacher Magazine* asked Danny to write an article, a short history of José Limón. He wrote a very personal article, and they loved it, deciding to print the entire article, which was about three pages. Danny spent time in the article talking about José and his choices of music.

Operas

A full list of the operas choreographed by Danny can be found in the Appendix. He got his start by filling in for José in Dallas, Texas.

An article in the *Dallas Times Herald* of September 28, 1972, titled "Limón to Choreograph" described Limón's plans to choreograph the opera *Dido and Aeneas* for the Dallas Civic Opera (DCO). The article stated that he would use the dance company from

Juilliard for the production. DCO general manager Lawrence Kelly also announced that Jack O'Brien, director of the APA Repertory Company in New York, would do the staging of the opera. The article went on to give Limón's history, dance training, and the formation of his company, plus his involvement with American Dance Theater in 1964. Tenor Jon Vickers would be starring in the production, along with Tatiana Troyanos, Graziella Sciutti, Joan Caplan, Rebecca Roberts, Christine Asher, Antonia Kitsopoulos, and Frank Little. However, José did not do *Dido and Aeneas*. Danny did. In 1971, Pauline had passed away, and José was not doing well, so Danny ended up doing the opera with Jack O'Brien. This was a great connection for Danny. They hit it off right away and got along really well throughout their professional relationship. Danny took Juilliard students with him to do the dancing in *Dido and Aeneas*. One of these dancers was Teri Weksler. He also took his dog Quay, who was just a puppy then. He put Quay in a box under the seat on the plane, and she chewed her way out of the box and ran all over the cabin. Unfortunately, on the way back home, she had grown a lot during the two weeks in Dallas, so she almost did not fit in the box.

In 1978, Danny did the opera *Aida* with Jack at the Houston Grand Opera (HGO), with music by Giuseppe Verdi, libretto by Antonio Ghislanzoni, producer David Gorky, conductor John L. DeMain (Danny and DeMain had gone to school together at Juilliard), and director Jack O'Brien. *Aida* was a huge production, including camels and elephants on stage and various choruses. They did the opera in English on certain nights and other nights in Italian. Bob Reiter convinced the HGO people to use Danny's company as the dancers for *Aida*, and the dancers were paid. There were many problems along the way with the production. The music they gave to Danny to work with in New York before coming to Houston did not match what the musicians did once they got to Houston. Also, during the triumphant march and the gladiator scene, the measurements they sent to Danny did not match the stage and set. Danny ended up having to redo the choreography of those sections once they were in Houston. Most of these dancers had never done opera, and they were uncomfortable with the rehearsal process, having to sit for long hours, and with the costumes, which were not built for dance. There were three ballets in the opera, and in the end, it was very successful.

Plays and Musicals

Danny always had an interest in dance and music forms beyond the modern dance genre, beginning with his work with Yiddish Theater. A list of his work in plays, musicals, and commercials can be found in the Appendix.

In 1977, Danny choreographed the Broadway show *Nefertiti*. This was the second production that Danny did with Jack O'Brien, after *Dido and Aeneas*. Jack brought Sherwin Goldman, David Spangler, and Christopher Gore to the Roundabout Theater on 23rd Street in New York to see Danny's company. When he saw *No Strings*, Jack liked the imagination, the way the chairs transformed, and the humor, and he recommended Danny to Goldman. Rehearsals began in New York in July at the Minskoff Theater, and the show opened in Chicago at the Blackstone Theater for the out-of-town tryout. The production staff included Jack O'Brien (director), Sherwin M. Goldman (producer), Daniel Lewis (choreographer), Nancy Scattergood Jordan (Danny's assistant), David Spangler (music composer), Christopher Gore (lyricist), John DeMain (musical direction), Robert Billig (orchestra conductor), and Sam Kirkpatrick (set design). It starred Robert LuPone, Andrea Marcovicci, Michael Nouri, Michael Smartt, and Jane White. The New York rehearsals went well, but when they got to Chicago, they realized the show was in trouble because it did not hold together and some of the music did not work. The reviews were terrible, and Goldman panicked, so he brought in historians who were experts in Egyptian history and culture. However, their comments had nothing to do with artistry or musicals. The show spiraled downward as it became more convoluted. They were making daily changes, going further and further from the original concepts. Finally, Goldman called a meeting and said that the show was going on hiatus. What he really meant was that the show was canceled. What Danny liked the least about this experience was being told by the producer to make the work more commercial when Danny wanted it to be artistic.

In 1981, Danny choreographed the musical *Crisp*. The original lyricist was Gault MacDermot (who was the lyricist for *Hair*), but they could not use his name because he was under contract to another company. On the program, book and lyrics are listed as Delores Prida. The director was Max Ferra, and the musical director was Tanya Leon, who was with the Brooklyn Philharmonic and was the musical director for Arthur Mitchell's Dance Theatre of Harlem. Danny really enjoyed this show because it introduced Danny to the Hispanic theater culture, and the actors were a delight to work with, especially Brent Collins and Manuel Martinez, who spoke almost no English at that point. From this work, Danny was offered the choreography for the Cottoncale television commercial.

The Limón Foundation

In 1982, it was the tenth anniversary of José's death. A special evening called "For José and Us" took place on December 2 at the Joyce Theater, staged by Carla Maxwell and Jennifer Scanlon, with lighting by Richard Nelson. The program contained the following statement: "An evening to celebrate the 35th anniversary of the founding of the José Limón Dance Company in 1947 and to mark the 10th year of José Limón's death on December 2, 1972." This was an important performance for two reasons. First, it was a celebration of José and his work and legacy. Second, it was the last time that Danny would ever perform as a dancer. Carla asked Danny to do his solo from *The Unsung* as part of the memorial to José. At this point, Danny had not danced in years, but he decided to do it because he had never performed at the Joyce Theater and he thought it would be good to honor José. He thought he had plenty of time to get in shape before the performance. However, that never happened. By the day of the performance, Danny had done nothing to prepare. He walked a couple of blocks from his home over to the theater, stood under a hot shower for an hour, and did a long, hard warm-up. The plan was for the company to do the opening Pantheon from *The Unsung*, then Danny's solo, and then Clyde Morgan's solo. They would finish the first half of the evening with the opening circle from *There Is a Time*. Many of Danny's Juilliard students who had never seen him perform came. Danny only walked through the work onstage in the afternoon; he figured if he tried to do it in the preparation time, he would injure himself and not be able to perform that night. He thought he could manage to do it full out just once. Therefore, he waited for the show to dance it full out, and he did a magnificent job. The only problem was that he came offstage at the end of the solo and couldn't breathe. His lungs froze up, and he was certain that death was imminent. He finally caught his breath just in time to go back onstage for the opening circle from *There Is a Time*. The whole time he was dancing the circle, he felt really dizzy. This was Danny's last performance! He swore never to get on the stage again. The irony is that for years he had been teaching students that they needed to be in shape and properly warmed up for performance. Danny claims this was the dumbest thing he ever did. He should have followed his own advice!

The evening brought together three generations of dancers, choreographers, teachers, educators, and administrators who had been vital to the persistence of the vision of Limón. The people there observing included Pauline Koner, Betty Jones, Martha Hill, Anna Sokolow, Murray Louis, Alwin Nikolais, Jennifer Muller, and Louis Falco. Lucas Hoving was not able to attend, but he sent a video that was played at the performance.

The evening opened with an introduction to the evening by Carla Maxwell, followed by a playing of the tape of José's Juilliard convocation speech from October 5, 1966. Then Sarah Stackhouse performed Limón's *Chaconne* (1942). Betty Jones introduced *The Moor's Pavane* (1949). Pauline Koner introduced a film of excerpts from *Lament for Ignacio Sanchez Mejias* and *There Is a Time*. Lucy Venable introduced three works: (1) Doris Humphrey's *Air for the G String* (1928); (2) "The Pantheon," "Sitting Bull," and "Geronimo" from Limón's *The Unsung* (1970); and (3) an excerpt from Limón's *Orfeo* (1972). The first half ended with an introduction by Jennifer Scanlon of a film of Doris Humphrey's convocation speech at Juilliard on October 10, 1956, and excerpts from Limón's *There Is a Time* (1956). After intermission, there was a taped introduction by Lucas Hoving for Limón's *Missa Brevis* (1958).

In her review of this evening's event in the *New York Times* on December 4, 1982, Jennifer Dunning said, "As to the memories, Miss Maxwell and Miss Scanlon created a gentle blockbuster of an Act I close by joining the company with earlier Limón dancers, summoned to the stage from the audience and wings. Holding hands, they watched with pride, sadness and absorption as, within their ring, their younger colleagues performed the closing circle dance from Mr. Limon's 'There Is a Time.' Nothing could have expressed so eloquently the evening's theme of continuity."

A letter from Frank Barth at this time asked Danny for his assistance, at the strong recommendation of Martha Hill. Prior to becoming involved with the Limón Company, Barth was a minister and, as such, had little experience or previous background with the dance world. At this point he had only been doing the job at Limón for about four months. In the letter, he commented about how impressed he was with the tenth-anniversary celebration at the Joyce. He went on to say that they were entering a period of serious reflection and analysis about the nature and impact of the future of the Limón Company. At this point, Carla had been directing the company ("firmly and heroically") for several years. The Limón Company was engaged in soul searching: What does the public look for from the Limón Company, and what has the company been saying? Does the company have a future, and what would that be? Barth was asking Danny to participate in this process, which he acknowledged would not be an exact science but rather the reactions of caring people like Danny to put together a story that speaks for the company. They planned to have a preliminary discussion at an all-day retreat in the near future. Danny did participate in this process, which was instrumental in the founding of the Limón Institute.

At this stage, they were also starting to put set prices on works that they would mount for other companies. They had already been selling works for some years, but by 1984–1985, they set up a consistent and thought-out plan and budget of what to charge for the various costs (mounting, reconstruction, execution, salaries, licensing, etc.).

Ruth Currier was the artistic director of the Limón Company from 1973 to 1978, and in those years, Danny was not happy with the look of the works when he would see the Limón Company, because the movement looked too soft for his taste. Then Carla Maxwell took over as artistic director in 1978 (and remained until 2016), and Carla's husband Frank Barth was the company manager. The business manager was Jeff Bush, the husband of Celia Ipiotis, and the two of them founded the television series *Eye on Dance*. Jeff and Frank were actually a good team, and they did great work for the company. Frank wanted to make the company more secure, so he spoke with Martha Hill, who told him that they should bring Danny Lewis back in, because he knew José better than anyone. In 1984, Danny was invited by Carla Maxwell to be a guest at the open house at the Limón Studio on January 30. Shortly after, Frank called Danny and asked him to start the José Limón Institute, which would be the part of the Limón Foundation responsible for the selling and staging of works and for the integrity of the works. Danny was therefore the founding director of the Limón Institute,[2] which he ran out of the studio and out of his house. As director, he was responsible for all the mounting of Limón works, nationally and internationally, on both ballet and modern dance companies as well as schools. Other responsibilities of directing the Limón Institute were The New Dance Series in New York City and classes at the Limón Studio.

When the Limón Foundation hired Danny to start the Limón Institute, part of that job was to organize the Limón Summer Dance Program, which began in 1985 with the Limón Company in residence. Martha Hill was instrumental in getting Bennington College to house this program in that first year. She made the phone calls to Bennington, where she had originally started her summer dance program, which would later become the American Dance Festival at Connecticut College before eventually moving to Duke University in North Carolina. Bennington was very interested in increasing their enrollments and starting something in the summers, so they were pleased when Martha contacted them. They had the backing of the president and considerable student interest. For the first summer, they brought in a lot of students, and Donna Krasnow was one of those students. At the end of the program, they did a showing of faculty work in what was called the Martha Hill Workshop.

Through His Friends' Eyes—Donna Krasnow

Danny choreographed Mind Over Matter *for students of the 1985 summer program. I recall what it was like to work on* Mind Over Matter *with Danny: "He was busy choreographing the group sections, and he told me that a certain section of music was to be my solo. 'I'll get to it later,' he said, 'just improvise for now.' After a few weeks, with the performance drawing near, I finally said, 'You're not actually going to choreograph my solo, are you?' He replied, 'No, I like what you're doing. Just go ahead and set it.' Although I was a bit terrified at this development, it was truly my introduction to Danny's collaborative way of working with dancers he trusted!"*

---

2. Danny remained the director of the institute until 1988.

The faculty Danny hired for the 1985 Limón Summer Dance Program included Jean Cébron, Lucas Hoving, Phyllis Lamhut, Barbara Roan, Jennifer Scanlon, and Sarah Stackhouse. In addition to the faculty concert, the Limón Company performed. The administrator of these events was Frank Barth. On the faculty program were *Brahms Waltzes*, choreographed by Isadora Duncan and staged by Sarah Stackhouse; *The Red Towel* choreographed by Remy Charlip, with Barbara Roan dancing; a solo choreographed and danced by Andrew Grossman; a solo choreographed and danced by Sarah Stackhouse; a duet choreographed by Jane Carrington and danced by Jane and Donna Krasnow; *Solitary Dancer*, a solo choreographed and danced by Donna Krasnow; a work by Ann Vachon; and finally *The Chaconne*, choreographed by Limón and danced by Sarah Stackhouse. Martha Hill was in Hong Kong at the time and sent a telegram about the program stating, "Right program, right place, right people."

Initially, Carla was strong as the artistic director, and the partnership of Frank Barth and Carla was quite solid. Then, in the midst of her tenure, they got divorced, and Danny stopped going into the studio for a while. Danny was employed by Barth, but his artistic relationship was with Carla, so it was a difficult situation. Eventually, Danny moved to Florida, and he moved the institute work to Miami with him, as he was mostly working from home by then.

He continued directing the Limón Summer Dance Program—in 1986 at the Limón Studio in New York, in 1987 at SUNY Purchase, and in 1988 and 1989 at New World School of the Arts. In 1986, at the same time that the Limón Summer Dance Program was scheduled, the Juilliard School was taking dancers to Hong Kong for the dance festival. Muriel Topaz asked Danny to come on the trip, but he was already committed to the summer dance program, so he agreed to go with her and left Jane Carrington in charge of teaching his summer classes and staging his work *Moments*. In the middle of all this, Risa Steinberg also had to leave, so Jane was teaching Danny's classes and Risa's classes and also staging *Moments*. Although Frank Barth was quite annoyed at this arrangement, Jane did an excellent job, and the program was a huge success.

8

New World
School of the Arts
The Beginning

The luck and joy of knowing Martha Hill once again took me to a new adventure. At her suggestion, I applied for the position of dean of dance at the newly forming New World School of the Arts in Miami, Florida. This began a new chapter in my life and called upon all of my previous talents as an artist, teacher, and administrator to create a new eight-year program and sustain it. I had a vision and philosophy for dance training of the multi-faceted dancer, and worked to fulfill that vision, while making important connections in the Miami dance community.—Danny Lewis

The Move to Miami and Personal Stories

In September 26, 1985, in a newsletter at Bennington College, it was announced that Martha Hill was officially retiring from Juilliard as the artistic director. She was named artistic director emeritus, although she would continue teaching her dance history course. (Bennington published this article because Martha Hill had started the dance program at Bennington.) It is important to realize that by this time, Martha Hill was an extraordinary figure in the dance world. She had started many important programs, and the dancers who came through Juilliard under her tutelage could be found all over the world in both professional and academic positions.

At this point, Muriel Topaz was named the new artistic director. All the faculty members were called to an emergency meeting in the office of Joseph Polisi, who was in his first year as president of the Juilliard School. Martha Hill and the entire dance faculty were all there. He told them that Topaz was being appointed but that it was not his doing. He preferred consultation with faculty before important decisions were made. However, the decision had been made before he was the president. At the meeting, they also discussed giving Martha Hill an honorary doctorate, something that Juilliard was not doing at that time. Now they give them every year.

Meanwhile, in Florida, educators and public officials were working on a groundbreaking project. In 1981, Seth Gordon was hired by the Miami Chamber of Commerce. One day he came to the office, and a group of men from the Chamber of Commerce was at his desk with a copy of *Time* magazine that had the cover story "Paradise Lost." It was focused on all the problems in Miami: crime and drugs and racial tensions. The magazine issue really gave the Chamber of Commerce a wake-up call, and it was the impetus for all of the changes that then took place in Miami. Two teachers, Kandell Bentley-Baker (Miami Dade College) and Marcy Sarmiento (Dade County public schools), came to Seth Gordon to see whether he could assist in drafting legislation to make an arts school possible—that is, to create an independent charter.

In 1987, Martha told Danny about a new school opening in Florida and suggested that Danny should apply for it. (Martha felt that Danny should go out and develop his own program, and she had previously suggested Australia several times.) Richard Klein, principal at the LaGuardia High School for Performing Arts, was to become provost of the New World School of the Arts (NWSA) in Miami. He came to see Danny teach a class at Juilliard, and Richard told him that he should apply. Richard also asked Martha whether she knew other people who should apply, and she said Danny was the only person who would be right for the job.[1]

Danny applied with ambivalent feelings. As soon as he did the three-day interview process in Miami, however, he wanted the job. It was virgin territory—a place where he could realize his own vision. He asked the people running the interview (senators, congressmen, dance educators) what kind of school they wanted, and they said they did not know. The search committee included Kandell Bentley-Baker, Marcy Sarmiento, Seth Gordon, Lee Wagner Brooke (Juilliard graduate and faculty member at Florida International University), Diane Brownholtz (faculty member at Miami Dade Community College, which would later become a four-year school called Miami Dade College), and state Senator Jack Gordon. Although the committee thought this lack of direction was a weakness, Danny saw it as the freedom to build what he wanted, and it is what sold him on the job. They would hire four deans (dance, music, theater, visual arts), and they would determine the type of school it would be. In the beginning, four institutions formed a partnership: Miami-Dade County Public Schools (one of the largest public school systems in the United States), Miami Dade College (the largest college in the United States), Florida International University, and the Florida legislature. This combination was an experiment and one of a kind. It became known as New World School of the Arts. It included a four-year high school diploma, a two-year associate's degree, and an upper-level two-year bachelor's degree. In addition, the high school students earned twenty-four college credits. They were both high school and college students simultaneously, and they were therefore able to fast-track their education when they arrived at the college full time. This was a unique way to get a new institution without actually creating one. All of the administrative and infrastructure parts were in place from day one. Miami Dade College was the fiscal agent, and the school was housed there. Upon the recommendation of school board members Betsy Kaplan and Janet McAliley, the school board agreed to allow high school classes to be taught by both high school teachers and college

---

1. Years later, Danny was able to pay tribute to Martha at Juilliard's Martha Hill Memorial on Monday, September 30, 1996. Performances included Juilliard School dancers (performing Okito, Ophelia's Dragon: A Character Study of Ophelia, Drawn, and See-line Woman), Martha Graham Dance Company (performing Lamentation, El Penitente, and Dark Elegies), Limón Dance Company (performing excerpts from There Is a Time), and Paul Taylor Dance Company (performing Fuga Ricercata). Other events included a photo exhibition in the library, a symposium, and an alumni reception. Danny conducted the symposium, and he was one of the evening speakers at the performance.

faculty, even though the latter were not accredited to teach at the high school level but were certainly qualified.

Danny did not get a call for a long time, so he thought he did not get the position as dean of dance. He had a job lined up at The Place in London, and three days before he left, Richard Klein called to tell him he was being offered the job. Danny jokingly asked if the delay was because everyone else turned it down. Richard told him that he was their first choice, but due to the administrative bureaucracy, the search process took longer than anticipated. After the committee submitted the recommendation of their three top choices (which included Danny) to provost Klein, Danny was offered the position.

Through His Friends' Eyes—Richard Klein

Richard Klein made these comments about Danny's appointment and work at NWSA: "I was very lucky when searching for someone to head the dance department at the New World School of the Arts at its beginning. I was very friendly with Martha Hill, then the director of the dance department at the Julliard School and a member of the advisory council of the High School of Performing Arts. I asked her for some suggestions and she said, 'Richard, you must hire Danny Lewis.' He was her assistant at the time, a former professional star of the José Limón Company, and a graduate of the High School of Performing Arts. He did a fantastic job of hiring a group of professional dancers for NWSA faculty and he remained at New World for twenty-five years before retiring. He had a great talent as a teacher. But, more importantly, he was a personal friend of every student in the dance department, inviting every one of them and their teachers (and my wife Rhoda and me) to his home at the Christmas break, and he had a special ability to recognize and encourage budding talent when he saw it. You can be sure he had a strong hand in the development of every dancer who reached the top!"

Danny and Jane went on to London that summer 1987, and they returned to the SUNY Purchase Limón Summer Dance Program. Right after that, they flew to Miami to start setting up the school and to find a place to live. NWSA opened in late August of 1987. At first Danny was nervous, because he was not sure he wanted to live in Miami; he had been in New York all his life and had never visited Florida. However, he wanted the position, because the potential to create a dance program with his vision was so incredible. As soon as they arrived in Miami, Jane got a call from Larry Berger, a Juilliard graduate, who ran the dance program at the University of South Florida in Tampa. He needed a teacher, so she went to Tampa for that first semester, returning to Miami on the weekends. After she returned for the second semester, she announced that she was leaving Danny for her tennis teacher. Danny was very hurt by what happened but was also relieved because it was difficult living with someone who was lying and drinking heavily. For a very long time, they had been a great team; she assisted him in staging works around the world and demonstrating for his classes, but her drinking just took over. Jane applied for a joint position at Florida International University (FIU) and NWSA, which she received. Later, when FIU split with NWSA, Jane became a faculty member of Miami Dade College and continued teaching at NWSA for several more years, but their personal partnership was over.

Alex Sink of North Carolina National Bank was on the executive board of NWSA. When Danny first arrived at NWSA, Alex was instrumental in getting North Carolina

National Bank to donate a bank building across the street from Miami Dade College. This building housed music, theater, and administrative offices. Dance was in the Diamond Center, another converted building that had been a jewelry exchange, and visual arts was housed in three storefronts. North Carolina National Bank eventually became Nations Bank and then Bank of America. This bank is the largest contributor to NWSA to date, including their sponsorship of the twenty-fifth anniversary gala.

After Danny went to Miami to start NWSA, Joy Davidson was hired as the NWSA director of opera. She came from the tradition in which at the start of a new show, you have a party in the dressing room. So at the start of the year, she had a wine and cheese party and invited all the deans. Danny was sitting in Joy's office, having a glass of wine, when he noticed a picture of *Aida* on the wall and realized that Joy had played the lead in the production he choreographed! They did not even meet at the time of the show.

Family was an important part of Danny's life, and in 1990, he and Maureen O'Rourke got married. Maureen was a former dancer who had developed a practice in body work for dancers and anatomy/kinesiology. In that same year, they bought a house—the one they live in to this day. They moved in, and a small truck dropped off all of their belongings. The next morning the doorbell rang, and a woman was standing there with a tall man next to her. The couple at the door introduced themselves as the Duncans (Dottie and Angus), who lived next door, and they had a cake with them to welcome Danny and Maureen to the neighborhood. Danny was a New Yorker and accustomed to the New York attitude of everyone leaving everyone else alone, so this hospitality surprised Danny. He jokingly asked, "Are you any relation to Isadora Duncan?" Angus responded that Isadora was his aunt! His father was Isadora's brother Augustin, and Angus knew Isadora. Angus was an actor and executive director of Actors' Equity Association from 1952 to 1972. He also played a beefeater at the 1939 World's Fair. Danny and Maureen went over to their house and saw many pictures and memorabilia of Isadora.[2]

The June 7, 1998, *Miami Herald* article by Gail Meadows announced the birth of Danny and Maureen's son, Quinn: "When you perform on stage a million times, it's hard to find an act that wows you more, but Danny Lewis, dean of dance at New World School of the Arts, found it Monday at Baptist Hospital with the birth of his son, Quinn Christopher Lewis. 'It tops them all,' Lewis said Tuesday as he rocked the six-pound newborn. Quinn was the first child for Lewis, 53, and his wife Maureen, 44, a New World teacher of anatomy and kinesiology."

Philosophy and Development of the New World School of the Arts

Danny had a clear vision and philosophy for the dance division of the New World School of the Arts. He wanted the primary focus of the program to be preparing dancers as performers and, in particular, to be well-informed, well-rounded performing artists. From José Limón, Martha Hill, and Anna Sokolow, he brought the idea of honoring the dance traditions while encouraging innovation and revolution. As soon as he saw his new environment—the multicultural landscape of Miami and Florida—Danny knew he wanted a program with a core of several ballet and modern forms and that

2. After Hurricane Andrew, Dottie and Angus moved to Texas to be with Dottie's daughter Pam.

also embraced all of the cultural and world forms: jazz, African, Afro-Caribbean and Afro-Cuban, Spanish, Brazilian, classical Indian, and tap. He was invested in moving dance education and training into the realm of health and sciences, developing a physical therapy section where dancers could go for treatment, as well as offering courses in anatomy and kinesiology. The first faculty members were Ted Kivitt, who danced *The Traitor* at ABT; Judith Newman; Peter London; Daniel Lewis; Jane Carrington; and Freddick Bratcher. Ted's wife was dancing with Miami City Ballet under the direction of Edward Villella. Ted and Judith taught ballet, Peter taught modern and Afro-Caribbean, Danny and Jane taught modern, and Fred taught jazz and modern. Ted convinced Danny that the students should have two-hour ballet classes, which they did at first, but Danny ended that practice after a few years.

Danny was particularly interested in creating an outreach program. This idea served to give the dance students a variety of performance opportunities, while also serving a wide range of communities, such as children, the local studio dancers, and people with disabilities. To give a national and international profile to NWSA, Danny began in the early years hosting major dance conferences and meetings at the school, bringing dancers, dance educators, and scholars from around the world to see this new model for dance education.

In the first year, 1987–1988, they started with just the high school, grades 10, 11, and 12. Danny inherited the students from the Performing and Visual Arts Center (PAVAC) in Miami, so he had students and he had two main studios and a small rehearsal studio, which were in the Diamond Center. Danny did quite a bit of the teaching in the studios

Martha Hill and Daniel Lewis at New World School of the Arts, 1989 (courtesy New World School of the Arts and Miami Dade College).

in that first year. He arrived before the school year started, coming to Miami right after he finished the job in England, and he interviewed and hired teachers. While in England he wrote a curriculum for grades 10, 11, and 12. He knew he only had the students for three hours per day; he would have grades 11 and 12 in the afternoon and grade 10 in the morning. This arrangement was difficult in terms of scheduling, but he managed it. But because he really needed the three grade levels at the same time to give them the curriculum they needed, during that first year he made the parents aware of this issue. The parents then went to Alan Weiss, the first NWSA principal, and complained. The principal was initially very angry at Danny for convincing the parents to go to him with the complaints. However, because parents have a voice, Weiss redid the schedule for the next year, putting all the levels in the three hours in the afternoon. He did the same for the theater, music, and visual arts divisions. Danny also brought up the question of adding grade 9, and Weiss had already been considering it. Therefore, the plans for the second year included adding grade 9, having all the classes in the afternoon, and starting a college program (with only freshman).

For the high school, they held an audition and accepted students for grades 9 and 10 for the next year. The previous year's grades 10 and 11 became grades 11 and 12. This increase in numbers and the added level meant that Danny needed more faculty members, and he spent most of the first year getting to know the Miami dance scene. He interviewed and spoke to almost everyone in dance in the city. He also invited teachers and dance school directors to come and see the classes, and he assured them that he would not be taking students out of their studios, because the dancers could still go to rehearsals in their usual studios in the later part of the evenings. He even

Daniel Lewis with Anna Sokolow in front of the first studio at New World School of the Arts (The Diamond Center), 1988 (courtesy Daniel Lewis archives).

Daniel Lewis teaching in the Diamond Center at New World School of the Arts (first studio), 1988 (courtesy New World School of the Arts and Miami Dade College).

hired some of these people as adjunct faculty at NWSA. (Adjunct faculty members work part time.) In that first year, the administration did not raise any objections about the technique teachers not having college degrees. They wanted a minimum of a master's degree for courses such as music and dance history, and the teachers for these courses did have graduate degrees. However, the technique teachers did not, because Danny was more interested in their professional backgrounds. Danny firmly believed that technique needed to be taught by professional dancers with years of experience performing and teaching, and few professionals in dance had graduate degrees at that time. Therefore, Danny got the administration to agree to professional experience equivalency for the technique classes. This situation would not exist today, because many experienced professionals now have graduate degrees, but in the late 1980s, that was not the case. Danny was a firm believer in not hiring "academic" faculty—that is, young people who were recent graduates with a bachelor's or master's degree but no professional experience. The one problem he had with hiring seasoned professionals was that they had no experience in academia, and they had no idea what it was like to teach in a college or university. Danny had difficulties because of this deficit in their backgrounds, but over the years, most were able to learn how to navigate an academic setting.

Through His Friends' Eyes—Lara Murphy

Lara Murphy attended the high school at NWSA. She went on to study at New York University and returned to Miami to dance with Maximum Dance Company. She eventually took a full-time position at NWSA. Lara said, "On first meeting Danny, I was struck by the unusual combination of his commanding presence and his warm, friendly, and welcoming nature. As a student in his classes, I saw that Danny had a gift for breaking down the material beautifully. Before I knew it, I was doing combinations that were significantly more complex, but it felt natural because of the progression. One of my most important memories of Danny was a time when I was injured with multiple stress fractures in both feet. It was hard, because I wanted to be dancing. However, as my teacher, Danny told me that I needed time to heal. He was very clear that it was in my best interest to sit out the performance. He really gave me perspective on the situation, and I realized that it was professional, not lazy, to take the time to heal. Another fond memory, after I became a NWSA faculty member, was at a national high school dance conference and festival in Philadelphia, where I taught some classes as part of the recruitment for the college. It was very cold, and Danny and I both really loved French onion soup. We ordered it wherever we went. We ended up doing the French onion soup tour of Philadelphia! Danny was a wonderful mentor to me as a faculty member. He kept throwing more and more at me, but because he had confidence in me, it gave me confidence in myself. Now I teach ballet, pointe, and composition, and I am choreographing and staging works on the students. It is rare that a ballet teacher is asked to teach composition, but Danny doesn't set those kinds of boundaries. What Danny created is something that will last way beyond him, because it was done thoughtfully and purposefully."

Finding college students was far more challenging than for the high school program, which was free. His challenge was convincing parents to send their children and pay for a college that did not exist, had no alumni, and had no track record. Danny advertised and had quite a few dancers come in for interviews. For these interviews, the child and the parents came, so Danny was explaining to the parents how exciting it was going to be that their child would be part of the first graduating class of an institution that was going to become famous. Additionally, although it would have the intensity of a conservatory approach in the training, they would also be getting a full academic program, because they were part of Miami Dade College, which required math and science. The students would be part of an educational experiment in which the dean would personally be evaluating their work as well as changing faculty and curriculum as they went along to make it all work. All the time that Danny was talking, the parents were taking notes. In the end, he managed to convince thirteen students and their parents to enroll in a college that did not yet exist! The school had a couple of factors in its favor. First, Miami loved outsiders, and even when seeing performances, they preferred imported to local companies. Danny was seen as an outsider at that point, which gave him leverage, and he talked about his connections around the world. He wanted NWSA to be a school that graduated students into the profession, nationally and internationally, not into practical or educational careers. All of the students who came that first year, one boy and twelve girls, wanted to be performers.

The problem Danny faced was that in order to make classes viable at the college level, he needed more than a dozen people in a class. At that time, the minimum class size was around eighteen. He had to convince Miami Dade College that because they were new, they could not meet those numbers; they said they would give him one year to increase his student body. Danny found an unusual solution; he began allowing part-time students who were not seeking degrees to attend. This meant he had professional dancers in the classes who were there simply for the benefit of the class. Danny had different course numbers for the same class and different costs, depending on how many times a week a student attended, so he had as many as six course numbers for the same class. This arrangement did in fact have some effect on the local dance community, but not on the high-school-age dancers from the local studios. Danny maintained this arrangement for about four years, until he had a full four-year college program going and the numbers to satisfy the administration. Then he had to stop this arrangement, because it was not fair to the full-time students, once the classes were full. Danny was quite the salesman and always found a way to make a situation work.

Danny explained to the administration that in a conservatory setting, generally when there are twenty first-year students, after four years there will be about ten graduates—that is, half attrition. In a larger academic institution, if the student moves to a different department, it is not counted as a loss. For example, a dance student might decide to move to English literature and therefore has not left the school. However, in a small conservatory setting, there are not numerous departments to which a dance student can transfer, so when a student leaves dance or music or theater, they leave the school. In a few cases at NWSA, a dancer would switch over to Miami Dade College, which had a small dance program, but this was not common. When the administration looked at other conservatory programs, like Juilliard, they began to understand the attrition rate at these schools. This high attrition rate can be attributed to several factors, but typically dropout occurs after students start as freshman and soon realize that this type of intense program is not what they were looking for. Every year, Danny would reevaluate the curriculum and continually improve the program, but they have always kept the broad range of dance styles from various cultures.

In 1988 when Danny was first developing the curriculum, he wanted to add Pilates classes. At that time, Pilates was not that well known, and the Pilates community was still in the controversy of who owned the name and the rights. Miami Dade College questioned what Pilates was and why Danny wanted it in the program; after he explained, they agreed to add it as a course. He also wanted a physical therapist on site to treat dance students, but there was no budget for it. (Note that later when the new building was constructed, it had a designated physical therapy room.) They told him he could have a physical therapist in the program, but it had to come out of his budget, and he did not have the funds for it. Danny also wanted musical accompanists. There was similarly no budget for accompanists, but Danny was good at raising funds and at juggling money within the budget, so he added both the physical therapist and accompanists to the program. There were not many accompanists at that time in Miami, although there were many musicians, so they ended up training on the job. Danny felt that live accompaniment was very important for the dancers' training, and in one year when he faced a major budget cut from the government, he cut a secretary rather than lose accompanists.

From the beginning, Danny thought that he had two or three years in which he would be able get away with doing what he wanted and even have some losses in the budget. In fact, he did go over budget in the first three years. Richard Klein was very understanding about it, and he worked to get the money Danny needed. Danny explained that at PAVAC, dance was always part of theater, and theater handled the budget, allotting funding for one dance performance per year and one guest choreographer. When NWSA began, dance was separate from theater. Danny was told that the theater program would take care of Danny's costume needs in dance, but when the new theater dean came in, he did not agree to this arrangement. Danny had never received funding for costumes in his own budget, but he found a way within his budget to make it all work and cover costuming.

One of the most significant changes that occurred in the beginning was to the technique classes. At first, they would have a mix of levels and forms at the same time; for example, intermediate modern and advanced ballet would take place simultaneously. However, to place students appropriately, it made more sense to have all the levels of ballet in one time, with each of the levels of modern in a different time slot. In this way, students could take a mixed-level program—that is, a student might need intermediate modern but be ready for advanced ballet. Also, they could move a student from one level to another during the year. This concept was hard for the administration to understand, especially since it added budgetary strains, such as needing more accompanists and faculty. It also meant that a student might appear on one registration list but be moved to another class, which complicated student records. Eventually the administration understood and accepted these policies, and it is now a general practice in many university dance programs.

Another difficulty was faculty load (how many courses teachers are assigned) in terms of credits. For example, if all the ballet classes were at the same time, it made it problematic to find enough credit hours for a given ballet faculty member to satisfy the contract demands. Regarding the dance academics (anatomy, kinesiology, music, composition, Laban), not all of the faculty could teach these courses, so there were teachers with nothing to do during those time periods, and Danny could not fill their credit loads. The choreography for the program fixed this situation, because when a teacher was a choreographer, they were paid for their work as such, and it counted as part of their load; two two-hour rehearsals per week counted as a three-credit course. If a teacher was not a choreographer, they became an assistant to a guest choreographer. Usually, works are rehearsed much more than four hours per week, plus they had the technical rehearsals and the performances at night that counted in their hours. In the end, faculty either met their load or were actually on overload. This process of counting rehearsals and performances as part of course load and pay was (and still is) highly unusual in a performing arts department.

At the end of fifth year, in 1992, NWSA had its first college graduating class of ten students.[3] After that first group, it averaged about fifteen students per class in the college, and eventually went to about thirty at the start of the class, with fifteen to twenty students graduating by the end of the four years.

Philosophically, it is important to note that the curriculum was not ballet or modern but a broader vision of dance training. The modern classes were not even called Graham, or Limón, or any particular technique—just *modern dance*—even though the faculty members who were hired did teach Graham and Limón. Danny wanted to avoid

---

3. Margarita Dosal-Owen moved to New Zealand and is still working in dance. Lynne Dreeson remained in Miami and continues to dance. Debra Baxter graduated, had a career as a costume designer, came back to NWSA to work as wardrobe mistress, and toured with NWSA to Taiwan. She was married for a while to lighting designer Eric Fliss, but now her whereabouts are unknown. Victoria Fernandez moved to the west coast of Florida and continues to teach and run a dance company. Sharon Zimbler became a marriage and family therapist who specializes in eating disorders. Sofi Haya, Tamara Sisler, and Heather Flynn live north of Danny. Sofi is doing individual and family therapy and movement therapy. Tamara moved to Sarasota and is raising a family. Heather moved to Georgia and became a professional personal trainer. Lewis Hooton taught dance in the public schools before coming to NWSA for his degree, and he has since passed away. Sara Reategui teaches in the public school system in Miami.

First graduating class at New World School of the Arts, 1992. From left: Margarita Dosal-Owen, Lynne Dreeson, Debra Baxter, Victoria Fernandez, Sharon Zimbler, Sofi Haya, Daniel Lewis, Tamara Sisler, Heather Flynn, Lewis Hooton, and Sara Reategui (courtesy New World School of the Arts and Miami Dade College).

any issues with students preferring a given technique. Additionally, every student had to take every class in every form, regardless of their preferences.

Through His Friends' Eyes—Peter London

NWSA faculty member Peter London commented, "As an administrator, Danny trusted that the faculty he hired were there for the students, and he knew that whatever the teachers were doing, it was to promote and move the students forward. He knew that the choreographers were making work that would help the students grow. Danny really understood the life of artists and what they needed. He did fit the role of the administrator, but he protected and advanced the artistic life of the teachers and the students. The freedom of the artistry was always the central focus and goal. As an artist, you must be a visionary. With Danny, his vision and sense of freedom lifted everyone."

An issue that can arise with dance teachers is a possible lack of anatomical knowledge, which can be a problem if the students are studying anatomy and think that what they are being taught in technique is contradictory to anatomical principles. When Danny hired these dance professionals, he encouraged them to get a BFA degree in dance, which they could easily do at no cost for the first two years at Miami Dade College, and then they paid regular fees to complete the degree at the upper level. By doing the BFA program, they would receive anatomy and kinesiology as part of their program of study. Peter London, Bambi Anderson, Tina Santos, Arnold Quintane, and Gerard Ebitz were among the faculty members who all earned their BFA degrees through NWSA while teaching. This also allowed Danny to defend his hiring of these people without degrees, because they were all in the process of earning them. Additionally, the faculty trusted

Maureen O'Rourke, who ran the physical therapy program, and they would go to her regularly with questions.

After Danny moved to Miami, he had to deal with all the local private schools and befriend them so they would not be alienated from NWSA. He was warned by several people that there was going to be friction. Also, the state already had good dance programs. One was at Florida State University (FSU) in Tallahassee, founded and directed by Nancy Smith Fichter, who can be called the mother of dance in Florida. She and Danny spoke a lot when he first came to Miami, and she explained to him the state's built-in transition from community college to a four-year college. (In Florida, if a student graduates from a community college, he or she is guaranteed admission to the upper level of any Florida state university.) Another dance program was under theater at the University of South Florida (USF) in Tampa, run by Larry Berger, who was a Juilliard graduate and a good friend of Danny's who used to stage manage the Lincoln Center Student Programs. And another dance program was at the University of Florida (UF) in Gainesville. At UF, they had good visual arts and theater programs; the dance program was part of the theater program.

One advantage for New World was the connection with Miami Dade Community College, which made it possible for the dance program to take someone with lower grades into the community college system and mentor them until they could move into courses at New World that were part of the upper-level UF program. This system really helped the dancers from underprivileged backgrounds, and it really helped the school grow.

Danny became acquainted with Florene Lithcut Nichols, director of the Inner-City Children's Touring Dance Company. This was an important company and private school in Miami when Danny arrived, and it had been around for years. She was a big help for Danny in seeking out students for NWSA from the inner-city areas, particularly Overtown, which is just northwest of downtown Miami and is the historic area of commerce for the black community. Two other teachers and their schools were highly important in these early NWSA years. One was Thomas Armour at the Miami Conservatory (later the Thomas Armour Youth Ballet), and the other was Martha Mahr at the Martha Mahr School of Ballet. They both became schools that would provide students to the high school. Finally, Maribel Diaz, principal of the Conchita Espinosa Academy, often consulted with Danny about dance educational issues. Danny and Maribel served on the board of directors of the Florida Dance Association.

Finally, it was very important to Danny to have a faculty with a diverse ethnic and cultural background, to mirror the climate of the student body and the Miami culture. Because the population of the city and the school was so mixed, it was important to have a faculty that the students could relate to, and this goal was a driving force in the development of the curriculum and the faculty.

The success of NWSA in fulfilling its mission to produce performers with diverse skills and interests can be seen in its graduates over the years. NWSA graduates have danced in many companies, including Alvin Ailey American Dance Theater, Dance Theater of Harlem, Joffrey Ballet, José Limón Dance Company, Les Grands Ballets Canadiens, Martha Graham Dance Company, Merce Cunningham Dance Company, Netherlands Dance Theater, O'Vertigo Danse, Paul Taylor Dance Company, and Twyla Tharp Dance. At one time, a sixth of the dancers in the Alvin Ailey Company were

NWSA graduates. NWSA graduates have danced in many major companies all over the world.[4]

The Funding of the New World School of the Arts

At the start of Danny's work as dean of dance at NSWA, there was no extra money in his budget for any events. He could only cover his curricular needs for the dance program, along with a few additions such as the accompanists and physical therapy. Danny created Miami Dance Futures, Inc. (MDF) as a 501(c)(3) nonprofit organization to finance the hosting of conferences, events, and projects such as touring, which would bring attention nationally and internationally to NWSA. He became the president and program director of MDF, and he received no remuneration for any of the MDF activities. He needed a nonprofit organization for which he could solicit funds, and he knew that using the Miami Dade College nonprofit system, called the Miami Dade College Foundation, was cumbersome and required various permissions to do anything. Through MDF Danny could apply for grants outside of the school in order to bring in guest artists and host events. Additionally, it allowed him to help the dance community—that is, the local schools and studios—and that helped Danny build contacts with community members who would support NWSA. Through both MDF and the Miami Dade College Foundation, Danny received some major grants to use for NWSA. This funding was very important to NWSA, as was the funding from the city of Miami and private organizations.

Additionally, for decades NWSA received grants annually from the Metro Dade Cultural Affairs Counsel, and these grants went through the Miami Dade College Foundation. The counsel gave numerous grants for various projects and visiting guest artists. Generally, faculty at schools and colleges are not permitted to do personal fundraising, but Danny managed to do it through the nonprofit MDF, so it was technically not as an employee of the college that he was raising funds. Danny put both the NWSA high school principal Ellery Brown and Maribel Diaz, the principal of Conchita Espinosa Academy, on the board of MDF, and they were in support of the ways that Danny wanted to use these funds. Because MDF was a 501(c)(3) nonprofit organization, it could accept these grants and then use these funds to support projects for NWSA and the community. MDF received nearly every possible grant.

Another source of funding was the Surdna Foundation, which wanted to use some of its funds for arts and education. Ellen Rudolph, program director of the Surdna Foundation's Thriving Cultures Program, visited several summer dance programs. In speaking to several dancers at these various programs who interested her, she found out that they all went to NWSA, so she called Danny to arrange a visit to NWSA. She asked Danny what he wanted, and he suggested that he was interested in interdisciplinary

---

4. Additional companies in which NWSA graduates have danced are Alonzo King Lines Ballet, Axis Dance Company, Ballet British Columbia, Ballet Hispanico, Ballett des Saarländischen Staatstheaters, Bayerisches Staatsballett, Bern Ballet, Buglisi Forman Dance Company, Cedar Lake Ensemble, Central Florida Ballet, Chen and Dancers, Chuck Davis Dance Company, Coconut Grove Ballet, Dallas Ballet, Dance Heginbotham, Demetrius Klein Dance Company, Garth Fagan Dance, Houston Ballet, Isadora Duncan Dance Ensemble, Jessica Lange Dance, Martha Graham Dance Ensemble, Maximum Dance Company, Pacific Northwest Ballet Company, Parsons Dance Company, TAKE Dance Company, Tanya Pérez-Salas Compañía de Danza Contemporanea, Urban Bush Women, and White Oak Dance Project.

arts. Ellen told him exactly how he should write the grant, and he received $187,000 from the foundation. Visual arts was the one that worked very successfully in interdisciplinary work with dance. Maurice Fraga, professor at Shenandoah University since 2009 and the artistic director of his own dance company, Ekilibre, was a dance faculty member at NWSA at the time. Danny hired him to write an interdisciplinary arts curriculum, and they created an interdisciplinary arts website. They had the high school students in dance, theater, and visual arts work together on various projects, and they used this grant money over a three-year period. Danny had to match the money to receive the grant. One day, he was having lunch with Ellen Rudolph and Olga Garay, who had worked as the director of cultural affairs at Miami Dade College and was, at this time, the founding program director for the arts at the Doris Duke Charitable Foundation in New York City. Danny casually turned to Olga and suggested that she match the $187,000 from the Surdna Foundation, which made the two women think about doing a joint project together. Danny received an invitation from both foundations to apply for a new grant called Talented Students in the Arts Initiative. Danny was interested in three areas: guest artists, mentoring for the high school students, and internships for the high school students. This money would be for dance, theater, and music—the three performing arts areas. If he received the grant, the Surdna Foundation would provide $75,000 each year for five years, and the Doris Duke Foundation would give $150,000 each year for five years, which had to be matched and put into the bank. At the end of the five years, there would be $1.5 million in the bank, which was an endowment. This money in the bank generated $75,000 in interest, so this grant would be ongoing, and each of the three divisions would receive $25,000 annually, which went up over the years. Because the Surdna Foundation partnered with the Doris Duke Foundation, the Surdna contribution covered the $75,000 for the first five years, until the endowment money became available. This grant was one of the largest Danny ever received, and it was very important to NWSA.

At one point, Danny and Mercedes Quiroga, who served as both NWSA college dean (2004 to 2006) and then provost (2006 to 2009), had lunch with R. Kirk Landon, a wealthy builder and a philanthropist in Miami. Landon came up with an idea called Key88, in which people would "buy" a piano key for $5,000. Landon promised to bestow a gift of $100,000 as soon as NWSA reached its first-year goal of $440,000 or 88 gifts of $5,000. The John S. and James L. Knight Foundation had been founded with a belief in the value of education, and they committed to matching Landon's $100,000 donation. Dennis Edwards, who was the president of the NWSA Foundation, the funding organization connected to NWSA, worked on selling the keys, and it was very successful. This fund went on for four years, raising large funds for NWSA. Danny considers Dennis a good friend, and he said that they were a great team together. Dennis and his partner Mark later got an award for philanthropy for all of their charitable giving to Miami, and they requested that Danny and Maureen be at their table at the ceremony.

Many other grants were received from government and community organizations, including National Endowment for the Arts, Florida Department of State, Division of Cultural Affairs, and Knight Challenge Grant for National Water Dance through Miami Dance Futures.

Because of the financial and artistic affiliation between NWSA and MDF, there is a certain amount of overlap in their activities. For simplicity of describing these years, the activities and events with an educational focus or that primarily utilize students will be discussed under NWSA, and the ones with a community and professional focus will be covered under MDF. It should be recognized, however, that NWSA and MDF were always working hand in hand for the benefit of both the dance students at the school and the dance community at large.

9

Outreach and
Special Events

I was lucky to have so many connections across the United States and throughout the world in the dance community. When I began hosting conferences and festivals, I could call on these connections to bring their talents and artistry to New World for these events. And by this time, I had the administrative skills to plan and operate functions involving hundreds of people. The connections also allowed me to offer touring opportunities for the New World students and many guests who were invited to the school. It was always my hope that I could encourage the students to follow their dreams, but also go down the unexpected, lucky road.—Danny Lewis

Conferences and Festivals

In addition to developing and managing NWSA's dance program, Danny wanted to encourage high visibility for NWSA in a number of ways, one of which was producing and hosting a large number of conferences at NWSA. He co-produced the highly successful Miami Balanchine Conference in 1989, and he produced the Dance History Scholars' Conference in 1991, the American Dance Guild Conference in 1992, the International Dance Musicians' Conference in 1993, the Congress on Research in Dance (CORD) Conference in 1995, and seven National High School Dance Festivals: 1994, 1996, 1998, 2002, 2006, 2010, and 2014. The one in 2010 was the largest high school dance festival held in the Americas. He also produced the International Association for Dance Medicine & Science (IADMS) Conference in 2000, the International Conference of Fine Arts Deans (ICFAD) in 2000, and the American College Dance Festival in 1997 and 2003.

Because Danny was still the director of the Limón Institute when he started at NWSA, he held the Limón Summer Dance Program at NWSA in the summer of 1988. During that summer, Danny also produced the Limón Company performance at the Colony Theater in July 1988, dancing *Suite from A Choreographic Offering, The Moor's Pavane,* and other works by various choreographers. This performance occurred while the Limón Company was in residence at the Limón Summer Dance Program. The Concert Association of Florida, headed by Judy Drucker, brought many dance and music groups to Miami, and she partnered with Danny and MDF to bring the Limón Company to Miami.

In November 1989, Danny and MDF produced and hosted the three-day Balanchine Conference, conceived and initiated by David Eden, former director of Miami's Dance Umbrella. That year's conference was titled "Tradition and Innovation," and it brought all of the dance critics from New York, California, and Chicago to Miami, as well as dance scholars from around the world. This event let the dance world know that NWSA was there and was starting an outstanding program. Richard Klein agreed to fund it, all of the NWSA students could attend for free, and it took place in the original NWSA building on the Miami Dade College campus. A performance of an all-Balanchine program danced by Miami City Ballet, directed by Edward Villella, opened the event on the Thursday evening before the first sessions. Important people attended the lectures and panels, who came to the conference because Danny had so many connections in the dance world and because of the focus on the legacy of George Balanchine. Speakers included Anna Kisselgoff (keynote speaker), Roger Copeland (keynote speaker), Francis Mason (editor of *Ballet Review*), Selma Jeanne Cohen (American dance historian), Dawn Lille Horwitz (dance historian), Nancy Reynolds (dance historian), Alan Kreigsman (dance writer), Ann Hutchinson Guest (well-known dance notation expert), as well as three leading Soviet dance scholars—Vera Krasovskaya, Elizabeth Souritz, and Vadim Gayevsky. There was an interview of former Balanchine dancers Esmeralda Agoglia, Marie-Jeanne, Elyse Borne, Suki Schorer, and Edward Villella. They recorded all of this fantastic event but were later told that they had to destroy the recordings because of copyright issues.

The next major conference Danny produced and hosted at NWSA was the Society of Dance History Scholars (SDHS) Conference in 1991, titled "Dance in Hispanic Cultures." Matteo, Danny's Spanish dance teacher at the High School of Performing Arts, gave a fabulous lecture.[1] Miami City Ballet performed for the SDHS conference. The keynote address "Dance and Poetry" was by Lynn Matluck Brooks, the Arthur and Katherine Shadek Humanities Professor at Franklin & Marshall College and founder of their dance program. The World Dance Alliance was represented at the SDHS conference, and they gave a breakfast to promote their organization. The proceedings from the conference were published under the title *Dance in Hispanic Cultures*, and Danny was listed as the editor.

This event was followed by the American Dance Guild Conference in 1992. In 1993, Danny produced and hosted another important conference, the International Dance Musicians' Conference. Max Vanderbeek was the music teacher for the dance program at NWSA, both for the high school and the college. He and a group of well-known musicians had the idea of forming a guild to support dance accompanists. The conference at NWSA was their second meeting, but it continues every year, and the group is now called the International Guild of Musicians in Dance. This group and the conferences that followed were major innovations developed by Danny and colleagues.

By the 1993–1994 school year, Danny was the only NWSA dean who did not have an assistant. Danny was doing all the administrative tasks for the dance division, even though he asked repeatedly for an assistant. He finally did get an assistant when Richard Klein left in 1994, as Richard signed off on the appointment before the end

---

1. In 1993, Gerri Houlihan used the Matteo lecture as background music for a work that Miami Dance Futures presented.

of his term. Danny's first assistant was Roberta Kjelgaard, and she did most of the organizing for the 1995 CORD conference. This event brought many professionals in the field to NWSA, and these professionals then went home and told others about NWSA. The result was that after Danny started producing and hosting conferences, the NWSA enrollment increased from word of mouth. The conferences also brought professional dance artists, who would sometimes hire the NWSA students after seeing them dance.

Kathryn Kearns, a professor at Penn State University, started the National High School Dance Festival (NHSDF) in Philadelphia at the School of the Arts in 1992. After the first festival, Danny suggested that he produce and host the second high school dance festival, and Kathryn loved the idea because she wanted to move the festival around. As a major contribution to dance education at the high school level, Danny hosted seven National High School Dance Festivals from 1994 to 2014. Danny was an amazing conference and festival host, understanding how to organize these events and how to get the entire community involved in helping with all the work. In each year that Danny produced and hosted the festival, he threw enormous parties for the dancers and faculty. At each of the festivals, they would have regular concerts, gala concerts, choreographic showings in the smaller theaters, and over a hundred master classes—all in three days.

At the first NHSDF at NWSA in 1994, Danny hosted 1,000 dance students and 250 faculty. The opening performance was held at Bayside Marketplace in the Amphitheater. After the show, Danny had music playing on loudspeakers, and there was enough pizza to serve all the dancers. For this event, the Coca-Cola Company sent a trailer with soda fountains inside, so the dancers had their fill of sodas.

Danny produced and hosted the sixth NHSDF at NWSA in March 2002, with 1,200 students and 250 faculty attending. One of the interesting aspects of these high school festivals, with such large numbers, was the quantity of items like toilet paper that were needed. Danny got Procter & Gamble to donate cases and cases of feminine hygiene products so that all the bathrooms were fully stocked. That year the festival gave over $100,000 in scholarships for dancers to go on to college. The attendees were mainly juniors and seniors; younger students could attend if they were in the work being performed, but they were not eligible for the scholarships. They had two different auditions held by the attending colleges: one for juniors, for the schools to see them dance and give them feedback for the following year, and one for seniors, where they were being auditioned for enrollment in the various colleges.

At the eighth NHSDF at NWSA in 2006, Danny arranged an outdoor dinner for the teachers. Inside the tent, a 16-by-16-square-foot area of pushed-together tables was filled with sushi that they kept refilling. In another area, they had a long table filled with fruits from a local farmer and enough Subway sandwiches to feed all the dancers. Danny got the Coca-Cola Company to provide soft drinks at a discount, and they brought cases and cases in a large truck. They also had a DJ at the event, and the dancers were all dancing outdoors.

At the tenth NHSDF at NWSA in 2010, Danny hosted 1,500 dancers and 250 faculty. The festival in 2010 was the largest high school dance festival held in the Americas. At the end of the final performance at each conference, the bows would finish, the curtain would come down, and then the curtain would go back up and the dancers would come onstage and dance to rock music. The Olympia Theater at the Gusman Center for the Performing Arts, where the performance was held, was supposed to put security at each corner to limit the number of dancers who came onstage, but at this year's final performance, a huge number of people jumped onto the stage. The orchestra pit area began to sway, so they cleared everyone in a hasty manner, which caused one girl to pass out. All the students went immediately to their hotels, and they did not get to eat the desserts Danny had bought for the final party. (The next morning, Danny had all the desserts delivered to the school and put out as an early treat.)

All the participants told Kathryn Kearns that the festivals at NWSA were the best they had ever attended, which is why she kept bringing the festival back to NWSA. Additionally, NWSA had magnificent spaces to host a 1,500-dancer festival.[2] These festivals were amazing in terms of the reputation of NWSA. The number of applications exploded, and they had to turn away prospective students.

The local community was appreciative of the influx of visitors, with all the dancers in the high school dance festivals visiting stores in the surrounding four-block radius, and Danny received calls from local vendors thanking him. There were even restaurants offering to stay open on Sunday to serve these dancers. At this point, the Greater Miami Convention and Visitors Bureau asked Danny to do an impact study; according to the statistics gathered, the festival brought downtown Miami $1.8 million in revenue in three days thanks to hotel rentals, restaurant visits, and retail sales. The mayor of Miami gave Danny an award for bringing this business to downtown Miami during the high school dance festival. As the publicity surrounding the festivals spread and companies and choreographers learned about the artistic culture Danny was developing in Miami, he began getting requests from all over the country from dance companies that wanted to come to Miami to perform, and from choreographers, some of whom Danny would hire to set work on the NWSA dancers.

Each time Danny produced and hosted the NHSDF, the Newtown High School of Performing Arts from Newtown, Australia, brought a group of students. Newtown is a suburb of Sydney's inner west section, a very nice area with lots of clubs, stores, and theaters. The two teachers who came with the students were Peter Cook and John Mullins. Danny and his wife, Maureen, became friendly with the Newtown faculty over the years of the festival, and Danny and Maureen eventually went to the Newtown High School to teach master classes.[3]

The Congress on Research in Dance (CORD) thirtieth-anniversary conference,

---

2. After Danny had retired, the fifteenth NHSDF was scheduled at NWSA for 2014. Even though he was no longer at NWSA, the provost, Jeffrey Hodgson, asked Danny to manage the event. Hodgson told Danny that the new dean of dance, Mary Lisa Burns, was in her first year and just learning the job, so she needed help with running the festival. Danny said he would help, but Hodgson asked him to run the whole event, and he provided MDF with an honorarium to cover expenses and fees for other assistants. Danny said yes, and thus ended up running the last NWSA National High School Dance Festival.

3. Melissa Toogood was the first Australian student to attend NWSA, and they found her a high-rise apartment in downtown Miami. The day she arrived, Danny picked her up at the airport and then dropped her off at the apartment; he told her that he would wait until she got her luggage upstairs, and then they would go out to dinner with Maureen. Danny waited outside a long time, but she did not appear. He finally went inside to look for her, only to find a group of people gathered in the lobby because the elevator was stuck. One of the women trapped in the elevator was claustrophobic, and she was having a panic attack. Security guards were there, but they were not doing anything; they were waiting for the elevator company to come and open the door. Danny calmly went to his car, got the lug wrench, went back inside, and jammed it into the door. Despite the security guard's yelling at him to not break the door, he did indeed break open the door to get everyone out. This was Melissa's first exposure to high rise perils and Danny's inventiveness. Welcome to Miami!

called "Dance, Myth, and Ritual in the Americas" was held November 2–5, 1995, at NWSA. Andrea Seidel was a professor at Florida International University (FIU), and she wanted to host the CORD conference. She came to Danny to see whether he would do it at NWSA. He asked her why she was not doing it at FIU, where they have a whole program in global dance, but she said that FIU did not have the capability to do such a huge event. Danny agreed to produce and host it at NWSA, and he decided that Rex Nettleford would be the best keynote speaker. Rex was a well-known Caribbean scholar, educator, historian, political analyst, choreographer, and cofounder of the National Dance Theatre Company of Jamaica. Rex was also on the UNESCO board of directors, which met in Miami at one point, and he spoke at that event. Further, Danny knew Rex personally from National Dance Theatre Company of Jamaica. It was difficult to get him for the CORD conference, because he was to be in Paris at the time for the UNESCO meeting. He agreed to fly in, do the lecture, and go right back to Paris. His keynote lecture attracted people from all over the world.

Another keynote speaker was VéVé Clark, an associate professor in the African American studies department at the University of California at Berkeley. A workshop on holistic methodology was conducted by Joann Kealiinohomoku, American anthropologist and educator, and cofounder of the dance research organization Cross-Cultural Dance Resources in Flagstaff, Arizona. There was a panel called "Dance, Myth, and Ritual in Time and Space" with panelists Joann Kealiinohomoku, Judy Matoma from the World Arts and Cultures Program at UCLA, and Edith Turner from the University of Virginia (who also gave a keynote called "Gentle Inviting—The Power of Dance— Off-Beat Stop: The Style and Meaning of Iñupiat Eskimo Dance"). Menaka Thakkar, a well-known classical Indian dancer from Toronto, attended. There were many other workshops, lectures, panels, and live performances. People came in from almost every state in the United States, as well as Canada, Mexico, South Africa, England, Brazil, Australia, and Japan.

Through His Friends' Eyes—Menaka Thakkar

Menaka Thakkar, renowned classical Indian dancer and founder and director of Nrtyakala, the Canadian Academy of Indian Dance, said the following about Danny and NWSA: "NWSA is an ideal place for a younger person who wants to dive into the world of dance as a professional artist. No matter which aspect of dance they would like to specialize in, they receive professional training in all aspects of the dance world: strong technique, performance, choreography, dance production, the openness of thought and the alertness of the mind and the body, the discipline, respect for old traditions of dance, respect for other artists, teachers, and guest choreographers. All this is possible because Danny brings his experience as a performing dancer with various companies for twenty-five years, along with his administrative ability and, above everything, his vision for dance. His ability to work hard, his relaxed personality, and his sensitivity for humanity make it easy to work with him and create a pleasant working atmosphere. He has a very talented and experienced faculty behind him to bring his vision alive! I can see many wonderful artists and dancers not only making their careers in dance, but also contributing in the field of dance on the basis of what they have learned from this institution."

It was an excellent conference, with content that was relevant to what was happening in Miami's dance scene. There were lessons learned. For example, Andrea had gotten the conference brochure, which included the application, printed on glossy paper.

Everyone filled out the application in ink, and the ink rubbed off in the mailing process, so there was a lot of missing information when they arrived. It took a lot of work to figure out the necessary information.

Danny hosted the American College Dance Festival Association (ACDFA) in 1997 and 2003. (This is now the American College Dance Association [ACDA]; they removed the word *Festival* in order to make it easier for faculty to get funding for their students to attend.) Lisa B. Palley, daughter of Myrna Palley (one of the original foundation board members at NWSA), wrote the press release, "Regional College Dance Festival Coming to Miami for the First Time," published in the *Miami Herald* in March 1997.

The festival had two evenings of dance, the Dance Celebration and the Festival Gala Performance. The event also included other dance concerts, master classes, and adjudication sessions, in which college ensembles competed for the chance to dance at the Festival Gala Performance at the Olympia Theater at the Gusman Center for the Performing Arts. Winners would compete at the national level at the Kennedy Center in Washington, D.C. The Dance Celebration showcased professional Miami-based dance companies. It also included Dance History Live, an acclaimed lecture/demonstration by Frank W.D. Reis, chair of dramatic arts and director of dance at University of California at Santa Barbara (UCSB). Reis had large dance history classes at UCSB in which he used costumes and dancers. Danny brought him to NWSA several times to give history lectures. He came to the National High School Dance Festival one year and gave a talk on Fred Astaire, wearing the actual tuxedo from one of Astaire's movies. Danny said that the master classes, concerts, and adjudications, as well as exchanges between dancers and faculty, were invaluable for the dance students, regardless of their level of experience. He added, "The great thing about this festival is that audiences can see both professional and student dancers from both here and from around the country. It's a wonderful opportunity for Miami to see where dance is right now and where it will be in the future. These students are tomorrow's dancers." Adjudicators included Carla Maxwell (artistic director of the Limón Company), Ethel Winter (member of the Juilliard School dance faculty and early dancer with Martha Graham Dance Company), and Jean-Pierre Bonnefoux (artistic director of the North Carolina Dance Theater and dancer with New York City Ballet). Local companies included Houlihan & Dancers, Ballet Español Rosita Segovia, Isadora Dance Ensemble, Ballet Cubano de Miami, and solo artist Gary Lund. For the 2003 festival, Danny brought Daniel Nagrin and Gerri Houlihan as adjudicators, and Danny got to know Nagrin as a result of this festival. Nagrin really liked Robert Battle's dance *Battlefield*. The volleyball team at Miami Dade College always made delicious large cookies to raise funds, and Danny thought one year it would be nice to keep as many of the festival purchases in house as possible. He asked the team if he could purchase 1,000 cookies. They actually managed to bake them, and they delivered them to a performance at Bayside Park. The next day, they had at least 500 cookies left over, so they put out a sign, selling water for $1 and giving away free cookies. One teacher walked by and said, "Things have changed; cookies used to cost money, and water was free!"

In October 2000, Danny produced the Annual Meeting of the International Association for Dance Medicine & Science (IADMS) at NWSA. Generally, it takes about two years in advance to plan a conference. Starting in 1998, Danny began the organization for the IADMS event. In 1999, the provost Karen Hays called him for a meeting,

Daniel Lewis (left) with Daniel Nagrin, keynote speaker, at the National Association of Schools of Dance (NASD) conference, Tucson, Arizona, 2004 (courtesy Daniel Lewis archives.)

with several people in attendance, including Donald McGlothlin, the dean of fine arts from the University of Florida (UF).[4] At this meeting, Danny was told that UF would be hosting the International Council of Fine Arts Deans (ICFAD). Because Danny had run so many conference and festivals, they wanted Danny to run it. However, the dates were the exact same weekend as the IADMS meeting. Danny ended up running both conferences simultaneously. That weekend, Danny literally ran back and forth between the two sites, with ICFAD at the New World Symphony in Miami Beach and IADMS in Building 3 of Miami Dade College. Both conferences worked out fine, and Danny managed to stay sane! NWSA did a performance for the opening of both conferences, held at the Olympia Theater at the Gusman Center for the Performing Arts. The concert was of multiethnic dance and included works by the Isadora Duncan Dance Ensemble, Diego Blanco, Peter London, Michael Uthoff, Rosa Mercedes, Angela Rhea, Juliana Azoubel, and Mohamed DaCosta. MDF, NWSA, and UF sponsored the performance. At the time of these two conferences, Danny had a wonderful male secretary named Jesus Rivera, who ran around saying, "The ICFADs are coming!"[5]

---

4. The dean after him was Lucinda Lavelli, who asked Danny in 2014 to donate his archives to the University of Florida.

5. Jesus had originally worked at Miami Dade College but had been laid off during a RIF (reduction in force). When Danny wanted to do a hiring, he was required to first interview anyone who had lost their position in the RIF. Danny ended up hiring Jesus as his secretary.

The National College Choreography Initiative

Suzanne Callahan—an arts consultant who worked with Dance USA, Joe Goode, Urban Bush Women, and Washington Ballet—wrote three reports on the three years of the National College Choreography Initiative between 2001 and 2005. This initiative funded choreographic projects at universities all over the country, and it was a partnership between Dance USA and the National Endowment for the Arts (NEA). In 2002, the cover of the publication was the NWSA production of *Inlets II*, the Cunningham work.

NWSA received funding for this production from the initiative, and they were singled out as one of the best in terms of how the grant was written and what they did with the funding. Banu Ogan came and staged the work, with Foofwa d'Imobilité assisting. Callahan wrote an article about the grant and the work *Inlets II*. Many schools received funding through this excellent project.[6]

Danny felt that NWSA was very fortunate to get the Cunningham work because it made the Cunningham Company aware of NWSA. Soon after the NWSA performance of *Inlets II*, the Cunningham Company came to Miami to perform at the Adrienne Arsht Center for the Performing Arts, and the NWSA dancers did *Inlets II* in the lobby prior to one of their performances. Then they did a new work called *Before Oceans*, choreographed by Robert Swinston, who danced with Cunningham for thirty years and was his assistant. Robert also studied with Danny at Juilliard. It was recognition, like this initiative and other projects and grants, that made NWSA famous around the country. Banu Ogan, Foofwa d'Imobilité, and Robert Swinston all fell in love with NWSA dancer Melissa Toogood (mentioned in the section on the National High School Dance Festivals), who danced in *Inlets II*. She was a natural Cunningham dancer. After she graduated, she went to New York and studied at the Cunningham School. She apprenticed with the company for about two years, and then Robert Swinston took her into the company. At the end of Cunningham's life, Melissa became a close assistant to him in the period in which he was bringing everything to a close. She did the final two years, known as the Legacy Tour. Her husband Kenneth Parris III went with the company on the tour and illustrated all of the dancers and the performances.

The Connection with Taiwan

Su-Ling Chou, director of the Tsoying Senior High School dance program in Kaohsiung, Taiwan, had visited NWSA in 1991 for a research project on dance education at American high schools. She then attended the first National High School Dance Festival in 1992 with about twenty of her students. Kathryn Kearns called Danny and said that

---

6. Some of the other schools that received funding from this initiative were the University of Alaska, Huntington College, Henderson State University, Arizona State University, the University of Colorado, California State University at Hayward, Trinity College, the University of Delaware, Brenau University, Ball State University (Isadora Duncan), University of Idaho (Bill Evans), University of Hawaii, University of Iowa (Lar Lubovitch), Wichita State (David Parsons), Loyola University (George Balanchine), University of Maryland (Doug Varone), Western Michigan University (George Balanchine and Paul Taylor), Bates College (Tere O'Connor), the Five College Dance Program (Pearl Primus and Jawole Willa Jo Zollar), Duke University (Tudor), University of Nebraska (Charles Weidman), Montclair State University (Sean Curran), Eastern New Mexico University (Martha Wittman), Sarah Lawrence College, the University of the Arts (José Limón), University of Rhode Island (Jack Cole and Danny Buraczeski), Washington Pavilion of the Arts and Sciences (Paul Taylor), and Southern University of the Arts (José Limón).

Su-Ling was taking these students from Taiwan on a trip to see other dance schools, and she would love for them to see NWSA. Su-Ling was looking for good schools to send her dance students to. Danny hosted these dancers from Taiwan, who performed for the NWSA dancers. It was a lovely visit for all involved.

During this visit, Su-ling Chou asked Danny to accept two of her students, Wen-shuan Yang and Wen-jinn Luo, to NWSA. He agreed, based on a video audition. Their application process was complicated because they needed student visas, a process that Danny had mastered over the years with the help of Miami Dade College. The two girls flew into Miami with Wen-jinn's mother, and Danny found them a place to stay, a condo near the house where Danny and Maureen lived. Within four days, Hurricane Andrew hit, so NWSA did not open when it was supposed to. Kuanghsi Wu, a Taiwanese professor at FIU who knew Su-ling, told the two girls to come and stay with him, because his place would be safer than their condo. Ironically, the place they went for safety ended up being at the edge of the eye of the storm. After the storm was over, it was difficult to find anyone; houses were destroyed and streets were flooded. Street signs were gone, trees were all over the place, and phones were not working. Danny finally made it over to Dr. Wu's house, and spoke to the mother, who spoke only a bit of English, and the two girls, who spoke no English at this point. Danny apologized about the storm, and the mother said it was just a typhoon, and they have them all the time! Despite this rocky start for the two Taiwanese girls, they completed the program within the four-year time period. Both Wen-shuan and Wen-jinn graduated in 1996, speaking excellent English.

Through His Friends' Eyes—Su-ling Chou

Su-ling Chou commented about Danny and the collaboration between their two schools: "I first met Danny Lewis when I visited New World School of the Arts in 1991, as I was doing research on dance education at American high schools. Danny and I arranged cultural exchanges called 'Miami Kaohsiung Dancing Together,' bringing students from each school to the other school for classes and performances. We exchanged different techniques, styles of dance, and the work habits of different cultures. This collaborative work provided an opportunity for students speaking different languages to work together and to find a common language in movement. It is a wonderful experience to work with Danny, as he is open-minded and very efficient. Both of us took a lot of time to arrange the schedules. We wanted to give the students many chances to understand the different cultural and artistic styles, since we know that these exchanges are so important to the growth of art around the world. He is a great friend to cherish and a wonderful partner with whom to work."

During their four years at NWSA, more and more Taiwanese students were coming to NWSA, and Dr. Wu was very good at getting them housing at the condo complex. At one point, he bought one of the condos, so if a student were short on money, he would give them an extension on the rent. Over the years, Danny had more than twenty Taiwanese students in the dance division. What he loved about these students is that they were entirely focused on their studies, doing homework on weekends while the American students were out dancing at the clubs. Mixing all these cultures together—students from Taiwan, from South America, from Europe, and from the United States—affected the behavior of all of them. Due to language issues, it often took some of the international students three years instead of two to get through the associate's degree program;

in the first year, all they did was dance classes and English as a second language (ESL) classes. The Taiwanese students who learned English at NWSA spoke it with a Cuban accent, because the ESL teachers were all Hispanic. Normally, students were required to complete the associate's degree program before they could enter the upper-level program. Danny worked with the administration to get special permission for the Taiwanese students to do courses in the upper-level program by year three, since they had already done two years of dance classes and were ready for the advanced classes.

These two students took very different paths after graduation. Wen-jinn attended the University of Illinois at Urbana-Champaign (UIUC) on scholarship. The UIUC head of dance, Patricia Knowles, did not even require the NWSA college graduates from Taiwan to audition for her program. After Wen-jinn completed her master's degree at UIUC, she returned to Taiwan, where her mother was a dancer and choreographer with her own company. Wen-jinn became the artistic director of the company in 1999, called Scarecrow Contemporary Dance Company, and was very successful.

Wen-shuan stayed in North America and danced with some major companies, such as O'Vertigo Danse, directed by Ginette Laurin in Montréal, Canada. When O'Vertigo Danse came to Miami to perform, Danny was astounded with how magnificently Wen-shuan was dancing. When the deans voted on the Rising Stars honoree during a dance year, Danny recommended Wen-shuan. They bought her a plane ticket to come and receive the award. Then there was a huge snowstorm in New York. She could not get out of New York to get to Miami. At the Rising Stars gala, when it was time for Danny to introduce her, he told the story of Hurricane Andrew and said that it was fate that she could not be there. He mailed her the award, and she was astounded by how beautiful the award was.

In July–August 1998, NWSA visited the Tsoying Senior High School in Kaohsiung, Taiwan. This exchange was done while Bennett Lentczner was the provost of NWSA. Works for the performance were choreographed by Freddick Bratcher (*Bluette*), Gerard Ebitz (*Waiting* and *Crossings*), and Gerri Houlihan (*Between Angels*), with lights by Eric Fliss and costumes by Debra Baxter. The Tsoying students performed *Encounter* by Susan Street, *Innermost Feeling* by Wen-jinn Luo, *When Wind Blows* ... by An-li Su, and *Beneath the Cloistered Moon* by Danna Frangione. Peter London was also there teaching modern classes. Maureen and Quinn were initially going to join Danny on this trip to Taiwan, but there was an outbreak of avian influenza, and Quinn was just an infant, so the two of them did not go. Danny and the students, both from NWSA and Tsoying, went on a bus tour through Nantou County, in the center of Taiwan. The town that they visited was an artisan center, and it would sadly disappear a year later due to an island-wide earthquake.

In June–July 2007, NWSA returned to the Tsoying Senior High School in Kaohsiung, Taiwan. They did a cooperative dance performance, "Miami Kaohsiung Dancing Together 2007." The NWSA dancers performed Robert Battle's *Primate*, Paul Taylor's *Esplanade*, and Freddick Bratcher's duet *Polyphony* with Solomon Dumas (who later danced with Garth Fagan and Alvin Ailey) and Crystal Karaginis (later Crystal Peattie, who would create *The Haunted Ballet* in Miami in 2015, produced by MDF). The Tsoying dancers performed choreography by Hsiao-ting Huang, Yueh-li Cheng, Hsien-fa Cheng, and Wen-jinn Luo, a graduate of Tsoying High School and a student at NWSA. Both groups of dancers performed in *Meditation in Autumn* by Ya-ting Chan. This was another wonderful joint venture of the two schools, and dancers from Tsoying would

New World School of the Arts dance faculty, April 8, 2011. Standing, from left: Bambi Anderson, Tina Santos-Wahl, Dale Andree, Elaine Wright-Roark, Maureen O'Rourke, Peter London, Arnold Quintane, Lara Murphy, Josee Garant, Susan D'Arienzo, Gerard Ebitz, Rebecca Cannan, Diane Brownholtz; seated: Daniel Lewis (courtesy Daniel Lewis archives).

come to do their college studies at NWSA as a result of these collaborations. Both Maureen and Quinn joined Danny on this trip to Taiwan.[7] During this visit, they had an NWSA alumni reunion with the past students and their parents. It was a very mixed group, with every ethnic group imaginable. Fourteen dancers and four faculty and staff were part of the tour. They did one performance in Miami with students from the Tsoying Senior High School in Kaohsiung, Taiwan, and then two performances in Kaohsiung and a lecture demonstration at a junior high school.

After the performances in Kaohsiung, they went on a bus trip and visited the countryside and the big cities. They visited several schools and museums, and they saw aboriginal dancers and the Cloud Gate Dance Company. The NWSA dancers also performed for Cloud Gate. Danny met with Lin Hwai-min, because he wanted to bring Cloud Gate to Miami. When Danny went home, he worked with Judy Drucker to try to make this happen, but it was never possible, because the company was just too expen-

---

7. All the students in Taiwan thought Danny's son looked like Harry Potter, with his round glasses. One day when he was going down the hallway, Quinn passed a room with several students having lunch. They yelled that it was Harry Potter and began chasing him! Quinn ran outside and hid in the bus.

New World School of the Arts and Taiwanese dancers and faculty at the airport in Kaohsiung, Taiwan, 2007 (courtesy Daniel Lewis archives).

sive. Although Judy was willing to bring the large ballet companies like ABT to Miami, she probably did not want to invest that kind of funding in a modern dance company. She did bring the Limón Company for the summer program in 1988. Everyone had a wonderful educational experience.

Students from Taiwan who came to NWSA have followed a myriad of career paths after graduating. Some went on to get higher degrees at other institutions. Many went on to dance with various companies in Taiwan, Canada, and the United States. Others opened Pilates studios in New York and other cities. Shu-Chen Chen, who graduated in 1997, started the successful company Gin Dance Company in Washington, D.C., and taught for the Washington Ballet as well as other schools in China and the United States.

Events

On March 31 and April 1, 1989, the first performance of the New World Dance Ensemble, college division, took place at the Colony Theater in Miami. Danny was the artistic director, Gerri Houlihan was the associate artistic director, and Richard Bergman was the lighting designer. At this time, the faculty at NWSA consisted of 14 members.[8]

In 1996, NWSA joined with the Leonard Bernstein Center for Education Through the Arts to do a research project to examine the relationship between the center's artful learning model and the artistic and academic success and joy of the students. Kathleen Quinlan-Krichels and Andrew Quinlan-Krichels were two of the people Danny had hired to do the riverboat trip in 1976, and they were working at the Leonard Bernstein Center, so it was lovely for Danny to reconnect with them on this project twenty years later. This exchange was another project that was done under the leadership of Bennett Lentczner, provost of NWSA.

8. Faculty included Freddick Bratcher, Jane Carrington, Tony Catanzaro, Gerard Ebitz, Ron Headrick, Gerri Houlihan, Daniel Lewis, Leslie Neal, Judith Newman, Maureen O'Rourke, Mariano Parra, Deborah Salkov, Rosita Segovia, and Andrea Seidel. Guest artists listed for that year were Mariano Alvarez-Brake, Thomas Armour, Maria Benitez, Ze'eva Cohen, Joel Giewartowski, Mark Haim, Nancy Jordan, Julia Levien, Peter London, Gary Lund, Martha Mahr, Donald McDonagh, Bebe Miller, Celeste Miller, Luciano Proano, Mitchell Rose & Company, Jeanne Ruddy, Marcia Siegel, Paul Taylor, Elizabeth Walton, and Lynne Wimmer.

Gerri Houlihan and Daniel Lewis at American Dance Festival in North Carolina, 2019 (courtesy Daniel Lewis archives).

The Aventura Marketing Council's Education Committee, led by Eric Beck of Cyber Doctors, would take 150 at-risk students from the Dade Partner schools on monthly trips around the country, including Krop Senior High, North Miami Beach Senior High, Highlands Oak Middle, VAB Highland Oaks Elementary, Madie Ives Elementary, David Lawrence, Jr. K–8 Center, Greynolds Park Elementary, and Ojus Elementary. David Lawrence served as the president of the executive board of NWSA. For many years each December, the committee brought the students to see a performance at NWSA, where the dancers would work with everything from 1950s music to original compositions. Danny also brought in the Connection, which was the musical theater group at the NWSA high school theater division, for these performances. Beck said that the trip to NWSA was the one that brought the greatest attendance.

Dawn Jenkins worked for Palm Springs Middle School in Hialeah, Florida, and she taught students with hearing impairments. Each year, Danny would bring dancers doing African dance to perform for them, because they could feel the vibrations of the drumbeats. They would then participate in an African dance master class. Danny received many thank-you cards from these students, who were so appreciative of the dance experience.

NWSA did a joint program each year with University of Florida (UF) in collaboration with Professor Joan Frosch and Agbedidi Africa, the West African music and dance ensemble at the university. NWSA would perform at UF, and Agbedidi Africa would come down to Miami to perform. It made the NWSA and UF collaboration much stronger, because Danny headed one of the few divisions that did events with UF. Another event Danny did with UF was an event in which NWSA dancers would go by bus to UF and perform two of their contemporary works, and UF dancers under the direction of Mohamed DaCosta would perform two of their African works; then Mohamed would create a work for the dancers from both schools. The UF dancers would then come down to Miami and they would all perform the same program. The NWSA faculty did not all like the event, because it took the students out of classes for several days and was not a typical concert. The administration, however, was very positive about all of the UF collaborations, and NWSA and UF spent significant money on these events.

Every year in March, NWSA did an event called Rising Stars, which combined dance, theater, music, and visual arts performance, all with NWSA students. (For a couple of years, Danny tied the National High School Dance Festival to the event.) On the Thursday night performance, all of the visiting high schools would get to see Rising Stars, and the tickets were free for the first two seasons. It became the most important performance of the year to see, because it was a showcase of the NWSA students. This event brought a lot of new students to NWSA, and it highlighted many well-known choreographers. For example, the 1998 Rising Stars dance program included Jennifer Vannucchi's *Variations and Departures*, directed by Mariana Alvarez Blake; Gerri Houlihan's and Pamela Pietro's *Subterranean*; Gerard Ebitz's *Waiting*; Freddick Bratcher's *Bluette*; *The Dying Swan*, adapted from the choreography of Michel Fokine; Michael Uthoff's *Three Easy Pieces*, staged by Nancy Jordan; and Peter London's *Urban Serengeti*. Rising Stars included all of the performing arts divisions. For the first few years, each division got one or two evenings in the week to do their own showcase of the students. Later, it was one show with all the divisions combined. Rising Stars happens each year, and they honor an alumnus from one of the divisions. The award rotated from one division to the next each year, except in the twenty-fifth- and thirtieth-anniversary years, when they gave an award for each division. Some of the Rising Stars from the dance division were Robert Battle (1997), Shirley Sastre (1998), Cheryl Rowley-Gaskins (2001), Wen-Shuan Yang (2007), Miguel Quinones (2011), Rosie Herrera (2014), Gaby Diaz (2017), and Jarmar Roberts (2018).

Through His Friends' Eyes—Robert Battle

Robert Battle met Danny as a student at NWSA, and he received the first NWSA alumni award at the Colony Theatre. He began his dance studies at Miami Northwestern (through the Performing and Visual Arts Center) for the ninth and tenth grades and then studied at NWSA for the eleventh and twelfth grades. Robert went on to dance with various professional companies, including Parsons Dance in NYC, formed his company Battleworks, and then became the artistic director of the Alvin Ailey American Dance Theater, being one of only three people to have held that prestigious position since the company opened in 1958, along with Alvin Ailey and Judith Jamison.

About his time at NWSA, Robert said, "While I was studying at NWSA, Danny told me that one day I should have my own company. Danny had the 'puppet strings'—in the best way; he was an operator making things happen. He was always present, observing, and encouraging. Danny had a very direct presence as a leader, and I hope that I have adopted some of that quality in my role as the artistic director of the Alvin Ailey American Dance Theater. I remember Danny's works on the college program as mysterious, in the same way Danny is. I had never seen anything like Danny's choreography, with its abstraction and starkness. It made me understand Danny's layers a bit more, because he is a complex man and yet very passionate. When I would return to NWSA to set a work in later years, sitting in the office talking with him was like watching a circus act. Danny would be doing multiple things at once—on the phone, solving problems, and making things possible. I came to appreciate this quality in my own life, the job of juggling many balls at once. I call Danny 'the conductor.'

Danny is cool, supportive, and humorous, always saying 'You'll be fine; you'll be great.' The sign of a great leader is the people he surrounds himself with, and this is why the faculty at NWSA was so magnificent. Danny's work in dance is who he is—his DNA compels him to be involved and make things happen."

In 2011, at Danny's retirement ceremony, Robert remarked about the time in his high school years when Danny suggested Robert should have his own company. He looked directly at Danny sitting in the audience, and said, "Alvin Ailey American Dance Theater—will that suffice?" He went on to say, about Danny retiring, "I can only quote the words of Patrick Henry, 'I know of no other way of judging the future but by the past,' and so I seriously doubt that Danny is retiring!"

Years before Tovaris Wilson became a well-known commercial dancer and choreographer, he attended NWSA. During his time at NWSA, his mother, Vernell Wilson, produced *The Chocolate Nutcracker* in Miami. The show gave a black perspective to the timeless tale that has been a holiday tradition for many years. Vernell approached Danny, saying she wanted to produce the show with NWSA. At that time, Danny could not offer much except some free rehearsal space, because he had no funding. The show took place at Dade County Auditorium, and it was a success.

The dance division was very involved in the community. Danny wanted to make sure that NWSA contributed to the community, and the publicity was good for the school's reputation. There were several thank-you letters from Miami Dade College and others about the hundreds of performances NWSA did in the community for other organizations. They did performances for Black History Month, Hispanic Heritage Month, Gay Pride Week, and many more. The MDC presidents, Robert McCabe and later Dr. Eduardo Padrón, were very supportive, and MDC was a huge backer of these performances.

One of the Hispanic Heritage Month performances was done at the request of the Immigration and Naturalization Service (INS). Danny felt that it was very important, living in the Miami community, to learn tolerance and acceptance of different languages and cultures. For the INS performance, the NWSA high school dancers did Spanish dances with castanets. NWSA students Diego Blanco and Ana Padron, who later won many international prizes and founded the company Tango for All, were among the dancers in this performance. As a thank-you, the INS gave all the dancers INS shirts with the official INS emblem. A few days later, Diego came to school and told everyone that he had gone out to eat in his INS shirt, and all the waiters ran out of the restaurant!

There were also many thank-you letters from local dance companies that Danny helped, with favors such as the loaning of a portable dance floor for a performance. One letter was from the College of Fine Arts and Communication in St. Louis, Missouri; the director had come to Danny for advice on improving their dance division. Another letter was from Mary Luft, the Founder of Tigertail Productions. Mary Luft was an important figure in the dance community, bringing many distinguished artists from South America and other international locations, and sending these guests to NWSA to do lectures and master classes.

Danny produced an end-of-year document each year that summarized the events. When the school first opened, they had no alumni, so Seth Gordon created an honorary alumni association, called STARS (School of the Arts Roster of Supporters). This became the group Danny could go to for assistance, like an alumni group, and to get connections in the community. It was really only meant to exist until they had actual alumni from the school and would have a true alumni association. Miami Arts Exchange (MAX) was another ongoing event that did build over time, bringing in many important guest artists and lecturers, but it was run by staff and Board members of NWSA. As their work for NWSA became more complex, they had to let go of this incredible event.

Patricia Penenori, president of the NWSA parent-teacher-student association, also happened to be a dance teacher with her own studio. She suggested to Danny that the high school do a fashion show to raise money. Danny laughed and thought this was a ridiculous idea. However, they went ahead with it, and it raised a large amount of money for NWSA (much to Danny's surprise), and so it became an annual event. Over the years, most of these shows were choreographed by Cynthia Dufault, an adjunct faculty member. The local stores provided the fashions each year, and it was amazing to see the teenagers walking down the catwalk in fabulous outfits and high heels. One year, David's Bridal Shop provided the gowns and tuxedos. Of course, all of the parents bought tickets to see the show, but so did outsiders. Myrna Palley and Beatrice Simon,[9] two of the NWSA Foundation board members, supported the fashion show, paying the bill for all of the expenses, such as the hotel and the food, so all of the income was profit.

Other important donors included Lydia Harrison, who created the Daniel Lewis Scholarship given to an NWSA college student each year; Betty Rowan, who created an endowment for students to pursue dance education; and Marsha Simon Kaplan, Billie Kirpich, and Mildred Levinson, who each created an endowment for dance student scholarships.

For the tenth anniversary of NWSA, in spring of 1997, Danny produced the first alumni newsletter, called *New World Journal of Dance*. The whole school was blown away by it, including the academic faculty, because nothing like it had been done before. They wanted it done every year after that first one. Ruth Wiesen assisted Danny in putting the journal together, and it contained stories by students and alumni.

Through His Friends' Eyes—Ruth Wiesen

Ruth Wiesen received her bachelor's degree in dance from NWSA and UF, and she performed with the Miami Ballet from 1984 to 1991. She is the director of the Thomas Armour Youth Ballet and is on the ballet faculty at NWSA. In speaking of Danny, she said, "From our first meeting, Danny was fast talking and energetic about everything. That sense of excitement about the future was palpable, and it has remained with him through all the years I have known him. He believed in my work at Thomas Armour Youth Ballet, so after he retired from NWSA in 2011, I asked him if he would be on the organization's board; then a year later, I asked him to be president of the board. Throughout the years, Danny was always positive, which was communicated to all of the students. He also made it clear that he was enthusiastic about each and every student and that he valued

---

9. Myrna and Sheldon Palley were major contributors to the NWSA dance program and Miami Dance Futures. Beatrice Simon used to donate to NWSA in the form of stocks, and Danny would take them to Northern Trust Bank (a high-end financial institution) so the bank could convert the stocks to cash.

them. I took Limón classes with Danny, and I felt like I was dancing 'at the edge of a cliff.' Danny was so good at teaching Limón, and his personal connection to José gave insight into what José was trying to express and where the movement came from. Danny has the ability to connect with people on a warm and human level. His approach is humble in that he has blue-collar roots, and this makes him a very 'let's get the job done' type of person. He was able to transition from the stage to leading a complex, educational institution. Danny did not consider one school of training to be better than another. He believes in any program that has good training. He sees quality. Danny brought icons of dance to NWSA to expose the students to the masters of modern dance. He was able to do that because of his contacts, and he made sure that there was no cost to the students for these opportunities. Danny and I both have a global vision when it comes to dance. Danny wants everyone to have the opportunity to dance."

During Danny's twenty-four years at NWSA, they did more than over thirty performances every year: two spring concerts (high school and college), the BFA concert, the Rising Stars event, two choreographic workshops (high school and college), and the senior showcase for the high school. Performance was the key to what the program was about, and NWSA was where dancers came who wanted to be performers rather than teachers. (There was one exception to this focus: Betty Rowan, who wrote several books on early childhood development and dance, sold her school in Miami, and gave an en-

Daniel Lewis teaching at New World School of the Arts, 2008 (photograph by Rose Eichenbaum).

dowment of $175,000 for scholarships at NWSA for students interested in becoming teachers.)

Tours and Opportunities

In addition to all of the performance events at NWSA, Danny was committed to giving the NWSA dance students the experience of traveling and performing in a variety of venues. In July 1994, Danny arranged for a tour of Australia en route to the Dance and the Child International (daCi) Conference in Sydney. Kathryn Kearns arranged for the NWSA high school dancers to perform at the Newtown High School of Performing Arts (an internationally known school in the suburbs of Sydney), and Danny also taught some classes. The NWSA students who Danny brought on this trip were twelve girls and one boy, Travis-Tyrell Thomas. Danny brought dancers from the Isadora Duncan Dance Ensemble who did works from their repertory, and other dancers from NWSA who did various works.

One evening, the students wanted to go to a night club, and Danny said no, because he did not want them out alone. Pam Pietro, an NWSA faculty member, said she would take them, so Danny agreed. Danny arranged for all of them to meet in the lobby at the same time, with the plan that he would order taxis and give them a specific hour that they had to return to the hotel. He waited and waited, and at 9:00 p.m., the students were still in their rooms getting ready. Finally, when they came down, Danny almost fainted when he saw the halter tops and extremely short skirts on all of the girls. Danny said they could not go until they had less skin showing! He felt responsible for them. When they returned, they were elegantly dressed, and Danny approved. He sent them off in a few different taxis, and Danny and Maureen figured that they had the evening to themselves. About ninety minutes later, though, they were all returning in taxis to the hotel. Travis-Tyrell had picked the night club, and he took them to a gay club. The girls danced with each other for an hour, and then they left!

Danny gave all the students a per diem cash allowance each morning for food, but they would go off to The Gap and purchase the same items they could buy at any mall at home. Danny said that if they were going to spend their per diem allowance on items other than food, they should at least purchase authentic Aboriginal and Australian goods. Danny did take them on a tour of Aboriginal music and dance, but they really could not relate to it, and did not have much interest.

After this trip to Australia, Danny never again toured with high school students outside the state of Florida. He had several reasons. First, if the dancers are under eighteen years old, they are minors, and written permission from the parents is needed to take them across international lines. Second, the differing laws and customs had proved to be an issue during the Australian tour. After checking in at their hotel, Danny went to the lobby to meet everyone for dinner, and the students were all at the bar having drinks, because eighteen-year-olds can legally drink in Australia; even the seventeen-year-old students were being served drinks. Danny took their drinks away, and they had huge arguments, especially the eighteen-year-old students, who could legally drink in that country. They came to a compromise; Danny bought one margarita at each dinner, and everyone got one sip. Also, Danny warned them all that the traffic drives on the opposite side of the road in Australia, so when they crossed the street, they had to look to the right before looking left. The students had a very difficult time remembering this safety rule.[10]

Other opportunities were offered to NWSA dancers outside the school. Judy Drucker, south Florida impresario and founder of the Concert Association of Florida in 1967, called Danny to say that she was going to be producing an evening of solos performed by Mikhail Baryshnikov on February 27, 2004, and he needed two dancers to be in one of the works. Judy wanted Danny to recommend the two dancers. Danny sent two dancers over to the Olympia Theater at the Gusman Center for the Performing Arts for the rehearsals, Lindsey-Lee Jolly and Diana Diaz, college students at NWSA. That night, Danny went to see the performance. One of Baryshnikov's solos involved two chairs on wheels that rolled around the stage. The two dancers were wheeling around as well as walking in the space. When the work was over, Baryshnikov took both of the dancers by hand, and they all bowed together; Danny was amazed and proud to see his two young dancers from the college bowing side by side with such an incredible and prominent dancer as Baryshnikov.

Through His Friends' Eyes—Michael Uthoff

Michael Uthoff was a dancer with Joffrey Ballet, creator of the Hartford Ballet in 1972, and artistic director of Dance St. Louis.

Michael said, "I met Danny in 1962 at Juilliard. Eventually, I went to Arizona to start Ballet Arizona, which was successful for seven years; then in 1999, my world crumbled, and my company work ended. Danny was very important to my career. It is during times of crisis that you know who your real friends are. Danny called and invited me to come to NWSA to work, and this generosity revived my love of and investment in dance. Although many dancers have natural gifts, it is being in the right environment in an ongoing way that develops one as a dancer, and this is what I saw at NWSA. I worked quite a bit at NWSA, teaching ballet and creating work for the high school and college. I was impassioned by the way Danny brought world cultures from all over Miami into the school, and all these students were able to work together and befriend each other, which was inspiring to see. Danny and I created a semiprofessional dance company made up largely of NWSA students and took them to Arizona, where I was living, so they could perform as professionals.

Danny was very influential in my life in many ways, and I am eternally grateful. While in the professional field, Danny showed me an incredible paradigm of how to work, and it was Danny and NWSA that inspired me to eventually start a dance school. I developed the Spring to Dance Festival in St. Louis, Missouri, for small, independent dance groups, and to showcase undiscovered and existing talent, and Danny helped curate the event throughout the nine years that I ran the program. He was one of three consultants who reviewed applications to form the best program.

One of Danny's truly special qualities is that he surrounded himself with excellent professional people, not necessarily college graduates, who helped the students move from classroom to the stage. He also encouraged all the students to study classical dance and

---

10. After the Australia tour, Danny sent the students home with Pam, and he and Maureen flew to Taiwan. First they went to Taipei and visited Ping Heng, the director of Taipei National University of the Arts; she had danced in Cloud Gate and was a student of Danny's at NYU. They went to the mountain studio of Cloud Gate Dance Theater of Taiwan, directed by Lin Hwai-min, and watched rehearsals and a performance. After Taipei, they went to Kaohsiung to visit Su-Ling Chou, to visit her school, to teach master classes, and to talk about her students coming to NWSA. Danny also staged The Beethoven Sextet on the students.

many dance forms in order to expand their horizons and skills. Danny has perseverance, objectivity, caring for the dancers and their development, and a willingness and desire to be surrounded by great artists. His commitment is to the beauty, growth, and excellence of dance."

Another trip that Danny took with the NWSA ensemble was to the Czech Republic in 2010, where they performed Robert Battle's *Battlefield* at the New Prague Dance Festival. They won the two top prizes: (1) the Grand Prix, worth 1,000 Euros, and (2) the Special Prize of the Director. In the words of the director of the festival, "The unique crystal main prize New Prague Dance Festival GRAND PRIX is for the best group (with a financial gift of 1000 EUR), which shall be awarded by a jury consisting of members of the Academy of Music and Dramatic Arts, Faculty of Dance, Charles University, Czech Culture, National Theatre Ballet in Prague and international members (Stuttgart Ballet, Grand Ballet Genéve, Bolshoi Theatre Moscow, Kasay Dancing Company)." The jury that awarded the Grand Prix prize said that NWSA was the only group for whom the entire audience rose to their feet and gave an ovation. These awards were a tremendous honor to the dancers representing NWSA abroad.

Guest Artists

Part of Danny's vision in bringing guest artists to NWSA was the hope that after getting the chance to work with the NWSA dancers, the guests would eventually hire many of them. This indeed happened. There was one period of time between 1998 and 2000 in which a fourth of the Martha Graham Dance Company, two dancers in the José Limón Company, six dancers in the Alvin Ailey American Dance Theater, and a fourth of the Parsons Dance dancers were all NWSA graduates.

The following list shows some of the most prominent guest artists and choreographers who have taught, lectured, performed, or choreographed for the students at NWSA: Jack Anderson, Robert Battle, Fernando Bujones, Katherine Dunham, Gus Giordano, Martha Hill, Deborah Jowitt, Allegra Kent, Bill T. Jones, Eleanor King, Julia Levien, Carla Maxwell, Jim May, Donald McKayle, Mia Michaels, Elisa Monte, Jennifer Muller, Daniel Nagrin, Larry Rhodes, Marcia B. Siegel, Anna Sokolow, Paul Taylor, Michael Uthoff, Sylvia Waters, and Lila York. Over the years, Danny invited dozens of well-known artists and scholars to lecture, teach, and mount work at NWSA.[11]

---

11. Additional guest artists and lecturers at NWSA during Danny's tenure included Thomas Armour, Mary Barnett, Letty Bassart, Tandy Beal, Mariaz Benite, Janis Bremer, Michel Brisnakoff, Jacqulyn Buglisi, Nai-Ni Chen, Elisa Clark, Ze'eva Cohen, Alice Condodina, Roger Copeland, Mohamed Da Costa, Barbara Dilley, Foofwa d'Imobilité, Roxane D'Orleans Juste, George Dorris, Cynthia Dufault, Katherine Dunham, Eiko & Koma, Bill Evans, Rosa Mercedes Fleischer, Michael Foley, Maurice Fraga, Shunojo Fujima, Israel Gabriel, Jimmy Gamonet, Robert Garland, Laura Glenn, Eric Bli Bi Gore, Mark Haim, Francie Huber, Ben Isaacs, Andrew Janbek, Hannah Kahn, Beatrize Kobme, Donna Krasnow, Gelan Lambert, Heather Ann Maloney, Susan Marshall, Sophie Maslow, Donald McDonagh, John McFall, Rosa Mercedes, Rick Michalek, Bebe Miller, Celeste Miller, Clyde Morgan, Jennifer Muller, Banu Ogan, Susan Olson, Joe Orlando, Stuart Pimsler, Troy Powell, Peter Pucci, Renee Rich, Jeanne Ruddy, Diego Salterini, Uri Sands, Rosita Segovia, Fujima Shunojo, Lynn Simonson, Stephanie Skura, Augusto Soledade, Sally Sommers, Sarah Stackhouse, Risa Steinberg, Elizabeth Streb, Elaine Summers, Robert Swinston, Abou Sylla, Menaka Thakkar, Marni Thomas Wood, Kevin Thompson, Nancy Topf, Talani Torres, Elizabeth Walton, Gretchen Ward-Warren, Randy Warshaw, Teri Weksler, Dudley Williams, Reginald Wilson, Ethel Winter, Ellis Wood, Reginald Yates, Bill Young, and Zig Zag Ballet.

Daniel Lewis (left) with Donald McKayle, when he came to New World School of the Arts to stage *Rainbow Round My Shoulder*, 2005 (courtesy Daniel Lewis archives).

In November 1990, Danny invited Martha Hill to visit NWSA to show her the school and get her opinion about the curriculum and how it was all working. On the first day, he gave her a full tour of the building, and then they sat down in Danny's office, where he asked her what she thought. She said, "Danny, you know best; do whatever you want to do. You're going to do a terrific job." During this visit, she gave a lecture to the students about the early days of modern dance. She also talked about how large and open the spaces in Miami were, compared to New York schools and studios.

In 1992, Danny wanted to bring Katherine Dunham to Miami, and she agreed to come because of the large Haitian population in the city. Earlier that year, Jean-Bertrand Aristide had been deposed as leader of Haiti after a military coup. While in St. Louis where she lived, Katherine Dunham (age 82 at the time) went on a fast to protest the United States' sending of Haitian refugees back to Haiti. When her plane arrived in Miami, they held a press conference because so many of the press were there to meet her. Her contract stated that in addition to teaching classes and lecturing at NWSA, she wanted time to rent a stadium. She did so, and 50,000 Haitians showed up to hear her speak. Dunham was an amazing artist but also a strong political activist. She was, however, quite demanding and had to have an entire hotel suite for her entourage: her assistant, two of her children, a chauffeur, and more. Her room also had to be wheel-chair accessible, because she was still quite weak from the hunger strike. When Danny went to the hotel one day, there was a huge line of people waiting to meet her as she lay in her bed. She had crystals all around her on the bed, for healing, and she was ba-sically holding court. To the NWSA dancers, she described what it was like to perform in Miami many years ago, when she had to use the hotel's service entrance because she was black.

In 2006–2007, Danny brought Darshan Singh Bhuller to NWSA. Darshan had danced in London Contemporary Dance Theatre, which was directed by Darshan's friend and associate Robert Cohan. Darshan had been a student of Danny's at Lon-don Contemporary Dance School. Danny invited Darshan to choreograph at NWSA because he worked with technology, which Danny was starting to introduce into the school. At that time, Peter London was staging *Diversion of Angels* (choreographed by Martha Graham in 1948) at NWSA. Darshan invited Robert Cohan, who had danced in the original version of the work, to see a rehearsal. Robert talked about Martha Graham's images and explained the reason for all of the tilts in the dance, saying that love is in a precarious balance.

NWSA Graduates

Thirty years after the school's inception, NWSA graduates were a major presence in dance, theater, visual arts, and musical theater. This was particularly apparent to Danny during a November 2010 visit to New York City. Danny was there for a site visit for the National Association of Schools of Dance (NASD) of Ballet Hispanico, and he went to a performance of Garth Fagan's Company at the Joyce Theater. In the company were both Juilliard and NWSA graduates who Danny knew, including a dancer named Vitolio Jeune. Vitolio had come to NWSA from Haiti, and his teacher in Haiti had been paying his way through college. When the political climate in Haiti changed with the over-throw of Jean-Bertrand Aristide's government, the money dried up. Eventually NWSA got him some scholarship funding. Then, Garth Fagan came to NWSA to set the work "From Before" and was very impressed by Vitolio's dancing. Garth agreed to help pay his accommodations for a short period of time during his education. In his senior year, Vitolio was accepted into the *So You Think You Can Dance* television competition, and eventually danced in Fagan's company.

Danny went to the Fagan rehearsal with Vincas Greene, founding director of Vytal Movement Dance Company in Spokane, Washington, since they were doing the site visit of Ballet Hispanico together. He stopped by his old apartment to show it to Vin-cas. Danny then received a phone call from Edgar David Grana, who told him that the film of Danny's work *Moments* was going to be projected on the side wall of a building around the corner from 34th Street. Danny walked up to 34th Street and watched the film with Edgar and Laura Glenn. He then walked up through the Broadway district to see the marquees of all the Broadway shows, many of which featured dancers who were NWSA graduates, such as Nina Lafarga in *In the Heights*. *In the Heights* had musical arrangement by Alex Lacamoire, a NWSA music division graduate who did musical

(From left) Daniel Lewis, Natalie Rogers, and Garth Fagan, when they staged Fagan's choreography *From Before* at New World School of the Arts, 2008 (courtesy Daniel Lewis archives).

arrangement for *Hamilton*. Several other Broadway shows, including *Lion King*, also had NWSA graduates.[12]

Danny then went up to 96th Street to Ballet Hispanico. The founding artistic director, Tina Ramirez, was a longtime friend of Danny's, and she was there through the whole site visit. The woman who met with them and was to take them through the tour was a NWSA graduate, and three of the dancers were from NWSA. Through the years, there have been NWSA graduates in the company and as part of the administration, and Melissa Fernandez from NWSA is still dancing with the company. Johan Rivera, a NWSA graduate, later became the associate artistic director.

Reviews and Articles

In the very beginning of the school's operation, NWSA received a lot of press. A preview feature article called "Spotlight on the Deans" was published November 3, 1987, in the *Miami Herald*. This article was about the original four deans: Danny (dance), John de Lancie (music), Ed Love (visual arts), and Richard Janaro (theater).[13]

---

12. NWSA graduates have also achieved success in other areas of arts and entertainment. For example, NWSA theater graduate Tarell Alvin McCraney wrote the film Moonlight, which won the Oscar for best film in 2017.

13. Richard Janaro and Thelma Altschuler wrote the first edition of the humanities textbook The Art of Being Human in 1979, and it is still widely used today.

These four deans remained for varying periods of time. Janaro was acting theater dean for one year and then was replaced by Jorge Guerra-Castro. Love was a dean through 1990, de Lancie through 1992, and Danny through 2011.

An article in the *New York Times* education section from December 7, 1988, was written by George Volsky just after the school had opened. Both Volsky and his wife were Miami residents for many years. The article was called "A School for Arts Matures in Miami" and had a picture of the four deans, plus Richard Klein (the provost). Because the *New York Times* is read nationally, NWSA began getting calls from all over the country.

For a while in Miami, Owen Goldman had a newspaper called Dancer, and it included cartoon images. The October 1990 issue featured the cartoon shown here.

The illustration was by Fernando Daza Osorio, a well-known artist from Santiago, Chile. His sons Raniero Daza and Ulysses Daza attended NWSA as dance majors, and Raniero graduated in 1992. Raniero did a lot of the graphics work for the dance program at NWSA, such as designing the first NWSA dance logo. This dance logo was used on all of the internal documents; on external documents they were required to use the official NWSA logo in addition to the dance logo.

Laurie Horn was an important and influential dance critic in Miami and often wrote about NWSA. In 1991, Horn wrote a review in the *Miami Herald* titled "Thank New World School for a Dance Transformation." She talked about what was happening to the Miami modern dance scene due to NWSA. She specifically mentioned NWSA dancers David Hernandez, Mary Spring, Gabrielle Malone, Gisela Genschow,

Illustration by the late artist Fernando Daza Osorio, published in a Miami newspaper called *Dancer*, October 1990 (courtesy Raniero Daza).

DANCER - OCTOBER, 1990 - PAGE 15

NOS DICE DANNY LEWIS NUESTRO DECANO DEL DEPARTAMENTO DE DANZA DEL NEW WORLD SCHOL OF THE ARTS: "SER BAILARIN.(BAILARINA) ES DIFICIL. SE DEBE TRABAJAR POR AÑOS EN SU PROPIO FISICO CUAL SI FUERA UN INSTRUMENTO PERFECTIBLE.
SE REQUIERE DE UNA ILIMITADA DEDICACION PARA QUE ESTE INSTRUMENTO LOGRE SU OBJETIVO QUE ES LA PERFECCION.
YO BAILE DURANTE 25 AÑOS Y CONOZCO, AMO Y RESPETO ESTA BELLA Y BRUTAL EXIGENCIA.

Danny Lewis, our Dean of the Dance Department of the New World School of the Arts, tells us:
"To be a dancer is difficult. One must work on his own physique for years as if it were a perfectionable instrument.
"It requires an unlimited dedication for this instrument to reach its objective of perfection.
"I danced for 25 years and I know, love and respect this fine and brutal requirement."

and Victoria Fernandez, who were dancing in the companies Mary Street Dance Theater, David Hernandez and Dancers, Ballet Randolph, Jane Carrington Dance, Freddick Bratcher, NWSA Dance Ensemble, and Houlihan and Dancers. In her words, "The common denominator here is New World's dance department, under the direction of Danny Lewis. The school's conservatory program is transforming modern dance in Miami into a 'look-at-me' art form. In particular, these dancers are showing Miami audiences that modern dance does *not* mean lumpy, half-trained people emoting ineptly, relying on facial expression instead of the body." At this point in time, the *Miami Herald* had a policy of not reviewing colleges in any of the performing arts areas. However, they did review NWSA because the *Miami Herald* saw it as a professional training school, and Laurie Horn fought for their inclusion in the paper, as did David Lawrence, the publisher of the paper. The *Miami Herald* won five Pulitzer prizes under Lawrence's leadership, and he later became president of the executive board of NWSA.[14]

Valerie Gladstone wrote an extended article about NWSA for the December 1993 issue of *Dance Magazine*, called "Dean of New World Dance." Given that this was *Dance Magazine*, this recognition was significant. The article states that Floridian dancers no longer needed to go north for professional training in dance, theater, music, and visual arts, noting that NWSA had achieved national acclaim in just six years. The article credited Danny's imaginative leadership as a contributing factor, stating that no area of dance was foreign to him, from teaching at Juilliard to heading the Limón Company to writing a book on the Limón technique. In the interview, Danny was quoted as saying, "Miami is a gateway to Europe, South America, and the Caribbean, and the community reflects that cultural diversity…. Our enrollment is about the same mix." Danny spoke of his pride in his staff: six full-time faculty members (Gerri Houlihan, Judith Newman, Rosita Segovia, Jane Carrington, Freddick Bratcher, and Andrea Seidel) plus 19 part-time faculty members. Additionally, he brought in as many visiting choreographers as he could afford. Danny spoke of his emphasis on injury prevention, with a full-time massage therapist and courses in Pilates. Performance, Danny stated, is at the heart of the curriculum. The article mentioned that in the previous year, *Redbook* magazine had named NWSA the nation's best arts high school.

The *Miami Herald* did a spread about NWSA for both the tenth anniversary and the twenty-fifth anniversary. The article on the tenth anniversary was published March 23, 1997, and it was called "New World Dean at Center of South Florida's Thriving Dance Scene," with the subtitle "Danny Lewis Has Built a Reputation as Well as a Community Spirit." The article was written by Jordan Levin, and it began by describing how incredibly busy a typical day in Danny's office was: visits and phone calls from a visiting dance teacher from Spain; a Canadian choreographer seeking grant-writing advice; visiting teacher Sophie Maslow (former dancer and choreographer), picking up her teaching itinerary; and Cuban ballerina Rosario Suarez, stopping by with flyers about her upcoming auditions. Levin stated, "In the 10 years since he started as dean of New World's brand new dance department, Lewis has expanded his realm from one studio, two teachers and fewer than 40 students to a nationally known school that places students in companies all over the country, including Alvin Ailey American Dance Theater,

---

14. Lawrence retired in 1999. The new publisher, Alberto Ibargüen, had been on the board of the Merce Cunningham Dance Company, so the newspaper continued to have an interest in Miami's up-and-coming dancers. After Laurie Horn died in 2002, Jordan Levin took over Laurie Horn's job as dance critic. Eventually they stopped reviewing college dance altogether.

Baryshnikov's White Oak Dance Project, and Twyla Tharp." The article included praise for the NWSA training from Benjamin Harkavy, Juilliard's dance director, and Denise Jefferson, director of the Alvin Ailey school. Levin went on to talk about the curriculum, and she described the numerous concerts, opportunities to choreograph for both faculty and students, as well as the annual concerts Danny produced for local choreographers through Miami Dance Futures. The article ended with Danny's words: "'The next generation is going to make a difference here, not what's going on now,' Lewis says. He believes wholeheartedly in these young dancers, and in Miami. 'They're coming to me and saying [that] they don't want to leave. They see a future here. They have visions. And hopefully they're taking whatever I'm giving them and taking that next step.'"

Another article published February 1, 2001, in the *Miami Herald* called "And the Dance Goes On" addressed the issue of NWSA facing major funding cuts. From the first days at NWSA, every year was a struggle to ensure that they had the needed funding. State funding was cut or reduced each year, often due to internal politics. Because NWSA was not a line item in the state budget, every year they had to fight to get money. The funding came from discretionary funds and never had its own definite place in the budget. Whenever the state budget had to be reduced, the first funds to go were the discretionary funds. The worst year was 2001. The legislature recommended an intermediate cut of $482,000, which was a significant reduction in total funding for NWSA for classes, instruction, and programming, all in the arts area. The school was very expensive to run, and people outside the school complained about the amount of money that was going to NWSA. This severe cut coincided with the arrival of Stephen Sumner as the new provost. Danny really liked Sumner as a provost, and Sumner really loved the dance division, but he couldn't deal with the politics and all of the difficult meetings. When he left after two years, Danny continued sending him flyers of all the NWSA dance performances. Sumner would always write back, "You're killing me!"

The February issue of *Dance Teacher* in 2011 covered Danny in a full article by Guillermo Perez called "Daniel Lewis: Innovator." The article began with Danny's history and how he ended up at NWSA. This article again emphasized Danny's vision in developing students who would be proficient across a broad spectrum of dance, a novel idea at the time. Another one of his ideas was to foster artistic expression in a range of body types, "tearing down the clichés about what a dancer looks like." At the end of the article, Danny stated, "I'm now on a personal crusade to put dance in every school K through 12."

In the May issue of 2011, *Dance Magazine* published the article "Moving On, but Still Moving" by Guillermo Perez. In Danny's words, "Kids in this generation are amazingly attuned to new media, and colleges have to be up on this to meet their changing needs." Tina Santos-Wahl, one of the ballet faculty members at NWSA, commented on her appreciation of how Danny upheld tradition while championing the latest digital media in dance education and production. The article focused on Danny's plans to keep working after his retirement from NWSA. Danny said, "I'm proud of leaving something really good behind in New World: a strong foundation for students that's well-respected and recognized. We—and I prefer using the plural given the remarkable efforts of my faculty—have made a lasting mark.... Creativity is what makes us different from other animals."

10

Other Facets of Danny's Life During the NWSA Years

In following my own dreams and paths, I discovered interests and talents in surprising areas. My long-time love of technology blossomed during these years and brought together other like-minded dance artists. This time also ushered in a period of receiving many awards and accolades, and in my acceptance speeches, I never failed to mention how lucky my life has been. As I say to my dancers, dreams are inspirational and wonderful, but make sure to waver from those dreams to go in the direction that life takes you.—Danny Lewis

Miami Dance Futures

Miami Dance Futures (MDF) produced and supported local dance companies, including Rosita Segovia's Ballet Español, Gerri Houlihan & Dancers, and the Isadora Dance Ensemble. MDF produced the annual Miami Dance Sampler, a showcase of local choreographers' work, which continues to this day as the Daniel Lewis Miami Dance Sampler, now produced jointly by the Florida Dance Education Organization (FDEO), NWSA, and Dance NOW! Miami. MDF also produced the Florida Dance Series and the Independent Dance Series from 1988 to 1999. Additionally, Danny was involved in several major community events, including those organized by Community Concerts and the Caribbean Dance Celebrations organized by Jamaica Awareness.

Through His Friends' Eyes—Gerri Houlihan

Gerri Houlihan was a former dean of American Dance Festival and a dancer with Lar Lubovitch. She made the following comments about Danny: "I met Danny in 1962 as a student with him at Juilliard; at first, I was intimidated, because he was so sophisticated and knowledgeable about dance. At the time, he was already doing Limón works, and he was passionate and poetic but also quite macho. After Juilliard, we went our separate ways, until 1987, when I saw an article about the development of NWSA. I called Danny and came to Miami to see what was happening. I got a tour of Bayside in Miami, saw the first two studios at NWSA, and watched dance classes. In 1988, I joined the faculty. When I first started at NWSA, I did all my clothing changes and warm-ups in a shared office, which horrified the secretary. When I started choreo-

191

graphing on the students, Danny convinced me that I should have my own company;
therefore, Houlihan & Dancers was Danny's idea. Danny handled the administrative
end of the company for me, and his support, vision, and confidence in my ability, ex-
pertise, and commitment made it possible. This was an eight-year investment that was
extraordinary for me."

Caribbean Dance Celebrations

The Caribbean Dance Celebrations began in 1999, and they go on to this day. These were impressive events, celebrating the dances of the African diaspora. MDF was one of the sponsors of the Caribbean Dance Celebration, and other sponsors including Metro-Dade Cultural Affairs and Florida Arts Council. The 2000 celebration, presented by Jamaica Awareness, took place at the Olympia Theater at the Gusman Center for the Performing Arts. In attendance were Sydney S. Roberts and Jan Mapou, the classic Haitian dance authority in Miami and the director of Sosyete Koukouy Miami, Inc. Others who attended in 2000 were Rex Nettleford (a well-known Jamaican scholar and choreographer), Harambee Dance Ensemble (a music and dance educational group that specialized in dances of the African diaspora), National Dance Theatre Company of Jamaica, Artcho Danse Repertoire (Haiti's premiere dance company), Sosyete Koukouy (a multidisciplinary folk art organization that focused on establishing Creole as the national language of Haiti), and Yvonne Jones Houston (the artistic director of Harambee Dance Ensemble and Danny's first secretary).

In 2002, the fourth annual celebration was organized by Sosyete Koukouy and Jamaica Awareness, Inc., and was sponsored in part by MDF. There were performances by the National Dance Theatre Company of Jamaica, the National Dance Theater of Trinidad and Tobago, Sosyete Koukouy (Haiti), the Ugundani Dance Company (Belize), and the Caribbean Performing Arts Company (Miami). Performances took place on April 6 and 7 at the North Miami Beach Performing Arts Center and on April 7 at the Coral Springs Civic Center. The president of Jamaica Awareness, Inc., was Sydney Roberts, and he was a good friend of Rex Nettleford. Sydney took Danny and Maureen to Jamaica, and they were at Bob Marley's estate for his birthday party, given by his wife after Marley had passed away. The entire party was filled with smoke from all the marijuana being smoked, and the music was fabulous. The Caribbean Dance Celebration continues to have events and is now called the Miami Broward One Carnival.

Miami Dance Samplers

When Danny arrived in Miami, modern dance was not very well known there. The few local modern dance companies were doing very "traditional" modern, and the local community only related well to ballet and jazz. The city was seeking innovative modern dance. In November 1995, MDF presented A Modern Dance Sampler at NWSA, and this series would later become the Miami Dance Sampler. It had works by Jane Goldberg (tap dance), Delma Iles, Dale Andree, Karen Peterson, Mia Michaels, Gina Buntz, Houlihan & Dancers, and Isadora Duncan. Mia Michaels had been a student at PAVAC years before, and Danny brought her several times to NWSA to choreograph. The Miami Dance Sampler series was produced each year by MDF, and it became an important event in Miami, showcasing local choreographers and companies,[1] and performing for sold-out houses. With the Miami Dance Sampler, the company fees were based on the number of dancers and choreographers.

After Danny retired, the Miami Dance Sampler was renamed the Daniel Lewis Miami Dance Sampler, by Dance NOW! Miami. The mission of Dance NOW! Miami is to promote the artistic vision of cofounders Hannah Baumgarten and Diego Salterini. The company creates, promotes, and produces contemporary dance of the highest caliber; the organization nurtures new talents, fosters artistic collaborations, and makes the art of dance accessible to diverse audiences locally, nationally, and internationally. The first performance with the new name of Daniel Lewis Miami Dance Sampler was in 2012, and it was presented by Dance NOW! Miami, the Florida Dance Association, and the Little Haiti Cultural Center. The event featured Carolyn Dorfman (guest choreographer), Brigid Baker WholeProject (located in little Havana), Arts Ballet Theatre (choreography by Vladimir Issaev), Karen Peterson and Dancers, Lara Murphy, Dance NOW! Miami (choreography by Hannah Baumgarten), Pioneer Winter (known for site-specific and mixed-abilities work), and NWSA graduates Afua Hall and Luis Alberto Cuevas.

Companies Produced by MDF and NWSA

Danny was committed to supporting developing dance artists and new companies in the Miami area. There were many of these companies over the years, and a large number of reviews were written about the companies that MDF produced and supported. Only a few will be highlighted.

One important company that MDF worked with over many years was the Isadora Dance Ensemble, directed by NWSA/FIU faculty member Andrea Seidel. She used many dancers from the NWSA high school. MDF produced them and sent them on a tour to Russia and to the Kennedy Center in Washington, D.C. One of the people who worked with the ensemble was Julia Levien, founder and artistic director of the Isadora Duncan Commemorative Dance Company. Hence, Danny was quite immersed in Duncan history and works during his tenure at NWSA. Danny found it so joyous to see these young teenagers dancing the work of Isadora in the way it was originally done, with a complete freedom of movement. Julia had danced with Isadora, and both she and Andrea were very particular that the work be authentically reproduced. The teens captured it brilliantly.

Through His Friends' Eyes—Andrea Mantell Seidel

Andrea Mantell Seidel is the artistic director of the Isadora Duncan Dance Ensemble, and she was Eleanor King's primary protégé for over sixteen years, serving as trustee of King's choreographic legacy. In 1990, Andrea took a full-time joint position with FIU and NWSA for four years, then moved full time to FIU. Andrea commented, "As I came

---

1. Example programs include the following: In the 1997 Miami Dance Sampler, the performers were Rosa Mercedes (dancer with Rosita Segovia), Esaias Johnson (hip-hop and contemporary dancer), Tamara Welch (NWSA graduate), Karen Peterson, Peter London, Ivonice Satie, Spencer Snyder, and Houlihan & Dancers. Donna Krasnow, performing in Montréal choreographer Motaz Kabbani's With-In-finity, and Peter London performed in the sampler in 1998. The 2000 event had works by Heather Maloney and featured Roberto Dias' group, Brazarte Dance Company; Ada Linares' group, Dance Mediterraneo; Cynthia Dufault; Gerard Ebitz; Michael Foley; Peter London; Momentum Dance Company; Karen Peterson Dance Company; and Rosario Suarez.

to know Danny, I realized that he was one of the most generous and supportive people I had ever known. When I formed the Isadora Duncan Dance Ensemble, he gave me studio space for rehearsals and made the ensemble a company in residence. He was incredibly giving and unselfish. When Hurricane Andrew hit Miami in 1992, I was in Homestead, Florida, which was hit very hard, so I had to move to a temporary place. Danny found out about it and drove out to bring batteries, supplies, and food. He jumped in more than any other friend. I was truly moved by his generosity and caring.

One of the great stories of my relationship with Danny occurred when the Isadora Duncan Dance Ensemble was performing at the Kennedy Center in Washington, D.C., on January 5 and 6, 1996. Danny decided to fly there for one performance and return home on the red-eye that night. When we left the theater, there was a terrible blizzard, and all the planes were grounded. We were snowed in for four days, with waist-high snow drifts, and Danny could not get out of Washington, D.C. He didn't have his laptop with him or any technology, which was unusual, but he had been expecting to be away from Miami for only a day. He did have his cell phone, but the charger was in Miami, and the phone was dead by the second day. Danny went into technology withdrawal! The hotel ran out of food, and the ensemble was running out of money. With me were ten dancers and Julia Levien, the company's mentor, who was over eighty years old at the time. We initially had double rooms, but we started putting four people into each room as the hotel bill was becoming too expensive. As Danny tells the story, they were threatening to put him in a room with Julia. He was pacing because he had no technology, and he was smoking like crazy. This was a real adventure for Danny.

I served on the board of MDF, and Danny was on the board of Dancearts Foundation, my nonprofit organization. The Isadora Duncan Dance Ensemble lasted about fifteen years, and the dancers referred to Danny as their benevolent godfather. In addition to his generosity, Danny was a great networker and politician, and he had the wisdom to know how not to alienate people who might help him at some point. He could deal with administration really well, and he knew how to get money and handle the budget. There were some old, cranky modern dancers in Miami, and Danny was inclusive and made them feel welcome. He had a sense of outreach and both local and international contacts."

In addition to her contribution to NWSA, Gerri Houlihan was a very skilled choreographer, and she brought a new kind of modern dance to Miami. It actually challenged the rest of the dance community in Miami to start creating new and innovative work. She was very popular with audiences and with the dancers, who loved working with her, and she received excellent reviews. This was why Danny encouraged her to start her company Houlihan & Dancers, and it made quite a difference in Miami. Because Gerri was so popular, Danny would pair her company with another dance group, and MDF could then produce them at the Olympia Theater at the Gusman Center for the Performing Arts and fill this very large venue. One of Gerri's dancers was Bill Doolin, who became the Florida Dance Association's interim director in 2007. An article in 1998 by Jordan Levin described a performance of a work by Gerri Houlihan, with eighteen dancers: Prior to the indoor concert, they did an outdoor performance of *Road Work* on Lincoln Road Mall, a major tourist attraction.[2] The company was significant in Miami because it was one of the few companies that was paying modern dancers. (Delma Iles

---

2. The performance was produced by Sheldon Schwartz, who was the director of the Florida Dance Association and the Florida Dance Festival. Schwartz had danced in Irving the Terrific at Juilliard.

was also paying modern dancers in her company Momentum Dance Company.) Over the years, MDF produced Houlihan & Dancers numerous times.

Through His Friends' Eyes—Gerri Houlihan

Gerri Houlihan said, "Miami Dance Futures blossomed during the early NWSA years. From MDF came amazing collaborations between Rosita Segovia Ballet Español, Isadora Duncan Dance Ensemble, and Houlihan & Dancers. During all this time, Danny's advice and knowledge were invaluable. Danny gave so many people encouragement and support, something he learned from his mentor Martha Hill, who always liked the oddballs and creative ones at auditions. Danny was amazingly loyal to everyone he worked with throughout the years. He always saw the possibilities of talent, desire, and passion in someone, and he would be steadfast in investing in that person."

When Danny and MDF produced Rosita Segovia's Ballet Español, she was very popular, dancing many forms of Spanish dance. For her 1993 concert, she had guest choreographer and dancer Paco Romero (who had his own company in Madrid) and dancers Rosa Mercedes, Cristina Masdueño (an NWSA graduate), José Junco, Maria Jesus Vallve, and Ada Linares (another NWSA graduate), plus the corps de ballet and the musicians. Paco Romero had begun dancing in Madrid at a young age, and he danced with the famous Spanish dancer Antonio, who developed his own technique, called *Antoniano*. Paco danced with Ballet Nacional for many years, and he toured as a guest artist internationally. Segovia's company performed at the Olympia Theater at the Gusman Center for the Performing Arts, and it had support from the Miami-Dade County Department of Cultural Affairs Council, the State of Florida Cultural Affairs Council, the National Endowment for the Arts, and the Tourist Office of Spain. These were sold-out performances. The shows were informal collaborations with Maribel Zubieta Diaz, director of the Conchita Espinosa Academy, who was also on the board of the Florida Dance Association. Her daughter Carol Diaz-Zubieta is the upper school principal, and her daughter Anna Diaz-Zubieta, who graduated from NWSA high school in 1989, is a licensed psychologist at the school. The philosophy of the school, which is K–8, is that the arts should be as strongly supported as academics, and every child should have an arts education. This is a full academic program with an arts academy as part of it. Rosita Segovia used to teach at this school, and Danny also hired her at NWSA. She had begun her training in Barcelona, and she became prima ballerina at the prestigious Liceo de la Opera de Barcelona and later at Ballets de Barcelona. She is a dual citizen of the United States and Spain. Rosita was very important to NWSA and MDF, and Danny produced her company for many years.

Karen Peterson and Dancers in Miami is a mixed-ability company, and Marjorie Burnett, one of her participants, went to FIU to get her degree because she could get a dance degree there doing solely dance academics. A founding member of Karen's company, she is wheelchair bound due to cerebral palsy. They have performed very touching works in the Miami Dance Samplers. Danny was a big supporter of performers with disabilities, and he was always happy to produce companies with dancers who had disabilities. He once gave a talk at the National Association of Schools of Dance (NASD) on the topic of the aesthetic of the body. Danny began by saying that it was not the great technical bodies who were his favorite dancers but rather those who danced with feeling. He showed a film of Marjorie and another dancer doing a duet on a pillow, and some of the audience began to dispute that it was good dance. The one person at the talk who defended Danny's definition of extraordinary dance was John Wilson from the University of Arizona, who said that their duet was some of the best rolling on the floor he had ever seen!

Dennis Edwards and Mark Steinberg were involved in the development of Maximum Dance Company, and Danny and MDF acted as the fiscal agent for the newly formed company. Danny convinced Dennis Edwards to be on the NWSA Foundation board, and Dennis revitalized the foundation into a totally organized group that raised major funds.

In 1995, Danny and MDF hosted the Florida Project, along with Community Concerts. Community Concerts brought in national level companies over a period of several years. In 1996, the series produced Mark Morris Dance Group, Isadora Duncan Dance Ensemble, Bill T. Jones/Arnie Zane, Eiko and Komo, Brno Chamber Orchestra (with Michiko Otaki on piano), Iceland Symphony, and Dance Theatre of Harlem. Danny went to see the Mark Morris Dance Group show, and he met a Japanese woman named Agnes Takako Youngblood, who was the president of the Friends of the Japanese Garden and the executive director of Community Concerts. She and Danny decided to work collaboratively to produce dance groups. Danny firmly believed that collaboration was the key to making things happen, and they worked wonderfully together since they had a similar vision of enhancing the arts in Miami. They ended up producing many dance performances together. In 1996, Community Concerts, NWSA, and MDF presented Menaka Thakkar, a classical Indian dancer, when she came to Miami to perform and mount work at NWSA, supported by a grant from the Canadian government. The work was based on Indian dance and American modern dance. (This is the same time that she performed in the Miami Dance Sampler.) Her musicians flew in from India to do these performances. In September 1998, Taipei Crossover Dance Company came to Miami, produced by Community Concerts and MDF, and performed at the Colony Theater. Crossover is an extraordinary company of mature dancers who have retired from Cloud Gate Dance Theatre of Taiwan but wish to continue their performing careers as they enter their late thirties, forties, and fifties. The company paid their way to the United States with a grant from the Taiwanese government, so MDF only had to cover production costs. The performance was very successful.

Rosie Herrera, a NWSA graduate, started a dance company in Miami, and her work was very unique. She was part of Danny's vision to develop a dance signature unique to Miami. Her company became very popular, touring and going to ADF each year. Rosie also studied opera, and Danny used her as a singer in two of his technology-based productions. She truly found her own choreographic voice. In 2017, the Limón Company commissioned a duet choreographed by her.

In November 1994, Miami Dade College brought H.T. Chen & Dancers to NWSA to perform, and Danny added a lecture and master classes at NWSA. The dance company was directed by H.T. Chen, married to Dian Dong, both of whom were Danny's students at Juilliard.

From 2000 on, Danny produced an African dance celebration each year. He wanted a balance to the annual *Nutcracker* performance. The African work was performed quite a bit, in black history month, and at both NWSA and UF. This work was spearheaded by Joan Frosh, an African dance and music historian and professor at UF.

After Hurricane Andrew, the Miami-Dade County Department of Cultural Affairs applied for funds from the state of Florida to help arts groups (including dance companies) that had lost money due to the hurricane, such as revenue from canceled performances. This endeavor, called Hurricane Andrew Recovery, was spearheaded by Michael Spring. Spring was the director at Miami-Dade County Department of Cultural Affairs, responsible for supervision of a public arts agency with an annual budget of more than $30 million. MDF was able to document their losses and thus received $25,000 from the Hurricane Andrew Recovery funds.

Spring later served as senior advisor for the county's Cultural Affairs and Recreation portfolio, including the arts, parks, and libraries. Spring served on numerous cultural and civic organizations, and he worked to pass a referendum for the Building Better Communities bond program in 2004. In 2007, he led Miami-Dade County's Outstanding Art in Public Places program, and in 2011 the department opened the Arquitectonica–designed South Miami-Dade Cultural Arts Center in Cutler Bay. In that same year, he assumed responsibility for three cultural facilities: Miami-Dade County Auditorium, Caleb Auditorium, and African Heritage Cultural Arts Center. Over the almost thirty years that he served the Department of Cultural Affairs, Michael Spring helped build Miami-Dade County's cultural community into a $1 billion annual industry made up of more than 1,000 nonprofit cultural groups and thousands of artists. Spring made a huge difference to the arts in Miami, and he was very supportive of dance. The department even paid critics to write dance reviews during the time the local papers would not do reviews of local dance companies.

MDF, along with the support of the Florida Dance Festivals and the Miami Dance Samplers, gave modern dance companies a chance to show what they had to offer. It also gave them a chance to bring together different audiences to see all of the work.

Florida Dance Association and Florida Dance Festival

Danny was president of the Florida Dance Association (FDA) for three terms, beginning in 1987, and also served as the treasurer. Nancy Smith Fichter had started the Florida Dance Association, which was housed in Tallahassee. The FDA mission statement says, "Florida Dance Association, a private nonprofit organization established in 1972, was incorporated in 1974 to serve and support the development of dance in Florida. Our mission is to encourage excellence, support artistic and cultural diversity in dance, and increase opportunities for all people to experience dance and the arts." The association supports festivals, workshops, and teacher training programs throughout Florida. FDA programs include the Florida Dance Festival, young dancer workshops, information referral and technical assistance, the Florida Dance Festival Scholarship Fund, teacher trainings, and publications.

When Danny arrived, Rebecca Terrell was the executive director, Thomas Thielen was the associate director, and John Cano was the director of membership services. Every year they would hold the Florida Dance Festivals in Tampa, which have gone on for at least twenty-five years. They also produced an excellent directory of everyone involved in dance in Florida. Danny was immediately asked to be on the board of directors. Along with Phyllis Penny, chair of dance at Douglas Anderson School of the Arts in Jacksonville, he was one of the longest serving board members. Rebecca had a dream of moving FDA from Tallahassee to Miami, and they moved into a beautiful building at the beach, with plans for the concerts to be held at the Colony Theater. One day Danny got a call from Rebecca, saying that they were going bankrupt. MDF helped bail them out, and they asked everyone to teach for no fee at the summer program that year, which everyone agreed to do. They managed to get FDA back on its feet. FDA moved out of the expensive rental on the beach into a downtown space that the city provided for free. Rebecca decided to leave, and they did a search for a new executive director. Sheldon Schwartz, who was the head of dance at the Kennedy Center, applied and was offered the position. He accepted the position and did impressive work with FDA. At one point, he complained to Danny that he had been misled into thinking there was financial support. At this point, Sheldon left the position. Tom Thielen applied, and they gave him the job. Unfortunately, Tom made some poor financial choices in his attempts to keep the organization afloat, and he did not pay the payroll taxes for a year. Next, Bill Doolin,[3] who had danced with Gerri Houlihan, took the executive director position. This also did not go well, because he became ill. At this point, Danny called Cindy Hennessy from Tampa, who was on the board, to see if she would take the position. MDF spent thousands of dollars getting FDA out of debt and paying back taxes, and MDF paid an accountant to clear up the books. The IRS made them pay every dime of taxes and penalties, which took a few years. Some dance companies who were owed money forgave the debts to help out. Eventually, FDA was healthy and functional again.

The Florida Dance Association moved to Miami and then Miami Beach, and FDA produced the Florida Dance Festival for several years. Danny was president of the board, starting in 1987. The goal of the festival was to present a wide diversity of dance at a high level. Its first concert series in Miami was held at the Colony Theater in 1998, and it included New York City Ballet, Mauricio Wainrot, Daniel Ezralow, Art Bridgman and Myrna Packer, Houlihan & Dancers, Rosario Suarez with Caridad Martinez, Koresh Dance Company, Voloshky Ukrainian Folk Dance Ensemble, Maximum Dance Company, and many more.

Conference Presentations

In 1990, Danny received a phone call from Jenny Coogan, one of his Juilliard graduates. The organizers of a conference in Germany had asked Martha Hill to come to the conference. Martha did not want to go, but she recommended Danny, so they called him in Miami. Danny gave a speech at the conference, called Symposion München (Munich), and the speech was transcribed into an article called "Dance Education in the USA, K–12," published in *Tanzund Gymnastik*. The article discussed the development of dance education in the school system in the United States. At a performance at the conference, Danny got to see the expressionist dance performed by major German artists that the Germans choreographed decades ago.

The March 1998 issue of *Medical Problems of Performing Artists*, Volume 13(1), published Danny's article "A Case Study: Dancing with a Prosthesis," based on a talk he gave at the fifteenth Annual Symposium on the Medical Problems of Musicians and Dancers. The article tells the story of Stephanie Bastos, an eighteen-year-old senior in

---

3. Bill was actually related to the outlaw Bill Doolin, founder of the Wild Bunch. Danny choreographed the opera "The Ballad of Bill Doolin" at Juilliard in 1980.

the dance division at NWSA and a dancer with the Isadora Duncan Dance Ensemble. On February 19, 1995, Stephanie was in a car accident, and her right foot was so seriously damaged that it could not be saved and was amputated above the ankle. She also suffered a fracture of her right femur. In spite of the loss of her foot, Stephanie was determined to continue her dance career. Three months after the surgery, she returned to school and began working with another dancer on two works of choreography that she could perform at her graduation. One was performed without a prosthesis, and the other was performed with a traditional foot prosthesis, which was frustrating due to a lack of flexibility. The next year, she entered the NWSA college program and continued working with the Isadora Duncan Dance Ensemble. Stephanie complained to her doctors that she needed more ankle flexibility, and the doctors spoke to Danny. He explained what she needed—more flexibility in the ankle from side to side and forward and back, and, if possible, the ability to point the foot. The doctors continued working on this issue, and Stephanie continued performing, executing East Indian choreography by Menaka Thakkar (1996), Ghanian work by Godwin Agbeli, and contemporary work by Mark Taylor, to name a few. Bill T. Jones came to NWSA to teach a master class, and during that class he told Stephanie to point her foot. He did not realize she was wearing a prosthesis, and Danny had to tell him. Stephanie continued improving her skills, learning appropriate compensations, and developing images that specifically addressed her challenges. In Danny words, "I'm not sure how long she will want to dance, or for whom or with whom. I do know that she will dance and make a major contribution to the art of dance. I also hope that she will share her knowledge about movement and the images she uses to make a lifeless limb as real as life."

Danny had additional personal comments about the whole experience. When he got the call about the accident from Andrea Seidel, he went at once to the hospital to see Stephanie, and she said on that day, "I am still going to dance." He had never seen such a positive attitude, especially given her loss of the foot. Danny told her the story of a Danish dancer who had continued dancing after the loss of his leg, and he said that they would make it happen for her. He then made phone calls, including to Stephanie's mother, saying that they needed to get attention to Stephanie's situation to be able to get funding for the specially developed prosthesis. Danny began getting calls from various organizations, like the Shriner's Club and the Masons, but these organizations only help people under eighteen years old. They did raise quite a bit of money from individuals, and she got her prosthesis. Stephanie started taking dance classes again, and her first performance was packed with both well-wishers and the media. However, she lost all of the scholarships she had been offered to attend university the next year. None of the schools that had accepted her wanted to take her. In contrast, NWSA high school had accommodated her by sending a school bus to pick her up for school and take her home each day. Eventually, this became a special service car. Danny explained to the faculty that they had to find ways to teach her; in the beginning, she did not even have the prosthesis yet. They were willing to work with her in classes. The issue of college, however, was her big concern, and Danny offered her a spot at the NWSA college. She got her dance BFA in three years, and the faculty worked with her beautifully. One of the most difficult issues for her was developing a sense of where the "foot" ended, because there was no sensation past the lower-leg area where the amputation occurred. She performed in every concert in the three years she attended NWSA college. Upon graduation, she was immediately approached by Axis Dance Company, a mixed-ability group in San Francisco. She had a fulfilling and wonderful career with them, as well as doing some film work; she was in a movie with Nicole Kidman in which she played a prostitute with one leg. When the Americans with Disabilities Act group came to NWSA to do their annual assessment, they were truly impressed by the lengths NWSA went to in assisting Stephanie and accommodating her needs.

In June 2002, Danny and Donna Krasnow were invited faculty at the Twentieth Annual Symposium on Medical Problems of Musicians and Dancers, in Aspen, Colo-

Cover of the NDEO brochure, Miami, October 2013 (courtesy National Dance Education Organization). Top left photograph of Doris Humphrey (far right) (courtesy Charles Woodford), top right photograph of José Limón (photograph by Daniel Lewis, courtesy Daniel Lewis archives), bottom left photograph of Ann Hutchinson Guest (front row, right) (photograph by Rose Eichenbaum), and bottom right photograph of Daniel Lewis (photograph by Rose Eichenbaum).

rado. Donna received a grant from York University to come to NWSA, with her musician Craig Ziebarth, to stage a Limón technique demonstration on some of the NWSA college dance students. She also staged this demonstration on dancers from Canadian Children's Dance Theatre and York University in Toronto. Once in Aspen, the three groups were joined. Danny gave a lecture on Limón training, and the students performed the demonstration. They were dancing at an altitude of 8,000 feet, and breathing was quite challenging, especially in the African dance work. It was a well-received and appreciated presentation, and the dancers had a wonderful experience. This was an excellent collaboration between Danny and Donna and of the three schools.

Richard Klein was involved in the creation of the International Network of Schools for the Advancement of Arts Education, which was formed to represent all the magnet schools around the country. (The organization was later called Art Schools Network.) Danny went to their annual meetings every year, because NWSA was part of this network, and he lectured at them for over a decade. He did many talks on technology and the arts, dance and the arts, and men in the arts.

Rose Eichenbaum and Daniel Lewis at a book signing at Miami Dade College, Miami, March 25, 2008 (courtesy Daniel Lewis archives).

Danny attended and presented at the National Dance Education Organization (NDEO) conferences almost every year for decades. In October 2005, the theme of the conference was "The Spirit of Creativity: Its Essence in Dance and Education," and it was held at the University of Buffalo. Danny met the photographer Rose Eichenbaum at this conference, and they immediately became really good friends. In 2008, he brought her to NWSA to give lectures to the high school and college dance students about her book *Masters of Movement*, a book signing, and a photography lecture for the visual arts division. Rose returned to NWSA in 2011 and spoke to the dancers again and to the acting division. Rose has several books of published photography, three of them about dance: *Masters of Movement* (2007), *The Dancer Within* (2008), and *Inside the Dancer's Art* (2017), and Danny was quoted on the back cover of the last one.

The cover of the NDEO brochure for the October 23–27, 2013, conference at the Hyatt Regency in Miami had photos of renowned artists and teachers: Doris Humphrey teaching a choreography class at the 92nd Street YMHA in New York, José Limón directing *The Moor's Pavane* with Royes Fernandez, Sallie Wilson, and Toni Lander at the State Theater, Lincoln Center, New York, Ann Hutchinson Guest teaching a movement session at the NDEO conference in Tempe, Arizona, and Danny Lewis teaching a Limón technique class at New World School of the Arts, Miami, Florida.

It is quite remarkable that Danny has taught and worked with thousands of people over the years and has managed to stay in touch with a majority of them.

Dance and Technology

Danny was involved in coordinating the use of internet technology to create new works in music and dance in collaboration with the Digital Worlds Institute at the University of Florida. (The full list of technological productions can be found in the Appendix.)

In 2003, Gene Hemp became the provost of NWSA. He was responsible for bringing technology to NWSA; he felt that it was important to bring interactive technology to NWSA for educational purposes, such as sharing classes with UF. Danny's interest in this technology was in its use for creative projects. This was the beginning of the collaborative work with the Digital Worlds Institute in the UF College of Fine Arts, which was headed by executive director James Oliverio.

David Lawrence had secured $6 million ($2 million from UF, from Dade County Public Schools, and from Miami Dade College) to improve the NWSA building. This is when they got the new lobby and the advanced networking equipment. Through the Internet2 Network, an organization that uses optical fiber to deliver network services for research and education, the school obtained a secure network testing and research environment. They got the equipment called Polycom that combined television monitors and cameras for distance communication. One example of the use of this technology was when Danny was out of town during one year's NWSA high school open house; he was still able to speak to the parents as he did each year, but this time he did so via the network.

By 2003, James Oliverio was creating *Non Divisi*, an international collaboration in the performing arts. *Non divisi* is a musical term meaning "not divided." Danny brought several dancers from NWSA to participate. At the time, some of his faculty members were very skeptical about why he was investing money to take students to this production at UF in Gainesville, Florida, rather than spending the money on purchases that they thought were a higher priority. The production turned out to be very successful, and Danny showed a video to the faculty, but it didn't really help change the minds of those opposed.

On October 15, 2003, UF's Digital Worlds Institute offered two performance demonstrations of the real-time-distributed collaboration *Non Divisi*, joining co-creators from three continents at the Indiana State Museum. Dancers in Korea rehearsed and performed with musicians, dancers, and engineers in North and South America to demonstrate how telepresence can effectively empower multinational collaborations in the performing arts. These performances were part of the ongoing work of Digital Worlds Institute in growing an international network of Access Grid nodes and Internet2 members interested in creating new works of multinational music and dance. Other partners included Korea Advanced Institute of Technology (KAIST), Sejong University, Red Universitaria Nacional (REUNA), and New World School of the Arts (NWSA), with major support from the staff at Digital Worlds Institute.

In 2004, the Universitaria Nacional (REUNA) in Santiago de Chile contacted Digital Worlds Institute about doing a duet simultaneously with dancers in the United States, and James Oliverio contacted Danny. REUNA emailed a video of the dance, and Danny had two of the NWSA dancers learn the same dance except in mirror image— that is, instead of doing it on the right side, they did it on the left side. The collaboration was called *Mask*, and it involved the two versions being played simultaneously from UF and from REUNA in Chile. The couple in Chile was dancing live in an auditorium during the opening ceremony of the Science, Culture, and Education on the Research and Development Network conference. The collaboration used MPEG-2 video running in real time over the Internet2 network. It appeared that the two couples were dancing together. It was an interesting performance, but it was crude technologically; it had skips and jerks, and the images were walking through each other at times.

In 2005, they did a work called *Hands across the Ocean: The Lost Chord*, with James Oliverio as artistic director and executive producer and with Danny as the Miami production executive director. The five locations for this work were Gainesville, Florida (Digital Worlds Institute, representing the United States and using bass, the classical string instrument); Miami, Florida (NWSA, representing South America and using Caribbean drums); Australia (Queensland University/Australian Centre for Interactive Design, using digeridoo, an Aboriginal wind instrument); Korea (Korean Advanced Institute of Science and Technology, using koto, a Japanese stringed musical instrument); and London, England (Doncaster College/Digital Knowledge Exchange, using violin). The work was loosely based on *Alice's Adventures in Wonderland*. In it, Alice falls asleep in class when her teacher is talking about musical chords. She goes on a journey through the internet and explores each of the five locations. There were actually five actors representing Alice—one at each location. At the end, the teacher wakes her up, and Alice explains that although each of these instruments (bass, drum, digeridoo, koto, and violin) cannot play a chord, if played together it creates harmony. At the end, all five Alices sang a song in unison over the internet. Due to the time delay caused by the various locations, it took a special metronome developed at UF to synchronize the singers. The production won the Inaugural Peoria Prize for Creativity in the Arts and Sciences. The only location where the audience saw all five Alices was in

London, England, which made Danny think about extending this type of event so that it would be full performance at each location.

By 2006, Danny was ready to realize this multisite concept with a project known as a Distributed Collaboration. The work was entitled *In Common Space*; Danny was the executive producer and artistic director, and the composer was James Oliverio, with original NOME programming by former Digital Worlds Institute associate director Andy Quay. NOME programming was a metronome system that allowed people on different continents to start singing simultaneously despite the time lags around the world. The choreographers were Dale Andree from NWSA, Kelly Drummond Cawthon and Neta Pulvermacher from UF, and Gary Galbraith from Case Western University in Cleveland, Ohio. In each location, there were live dancers from that location in the center of the stage, and a screen on each side showed life-size video of the dancers in the other two locations. Dancers could talk, see, and relate to each other in real time, and the three audiences could talk to each other during intermission. In Miami, the event was premiered at the conference for The Network of Visual and Performing Arts, hosted by NWSA.

In 2007, dancers from NWSA and musicians from UF's School of Music opened the festivities for Merce in Miami, a city-wide arts festival celebrating the work of Merce Cunningham and the Miami debut of the Merce Cunningham Dance Company Legacy performance. They did the premiere performances of the site-specific work *One Hand Clapping* in the lobby of the Ziff Ballet Opera House. The large-scale environmental event was created by NWSA choreographer Dale Andree in collaboration with the Digital Worlds Institute's multimedia composer, James Oliverio, and it was produced by Danny.

In 2011, the National Water Dance project began, with Danny as the founding producer and Dale Andree from NWSA as the choreographer. The first rendition was state-wide and was done at eight different sites. The goal was to bring attention to ecology and the waterways. The next version, in 2014, went nationwide and included dancers from seven-year-old children to professionals. In 2016, the third year of the project, they had over 100 institutions, including professional companies, three arts-in-education programs, and a program for students with learning disabilities. Twenty-six states were involved in the performances, and all performances were distributed internationally over the internet and seen in real time. The number of internet views was many times the number of audience members that could be possible in a theater setting for a live performance.

Through His Friends' Eyes—Dale Andree

Dale Andree graduated from Boston Conservatory and then danced with May O'Donnell. She taught at the School of the Paris Opera Ballet before returning to Miami to form her company Mary Street Dance Theatre. Dale commented, "I met Danny in the late 1980s and then came to NWSA to teach composition. Due to Danny's support and encouragement in terms of curricular development, I eventually ended up teaching improvisation and composition, as well as creating special projects and choreographing on the NWSA students. I found Danny's open attitude to be quite unusual. Once he determined that a project would go forward, he was very hands off and would let the person work independently. The National Water Dance project was a project that the two of us were very involved in together. Danny helped with getting funding, and from the start it was at multiple locations and involved technology. We later worked on other interactive technology projects with UF. Danny was supportive throughout all of these projects. He has great respect for dance, but he is not precious about it. Dance is so many things to Danny, and he has reverence for it; dance is really his existence. He loves to nurture and support people. His door is always open."

Right before Danny retired, he arranged for NWSA to host the International Digital Media and Arts Association (iDMAa) conference, as he was a member of the advisory board of iDMAa. As part of this conference, there was a performance project called *Icons of Innovation*, a collaboration that provided a tribute to the great innovators throughout time and brought together dancers, computer scientists, technologists, and people who worked with game engineering, design, and animation. Technology for this event involved the Microsoft Kinect, which was adapted and combined with the gaming engine the Unreal Development Kit. This technology allowed performers to inhabit avatars of famous inventors or innovators from different periods in history. Danny said, "I was extremely excited by the collaboration of New World and Digital Worlds. I saw this as a possibility that I could expose students to technology at its best. I felt like I left a little legacy at New World."

Awards

Danny has received many awards in his lifetime for his work in the dance field. The full list can be found in the Appendix.

In 1962, as Danny was finishing his years at the High School of Performing Arts, he received two awards from the school: the Award in Dance Production and the Award in Performance. Although he has a clear memory of receiving the production award, he does not actually recall receiving the performance award. Many years later, at the Society of Dance History Scholars conference in Miami in 1991, Ann Hutchinson Guest attended the conference. They went out to dinner, and she pulled out a box. She told Danny that she was staying in a room at Jacob's Pillow, and she found this box under the dresser. When she opened the box, she found the High School of Performing Arts Award for Performance with Danny's name engraved on it. She noted that Danny must have left it there, but Danny had not been to Jacob's Pillow at that time, so it was a mystery how the box got there. Thus, he learned many years later that he had received not one but two awards from the high school.

Dance4Life, a gala evening of dance performances to benefit the American Red Cross HIV/AIDS education programs and the South Florida Dance4Life Dancer's Fund, was held November 3, 2002. Danny was the honorary chairman and Daisy Olivera, a newspaper columnist, was the mistress of ceremonies. The producer of the event was Ellen Wedner, and lighting design was by Travis Neff. The event sold out at the Olympia Theater at the Gusman Center for the Performing Arts, with seating for just under 1,450 people. The evening featured Ballet Rosario Suarez,[4] Duende Ballet Español with Rosa

---

4. Rosario Charin Suarez was a contemporary and friend of Alicia Alonso, both famous dancers in Cuba. Rosario taught at NWSA and Thomas Armour Youth Ballet for many years. There is a documentary film about her called Queen of Thursdays, which premiered March 5, 2016, at the Miami International Film Festival the Olympia Theater at the Gusman Center for the Performing Arts. Danny sponsored her for many years, including her performances in the Miami Dance Samplers.

Mercedes, Karen Peterson & Dancers, Live in Color, Maximum Dance Company, and Miami City Ballet, with a special solo performance by Calvin Kitten from the Joffrey Ballet of Chicago. The finale was the South Florida Dance4Life Dancers in an original work by Paulo Manso de Sousa. The performance was dedicated to the memory of Laurie Horn, a reviewer for the *Miami Herald*. Danny received the Lifetime Achievement Award, and the program included a tribute to Danny. Judy Drucker of the Concert Association of Florida introduced him, and they showed a video produced by Shelley Gefter.

Through His Friends' Eyes—Dennis Edwards

Dennis Edwards was the first marketing manager of Miami City Ballet, and his husband Mark Steinberg was Miami City Ballet's first president. Dennis said, "I met Danny in 1988 when Danny was staging The Moor's Pavane *on Miami City Ballet. A few years later, Mark and I were involved with the launch of Maximum Dance Company. Danny, through MDF, was the fiscal agent for the company for its first year. We also worked on Dance4Life together. Danny and I still laugh about that night in 2002 when Danny was given the Dance4Life Lifetime Achievement Award. Several of us had scripted a tribute to Danny. Judy Drucker was an impresaria who had founded the Concert Association of Florida, and we asked her to introduce Danny. But on the night of the Dance4Life event, she got up and only talked about herself! He never got his full tribute. I was on the board of NWSA for eight years, and both Danny and I were on the board for the Thomas Armour Youth Ballet. Danny is forever an optimist and a dreamer. He always sees the big picture, whether it is creating an opportunity for thousands of young dancers at the national high school dance festivals or working to get accreditation for the Thomas Armour Youth Ballet. He always dreams big and does not think anything is impossible."*

In October 2010, Danny received the Lifetime Achievement Award from the National Dance Educators Organization (NDEO). He gave an acceptance speech filled with warmth, humor, and, above all, a sense of deep respect for his audience and colleagues. The theme of this acceptance speech was luck, and he spoke of how luck has driven his life story, including the fact that he was born with a club foot. He briefly described his life and career, demonstrating that along the way, accidental and fortunate events had helped create his path. He said that he has frequently been offered considerable fees by corporations to come teach their executives creativity. He responds that he can't, because it is too late. He said that creativity is not something that can be taught, and children develop creativity at a very young age, from age one through the early school years. He went on to tell a story, initially told to him by Betty Rowan, that has stayed with him throughout his years as an educator. The story was about a class in creative movement for five-year-old children, where they did various movement improvisations. At the end of the class, the teacher would lie down on the floor in front of the exit door. She would have the children line up and, one by one, run and leap over her to leave the studio. The children loved doing this exit. One day, the teacher instructed them to scream as they were leaping over her that day. The first little girl in line walked up to her and asked, "When I scream, do you want me to scream with my voice or with my body?" Danny went on to say that this type of work teaches a child how to be creative, how to be a strong leader, and how to think outside the box. Danny acknowledged that what arts educators do is teach children how to be good corporate presidents and politicians, and it is arts education at an early age that is going to save the nation. And in his gracious way,

Danny credited the NDEO for their ongoing fight to get the arts into early education. In his concluding thoughts he stated that one can only wonder how things would have turned out if he had not been born with a clubfoot. How would his life have changed, and what would have become of everyone touched by him? It is not only Danny Lewis but many in the dance world who were lucky that Danny was born with a clubfoot!

In 2011, Danny was awarded the Martha Hill Lifetime Achievement Award, presented at the Martha Hill Gala in New York. This award was very important to Danny, because Martha Hill was Danny's artistic "mother," and he owed his career and education to her. It was Martha who encouraged Danny to seek out the position at NWSA, one of the best decisions of his life. He had the opportunity to affect the lives of thousands of young dancers.

In 2013, Danny received the Education Advancement Award from the José Limón Dance Foundation. The award was presented by Robert Battle in New York City on April 29, 2013.

Service

Danny served as a consultant from 1980 to 1985 for the Council for International Exchange of Scholars–Fulbright Opportunities Abroad. He sat on the Advisory Screening Committee by invitation of Roy Whittaker, the director of the Council for Interna-

Daniel Lewis receiving the Martha Hill Lifetime Achievement Award, Manhattan Penthouse, New York, November 2008. Back row, from left: Daniel Lewis, Mercedes Ellington, Ernesta Corvino, front row, from left: Maureen O'Rourke, Carla Maxwell, Roxanne D'Orléans Juste (courtesy Daniel Lewis archives).

tional Exchange of Scholars. This is the group that administers the Fulbright Scholar Program, and Danny was involved in reviewing hundreds of Fulbright applications, not just in dance but also in theater and other areas of the performing arts.

In 1982, Danny was adjudicating performances for Canada Council for the Arts, Canada's federal arts funder. The council really appreciated his reports, because they felt he was honest and to the point. He reviewed Margie Gillis, and he also saw Anna Wyman in Vancouver that year. This relationship between Danny and the council went on for many years, and he saw many of the well-known companies in Canada. In 1983, he went to both Toronto and Québec City.[5] One of the companies he saw was Toronto Independent Dance Enterprise (TIDE). In 1984, Danny wrote a report about Anne Ditchburn for the council, and in 1985 he reported on Anna Wyman. Then in 1986, he did a whole series of adjudications, including Les Ballet Jazz, Danny Grossman, BCBC Festival, and Margie Gillis; the correspondence was with Barbara Laskin (later Barbara Laskin-Plumptre) at Canada Council for the Arts. Danny's report in 1987 on Robert Desrosiers looked at three works that Danny saw at the National Arts Centre in Ottawa; these included *Brass Fountain*, which was much improved since its first showing at Premiere Dance Theatre (PDT) in Toronto, and *Bad Weather*, also first seen at PDT, which was not much changed but had a wonderful score and good movement. Danny also reported on Fortier Danse-Création in Montréal and Danse Partout in Québec City. Other people who served on these juries with Danny included Peter Randazzo, Mary Yago, Daniel Jackson, Arnold Spohr, Jean Geddes, and Gary Semeniuk. Throughout the 1980s, Danny continued reviewing companies, including Pacific Ballet, Robert Desrosiers, Les Grands Ballets Canadiens de Montréal, Experimental Dance and Music (EDAM), and Eddy Touissant. There were mixed feelings in Canada about some of these companies, and the council needed an outside eye. Everyone in Canada knew each other, so there was little objectivity in the Canadian dance community. Danny provided that objectivity.

In 1987, Danny attended all of the Dance Notation Bureau's Professional Advisory Committee meetings. Other committee members included Ann Hutchinson Guest, Peggy Hackney, Rhonda Ryman, Odette Blum, Irene Fox, Penelope Henstead, Denise Jefferson, Muriel Topaz, and Lucy Venable.

In 2006, Canadian Children's Dance Theatre (CCDT) needed an external evaluation for a grant, so Danny went up to Toronto to do the review. The CCDT had worked with various choreographers from Toronto Dance Theatre, Holly Small, Danny Grossman, Maxine Hepner, and Dancemakers. This was a very different type of review because Danny was looking at the school and company rather than a particular choreographer.

Danny served on many panels and boards, and he was a member of several organizations throughout his career. The full lists can be found in the Appendix.

After Retirement from NWSA

On February 11, 2011, NWSA celebrated Danny's time at the school with an event called Daniel Lewis: A Life of Dance, which include a tribute concert at the Gusman

---

5. On a personal note, every time Danny went to Canada, he brought home another piece of Eskimo art, and he developed a love and passion for Eskimo carvings. To this day, they are displayed in his home in Miami.

Center for the Performing Arts and a VIP reception, held at La Loggia Restaurant. At the concert, NWSA announced the newly created Daniel Lewis Dance Scholarship Fund. At that time, Danny was the first founding dean to retire from the school, having served for twenty-four years, since NWSA opened in 1987. Jeffrey Hodgson, interim provost at New World School of the Arts, stated, "Danny Lewis has been a cornerstone in the development of New World School of the Arts since its inception. As a former dean, I had the privilege to observe how his love for the school, its faculty, and students translates into passionate leadership. It is an honor to work with him and to support him as provost in his quest to nurture and train the performing artists of the future. Danny's legacy will live on in the accomplishments of all of the students who have passed through our studios and classrooms."

Danny said, "Having the opportunity to create an eight-year program at NWSA has been one of the most rewarding and challenging experiences of my adult life. This has enabled me to completely immerse myself in developing a program for dancers and choreographers who will be the next generation of artists and leaders in the field. Being around young students most of my life, first as a dancer, choreographer, and then as an educator has allowed me the opportunity to help them explore and realize their artistic dreams. As an artist, I feel I understand the needs, aspirations, and frustrations of young developing artists."

(From left) Donna Krasnow, Daniel Lewis, and Laura Glenn at Daniel's retirement afterparty, 2011 (courtesy Daniel Lewis archives).

(From left) Jim May, Eddie Effron, Carla Maxwell, Daniel Lewis, Maureen O'Rourke, Hope and Bob Lewis, at Daniel's retirement after-party, 2011 (courtesy Daniel Lewis archives).

Joseé Garant, a NWSA faculty member and choreographer, directed and organized the concert, which featured performances by world-acclaimed dance companies, dancers, and choreographers, including Gerri Houlihan, Michael Uthoff, Jim May, Robert Battle, Carla Maxwell, the Martha Graham Dance Company, the José Limón Company, Rosie Herrera Dance Company, Tango for All Company, and choreographers and alumni from NWSA. Garant said, "It is a real privilege to be the artistic director of Daniel Lewis: A Life of Dance. The process of gathering the artists to perform at this historical concert celebrating the retirement of dean Lewis from NWSA has been one of constant amazement and awe! The love, admiration, and respect demonstrated throughout the nation and abroad toward Daniel Lewis—the dancer, choreographer, director, educator, the friend and dean of dance at NWSA—is endless and endearing. I have had both national and international artists wanting to be part of this concert."

Within three months of Danny's retirement, he received numerous offers for guest residencies, speaking engagements, and work in directing, mounting and choreographing dance works, and consulting. In addition, several Miami nonprofit organizations solicited him for their boards of directors. As calls came in with work offers, Danny limited his work to projects involving the creative process and to arts education. For the first time, Danny was very selective in accepting what he would and would not do. His first obligation was to serve children in the arts, partly because of his own start in dance was as a young boy. Danny wanted to make sure that all children had an opportunity to explore the arts and have choices in their future careers. He accepted positions on three boards: Arts for Learning, Florida Dance Education Organization (FDEO), and the Thomas Armour Youth Ballet. Arts for Learning is an organization in South Florida solely dedicated to connecting professional visual and performing artists to children and educators. Danny joined the board in 2012 and became vice president five years later.

The FDEO is affiliated with the NDEO. It is dedicated to the advancement of high-quality education in the art of dance, and it promotes the idea that everyone should have access to dance education regardless of gender, age, race, culture, socio-economic status, or ability. Danny was a board member, and he served as treasurer for three years. He then became general manager. After one year, the board gave him the dual role of treasurer and general manager, and during this time, he brought the FDEO to a secure financial position. The National Honor Society for Dance Arts (NHSDA) is a program of NDEO, and it has a branch with FDEO. It recognizes outstanding artistic merit, leadership, and academic achievement in students studying dance in public and private schools in K–12 education, dance studios, cultural/community centers, performing arts organizations, and postsecondary education.

Thomas Armour Youth Ballet (TAYB) has been a major project of Danny's for many years. When he was about to retire, he made an arrangement with Ruth Wiesen and Dennis Edwards, writing a letter of agreement that the relationship between NWSA and Thomas Armour Youth Ballet would be ongoing and permanent after Danny retired. The arrangement was specifically about the production of *The Nutcracker* each year. This ballet was a collaboration between NWSA and TAYB for many years. The letter Danny wrote supported the collaboration, and the new dean of dance, Mary Lisa Burns, recognized its value and has continued the tradition.

In 2011, Danny directed Concert for a New Renaissance: Symphonic Dances, Prayers, & Meditations for Peace. This event was originally conceived by Grammy Award–winning flautist Nestor Torres and included performances by Torres, Greater Miami Youth Symphony, Thomas Armour Youth Ballet, Miami Children's Chorus, New World School of the Arts, Brazilian Voices, and Florida Grand Opera Young Artist Studio. This work was very satisfying to Danny for four reasons. First, Danny knew Torres' work and greatly appreciated his artistry. Second, it involved a creative process. Third, several

Daniel Lewis (left) and Robert Battle at Daniel's retirement after-party, 2011 (courtesy Daniel Lewis archives).

children's groups were included. Fourth, as director, he had creative control. When Danny expressed his vision of how the work would be developed, Nestor was in complete agreement, and they worked together well. The performance took place on November 11 and was a major collaboration and a huge artistic success.

In the fall of 2011, Danny was called to consult for a company called Acceptd, which helped high school students build their résumés online; colleges and universities would then pay the company to find students who fulfilled their criteria. Danny took the company to meetings such as NDEO and the National High School Dance Festivals and assisted them in forming partnerships. This work was another way that Danny helped young dance students.

Dance NOW! Miami, a local dance company, asked Danny to teach and mount dance works on their dancers. Danny accepted this work, partly because they pay their dancers on a regular basis, and he appreciated the integrity of this group. They also took over the Miami Dance Sampler event and renamed it the Daniel Lewis Miami Dance Sampler. Dance NOW! Miami is the only professional dance company in Miami that Danny works with on a regular basis as an artistic advisor.

On December 14, 2012, Danny was awarded an honorary doctorate in Fine Arts from the University of Florida. The ceremony was headed by the president, Bernie Machen, who was president from 2004 to 2014. Danny was the 14th person to receive an honorary doctorate in Fine Arts, since 1945, and to support him, Jeffrey Hodgson, the provost at NWSA and Mary Lisa Burns the new dean of dance at NWSA were both in attendance, along with Danny's family.

Danny has also continued to pursue his work with technology in dance, a lifelong passion for him. He acts as an advocate for the use of technology in the arts and its

Daniel Lewis receiving his Honorary Doctor of Fine Arts Degree from the University of Florida, 2012. From left: James Oliverio (Director Digital Worlds Institute UF), Joan Frosch (Faculty Dance UF), Lucinda Lavelli (Dean of Fine Arts UF), Maureen O'Rourke (faculty NWSA), Dr. Daniel Lewis (Founding Dean of Dance NWSA), Jeffrey Hodgson (Provost NWSA) Mary Lisa Burns (Dean of Dance NWSA), Donald McGlothlin (Retired Dean of Fine Arts UF), Robert Lewis, Quinn Lewis, Hope Lewis (courtesy Daniel Lewis archives).

ability to enhance the creative process. He has also stayed involved with the National Water Dance Project.

Finally, Danny continues to travel on a regular basis for guest residencies, speaking engagements, and mounting and choreographing dance works. In the words of Robert Battle, "I know of no other way of judging the future but by the past, and so I seriously doubt that Danny is retiring!"

Appendix
Professional Accomplishments,
1960–2017

Danny staged José Limón's and Doris Humphrey's choreography at the following schools and companies from 1968 to 2017:

- 1967–1972: José Limón Dance Company, New York City
- 1967–1987: Juilliard School, New York City (*Missa Brevis, A Choreographic Offering, Emperor Jones, The Traitor, There Is a Time,* and more)
- 1977–1983: London School of Contemporary Dance, England (*Missa Brevis, A Choreographic Offering,* and *There Is a Time*)
- 1968: National Ballet of Canada, Toronto, Canada (*The Moor's Pavane*)
- 1969: Repertory Dance Theater, Salt Lake City, Utah (*There Is a Time*)
- 1969: Batsheva Dance Company, Israel (*La Malinche* and *The Exiles*)
- 1969: First Chamber Dance Company, New York City (*The Moor's Pavane* and *La Malinche*)
- 1969, 1970: American Ballet Theatre, New York City (*The Moor's Pavane* and *The Traitor*)
- 1970: University of California, Los Angeles (*Missa Brevis*)
- 1970, 1971, 1973: Royal Swedish Ballet, Sweden (*There Is a Time, The Exiles, Missa Brevis,* and *The Moor's Pavane*)
- 1971: Repertory Dance Theater, Salt Lake City, Utah (*There Is a Time, Ritmo Jondo*)
- 1972: Alvin Ailey American Dance Theater, New York City (*Missa Brevis*)
- 1972: Royal Danish Ballet, Denmark (*The Moor's Pavane*)
- 1972: American Dance Festival, New London, Connecticut (*The Emperor Jones*)
- 1980: Danzahoy, Caracas, Venezuela (*Night Spell*)
- 1981: Reed College, Portland, Oregon (*Night Spell*)
- 1984, 1986: University of Calgary, Canada (*A Choreographic Offering* and *There Is a Time*)
- 1984, 1986: National Ballet School, Toronto, Canada (same as UC above)
- 1985: Danskern, Amsterdam, Holland (*Day on Earth*)
- 1988: Miami City Ballet, Florida (*The Moor's Pavane*)
- 1988, 1993: Hong Kong Academy of the Performing Arts, Hong Kong (*Missa Brevis*)

- 2011: COCA, St. Louis, Missouri (sections from *A Choreographic Offering*)
- 2013: San Diego School of Creative and Performing Arts (*The Waldstein Sonata*)
- 2014: Mercyhurst University, Erie, Pennsylvania (*The Waldstein Sonata*)
- 2015, 2016: Dance NOW! Miami (*The Beethoven Sextet*, sections from *There Is a Time*, and *Ritmo Jondo*)
- 2017: San Diego Civic Dance Company (*Beethoven Sextet*)

Danny created the following dance works from 1966 to 1988:

- 1966: *Man Made* (Barnard College)
- 1967: *The Minding of the Flesh Is Death* (Lincoln Center Student Programs)
- 1970: *The Bokinski Brothers* (Barnard College)
- 1972: *My Echo, My Shadow, and Me* (NEA Choreographic Fellowship, Barnard College)
- 1972: *Irving the Terrific* (UCLA)
- 1974: *And First They Slaughtered the Angels* (Contemporary Dance System)
- 1974: *No Strings* (Barnard College)
- 1976: *Cabbage Patch* (American Wind Symphony)
- 1976: *Proliferation* (Juilliard School)
- 1978: *Life and Other Things* (Daniel Lewis Dance: A Repertory Company)
- 1979: *Mostly Beethoven* (Juilliard School)
- 1980: *Beethoven Duet* (Benefit Concert Honoring Doris Humphrey and Charles Weidman)
- 1980: *There's Nothing Here of Me but Me* (Amherst College)
- 1981: *Open Book* (Daniel Lewis Dance: A Repertory Company)
- 1982: *Moments* (The Juilliard School)
- 1982: *To Doris and Charles* (Portland State)
- 1984: *Textured Lighting* (Daniel Lewis Dance: A Repertory Company)
- 1984: *Atomic Ambience* (University of Calgary)
- 1985: *Women* (Juilliard School)
- 1985: *Mind over Matter* (Bennington College Summer Dance Program)
- 1986: *Bibleland* (The University of Calgary)
- 1987: *Air Raid* (SUNY Purchase)
- 1988: *The Morning after the Night Before* (Towson State College)

Danny staged and directed his work at the following schools and companies:

- Towson State College, Baltimore, Maryland
- Swarthmore College, Swarthmore, Pennsylvania
- José Limón Dance Company
- Barnard College, New York
- Teachers' College, Columbia University, New York
- University of Michigan, Ann Arbor, Michigan
- Hampshire College, Amherst, Massachusetts
- New World School of the Arts, Miami, Florida
- Juilliard School, New York (*Irving the Terrific, Proliferation, Women, Moments,* and *Mostly Beethoven*)
- UCLA, Los Angeles, California (*Irving the Terrific*)

- Tsoying Senior High School, Tsoying District, Kaohsiung, Taiwan (*The Beethoven Sextet*; also staged the fast dance and the slow dance from Limón's *A Choreographic Offering*)
- San Diego School of Creative and Performing Arts, California (*The Waldstein Sonata*)
- Governor's School for the Arts, Norfolk, Virginia (first movement from *The Waldstein Sonata*)
- Mercyhurst University, Erie, Pennsylvania (first movement from *The Waldstein Sonata*)
- Daniel Lewis Dance: A Repertory Company
- Contemporary Dance System
- New World School of the Arts
- Dance NOW! Miami (*The Beethoven Sextet* and *Ritmo Jondo*)
- Danzahoy, South America (*Night Spell*)
- Companies in England (*There Is a Time* and *Missa Brevis*)

Danny wrote the following publications from 1984 to 2006:

- 1984: *The Illustrated Dance Technique of José Limón*, published by Harper and Row
- 1986: *The Illustrated Dance Technique of José Limón* videotape, produced by Video D
- 1990: *Illustrierte Tanztechnik von José Limón*, published by Florian Noetzel Germany
- 1990: "Dance Education in the USA K–12," paper presented at International Symposion Munchen, published by Tanztendenz (This paper was also published in *Tanzund Gymnastik*, issues 3/90 and 4/90, in Switzerland.)
- 1993: *The Illustrated Dance Technique of José Limón*, published by Japan UNI Agency, Inc.
- 1994: *Dance in Hispanic Cultures*, Proceedings of the Society of Dance History Scholars Fourteenth Annual Conference, published by Harwood Academic Publishers
- 1995: *The Illustrated Dance Technique of José Limón*, published by Consejo Nacional para la Cultura y las Artes, Mexico
- 1998: two papers published in *Medical Problems of Performing Artists*: September, "Health Care for Dance Students at a Performing Arts Academy," and March, "Dancing with a Prosthesis"
- 1999: *The Illustrated Dance Technique of José Limón, Second Edition*, published by Princeton Book Company
- 2000: Article "Remembering Martha Hill (1900–1995)," in *Ballet Review*
- 2005: *The Illustrated Dance Technique of José Limón* DVD, produced by Video D in DVD format
- 2006: Article in *Dance Teacher Magazine* on the life of José Limón

Danny choreographed the following operas from 1972 to 1985:

- 1972: *Dido and Aeneas*, Dallas Civic Opera
- 1978: *Aida*, Houston Grand Opera
- 1980: *Le Rossignol*, American Opera Center at Lincoln Center

- 1980: *The Ballad of Bill Doolin,* The Juilliard School, New York
- 1980: *Feathertop,* American Opera Center at Lincoln Center
- 1982: *Mannon,* American Opera Center at Lincoln Center
- 1985: *Il Tabarro,* American Opera Center at Lincoln Center

Danny choreographed these plays, musicals, and commercials from 1977 to 2011:

- 1977: *The Tempest,* Amherst College (choreographer)
- 1977: *Nefertiti,* Sherwin M. Goldman Broadway Production (choreographer)
- 1981: *Crisp,* Intar Production, Off Broadway (choreographer)
- 1982: Cottoncale TV commercial, J.P. Stevens (choreographer)
- 2011: *Concert for a New Renaissance* (director)

Danny's work in dance and technology from 2003 to 2012:

- 2003: *Non Divisi* (Miami coordinator)
- 2004: *Mask* (Miami coordinator)
- 2005: *Hands across the Ocean: The Lost Chord* (Miami production executive director)
- 2005: *In Common Time* (Miami producer)
- 2006: *In Common Space* (executive producer and artistic director)
- 2011–2016: National Water Dance Project (founding producer)
- 2012: Icons of Innovation

Danny's awards from 1962 to 2017:

- 1962: Award in Dance Production, High School of Performing Arts
- 1962: Award in Performance, High School of Performing Arts
- 1963: Royal Knight of Cambodia, knighted by Prince Norodom Sihanouk in Phnom Penh
- 1985: Distinguished Professor, Reed College, Portland, Oregon
- 1990: Gold medal for Lifelong Achievement in Dance, National Society of Arts and Letters
- 1991, 2000: Award for outstanding service, Florida Dance Association
- 2000: Award for outstanding service in the development of the festival, National High School Dance Festival
- 2001: Florida Arts Recognition Award (Note that this is award—for outstanding initiative, leadership, and excellence in supporting the arts in Florida—is given by the legislature of the state of Florida and is highly prestigious.)
- 2002: Nancy Smith Award, for consistently demonstrating outstanding leadership and excellence in dance in Florida
- 2002: Lifetime Achievement Award, Dance4Life
- 2006: Salutes to Daniel Lewis by Mayor of Miami Manuel Diaz
- 2010: Lifetime Achievement Award, National Dance Education Organization
- 2011: Two awards declaring February 5 Daniel Lewis Day in Miami and in Miami-Dade County, presented during A Tribute to Daniel Lewis
- 2011: A proclamation from the floor of the Florida State Senate for his work in the arts in Florida by Senator Anitere Flores
- 2011: The Nestor Torres Miami-Dade County Days Ambassador of the Arts Award, presented at Dade Days in Tallahassee

- 2011: The Martha Hill Lifetime Achievement Award, presented at the Martha Hill Gala in New York
- 2012: Honorary Doctor of Fine Arts Degree, the University of Florida
- 2013: Education Advancement Award, José Limón Dance Foundation
- 2017: The Doris Leeper 2017 Award, Florida Alliance for Arts Education (FAAE)
- 2018: Award from Dance NOW! Miami for bringing the legacy of time and culture to South Florida

Danny served on the following panels and boards:

- 1975–1996: Canada Council, individual fellowships, site visits
- 1975–2005: National Endowment for the Arts, choreography fellowships, mentor teacher, panel member, chair, site visits, and chair of the Interdisciplinary Arts Panel
- 1980–1985: Fulbright Screening Committee
- 1987–2007: Florida Dance Association, president for three terms, treasurer, and board member
- 1987–present: Metro-Dade Cultural Affairs Council, community grants, Hanable Cox and advancements grants, festival grants, and major cultural institutions (MCI) grants
- 1988–1993: Florida Department of State, Division of Cultural Affairs, Dance Panel
- 1988–1997: National Society of Arts and Letters, Advisory Board
- 1993: South Carolina Arts Commission, Interdisciplinary Panel
- 1997: Kentucky State Arts Council, Interdisciplinary and Dance Panel
- 1997: North Carolina State Arts Council, Dance Panel
- 1997–1999: American College Dance Festival, board of directors
- 1997–2011: National Association of Schools of Dance (NASD), board of directors, treasurer, vice president, and president for nine years
- 2002–2012: Accrediting Commission for Community and Pre-collegiate Arts Schools (ACCPAS)
- 2005–2011: Council of Arts Accrediting Associations (CAAA), as vice president and then president of NASD, Danny was a board member of CAAA
- 2005–2015: International Digital Media & Arts Association (iDMAa), advisory board
- 2007–2011: Commission on Multidisciplinary and Multimedia in the Arts (CAAA), member
- 2012–present: Thomas Armour Youth Ballet, president
- 2012–present: Arts for Learning, vice president
- 2013–present: Florida Dance Education Organization, treasurer and general manager
- 2015–present: Editorial Board of the National Dance Education Organization journal called Dance Education in Practice

Danny has been a member of the following organizations:

- 1960–1964: Hebrew Actors Union
- 1962–present: American Guild of Musical Artists
- 1968–1975: American Federation of Television and Radio Artists

- 1972–1989: Society of Stage Directors and Choreographers
- 1987–2011: National Association of Schools of Dance
- 1990–1995: American Dance Guild
- 1990–1995: Society of Dance History Scholars
- 2011–present: Retired membership with the National Dance Education Organization

Index

Abrahams, Ruth 91, 91*n*
ABT *see* American Ballet Theatre (ABT)
ACDFA (American College Dance Festival Association) 170
Acme (dance company) 117
Adams, Carolyn 135
ADF *see* American Dance Festival (ADF)
Adirondack Champlain Festival 54
Agbeli, Godwin 199
Agoglia, Esmeralda 166
Aida 121, 145, 153
Ailey (Alvin) American Dance Theater 13, 36, 48, 75, 90–91, 111, 123, 161–162, 178, 179, 184, 189
Albee, Edward 52
Alenikoff (Francis) Studio 108
Alleyne, John 96
Alonso, Alicia 119
Alvarez Blake, Mariana 178
Amaral, Joseph 36
American Ballet Theatre (ABT) 48, 69, 82–84, 154
American College Dance Festival Association (ACDFA) 170
American Dance Festival (ADF) 15, 16–18, 35, 45, 73, 110, 127, 148, *177*, 191
American Dance Theater 36–37, 145
American Wind Symphony 129
Amherst College 137–138, 139
And First They Slaughtered the Angels 106, *106*, 109, 111, 114, 115, *115*, 116, 117, 118–119, 121, 122, 127, 128, 130, 134
Anderson, Bambi 160, *175*
Anderson, Jack 184
Andersson, Gerd 85, 85*n*, 86, 118

Andree, Dale *175*, 192, 204–205
Anthony (Mary) Dance Theater 124
Antonio 195
APA Repertory Company 145
Arenal, Julie 36
Armour, Thomas 161
Armour (Thomas) Youth Ballet (TAYB) 180, 205*n*, 206, 211
Arpino, Gerald 105
Artcho Danse Repertoire 192
artistic director roles: Daniel Lewis Dance: A Repertory Company 114, 125; Limón Dance Company 28*n*, 44, 56, 65, 65*n*; Lincoln Center Student Programs 38–39
Arts Ballet Theatre 193
Arts for Learning 211
As I Remember 125
Asakawa, Takako 111
Asher, Christine 145
Ashton, Frederick 119
Asia tour 25, 26–33
Atomic Ambience 97
Augustyn, Frank 96
Australia 26, 33, 182–183
awards 205–207, 218–219
Axis Dance Company 199–200
Azoubel, Juliana 171

Babiuk, Roxolana 104
Bagnold, Lisbeth 88
Baker, Elmer 91
Balanchine, George 105, 119, 166
Balanchine Conference 166
Balcena, Antony (Tony) 104, 107, 121, 122, 131, 133, 133*n*
Bales, William 121, 126
Ballad of Bill Doolin 198*n*
Ballade 111, 113
Ballet Hispanico 187
Ballet Nacional 140
Ballet Rambert 93
Ballet Randolph 189

Ballet Rosario Suárez 205
BAM *see* Brooklyn Academy of Music (BAM)
Bargain Counter 75
Barnard College 75–79, 92, 130
Barnes, Clive 51–52, 83, 104, 119
Barr, Howard 26, 30
Barr, Richard 52
Barreau, Pierre 104, *108*, 109, 111, 114, *115*, *116*, 117, 118, 119, 131, 139
Barrios, Maria 89
Barro Rojo Arte Escénico (dance company) 140
Barth, Frank 127, 147–148, 149
Baryshnikov, Mikhail 183
Bastida, Socorro 140, *141*
Bastos, Stephanie 198–200
Batsheva Dance Company 81–82
Battle, Robert 170, 174, 178–179, 184, 210, *211*, 213
Bauman, Arthur (Art) 111, 120
Baumgarten, Hannah 140, *141*, 193
Bausch, Pina 75
Baxter, Debra 159*n*, *160*, 174
Beck, Eric 177
Beethoven Duet 69, 120, 131
Beethoven Sextet 69, 120, 183*n*
Beethoven Trio 69, 121
Before Oceans 172
Belle, William 104
Bellini, Juan Carlos 17, 25
Bennett, Charles 39, 39*n*
Bennett, Sydney 39*n*
Bennett-Gaehler, Amy 95
Bentley-Baker, Kandell 151
Berg, Alban 103, 113
Berger, Larry 39*n*, 102, 152, 161
Bergmann, Elizabeth (Liz) 105
Berke, Stanley 16
Berliner, Charles 23, *24*, 121
Berlingeri, Julio 54, 54*n*
Berlioz, Hector 130

Bern, Mina *16*, 35
Bernhard-Link Studio 108
Bernissant, Bob 8–9, 9*n*
Bethke, Veit 118
Bettis, Valerie 36
Bikel, Theodore 35
Billig, Robert 146
Billy Rose Theatre 52–53
Bird, Bonnie 126
Bjørnsson, Fredbjørn 38, 38*n*
Blair, Shareen 17
Blanco, Diego 171, 179
Blum, Odette 208
Bolshoi Ballet 18
Bondi, Don 16
Bonnefoux, Jean-Pierre 170
Bonus, Ben *16*, 35
Borg, Kristen 121
Borne, Elyse 166
Bouck, Sharon 78–79
Boudreau, Robert 129, 130
Brandenburg Concerto 27
Bratcher, Freddick 154, 174, 178, 189
Bratches, Daryl 79
Brazilian Voices 211
Breazeale, Helene 139
Brittain, Laura 91
Brno Chamber Orchestra 196
Broadway 52–53, 145–146, 186–187
Brooklyn Academy of Music (BAM) 9, 48, 51–52, 53–54, 93
Broquet, Jacques 94
Brown, Ellery 162
Brown, Shirley 104
Brown, Tom 99
Brown, Trisha 110
Brownholtz, Diane 151, *175*
Bruhn, Erik 95
Bryant, Paul (Bear) 139
Buglisi, Jacqulyn 13, 184*n*
Bujones, Fernando 184
Buntz, Gina 192
Burnett, Marjorie 195
Burns, Mary Lisa 168*n*, 211, 212, *212*
Bush, Jeff 148
Butler, Diane 124
Butler, John 90
Byer, Diana 37

Cabbage Patch 129
Caceres, Richard 113
Cage, John 17
Cahan, Cora 13
Callahan, Suzanne 172
Cambodia 28–29, *29*, 32, 67
Camera Three (TV show) 10
Campbell, Neve 96
Canada 34, 89–90, 95–97
Canadian Children's Dance Theatre (CCDT) 208

Cannan, Rebecca *175*
Cano, John 197
Caplan, Joan 145
Capozzoli, Donato 17, 25, *26*
Carbee, Brian 126, 131, 133
Carden, Betsy 126
Caribbean Dance Celebrations 192
Caribbean Performing Arts Company 192
Carlota 64, 68
Carr (Deborah) Theatre Dance Ensemble 124
Carrington, Jane 1, 86, 91, 93, 94, 95, 97, 101*n*, 102, 114, 120, 121, 122, *123*, 124, 125, 126, 127, 131, 133, 133*n*, 135–136, 139, 149, 152, 154, 189
Carrington (Jane) Dance 189
Carter, William (Bill) 69, 120
Casey, Kathleen 121, 124
Castalia Enterprises 103
CCDT (Canadian Children's Dance Theatre) 208
CDS *see* Contemporary Dance System (CDS)
Cébron, Jean 149
Cenidi Danza José Limón 140
Centro Superior de Coreografia Grupo Piloto de Danza Contemporanea 140
Cernovich, Nick 13, 51, 52
Chaconne 147, 149
Chamberlain, John 126
Chan, Ya-ting 174
Chanukah Festival 35
Charleston 129
Charlip, Remy 17, 149
Chávez de la Lama, Ofelia 140, *141*
Chen, Hsueh-Tung 104
Chen, Shu-Chen 176
Chen (H.T.) & Dancers 196
Cheng, Hsien-fa 174
Cheng, Yueh-li 174
Chicago Tribune 72–73
A Choreographic Offering 18, 28, 35, 36, 49, 50, 53, 61, 62, 65, 66, 93, 96, 97, 99, 165
Chou, Su-Ling 172–173, 183*n*
Christopher, Patricia 17, 25, 27, 36, 118
Clark, Nathan 78, 78*n*, 135
Clark, VéVé 169
Clarke, Martha 34, 38*n*
Cleveland Ballet 71
Cloud Gate (dance company) 42–43, 175, 183*n*, 196
Clouser, James 22, 37
Cobb, Stephen 125
Cohan, Robert 94, 94*n*, 186
Cohen, Moss 139
Cohen, Nurit 81

Cohen, Selma Jeanne 166
Cohen, Ze'eva 121, 126
Collins, Brent 146
Comedy 18, 44–45, 48, 52
Como, William 121, 126
Concerto Grosso in D Minor 25, 56
Condodina, Alice *14*, 25, 35, 36, 49, 51*n*, 52*n*, 53*n*, 66, 74
conference presentations 198–202
Congress on Research in Dance (CORD) conference 168–168
Connor, Colin 80
Contemporary Chamber Ballet of Caracas 121
Contemporary Dance System (CDS) 91, 100–136, *102*, 110, 123
Coogan, Jenny 198
Cook, Peter 167
Cook, Ray 105
Copeland, Roger 166
CORD (Congress on Research in Dance) conference 168–168
Corea, Chick 125
Corey, Winthrop 89
Corning, Beth 86
Coronado, José 109, 111, 113, 114
Corvino, Alfredo 22, 43, 126
Corvino, Ernesta *207*
Craske, Margaret 17, 22
Cratty, Bill 124
Crawford, Ellen 98
Crisp 146
Crofton, Kathleen 22
Cuevas, Luis Alberto 193
Cullberg Ballet 96
Cummings, Blondell 75
Cunningham, Merce 17, 36, 64, 110, 172
Cunningham (Merce) Dance Company 17, 25, 48, 161, 172
Currier, Ruth 17, 25, 27, 28*n*, 31, 32, 61, 65, 67, 75, 93, 148
Cutler, Robyn 38*n*, 67, 114
Cuyahoga Community College 102–103

DaCosta, Mohamed 171, 177
Dallas Civic Opera (DCO) 144–145
Dance Conduit (dance company) 105
Dance Fusion (dance company) 105
Dance Magazine 33, 40–41, 46, 126, 189, 190
Dance Notation Bureau (DNB) 25, 54–56, 54*n*, 69, 105, 108, *108*, 208

Dance NOW! Miami 140, 191, 193, 212
Dance St. Louis 183
Dance Sextet 101
Dance Teacher 144, 190
Dance Theater Workshop 108, 111
Dance Theatre of Harlem 110, 146, 161, 196
Dance Uptown 75–79
Dancearts Foundation 194
Dance4Life Dancers 206
Dancemakers 121, 208
Dancer 188, *188*
Dances for Isadora 56, 124
D'Anne, Beverly 135
Danse Partout 208
Danskern (dance company) 98
Danzahoy (dance company) 94
D'Arienzo, Susan *175*
Davidson, Joy 153
Davies, Siobhan 93–94
Davis, Johnny 139
Day on Earth 75, 98, 109, 113, 114, 116, 118, 119, 120, 124, 135
Daykin, Judy 51
Daza, Raniero 188
Daza, Ulysses 188
Daza Osorio, Fernando 188, *188*
DCO (Dallas Civic Opera) 144–145
Dead Heat 109, 111, 112, 116, 118, 139
Dean, Laura 13
de Blois, Kat 107, 121, *123*, 129, 131, 133, 140
Debussy Dances 114, 116, 117
December Prose 103
de Lancie, John 187–188
Delanghe, Gay 76–77
Dela Peña, George 13
Dello Joio, Norman 68
DeMain, John L. 145–146
The Demon 47, 61
Denis, Agnes 130
Denmark 88–89
Dennis, Paul 137*n*
De Rothschild, Batsheva 81
DeSola, Carla 16
DeSoto, Edward *45*, 46, 51*n*, 52, 52*n*, 53, 53*n*, 54, 56, 58–59, 64, 66–67, 74, 75, *75*, 89, 111
de Sousa, Paulo Manso 206
Desrosiers, Robert 96, 208
de Valois, Ninette 119
Dialogue 120
Diamond, Matthew 109, 111–113, *112*, 113, 116, 118–119, 139

Diaz, Diana 183
Diaz, Gaby 178
Diaz, Maribel 161, 162, 195
Diaz-Zubieta, Anna 195
Diaz-Zubieta, Carol 195
Dido and Aeneas 121, 144–145
Diggs, Jennifer 139
Digital Worlds Institute 202–204
d'Imobilité, Foofwa 172
Dissette, Alyce 121
Ditchburn, Anne 208
Ditson, Les 87, 88
DLDRC *see* Lewis (Daniel) Dance: A Repertory Company (DLDRC)
DNB *see* Dance Notation Bureau (DNB)
Dong, Dian 75, 104, 196
Doolin, Bill 194, 198, 198*n*
Dorfman, Carolyn 193
D'Orléans Juste, Roxanne *207*
Dosal-Owen, Margarita 159*n*, *160*
Dove, Ulysses 90
Dózsa, Imre 86
Drake, Lisa 96
Draper, Paul 35
Draper, Ruth 75
Dreams 98, 118, 120, 122
Dreeson, Lynne 159*n*, *160*
Driver, Senta 25, 135
Drucker, Judy 175–176, 183, 206
Druckman, Jacob 61
Drummond Cawthon, Kelly 204
Duato, Nacho 110
Dudley, Jane 32, 32*n*, 78, 81, 92–93
Dudley-Maslow-Bales Trio 126
Duende Ballet Español 205
Dufault, Cynthia 180
Duke (Doris) Foundation 163
Dumais, Dominique 96
Dumas, Solomon 174
Dunbar, Christine 91
Dunbar, June 22, 37
Duncan, Angus 153, 153*n*
Duncan, Isadora 47, 119, 149, 153
Duncan, Jeff 105, 111
Duncan (Isadora) Commemorative Dance Company 193
Duncan (Isadora) Dance Ensemble 171, 182, 191, 193, 194, 196, 199
Duncan (Jeff) Repertory Dance Company 111
Dunham, Katherine 184, 185–186
Dunn, Judith 17

Dunning, Jennifer 41, 120–121, 121–122, 125–126, 147
Duran, Lynn 140

Earle, David 75, *75*, *76*
Ebitz, Gerard 96, 160, 174, *175*, 178
EDAM (Experimental Dance and Music) 208
Eddy, Martha 91
Eden, David 166
Edmands, Virginia 104
Edwards, Dennis 163, 196, 206, 211
Effron, Eddie 75, *75*, 76, 101, *102*, 103, 108, 109, 110–111, 114, 119, 125, 131, *210*
Eichenbaum, Rose *201*, 202
Ellington, Mercedes *207*
The Emperor Jones 18, 25, 27, 41, 56, 61, 64, 67, 98
ENDCC (Escuela Nacional de Danza Clásica y Contemporánea) 140
Endo, Akira 83
England 77–78, 92–95
Englander, Roger 18
Epstein, Susan 75
Erwin, John 126
Escuela Nacional de Danza Clásica y Contemporánea (ENDCC) 140
Esposito, Giovanni 30
Etudes 113–114
The Exiles 30–31, 46, 53, 54, 57, 65, 72, 80, 81, 85, 86, 98, 121, 126, 143
Experimental Dance and Music (EDAM) 208

Fagan, Garth 127, 135, 186, *187*
Fagan (Garth) Company 186
Falco, Louis 13, 17, 25, 27, 30, 31, 35, 36, 37*n*, 44, 45, 46, 51, 51*n*, 52, 52*n*, 53, 53*n*, 61, 65–66, 72, 73, 73*n*, 74, 121, 126, 147
Fandiño, Luis 140, *141*
Fargnoli, Margie 77, *102*, 103
Fauré, Gabriel 131
FDA *see* Florida Dance Association (FDA)
FDEO *see* Florida Dance Education Organization (FDEO)
Feigenheimer, Irene 101, 103
Fein, David 117
Feld (Eliot) Ballet 122
Feld, Eliot 13, 114, 119
Ferguson, Michael 130
Fernandez, Royes 83, 84, *200*
Fernandez, Victoria 159*n*, *160*, 189

224

Index

Ferra, Max 146
Festival of Dance 48
Fibich, Felix 14, 18, 34–35, 49, 121, 122
Fibich (Felix) Dance Company 14, 34
Figgott, Francine 130
Fine, Vivian 48
Finland 93, 118
First Chamber Dance Quartet 39n, 45
Fischer, Lindsay 96
Fisher, Carl 113
Fisher, Elizabeth (Betsy) 109–110
Five by Two (dance company) 106
Fleischer, Leonard 127
Flindt, Vivi 88, 89
Fliss, Eric 174
Flores, Rocío 140, 141
Florida Dance Association (FDA) 194, 195, 197–198
Florida Dance Education Organization (FDEO) 191, 211
Florida Dance Festival 197–198
Florida Grand Opera Young Artist Studio 211
Flynn, Heather 159n, 160
Fogel, Jessica 77
Fokine, Michel 105, 175
Fonaroff, Nina 92–93
Foreman, Charles 97
Fortier Danse-Création 208
Fournier, Jennifer 96
Fox, Irene 208
Fraga, Maurice 163
France, Bruyere 139
Frangione, Danna 174
Friedman, Esther 95
Frosch, Joan 177, 212

Galbraith, Gary 204
Gamson, Anabelle 119
Garant, Josee 175, 210
Garay, Olga 163
Gayevsky, Vadim 166
Geddes, Jean 208
Gefter, Shelley 206
Gennaro, Peter 22
Genschow, Gisela 188
Gershunoff, Max 105–106
Gi, Pang 130
Giannini, A. Christina 99
Gielgud, Maina 119
Giffin, John 39n, 75
Gifford, John 22
Gillespie, Karen 91
Gillis, Margie 208
Gin Dance Company 176
Giordano, Gus 184
Giselle 83
Gladstone, Valerie 189

Glastonbury Festival 77–78, 92
Glenn, Laura 14, 22, 34, 36, 37n, 48–49, 51n, 52n, 53n, 54, 55, 56, 57, 71, 74, 75, 76, 77, 81, 81, 82, 82n, 84–86, 87, 90, 101, 102, 103, 104, 106, 108, 108, 113, 114, 116, 117, 118, 119, 126, 129, 139, 184n, 186, 209
Glenn, Martha 77
Glint 120
Godreau, Miguel 36, 91, 111
Goldberg, Jane 192
Goldman, Owen 188
Goldman, Sherwin 145, 146
Goodman, Saul 131
Gordon, Jack 151
Gordon, Seth 151, 179–180
Gore, Christopher 145
Gorky, David 145
Goslar, Lotte 52, 67, 126
Goslar (Lotte) Dance Company 45
Graff, Jens 86
Graham, Martha 47, 63–64, 81, 94n, 105, 186
Graham (Martha) Dance Company 12, 41, 48, 69, 92, 111, 127, 139, 151n, 161, 170, 184, 210
Grana, Edgar David 41, 125, 126, 134, 186
Grande, Maria 135
Grands Ballets Canadiens 13, 139, 161, 208
Greater Miami Youth Symphony 211
Green, Ray 98
Greenberg, Mara 124
Greene, Vincas 186
Greenhouse Dance Ensemble 121
Greyeyes, Michael 96
Griffiths, Daniel E. 127
Grossman, Andrew 149
Grossman, Danny 208
Guerra-Castro, Jorge 188
Guest, Ann see Hutchinson Guest, Ann

Hackney, Peggy 208
Hall, Afua 193
Hall, David 87
Hammack, Patricia 36
Hampton, Eric 37, 38n, 39n
Hands Across the Ocean: The Lost Chord 203
Hangin, Keir 130
Hankins, Judy 56, 64
Hansen, Reed 22–23
Harambee Dance Ensemble 192
Harkarvy, Ben 40, 190

Harkness, Rebecca 61
Harrington, Rex 96
Harris, Bruce 42
Harrison, Lydia 180
Hartford Ballet 183
Has the Last Train Left? 27
Hawkins, Alma 23
Hawkins, Erick 126
Hawkins (Erick) Dance Company 48
Haya, Sofi 159n, 160
Hays, Karen 170–171
Hayward, Charles 52n, 53, 53n
Healey, Peter 104, 104, 106, 108, 114, 115, 116, 117, 118, 119
Hechavarría, Rodolfo 140, 141
Heinonen, Markku 86
Hemp, Gene 202
Hemsley, Gilbert Vaughn 121
Heng, Ping 183n
Hennessy, Cindy 198
Henstead, Penelope 208
Hepner, Maxine 208
Hernandez, David 188
Hernandez (David) and Dancers 189
Herrera, Rosie 178, 196
Hess, Carol 77
Hess, Susan 34
HGO (Houston Grand Opera) 145
HI Enterprises 56, 64
High School of Performing Arts (HSPA) 10, 12–14, 98, 205
Hill, Martha 20–24, 40, 42, 43, 43, 68, 78n, 92, 100, 101, 103, 104n, 120, 122, 126, 127, 131, 134, 138, 147, 148, 149, 150, 151n, 152, 154, 184, 185, 195, 198, 207
Hill (Martha) Dance Fund 121
Hill (Martha) Foundation 121
Hill (Martha) Lifetime Achievement Award 207, 207
Hinkson, Mary 22
Hinton, Mercie 130
Hirabayashi, Kazuko 22, 23, 34, 93, 104
Hirabayashi (Kazuko) Studio 108
Hirsch, Steve 101
HKAPA (Hong Kong Academy of the Performing Arts) 98–99
Hodes, Linda 17
Hodes, Stuart 67
Hodgson, Jeffery 168n, 209, 212, 212
Hogan, Kelly 36
Holm, Hanya 22, 131
Holst, Gustav 123, 131
Hong Kong 42–43, 98–99

Hong Kong Academy of the Performing Arts (HKAPA) 98–99
honorary doctorate 212, *212*
Hooton, Lewis 159*n*, *160*
Horn, Laurie 188–189, 189*n*, 206
Horne, Nat 1
Horst, Louis 21, 35, 125
Horton, Lester 105
Horwitz, Dawn Lille 166
Houlihan, Gerri 170, 174, *177*, 178, 189, 191–192, 194, 195, 198, 210
Houlihan and Dancers 189, 191, 192, 194–195, 198
Houston Grand Opera (HGO) 145
Hoving, Lucas 17, 25, *26*, 27, 30, 36, 74*n*, 83, 84, 118, 120, 147, 149
Howard, Robin 92
HSPA *see* High School of Performing Arts (HSPA)
Huang, Hsiao-ting 174
Hulburt, Dianne 79, 104, 113
Humphrey (Doris) Repertory Group 17
Humphrey, Doris 36, 38–39, 38*n*, 39*n*, 47, 73, 94, 95, 98, 105, 111, 113, 116, 118, 119, 120, 124, 140, 143, *200*
Hunt, Susan 138
Hurok, Sol 89
Hutchinson Guest, Ann 12, 166, *200*, 202, 205, 208
Huth, Lola 17, 25
Hwai-min, Lin 42–43, 105, 175, 183*n*

IADMS (International Association for Dance Medicine & Science) 170–171
Icarus 118, 120
Iceland Symphony 196
ICFAD (International Council of Fine Arts Deans) 171
Icons of Innovation 205
Ide, Letitia 31, 36, 53, 65
iDMAa (International Digital Media and Arts Association) 205
Iles, Delma 192, 194–195
The Illustrated Dance Technique of José Limón 69, 98, 126, 142, *142*, 144, 217
In Common Space 204
INBA *see* National Institute of Fine Arts (INBA)
Ingram, Mary Jane 64
Inkey, Peter 30
Inlets II 172
Insects and Heroes 17

International Association for Dance Medicine & Science (IADMS) 170–171
International Council of Fine Arts Deans (ICFAD) 171
International Digital Media and Arts Association (iDMAa) 205
Internet2 Network 202
Ipiotis, Celia 148
Irving the Terrific 23–24, *24*, 36, 121, 130, 134, 194*n*
Iscove, Robert 39*n*
Israel 81, *81*, *82*
Issaev, Vladimir 193
Italy 89, 140–141

Jackson, Daniel 208
Jago, Mary 89
James, Kenneth 77
Jamison, Judith 90
Janaro, Richard 187–188
Japan 29
Jefferson, Denise 190, 208
Jelly Roll 129
Jenkins, Dawn 177
Jeune, Vitolio 186
Joffrey Ballet 109, 111, 139, 161, 183, 206
Johnson, Hank 51, 72
Jolly, Lindsey-Lee 183
Jones, Betty 17, 22, 25, *26*, 27, 35, 36, 37*n*, 51, 62–63, 74*n*, 90, 111, 147
Jones, Bill T. 184, 199
Jones Houston, Yvonne 192
Jorasmaa, Serpa 38
Jordan, Nancy *see* Scattergood Jordan, Nancy
Jowitt, Deborah 77, 79, 184
Juilliard School 19, 20–43, 46–48, 69, 80, 104, 104*n*, 108, 110, 117, 124, 127, 128, 131, 134, 146, 147, 150, 151*n*, 170, 190, 191
Junco, José 195
Jürgensen, Knud Arne 89

Kaddish 125
Kåge, Jonas 85
Kahn, Alfred 135
Kahn, Hannah 77, 104, 109, 113, 114, 116, *116*, 117, 118, 119, 120
Kahn, Mary 135
Kans, Adriaan 98
Kaplan, Betsy 151
Karaginis, Crystal 174
Kasdan, Michael 52
Kauser, David 109–110
Kealiinohomoku, Joann 169
Kearns, Kathryn 167–168, 173, 182

Keen, Elizabeth 17, 113, 121
Kelly, Lawrence 145
Kent, Allegra 184
Kent, Linda 39*n*
Keyssar, Helene 138
Khachaturian, Aram 18
Killough, Richard 38
King, Eleanor 184, 193
Kirkpatrick, Sam 146
Kirov Ballet 57
Kirpich, Billie 180
Kisselgoff, Anna 126, 144, 166
Kitsopoulos, Antonia 145
Kitten, Calvin 206
Kivitt, Ted 154
Kjelgaard, Roberta 167
Klavsen, Verner 85, 86
Klein, Richard 151, 152, 166, 201
Knapp, Sue 38*n*
Knowles, Patricia 174
Kodály, Zoltán 120
Koner, Pauline 27, *50*, 51, 70, 74*n*, 121, 124, 126, 147
Korea 31
Koresh Dance Company 198
Kosminsky, Jane 106
Krasnow, Donna 1–3, 89, 95, 97, 126, 127, 148, 149, 184*n*, 193*n*, 200–201, *209*
Krasovskaya, Vera 166
Krasovsky, Emanuel 104, 117
Kraus, Michael 124, 126
Kraus, Rae (Carol-rae) 77, 78, 79, 91, 92, *102*, 103, 109, 111, 113, 129
Kreigsman, Alan 166
Kronstam, Henning 88
Kuch, Richard 36
Kudelka, James 96
Kurtz, Marcia 16

Lacamoire, Alex 186–187
Lafarga, Nina 186
Lallan Schoenstein Presents the Bokinski Brothers 77
Lamb, Judith 117, 117*n*
Lament for Ignacio Sanchez Mejias 53, 147
Lament for the Death of a Bullfighter 125
Lamhut, Phyllis 126, 149
Lamhut (Phyllis) Company 117
Lamp Unto My Feet (TV show) 10, 15, 69
Lamy, Martine 96
Lander, Toni 83, 88, *200*
Landon, R. Kirk 163
Lang, Pearl 36–37
Laskin, Barbara 208
Lasko, Judy 75
Latimer, Lenore 17, 25, 36, 37*n*, 51*n*, 52*n*, 53*n*, 74

Lauria, Louise (Danny's mother) 7, 8, 10, 12, 15
Laurin, Ginette 174
Lavallade, Carmen de 35, 75
Lavelli, Lucinda 171*n*, *212*
Lawrence, David 189, 202
Lawrence Limón, Pauline 25, 27–28, 28*n*, 30, 33, 33*n*, 38*n*, 45, 47, 51, 53, 60, 63, 65, 69*n*, 72, 79*n*, 83, 84
LCDS *see* London Contemporary Dance School (LCDS)
lectures/demonstrations 49, 109
Lee, John 41
Legend 18, 44, 53, *66*
Lentczner, Bennett 174
Leon, Tanya 146
Lerner, Marsha 14, 16
Lester, Eugene 73
Leventhal, Marcia 91
Levien, Julia 184, 193, 194
Levin, Jordan 189
Levin, Louis 125
Levinson, Mildred 180
Levow, Fay 139
Lewis, Bob (Danny's brother) 8, 9, 12, *210*, *212*
Lewis, Candy 77
Lewis, Jerome (Danny's father) 7–8, 10, 15, 135
Lewis, Louise (Danny's mother) 7, 7*n*, 8, 10, 12, 15
Lewis, Nancy 36
Lewis, Quinn (Danny's son) 21, 107*n*, 153, 174, 175, 175*n*, *212*
Lewis, Steven (Danny's brother) 8, 9, 12, 77
Lewis (Daniel) Dance Research Collection 91
Lewis (Daniel) Dance: A Repertory Company (DLDRC) 36, 39, 85*n*, *91*, 100–128, *108*, *116*, 122, 135, 138, 139
Lewis (Daniel) Miami Dance Sampler *see* Miami Dance Samplers
Licenciatura en Danza Contemporánea 140
Life and Other Things 120–121
Life Is an Open Book see Open Book
lighting 13, 76, 110
Limón, José *50*, *81*, *82*, *84*, *200*; as artistic director 36, 37; as choreographer 18, 22, 26, 34, 35, 36–37, 40, 54–56, 60–62, 68–74, 81, 90, 103–104, 105, 119, 124, 126, 149; as dancer 25, 30, 34, 36, 38*n*, 41, 44, 52, 53, 62, 74*n*; as Juilliard instructor 19, 22;

as mentor and friend 21, 22, 46, 60, 84, 89, 101, 128
Limón, Pauline *see* Lawrence Limón, Pauline
Limón (José) Dance Company 13, 17, 25, 26–33, 35, 36, 41, 44–59, 60–79, 80, 94*n*, 110, 111, 114, 135, 137*n*, 147–148, 149, 151*n*, 161, 170, 176, 184, 210
Limón Foundation 54*n*, 56, 80, 104*n*, 113, 127, 146–149
Limón Institute 55, 86, 147, 148, 148*n*, 165
Limón Studio 127, 148, 149
Limón Summer Dance Program 148–149, 152, 165
Limón Teachers Workshop 67–68
Limón technique 1–2, 38, 40, 140, 143–144, 159, 201
Linares, Ada 195
Lincoln Center Student Programs 37–39, 69, 102, 131, 161
Lithander, Margit 86
Lithcut Nichols, Florene 161
Little, Frank 145
Live in Color 206
Living on the Ceiling 97
Ljung, Viveka 86
Lloyd, Norman 53, 126
Lloyd, Ruth 126
Locatelli, Pietro Antonio 131
Londino, Gloria 101, 101*n*
London, Peter 36, 41, 42, 43, 94*n*, 154, 160, 171, 174, *175*, 178, 186
London Contemporary Dance School (LCDS) 32*n*, 92–95, 186
London (Peter) Global Dance Company 41
Louis, Murray 109, 147
Love, Ed 187–188
Love, Tom 73
Lubovich, Lar 119
Ludin, Fritz 17, 25, 35, 36, 37*n*, 51*n*, 74, 111
Luening, Otto 130
Luft, Mary 179
Luo, Wen-jinn 173, 174
Lupone, Robert 38*n*, 39*n*, 146
Luther 69
Lynchtown 75
Lyric Suite 103, 109, 111, 113
Lyrica String Quartet 26, 30

Mac Aber's Dance 61
MacDermaid, Susie 88
MacDermot, Gault 146
Machen, Bernie 212
Maddox, Doug 30

Mahr, Martha 161
Malaysia 26–27
La Malinche 37, 39*n*, 46, 54, 69–72, *71*, 77, 98, 119
Malone, Gabrielle 188
Man Made 75–77
Manion, David K. 121
Mapou, Jan 192
Marcovicci, Andrea 146
Marks, Bruce 13, 83, 84, *84*, 88
Martin, Keith 1, 95
Martinez, Manuel 146
Mary Street Dance Theater 189, 204
Masdueño, Cristina 195
Mask 203
Maslow, Sophie 37, 67, 124, 189
Maslow (Sophie) Dance Company 35
Mason, Francis 166
Massenet, Jules Émile Frédéric 131
Matluck Brooks, Lynn 166
Matoma, Judy 169
Matteo 35, 126, 166
Maule, Michael 21
Maxim Teatern 118–119
Maximum Dance Company 156, 196, 198, 206
Maxwell, Carla 37, 45, 46, 51*n*, 52*n*, 53, 54, 55–56, 57, *57*, *62*, 65, 67, 70, 74, 75, 88, 89, 93, 98–99, 113, 121, 124, 126, 146, 147, 148, 149, 170, 184, *207*, *210*
May, Jessica 118, 119
May, Jim *14*, 34, 39, 67, 74, 76, 91*n*, 104, *104*, 108, 114, *116*, 118, 119, 121, 122–124, *123*, 125, 125*n*, 126, 127, 130, 131, 132, 133, 184, 210, *210*
May, Lorry 118
McAliley, Janet 151
McBride, Patricia 48
McCallum, Halan (Harkey) 17, 25, 27, 32, 61
McGlothlin, Donald 171, *212*
McIntyre, Dianne 79
McKayle, Donald 36, 184, *185*
McKayle (Donald) Dance Company 25, 36, 67
McPherson, Dunya *see* Hulburt, Dianne
McPherson, Elizabeth 21
MDF *see* Miami Dance Futures (MDF)
Melikova, Genia 1, 22
Mendez, Alberto 119
Mennin, Peter 23–24, 68, 104
Mercedes, Rosa 171, 195, 205–206
Mercury Ballet 121

La Meri (dance company) 17
The Merry Mailman Show (TV show) 10
Mester, Jorge 37
Mexico 70, 140, *141*
Mezzacappa, Carol 124
Miami Children's Chorus 211
Miami City Ballet 166, 180, 206
Miami Dade College 151, 152, 157–158, 160, 162, *201*
Miami Dance Futures (MDF) 162, 163–164, 174, 190, 191
Miami Dance Samplers 192–193, 195, 205*n*
Miami Herald 153, 170, 189–190, 206
Michaels, Mia 184, 192
Miller, Andrew 79, 113
Miller, Joan 36
Mind Over Matter 148
The Minding of the Flesh Is Death 75–77, 103
Minor Latham Playhouse 75–79
Missa Brevis 25, 27, 29, 36, 37, 41, 48, 50, 51, 52, 61, 62, 72, 85, 87, 88, 90, 93, 99, 120, 134, 147
Mitchell, Arthur 13
Mittelholzer, Anna 75
Möbius (dance company) 1
Modern Quartet 129
Mohrmann, Diane 37, 38*n*, 39*n*, 51*n*, 52, 52*n*, 53*n*, 74
Moments 36, 40–41, 53, 134, 149, 186
Momentum Dance Company 195
Momix 41
Monk (Meredith) Dance Company 48
Monte, Elisa 135, 184
Moods 111
Moore, Jack 111
Moore (Jack) Dance Company 17
The Moor's Pavane 27, 37, 39*n*, 51, 51*n*, 52–53, 54, 56, *57*, 59, 62, *62*, 64, 67, 74, 74*n*, 82–83, 86, 88, 89, 98, 147, 165, 202, 206
Morales, Joe 95
Morgan, Clyde 44, 45, 46, 51, 51*n*, 52, 52*n*, 53, 53*n*, 54, 66–67, *66*, 74
The Morning After the Night Before 134, 139
Morris, Elbert 36
Morris, Mark 42, 120, 127
Morris (Mark) Dance Group 106, 196
Moss, Julian 93

Mostly Beethoven 36, 122, 131
Moving Earth (dance company) 117
Muller, Jennifer 17, 22, 25, 35, 36, 37*n*, 45, 51*n*, 52, 52*n*, 53*n*, 61, 69, 73, 74, 110, 111, 121, 147, 184
Mullins, John 168
Murphy, Lara 156–157, *175*
Murphy, Thelma Dickson 126–127
Musical Artists 25, 30, 56*n*
My Echo, My Shadow, and Me 103, 107, 114, 121, 129, 131
My Son, My Enemy 18, 48, 61–62, 63

Nadel, Myron 22
Nagrin, Daniel 18, 170, *171*, 184
Naharin, Ohad 36
Nahat, Dennis 37, 70, 71–72
National Association of Schools of Dance (NASD) 110, *171*, 186, 195–196
National Ballet of Canada 89–90, 95–97
National Ballet School of Canada (NBS) 95–97
National Center for Research, Documentation and Information of the José Limón 140
National College Choreography Initiative 172
National Dance Education Organization (NDEO): Lifetime Achievement Award 12, 206–207; national conferences 89, *200*, 202
National Dance Theater of Trinidad and Tobago 192
National Dance Theatre Company of Jamaica 169, 192
National Endowment for the Arts (NEA) grants 109, 114, 120, 135, 136, 138, 163, 172
National High School Dance Festival (NHSDF) 167–168, 168*n*, 170, 172, 212
National Institute of Fine Arts (INBA) 140, *141*
National Water Dance project 204, 213
NBS (National Ballet School of Canada) 95–97
NDEO *see* National Dance Education Organization (NDEO)
NEA *see* National Endowment for the Arts (NEA) grants
Neal, Leslie 136
Nefertiti 95, 119, 121, 145–146
Neff, Travis 205

Nelson, Rick 13, 146
Netherlands 98
Netherlands Dance Theater 96, 161
Nettleford, Rex 169, 192
New Dance Group 16
New London Day 73–74
New World School of the Arts (NWSA) 66, 93, 94, 94*n*, 96, 134, 149, 150–190, *154*, *155*, *156*, *160*, *175*, *176*, *181*, *185*, 191–192, 196, 199, 201, 202–205, 208–210, 211
New York City Ballet 48, 170, 198
New York magazine 45
New York Post 52
New York State Council on the Arts (NYSCA) 135
New York Times 41, 45, 51–52, 52–53, 74, 83, 101, 104–105, 111, 117, 120–121, 121–122, 125–126, 147, 188
New York Tribune 126
New York University (NYU) 10, 11, 91–92
Newman, Judith 154, 189
Newman, Maggie 17
Newsome, Ozzie 139
Newtown High School of Performing Arts 168, 182
NHS *see* National High School Dance Festival (NHSDF)
Nielsen, Lavina 30
Night Spell 27, 35, 54, *55*, 94, 95, 109, *109*, 111, 116, *117*, 121
Nikolais, Alwin 37, 111, 147
Nikolais (Alwin) Dance Company 48
Nikolais Dance Theatre 88
92nd Street Y 103, 141
No Strings 79, 121, 122, 130–131, 139, 145
Non Divisi 202–203
North, Robert 93
Northwest Repertory Dance Company 95
Northwest Summer Dance Workshop 1–2
Norton, Jack 93
Nouri, Michael 146
Nrtyakala, Canadian Academy of Indian Dance 169
Nunley, Stephen 124, 126
Nureyev, Rudolf 89–90
NWSA *see* New World School of the Arts (NWSA)
Nye, Libby 17, 22, 25, 28, *29*, 31, 32, 35, 36, 37*n*, 61, 67
NYSCA (New York State Council on the Arts) 135
NYU *see* New York University (NYU)

Oakland, Gail 91
O'Brien, Jack 121, 134–135, 145
Oder, Bonnie 65
O'Donell, May 98
Off the Wall Dance Company 41
Ofsowitz, Judyth 75
Ogan, Banu 172
Old Globe Theatre 134
Oliphant, Betty 95, 96
Oliva, Sonia 140, *141*
Olivera, Daisy 205
Oliverio, James 202, 203, 204, *212*
Olsen, Andrea 97
Olsen Santillano, Solveig 42–43
Olvin, Lawrence 13, 13*n*
Omega Liturgical Dance Company 16
Once Upon a Mattress 22
One Hand Clapping 204
Open Book 101, 107, 121–122, 128, 129, 132–134
operas 144–145, 217–218
Orfeo 56, 64, 68, 147
Orlando, Mariane 86
O'Rourke, Maureen (Danny's wife) 9*n*, 28, *30*, 107*n*, 153, 161, 163, 168, 168*n*, 173, 174, *175*, 176*n*, 182, 183*n*, 192, *207*, *210*, *212*
Orta, Carlos 94*n*
Osborne, Aaron 54, 57, 77, 103
Otaki, Michiko 196
Otley, Jane 16
Ottmann, Peter 96
outreach 124–125, 154, 165–190
O'Vertigo Danse 161, 174

Pachelbel, Johann 130
Pacific Ballet 208
Padron, Ana 179
Pagnano, Ernest 121
Palladian, Chris 77
Palley, Lisa B. 170
Palley, Myrna 170, 180, 180*n*
panels and boards 219
Paredes, Marcos 36
Paris Opera Ballet 90
Parker, Randall Faxon 104, *104*, *106*, *108*, 111, 117, 118, 119, 121, 122, *123*, 124, 126, 127, 131, 133
Parks, John 35, 36, *45*, 61, 90
Parsons Dance 178, 184
Partridge (Martha) Company 127
Passacaglia and Fugue in C Minor 25, 26, 27, 47, 138
Passow, Aviva 15, 15*n*
Patterson, Kraig 42, 126, 127

Paxton, Steve 17, 139
Payton, James (Jim) 67–68, 110
Peattie, Crystal *see* Karaginis, Crystal
Penenori, Patricia 180
Penny, Phyllis 197
Pentacle 124
Perea, Mireya 140, *141*
Perez, Guillermo 190
Perez, Renee 135
Perlman, Ronald 11–12
Perlow, Paul 100
Perron, Wendy 18*n*
Persson, Johan 96
Peterson, Karen 192
Peterson (Karen) and Dancers 193, 195, 206
Petronio, Stephen 139
Philippines 28
Phoenix Dance Theater 93
Piché, Jean 97
Pietro, Pamela 178, 182
Pilafian, Christopher 110
Pilla, Janet 105
Pimsleur, Sue 25, 30, 56*n*, 89, 90
Piperno, Elsa 140
The Place *see* London Contemporary Dance School (LCDS)
plays and musicals 145–146, 218
Plisetskaya, Maya 18
Poem 124
Poletti, Jessica 124
Polisi, Joseph 104*n*, 150
Pollack, Claudia 16, 25
Pomare, Eleo 13
Posin, Kathryn 15, 101, *102*, 103, 110
Preiss, Marcia 135
professional accomplishments 215–219
Proliferation 36, 131
Psalm 18, 52, 72
publications 142–144, 217
Puertollano, Lulu 38*n*
Pulvermacher, Neta 204
Purcell, Henry 83

Quay, Andy 204
Quinlan-Krichels, Andrew 130, 130*n*
Quinlan-Krichels, Kathleen 130, 130*n*
Quinones, Miguel 178
Quintane, Arnold 160, *175*
Quiroga, Mercedes 163
Quitzow, Vol 15–16

Rabin, Linda 25, 38*n*, 75–76, *81*, *82*, *102*

Rainer (Yvonne) Dance Company 48
Ralph, Richard 93
Ramirez, Tina 187
Ramsey, Jim 117
Ramsey, Maggie 117
Randall, Tony 126
Randall's Island 121
Randazzo, Peter 36, 208
Rauschenberg, Robert 17
Ravel, Maurice 125
RDT (Repertory Dance Theater) 109
Reategui, Sara 159*n*, *160*
Red Universitaria Nacional (REUNA) 203
Redlich, Don 38*n*, 126
Redlich (Don) Dance Company 48, 117
Reed College 1–2, 93, 95, 141
Regnier, Patrice 83
Reinhardt, Stephen 38*n*
Reinhart, Charles 52, 127
Reinhart, Stephanie 127
Reis, Frank W.D. 170
Reiter, Bob 105, 114, 117, 117*n*, 119, 137–138, 145
Repertory Dance Theater (RDT) 109
Repertory Dancers 75
retirement 208–213, *209*, *210*, *211*
REUNA (Red Universitaria Nacional) 203
reviews 40–41, 44, 45–46, 51–52, 72–73, 73–74, 76–77, 83, 95, 103, 104–105, 111, 117, 118, 119, 120–121, 121–122, 125–126, 144, 147, 187–190, 189*n*
Revueltas, Silvestre 125
Reynolds, Nancy 166
Rhea, Angela 171
Rhodes, Larry 184
Richardson, Larry 25, 36
Richardson (Larry) Dance Gallery 141
Richardson (Larry) Studio 108
Rigney, Jane 126, 144
Ritmo Jondo 140
Rivera, Jesus 171, 171*n*
Rivera, Johan 187
Riverside Dance Festival 94, 121, 126
Roan, Barbara 149
Roberts, Jarmar 178
Roberts, Rebecca 145
Roberts, Sydney 192
Robinson, Alma 36
Robinson, Chase 17, 25, *26*, 36, 37, 61, 118
Rocha, Laura 140, *141*
Rodgers (Rod) Dance Company 117–118

Rogers, Natalie 126, 127, *187*
Romero, Paco 195
Ron, Rahamim 81
Ronen, Oshra Elkayam 34
Rooks, Wayne 101
Rooms 111, 116, 117, 119
Rose, David 131
Rosenberg, David 108, 111, 114
Rosenwald, Peter 135
Ross, Bertram 22
Ross, Jerrold 127
Roumain, Martial 91, 113
Roundabout Theater 115–118, 145
Rowan, Betty 180, 181–182, 206
Rowe, Patricia 91, 91*n*, 127
Rowley-Gaskins, Cheryl 178
Royal Danish Ballet 88–89
Royal Swedish Ballet 84–86, 95, 118
Royal Winnipeg Ballet 139
Rudner, Sara 75
Rudolph, Ellen 162
Ruins and Visions 34
Ryman, Rhonda 208

Sabado, Steven 121
Sadoff, Simon 25, 26, 29, 30, 31, 36, 51, 52, 53, 63, 72, 83
Safer, Morley 126
Salatino, Tony 38
Salterini, Diego 140, *141*, 193
Sanasardo, Paul 111
Sanasardo (Paul) Studio 108
Santillano, Solveig *see* Olsen Santillano, Solveig
Santos, Tina 160, *175*
Sapiro, Dana 90
Sarmiento, Marcy 151
Sastre, Shirley 178
Scanlon, Jennifer 17, 25, 26, 36, 38, 51*n*, 52*n*, 53*n*, *55*, 56, 66, 74, 86, 146, 147, 149
Scarecrow Contemporary Dance Company 174
Scattergood Jordan, Nancy 40, 42, 79, 93, 100–101, 102, 105, 108, 114, 119, 123, 125, 126, 133, 135–136, 138, 140, 145, 178
Schleigh, Kelly 95
Schoenberg, Arnold 53
Schoenstein, Lallan 77
Schorer, Suki 166
Schubert, Mark 37
Schulle, Gunther 84
Schumacher, Michael 134
Schuman, William 104*n*
Schwartz, Judith 91, 91*n*
Schwartz, Sheldon 194*n*
Schwenk, Joan 130
Sciutti, Graziella 145

Scott, Marion 25
Scottie, Phil 101, 101*n*, 126
Scriabin 108, 109
Scriabin, Alexander 119
Scripps, Louise 91
SDHS (Society of Dance History Scholars) Conference 166
Segovia, Rosita 189
Segovia (Rosita) Ballet Español 191, 195
Seidel, Andrea 169, 189, 193–194, 199
Seldes, Marian 42, 53, 126
Semark, Philip 135
Semeniuk, Gary 208
Sergeyev, Konstantin 57–58
service 207–208
Setterfield, Valda 17
Shang (Ruby) and Dancers 41
Shapiro, Joan (Danny's cousin) 133
Shawn, Ted 119
Shea, John 126
Shepard, Evelyn 124, 125, 126, 127
Shulman, Clifford 121, 122, 124, 126, 127
Shurr, Gertrude 98
Siegel, Marcia B. 184
Simon, Beatrice 180, 180*n*
Simon Kaplan, Marsha 180
Sims, Howard (Sandman) 129
Singapore 26, 27, 33
Singh Bhuller, Darshan 93, 186
Sink, Alex 152–153
Sisler, Tamara 159*n*, *160*
Skelton, Tom 13, 17, 25, 30, 37, 45, 51
Small, Holly 208
Small, Robert 88
Smartt, Michael 146
Smith, Peter 126, 127
Smith, Raymond 96
Smith Fichter, Nancy 161, 197
Soares, Janet 75, 77, 79, 92
Society of Dance History Scholars (SDHS) Conference 166
Sokolow, Anna 21, *23*, 36, 37, 38, 39, 39*n*, 67, 97, 98, 101–102, 102*n*, 103, 104, 105, 108, *108*, 109, 110, 111, 113, 114, 116, 117, 118, 119, 120, 121, 122, 125, 128, 129, 138, 147, *155*
Sokolow (Anna) Dance Company 17, 36, 48, 101, 111
Sokolow (Anna) Player's Project 41
Sokolow Theatre Dance Ensemble 122
Solino, Louis 51*n*, 52*n*, 53, 53*n*
SoMar Dance Works 41

Sommers, Ben 127
Sommers, Estelle 127
Songs for Young Lovers 74–75, *75*, *76*
Sorkin, Naomi 69, 120
Sosyete Koukouy 192
Souritz, Elizabeth 166
Soviet Union tour 56–59
Spangler, David 145
Sparling, Peter 56, 77, 78, 79, 91, 92, *102*, 103, 113, 126
Spartacus 18, 18*n*
Spence, Chenault 13, 53
Spohr, Arnold 208
Spoleto Festival 119
Spriggs, Linda 104
Spring, Mary 188
Spring, Michael 197
Spurlock, Estelle 90
Square Dance 129
Stackhouse, Sarah 17, 25, 27, 30, 31, 35, 36, 37*n*, 44, 45, 46, 50–51, 51*n*, 52, 52*n*, 53, 53*n*, 61, 63, 65, 66, 72, 73*n*, 74, 90, 147, 149
Staines, Mavis 95, 96, 97
State Department tours: Asia 25, 26–33; Soviet Union 56–59
State Theater 83, *84*
Steinberg, Mark 196, 206
Steinberg, Risa 56, 59, 102, 105, 124, 125, 126, 127, 149
Stenberg, Torbjörn 42
Steps of Silence 109, 116, 117, 118
Stevens, Mark 77, *102*, 103
Stevens, Nancy 36
Stodelle, Ernestine 91, 126
Strange, to Wish Wishes No Longer 27
Stratton, Sandra 139
Street, Susan 174
Strickler, Fred 25
Su, An-li 174
Suarez, Rosario 189, 198, 205*n*
Sullivan, Catherine 104
Sullivan, Sally 42
Summerdance 97
Sumner, Janet 38*n*
Sumner, Stephen 190
Surdna Foundation 162–163
Sussman, Stanley 109, 111, 117
Sweden 84–86, 93, 118
Swerdlow, Martin 42
Swifts 52
Swinston, Robert 104, 172
Sygoda, Ivan 124

Taipei Crossover Dance Company 196
Taipei Festival of International Dance Academies 42

Taiwan 31–32, 172–176, *176*
Taking the Air 113, 121
Taliaferro, Clay 18, 67
Taliaferro (Clay) Company 127
Tango for All 179, 210
TAYB (Thomas Armour Youth Ballet) 180, 205*n*, 206, 211
Taylor, Mark 199
Taylor, Paul 17, *17*, 63, 105, 121, 174, 184
Taylor (Paul) Dance Company 17, 25, 45, 48, 151*n*, 161
technology 202–205, 218
television appearances 10, 15–16, 69, 118
Terrell, Rebecca 197–198
Tesman, Betty 120
Tetley, Glen 75, 119
Tetley (Glen) Dance Company 48
Textured Lighting 125
Thakkar, Menaka 97, 169, 196, 199
Tharp (Twyla) Dance Company 48, 161
Theodore, Lee 126
There Is a Time 22, 25, 26, 27, 32, 36, *45*, 48, 50–51, 52, 56, 61, 68, 85, 93, 94, 95, 96, 97, 98, 146, 147, 151*n*
There's Nothing Here of Me but Me 100–101, 107, 121, 122, 123, *123*, 126, 128, 129, 131, 132
Thielen, Thomas 197, 198
Thomas, Travis-Tyrell 182
Thompson, Clive 90, 135
Thompson, Rell 30
Thomson, Virgil 114, 121
TIDE (Toronto Independent Dance Enterprise) 208
Tigertail Productions 179
Tipton, Jennifer 25, 27, 30
Tjon, Walther 130
Tokunaga Dance Studio 108
Tomlinson, Charles (Chuck) 25, 27, 30, 51, 83
Toogood, Melissa 168*n*, 172
Topaz, Muriel 20, 40, 42, 54*n*, 61, 149, 150, 208
Topf, Nancy 77–78
Toronto Dance Theatre 36, 139, 208
Toronto Independent Dance Enterprise (TIDE) 208
Toronto Star 95
Torres, Nestor 211
Touissant, Eddy 208
tours: Limón Company 25, 26–33, 48–51, 53, 56–59; Lincoln Center Student Programs 37–39; NWSA 182–184

Towson State College 139
Tragedy see My Son, My Enemy
The Traitor 25, 26, 27, 41, 42, 46, 82, 84, 154
Troyanos, Tatiana 145
Tudor, Antony 19, 22, 37, 39*n*, 83, 122
Turek, Allen M. 101
Turkey 81–82
Turner, Edith 169
Turocy, Catherine 135
Two Essays for Large Ensemble 34, 35, 61

UCLA *see* University of California at Los Angeles (UCLA)
Ugundani Dance Company 192
University of Alabama 139
University of Calgary 97
University of California at Los Angeles (UCLA) 23, 53, 87–88
The Unsung 49, 56, 63–64, *63*, 67, 68, 98, 129, 132, 146, 147
Urdaneta, Adriana 94, 139
Urdaneta, Luz 94
Utah Repertory Dance Theater (URDT) 112
Uthoff, Michael 35, 36, 40, 42, 61, 127, 171, 178, 183–184, 210

Vachon, Ann 17, 25, 37*n*, 64, 75, 105, 149
Vallve, Maria Jesus 195
Van Buren, Marcia 101
van Fleet, Alice 95
Van Kuiken, Henry 77
Vannucchi, Jennifer 178
Vargas, Victor *106*, *108*, 118, 119
Variations on a Theme of Paganini 61
Vaughan, David 135
Vega, Suzanne 77
Venable, Lucy 17, 25, 27, 147, 208
Venezuela 94
Vered, Avner 51*n*, 52*n*, 53, 53*n*, 74
Vereen, Ben 13
Vickers, Jon 145
Villella, Edward 13, 48, 154, 166
Voloshky Ukrainian Folk Dance Ensemble 198
Volsky, George 188
von Bardeleben, Armgard 1
Von Honts, Jacqui 91, *91*
Vytal Movement Dance Company 186

Wagner, Lee 38*n*, 39*n*, 151
Wagoner, Dan 17, 105
The Waldstein Sonata 36, 64, 67, 68, 69, 86, 93, 100, 103–105, 114, 116, 117, 119
Walker, David Hatch 111
Walker, Norman 105
Wallach, Eli 35
Walton, Elizabeth 17, 176*n*, 184*n*
Warren, Leigh 79, 104, 112, 113
Washington, Shelly 106
Washington Ballet 176
The Washington Post 74, 65*n*
Waters, Sylvia 90, 184
Watt, Nina 67, 87–88
Wayne, Dennis 119
Wayne, Linda 126
The Wedding Dance *14*
Wedner, Ellen 205
Weidman, Charles 75, 124
Weinreich, Dennis 87, 87*n*
Weinreich, Michael 87
Weiss, Alan 155
Weiss, Barry 104
Weksler, Teri 20, 79, 86, 91, 92, 104, *104*, 106–107, *108*, 109–110, 113, 114, *116*, 117, *117*, 118, 119, 120, 145
Westergard, Lance 38*n*
Wetzler, Peter 125
White, Jane 146
White House performance 74
White Oak Dance Project 190
Wickoff, Bonnie 139
Wiesen, Ruth 180–181, 211
Wiesner, Theodore (Teddy) 78*n*
Wiley, Dyan 126
Williams, Dudley 13, 90
Williams, Holly 77
Williams, Megan 126, 127
Willis, Judith 14, 74–75
Wilson, Andrea 91
Wilson, John 196
Wilson, Sallie 83, *200*
Wilson, Tovaris 179
Wilson, Vernell 179
The Winged 18, 36, 48, 51, 52, 63, 72–73, 74*n*
Winter, Ethel 22, 42, 92, 111, 170
Wishy, Joseph (Joe) 119, 119*n*
Witkowsky, Gizella 96
Wittman, Joseph 45, 48
Wolenski, Chester 17, 27, 101, 103
Wolz, Carl 42, 98
Women 36, 42
Wood, David 12, 16
Wood (David) Dance Company 16–17

Woodford, Charles 91
The Works (dance company) 110, 111, 117
World Dance Alliance 166
Woshakiwsky, Tamara 51*n*, 52*n*, 53*n*, 74
Wright-Roark, Elaine *175*
Wu, Kuanghsi 173
Wyman, Anna 208
Wynne, David 17, 25, 32, 61

Yago, Mary 208
Yang, Wen-shuan 173, 174, 178
Yarborough, Sara 90
Yerma 69
Yglesias, Collette 104
Yiddish Theater 14–16, 34–35, 122, 128
Yocom, Rachel 13
York, Lila 40, 184
Youngblood, Agnes Takako 196

You-yu, Bao 42
Yukihiro, Ko *108*, 111

Zeidman, Anita 126
Zera, Hortense 127
Ziebarth, Craig 201
Zimbler, Sharon 159*n*, *160*
Zubieta Diaz, Maribel *see* Diaz, Maribel